MATHEMATICS
FOR
ECONOMISTS

Lyliana Gayoso

This is a volume in
ECONOMIC THEORY, ECONOMETRICS, AND
MATHEMATICAL ECONOMICS
A Series of Monographs and Textbooks

Consulting Editor: Karl Shell, *Cornell University*

A complete list of titles in this series appears at the end of this volume.

MATHEMATICS
FOR
ECONOMISTS

William Novshek
Department of Economics
Krannert Graduate School of Management
Purdue University
West Lafayette, Indiana

Academic Press
San Diego New York Boston
London Sydney Tokyo Toronto

Copyright © 1993 by ACADEMIC PRESS, INC.

All Rights Reserved.

No part of this publication may be reproduced or transmitted in any form or by any means, electronic or mechanical, including photocopy, recording, or any information storage and retrieval system, without permission in writing from the publisher.

Academic Press, Inc.
A Division of Harcourt Brace & Company
525 B Street, Suite 1900, San Diego, California 92101-4495

United Kingdom Edition published by
Academic Press Limited
24–28 Oval Road, London NW1 7DX

Library of Congress Cataloging-in-Publication Data

Novshek, William.
    Mathematics for economists   William Novshek
        p.   cm. -- (Economic theory, econometrics, and mathematical economics)
    Includes bibliographical references and index.
    ISBN 0-12-522575-X
    1. Economics, Mathematical. 2. Econometrics. I. Title.
II. Series.
HB135.N68 1993
330'.01'51--dc20   93-16696
                                                           CIP

Transferred to digital printing 2006
    95 96 97 BB 9 8 7 6 5 4 3 2

To Lynda

CONTENTS

2 LINEAR ALGEBRA

3 BASIC ANALYSIS

4 CORRESPONDENCES

5 CALCULUS OF SEVERAL VARIABLES

6 NONLINEAR PROGRAMMING SUMMARY

7 COMPARATIVE STATICS

8 COMPARATIVE STATICS SUMMARY

9 LINE INTEGRALS

10 STABILITY

11 DYNAMIC PROGRAMMING

APPENDIX: SAMPLE SOLUTIONS

PREFACE

This book contains the mathematical material necessary as background for the topics covered in graduate-level microeconomics courses. The intended audience includes graduate students in economics, agricultural economics, accounting, finance, marketing, and so on, as well as individuals who need an appropriate mathematical reference to understand a microeconomic topic in their work. The material is accessible to readers with knowledge of basic calculus and linear algebra.

The book is intended for use in a one-semester mathematics course that accompanies first-semester Ph.D. microeconomics courses, and the topics have been chosen to match the requirements of such courses. Every topic covered in this book either is directly applicable in microeconomics or is used to develop relevant topics. The extent of the coverage of any particular topic matches its importance in a first-semester microeconomics course. For example, to understand surplus measures or the integrability problem in microeconomics, students need to see line integrals and upper semicontinuous functions, respectively. But because these mathematical topics are not central to the development of microeconomics, their treatment is brief. On the other hand, optimization subject to constraints and comparative statics are crucial mathematical tools for economics topics. These areas are covered at length in the text, including extensive examples and summary chapters (Chapters 6 and 8) that provide step-by-step procedures for solving optimization and comparative statics problems.

One strength of the book is the set of examples and problems used. The examples included provide ample practice and they often illustrate new economic or mathematical points. Almost all parts to all problems at the end of each chapter have solutions in the Appendix. Most solutions have at least a sketch of the procedure followed to obtain the final answer. For many problems, the solution is very complete, laying out the procedure in detail. This is especially true for the initial problems in the summary chapters for optimization and comparative statics (Chapters 6 and 8). The problems and detailed solutions can be used as additional examples to help students understand how to approach problems and why particular techniques work.

Students with different levels of preparation will get different things from the book. The material is presented in a manner that allows all students to understand the intuition behind the results. (For example, hyperplanes and diagonal matrices are used to provide insights into optimization.) Some advanced material is included for students who are able to take advantage of it. Over several years of teaching this material to students with a wide range of backgrounds, I have found that, at the very least, students are able to develop a good understanding of constrained optimization and comparative statics.

I am grateful to Lynda Thoman, who read much of this material and made substantial suggestions on several chapters. Many versions of the manuscript were typed over several years, and I wish to thank Fern Poppe, Betsy Bryant, Janet Yoakum, and Julie Huffer.

William Novshek

INTRODUCTION AND NOTATION

This book contains the mathematical material necessary as a background for the topics in a graduate level microeconomics course. Graduate level microeconomics makes extensive use of optimization subject to constraints and comparative statics. It also uses a wide variety of other special topics in mathematics.

One main focus of this book is the development of nonlinear programming (optimization subject to constraints). A thorough understanding of optimization requires an understanding of (1) the first-order conditions used to identify potential optimizers (background for this topic is developed in the material on subspaces and hyperplanes in Chapter 2); (2) the second-order conditions used to determine whether a solution to the first-order conditions is a maximizer, a minimizer, or neither (background for this topic is developed in the material on eigenvalues and quadratic forms in Chapter 2); and (3) the methods available to determine whether a local optimizer is a global optimizer (background material for this topic is developed in the basic analysis topics in Chapter 3 and in the section on concave and quasiconcave functions in Chapter 5). Chapter 6 brings all this material together in a summary and provides a step-by-step procedure for solving optimization problems.

A second main focus of this book is the development of comparative statics. Comparative statics concerns two types of questions. How do optimal choices (or equilibrium values) change when a parameter changes? How does the optimized value of the objective function change when a parameter changes? For a competitive firm, the optimal choices would be input and output levels (input demands and output supplies) and the optimized value of the objective function would be the corresponding profit. Since the firm is competitive, the input and output prices would be parameters. The maximum theorem in Chapter 4 provides conditions under which the optimal choices and the optimized value will be continuous functions of the parameters. The implicit function theorem in Chapter 7 provides conditions under which the optimal choices and the optimized value will be differentiable functions of the parameters. When the functions are differentiable, a simple procedure allows us to determine the comparative statics effects. This is summarized in Chapter 8, which includes a step-by-step procedure for answering both types of comparative statics question. Comparative statics for equilibrium problems is useless unless the equilibrium is stable under an appropriate dynamic adjustment process. Stability is examined in Chapter 10.

Many other topics are covered in this book. Some of these topics, such as the chain rule and Taylor's theorem in Chapter 5, are needed as background for some of the other topics already discussed. Additional topics, such as line integrals in Chapter 9 and dynamic programming in Chapter 11, are included because they are useful for certain topics in microeconomics (surplus measures in the case of line integrals and sequential optimization as in discrete time capital theory in the case of dynamic programming).

In general, to aid in the development of intuition for many types of problems, it is best to consider linear cases or, for matrices, to consider diagonal matrices. Once one has developed the appropriate intuition in these special cases, the general case is covered by dealing with the tangent hyperplane approximation to the graph of a function (replacing a general function with its best linear approximation) or by thinking of the eigenvalues of a general matrix rather than the diagonal entries of a diagonal matrix. Several of the major topics in this book are approached in this manner.

The reader is assumed to be familiar with basic linear algebra and calculus of one variable. Since many topics in calculus of several variables have single-variable counterparts, Chapter 1 provides a review of many of these topics. When appropriate, the presentation in Chapter 1 provides an introduction to the approach that will be used when we meet the topic again in calculus of several variables. Chapter 1 also includes topics such as differentiation of integrals which may not be review, but are of interest in their own right for use in microeconomic applications.

Several sections of the book contain extensive examples, and virtually all problems at the end of each chapter have solutions in the Appendix. For many problems, the solution is very complete, laying out the procedure in detail. This is especially true for the initial problems in the summary chapters for optimization and comparative statics (Chapters 6 and 8, respectively). The problems and detailed solutions can be used as additional examples to help the reader understand how to approach problems and why particular techniques work.

The references at the end of this book list not only the works cited in the text but also some sources for additional material on many of the topics.

Throughout this book, the reader is assumed to be familiar with the following notation and concepts.

$:=$, "is defined to be equal to"

$\equiv$, "is identically equal to" [e.g., for $f(x) = [(x + 1)(x - 1) + 2]/(x^2 + 1)$, $f(x)$ is one for all x so $f(x) \equiv 1$]

$\neq$, "is not equal to"

$\mathbb{R}$, the real numbers

Set notation such as $\{x \in \mathbb{R} | x \leq 0\}$, which is read "$x$ in $\mathbb{R}$ such that x is less than or equal to zero"

$\mathbb{R}^l$, the set of l-vectors of real numbers ($l \geq 1$) (this is also called Euclidean l-space and is sometimes written E^l). Vectors will be written in boldface type to distinquish them from scalars (e.g., $\mathbf{a} \in \mathbb{R}^l$ versus $a \in \mathbb{R}$).

$\mathbb{R}^l_+ = \{\mathbf{x} \in \mathbb{R}^l | x_i \geq 0, i = 1, \ldots, l\}$, the nonnegative orthant of $\mathbb{R}^l$

$\mathbb{R}^l_{++} = \{\mathbf{x} \in \mathbb{R}^l | x_i > 0, i = 1, \ldots, l\}$, the strictly positive orthant of $\mathbb{R}^l$

Intervals in $\mathbb{R}$, for example $[0, 1] = \{x \in \mathbb{R} | 0 \leq x \leq 1\}$, $(0, 1] = \{x \in \mathbb{R} | 0 < x \leq 1\}$, $[0, 1) = \{x \in \mathbb{R} | 0 \leq x < 1\}$, and $(0, 1) = \{x \in \mathbb{R} | 0 < x < 1\}$. This last example must be distinguished from $(0, 1) \in \mathbb{R}^2$. Usage should be clear from the context.

$\in$, "is an element of" and $\notin$, "is not an element of"

$\subset$, "is a subset of" and $\not\subset$, "is not a subset of"

$\varnothing$, the empty set

For $X \subset \mathbb{R}^l$, $Y \subset \mathbb{R}^l$, and $\alpha \in \mathbb{R}$,

$$\alpha X := \{\mathbf{z} \in \mathbb{R}^l | \mathbf{z} = \alpha \mathbf{x} \text{ for some } \mathbf{x} \in X\},$$

$$X + Y := \{\mathbf{z} \in \mathbb{R}^l | \mathbf{z} = \mathbf{x} + \mathbf{y} \text{ for some } \mathbf{x} \in X \text{ and some } \mathbf{y} \in Y\},$$

$$X - Y := X + (-Y) = X + [(-1)Y],$$

$\mathbb{R}^l \setminus Y := \{\mathbf{z} \in \mathbb{R}^l | \mathbf{z} \notin Y\}$, the complement of Y, also written Y^c

$X \cap Y := \{\mathbf{z} \in \mathbb{R}^l | \mathbf{z} \in X \text{ and } \mathbf{z} \in Y\}$, the intersection of X and Y,

$X \cup Y := \{\mathbf{z} \in \mathbb{R}^l | \mathbf{z} \in X \text{ or } \mathbf{z} \in Y \text{ or both}\}$, the union of X and Y.

For $X \subset \mathbb{R}^l$ and $Y \subset \mathbb{R}^m$,

$$X \times Y := \{(\mathbf{x}, \mathbf{y}) \in \mathbb{R}^{l+m} | \mathbf{x} \in X \text{ and } \mathbf{y} \in Y\} \quad (\text{e.g., } \mathbb{R} \times \mathbb{R} = \mathbb{R}^2)$$

Σ, the addition symbol (e.g., $\Sigma_{i=1}^3 i = 1 + 2 + 3$)

$|z|$, the absolute value of the number z

$\|\mathbf{z}\|$, the length of the vector $\mathbf{z}$

$\mathbf{x}'$, the transpose of the vector $\mathbf{x}$ (i.e., $\mathbf{x}$ as a row rather than column vector). This must be distinguished from the notation for a derivative. Usage should be clear from the context.

The following symbols are used to shorten the writing of solutions to problems. They are used only in the Appendix.

$\forall$, the logical quantifier "for all"

$\exists$, the logical quantifier "for some" (or "there exists")

$\nexists$, "there does not exist"

$\Rightarrow$, logical implication (e.g., A implies B is written $A \Rightarrow B$)

1

REVIEW OF CALCULUS
OF ONE VARIABLE

1.1 INTRODUCTION

This chapter contains a brief review of topics in calculus of one variable. Most of the material should be familiar, though some of it might be unfamiliar or presented in an unfamiliar way. Many of these topics are important as special cases of the more general versions we will treat in calculus of several variables. A thorough understanding of the one-variable case will make the several-variable case much simpler. A few topics, such as differentiation of integrals, might not be review but have important applications in economics.

1.2 FUNCTIONS

Given a set S (for example, the set of students in a class) called the domain and a set T (for example, the set of possible first names for people), a *function* f from S to T (written $f: S \to T$) is a rule for assigning a unique element of T to each element of S (for example, the rule assigning a first name to each student). Note that every element of S is assigned exactly one element of T (every student has one first name), while an element of T may be assigned to any number of elements of S (two students may have the same first name, while no student may have the name Helen). The range of the function is the set of elements of T that are assigned to at least one element of S (the set of actual first names of the students). If we use the variable x to represent elements of S and the variable y to represent elements of T, then the function can be represented as $y = f(x)$ where x is the independent variable and y is the dependent variable.

1.3 GRAPHS

If the sets S and T are sets of numbers, then the *graph* of a function f from S to T is the set of points whose coordinates form a pair (x, y) such that $y = f(x)$. Note that for historical reasons, economists draw graphs of demand functions with the axes flipped. If p represents price and q represents quantity demanded, then the demand function is $q = f(p)$, but economists draw the graph with q on the horizontal axis and p on the vertical axis.

1.4 SLOPE

The *slope* of the line through the points (x, y) and (x', y') is $m = (y - y')/(x - x') = (y' - y)/(x' - x)$.

1.5 LIMITS

Let $|b|$ denote the absolute value of b, i.e., $|b| = b$ if $b \geq 0$ and $|b| = -b$ if $b < 0$. The function f has the *limit* L as x tends to c [written "$\lim_{x \to c} f(x) = L$" or "$f(x) \to L$ as $x \to c$"] if for any $\varepsilon > 0$ there exists a $\delta > 0$, depending on ε, such that $|f(x) - L| < \varepsilon$ for all x satisfying $0 < |x - c| < \delta$. We say f converges to L as x converges to c. When this is true, we can guarantee that the value of the function is arbitrarily close to L (within distance ε from L) by picking x sufficiently close to c (within distance δ from c). Note that f need not be defined at c to have a limit as x tends to c. For example, $f(x) = (x^2 - 1)/(x - 1)$ is not defined at $x = 1$ (division by zero) but $f(x) \to 2$ as $x \to 1$. Not every function has limits everywhere. For example, if $f(x) = -1$ for $x < 0$ and $f(x) = 1$ for $x > 0$ then f has no limit as x tends to 0 (looking from the right, L must be 1, while from the left L must be -1).

1.6 CONTINUITY

A function f is *continuous at c* if f is defined at c and $f(x) \to f(c)$ as $x \to c$. Continuity requires both that f have a limit L as x tends to c and that the limit equals $f(c)$. The two examples in Section 1.5 are not continuous, the first because $f(c)$ is not defined, the second because f does not converge to a limit as x converges to c. The first example can be modified by defining a new function, g, by $g(x) = f(x)$ if $x \neq 1$ and $g(1) = 2$. Then g is continuous at 1. If f is continuous at each point in its domain, we say f is *continuous*.

1.7 DERIVATIVE AT A POINT

The *derivative* of the function f at the point x is

$$f'(x) = \lim_{\Delta x \to 0} \left(\frac{f(x + \Delta x) - f(x)}{\Delta x} \right).$$

Note that what we usually think of as a variable, x, is held constant while Δx varies and converges to zero. The derivative of f at x is the slope of a line tangent to the graph of the function f at the point $(x, f(x))$. It is crucial to understand the implications of the existence of the derivative at a point x. First of all, the function must be smooth at x (the absolute value function has a kink at 0 and is not differentiable there). Second, the tangent line provides a good approximation to the graph of the function near x. Without other information (i.e., the function itself) the tangent line gives the best estimates of the graph.

In real-world economic applications we almost never know the actual function, though we do know the value of the function at some initial point and econometricians can estimate the derivative of the function. The tangent line approximation can then be used to help analyze policy issues. For example, suppose the United States imports all its widgets from abroad and long-run world supply is horizontal at price (in dollar terms) $20 per unit. Current consumption in the United States is 10,000 units per month and econometricians estimate the derivative of the U.S. demand function at price $20 is -500 units per month per dollar. In the long run, what happens to the quantity demanded in the United States if an import tariff of $0.50 per unit is introduced? Since long-run supply is horizontal at price $20 per unit, the tariff raises the U.S. price to $20.50. The tangent line approximation for the change in quantity demanded is

$$\Delta Q = (\text{derivative of demand})(\Delta p)$$

$$= \frac{-500 \text{ units}}{(\text{month})(\$)}(\$0.50) = \frac{-250 \text{ units}}{\text{month}}.$$

Thus our best estimate is that the tariff will lead to a 250 unit per month reduction in the quantity of widgets sold.

In general, if we know the function f is differentiable at c, then the tangent line approximation to f at c is $y = f(c) + (x - c)f'(c)$, where $c, f(c)$, and $f'(c)$ are constants, x is the independent variable, and y is the dependent variable.

1.8 DERIVATIVE AS A FUNCTION

If for each x in the domain of f the derivative of f at x exists, then we have derived a new function which assigns value $f'(x)$ to x. Several different notations are commonly used to denote this derivative function. In addition to $f'(x)$, one may also see y', Dy, Df, or dy/dx. For the derivative function, $f'(x)$, x is again an independent variable. Many important concepts in economics are based on derivative functions. For example, if $C(q)$ is the function specifying the total cost of producing output q, then $C'(q)$ is the marginal cost function.

1.9 BASIC RULES OF DIFFERENTIATION

The following are commonly used rules of differentiation:

For $y = f(x) + g(x)$, $y' = f'(x) + g'(x)$;
For $y = f(x)g(x)$, $y' = f'(x)g(x) + f(x)g'(x)$;
For $y = f(x)/g(x)$, $y' = f'(x)/g(x) - f(x)g'(x)/[g(x)]^2$
                               provided $g(x) \neq 0$;
For $y = $ constant, $y' = 0$;
For $y = x^n$, $y' = nx^{n-1}$;
For $y = e^x$, $y' = e^x$;
For $y = \ln x$, $y' = 1/x$.

1.10 EXPONENTIAL AND NATURAL LOGARITHM FUNCTIONS

Recall the properties of the exponential and natural logarithm functions. The exponential function $f(x) = e^x$ has domain including all numbers, positive and negative, but range equal to the set of strictly positive numbers. Its properties include $e^0 = 1$ and $e^{a+b} = e^a e^b$. The natural logarithm function $f(x) = \ln x$ has domain consisting of strictly positive numbers and range all numbers. Its properties include $\ln(ab) = \ln(a) + \ln(b)$, $\ln(a^b) = b \ln(a)$, and $\ln(1) = 0$. The exponential and natural logarithm functions are inverses of one another: $e^{\ln a} = a$ and $\ln(e^b) = b$ for any positive a and for any b.

1.11 CHAIN RULE

When $z = f(y)$ and $y = g(x)$, we use the chain rule to determine dz/dx. When x changes by Δx, y changes by approximately $\Delta y = g'(x)\Delta x$ (using the tangent line approximation). When y changes by Δy, z changes by approximately $\Delta z = f'(y)\Delta y$ (again using the tangent line). Thus $\Delta z = f'(y)g'(x)\Delta x$. In the limit we obtain the *chain rule*:

$$\frac{dz}{dx} = f'(y)g'(x) = f'(g(x))g'(x).$$

This result is very useful in economics since many of the functions used are composite functions, consisting of one function, f, evaluated at the outcome of another function, $g(x)$, to obtain $f(g(x))$. For example, to differentiate e^{x^3} with respect to x we could consider the composite function $f(g(x))$ where $f(y) = e^y$ and $g(x) = x^3$. By the chain rule, the derivative of e^{x^3} is $f'(g(x))g'(x) = e^{g(x)}3x^2 = 3x^2e^{x^3}$. When dealing with composite functions it is especially important to understand the meaning of the notation. By $f'(g(x))$ we mean "take the derivative function $f'(y)$ and evaluate it at the point $y = g(x)$." The order—differentiate first, then evaluate at a specific point—is crucial.

1.12 HIGHER-ORDER DERIVATIVES

Once we have found the derivative function, $f'(x)$, we can find the derivative of $f'(x)$ with respect to x. This is the second derivative of f at x, written $f''(x)$ (or y'', or D^2y, or D^2f, or d^2y/dx^2):

$$f''(x) = \lim_{\Delta x \to 0}\left(\frac{f'(x + \Delta x) - f'(x)}{\Delta x}\right).$$

If $f''(x)$ exists for all x, then we can find the third derivative of f at x by differentiating $f''(x)$, etc. This process can be repeated to find higher-order derivatives as long as the derivative functions exist.

1.13 TAYLOR SERIES

If derivatives of all orders exist for the function $f(x)$ at the point b then the *Taylor series expansion* of f about the point b is

$$f(b) + (x - b)Df(b)/(1!) + (x - b)^2 D^2f(b)/(2!)$$

$$+ (x - b)^3 D^3f(b)/(3!) + \cdots + (x - b)^n D^nf(b)/(n!) + \cdots.$$

where $j!$, j *factorial*, is the product of the integers from 1 to j: $j! = j(j - 1)(j - 2) \cdots (3)(2)(1)$. Under certain conditions, $f(x)$ is equal to this infinite sum of terms. Taylor's theorem provides an expression for the error (remainder) if we only use a finite number of terms. For example, if we only use two terms, then there is a number c between x and b such that $f(x)$ differs from $f(b) + (x - b)Df(b)$ by exactly $(x - b)^2 D^2 f(c)/2$. Note the remainder is very similar to the next term in the expansion, but it has $D^2 f$ evaluated at c rather than b.

The important implication of this result is that (for the types of functions we will be dealing with) the shape of the graph of the function f near b can be determined by the derivatives of f at b. The graph is upward sloping at b if $f'(b) > 0$, downward sloping at b if $f'(b) < 0$. The curvature of f at b depends on $f''(b)$. This should be familiar from the practice of curve sketching (i.e., using the signs of f' and f'' to generate a rough picture of the graph of f). If $Df(b) = D^2 f(b) = D^3 f(b) = \cdots = D^{n-1} f(b) = 0$, but $D^n f(b) > 0$, by Taylor's expansion $f(x)$ "looks like" $(x - b)^n$ near b [if $D^n f(b) < 0$, $f(x)$ "looks like" $-(x - b)^n$ near b]. Near b, the general shape of f is determined by the first nonzero derivative of f at b.

1.14 OPTIMIZATION

The fact that the first nonzero derivative of f at b determines the general shape of f near b provides the insight needed to understand the conditions for *optimization*. If $f'(b) \neq 0$, then f is increasing [if $f'(b) > 0$] or decreasing [if $f'(b) < 0$] near b, and b cannot be either a maximizer or a minimizer of f. If $f'(b) = 0$ but $f''(b) \neq 0$, then f looks like $(x - b)^2$ [if $f''(b) > 0$] or $-(x - b)^2$ [if $f''(b) < 0$] near b, and b is a local minimizer or local maximizer for f, respectively. If $f'(b) = f''(b) = 0$, then we look at the first nonzero derivative of f, say $D^n f(b)$. Then near b, f looks like $(x - b)^n$ if $D^n f(b) > 0$ and $-(x - b)^n$ if $D^n f(b) < 0$. If n is odd, then b is just an inflection point (as in x^3 at $b = 0$), while if n is even, b is a local maximizer of f if $D^n f(b) < 0$ and a local minimizer if $D^n f(b) > 0$.

We usually consider only the first and second derivatives. The results are summarized as follows:

1. If b is a local maximizer of f, then $f'(b) = 0$ and $f''(b) \leq 0$.
2. If b is a local minimizer of f, then $f'(b) = 0$ and $f''(b) \geq 0$.
3. If $f'(b) = 0$ and $f''(b) < 0$, then b is a strict local maximizer of f.
4. If $f'(b) = 0$ and $f''(b) > 0$, then b is a strict local minimizer of f.

The words strict local maximizer mean that for all $x \neq b$ but sufficiently near b, $f(b) > f(x)$ [for strict local minimizer switch the inequality to $f(b) < f(x)$]. This need not be true at a local maximizer. As an extreme example, for the constant function $f(x) = 1$ for all x, every x is a local maximizer (and minimizer), but no x is a strict local maximizer (or strict local minimizer). Conditions 1 and 2 are often referred to as the necessary conditions for maximization and minimization, respectively. Conditions 3 and 4 are often referred to as the sufficient conditions for maximization and minimization, respectively.

To find the global maximizer we must (a) find all local maximizers, (b) compare the value of the function at the different local maximizers to find the best one, and (c) determine whether the best local maximizer is dominated as x approaches the bounds of the domain (i.e., as x approaches $+\infty$ or $-\infty$). If f is a polynomial, the procedure is greatly simplified. First find the highest power of x appearing in the polynomial, say x^n. If n is odd, then there is no global maximizer or minimizer (as for x^3). If n is even and the coefficient of x^n is positive, there is a global minimizer but no global maximizer. If n is even and the coefficient of x^n is negative, there is a global maximizer but no global minimizer. For example, if $f(x) = 2x^3 - 15x^2 - 84x + 3$, then there is no global optimizer. Setting $f'(x) = 6x^2 - 30x - 84 = 0$ and solving, $f'(-2) = f'(7) = 0$. Checking the second derivative, $f''(x) = 12x - 30$, $f''(-2) < 0$ and $f''(7) > 0$. Thus -2 is a strict local maximizer and 7 is a strict local minimizer, with no global maximizer or minimizer.

Finding global optimizers is also easy when the second derivative is always positive or always negative. By Taylor's theorem with remainder, given b and any x, there is some c between b and x such that $f(x) = f(b) + (x - b)f'(b) + (x - b)^2 f''(c)/2$. If f'' is strictly negative everywhere, then any b such that $f'(b) = 0$ is a strict global maximizer $[f(x) = f(b) + (x - b)0 + (x - b)^2 f''(c)/2 = f(b) + (x - b)^2 f''(c)/2 < f(b)$ by $f'' < 0$ everywhere]. Similarly, if f'' is strictly positive everywhere, then any b such that $f'(b) = 0$ is a strict global minimizer.

1.15 IMPLICIT DIFFERENTIATION

One of the most useful tools in economic policy analysis is comparative statics. A typical policy problem would be to predict the effect on the price paid by consumers of a change in a tax rate. Because of various market interactions, the tax change is unlikely to be completely passed on to consumers in equilibrium. Analysis of such problems uses a generalization of the following technique. For one variable, the procedure uses *implicit differentiation* to find the slope of a curve. A thorough understanding of the one-variable case is necessary before we can deal with the several-variable case.

When the relationship between x and y is given implicitly by an equation, this technique is used to check whether y is a differentiable function of x and to find the derivative. For example, consider the curve defined by $x + y + y^5 = 3$. This defines an implicit relationship between x and y (as opposed to an explicit relationship such as $y = x^2 + 4$), but we cannot solve the equation to find y as a function of x. Is it possible to determine whether an explicit relationship exists (even if we cannot find it) and to determine dy/dx at an initial point $(x^0, y^0) = (1, 1)$? If the conditions of a mathematical result known as the implicit function theorem hold, the answer is yes. A step-by-step procedure is outlined below. The procedure may seem a little overblown for this simple one-variable problem, but an identical procedure will be used in the case of several variables, so it is useful to see and understand the procedure in the simple case first. The steps are as follows.

   1. Check that the desired point satisfies the equation. For the example, $1 + 1 + 1^5$ is equal to 3.
   2. Act as if the explicit relationship $y = f(x)$ exists (even though we don't know the form of f) and replace y in the original equation with $f(x)$ to create an identity. An identity is an equation that always holds. For example, $(x^2 - 1)$ is equal to $(x - 1)(x + 1)$ for every value of x. Thus it is an identity and is written $x^2 - 1 \equiv (x - 1)(x + 1)$. On the other hand, $x^2 = 1$ is an equation, but not an identity, since it holds only when x is 1 or -1. In trigonometry, one becomes familiar with many identities such as $\sin^2 \theta + \cos^2 \theta \equiv 1$. In our problem, if the explicit relationship $y = f(x)$ exists, then when we replace y in the original equation with $f(x)$, the resulting equation (in x alone) always holds, so it is an identity. For the example, the identity is $x + f(x) + [f(x)]^5 \equiv 3$.
   3. Act as if $f(x)$ is differentiable and differentiate both sides of the identity with respect to x. Since the identity always holds, the derivative of the left-hand side must always equal the derivative of the right-hand side. Thus we have generated a new identity. For the example, the derivative of the left-hand side is $1 + f'(x) + 5[f(x)]^4 f'(x)$ and the derivative of the right-hand side is zero. Thus the new identity is $1 + f'(x) + 5[f(x)]^4 f'(x) \equiv 0$. Note that we used the chain rule to determine the derivative of the left-hand side. This is commonly necessary.
   4. Evaluate the identity in step 3 at the original point, (x^0, y^0), recalling $y^0 = f(x^0)$. For the example, $x^0 = 1$ and $1 = y^0 = f(x^0) = f(1)$. The resulting equation is $1 + f'(1) + 5[1]^4 f'(1) = 0$ or $1 + 6f'(1) = 0$. This is now an equation rather than an identity because a specific value for x has been used. It is an equation in the desired derivative, $f'(1)$, not in x.
   5. Solve for the desired derivative. In the example, the solution is $f'(1) = -1/6$. Whenever the answer is well defined (i.e., whenever we do not need to divide by zero to solve the equation in 4), the previous steps are all justified and y can be expressed as a differentiable function of x at

least near the starting point. Even though we cannot explicitly solve to find the function f, we have found its derivative at $x = 1$.

If the solution involves division by zero, then y is not a differentiable function of x and $f'(x^0)$ does not exist. (It is still possible that y is an explicit, nondifferentiable function of x, but we would be unable to check this.) For example, if we started with the equation $x - y^2 = 0$ and initial point $x = y = 0$, the steps in our procedure would be

1. $0 - 0 = 0$;
2. $x - [f(x)]^2 \equiv 0$;
3. $1 - 2[f(x)]f'(x) \equiv 0$;
4. $1 - 2[0]f'(0) = 0$ or $1 - 0f'(0) = 0$; and
5. solving for $f'(0)$ involves dividing by zero, so y is not a differentiable function of x.

In the graph of the set of points satisfying $x - y^2 = 0$, the tangent line to the graph at $(0, 0)$ is vertical, which is not possible for a differentiable function.

1.16 DIFFERENTIALS

When $y = f(x)$, the differential of x, dx, is any number and the differential of y, dy, is a function of x and dx given by $dy = f'(x)\,dx$. We can think of dx and dy as changes in x and in y, starting from $(x, f(x))$, such that the new point remains on the tangent line approximation to the graph of f at x. Since the tangent line at x has slope $f'(x)$, the changes in y and in x must satisfy $dy/dx = f'(x)$. These differentials must be distinguished from the alternative notation for a derivative, dy/dx, which is a single piece of notation that cannot be separated. Differentials on the other hand, can be separated but are related by the equation $dy = f'(x)\,dx$.

1.17 DEFINITE INTEGRAL

If $b \geq a$ and $f(x) \geq 0$ for all x between a and b, then the notation $\int_a^b f(x)\,dx$ represents the area under the graph of $f(x)$ and above the x-axis between $x = a$ and $x = b$. The notation is called a *definite integral*. (Note: if $f(x) < 0$, then we count the area as negative, while if $b < a$, we define $\int_a^b f(x)\,dx = -\int_b^a f(x)\,dx$.) To determine the exact area we can proceed as in the following example. To evaluate $\int_0^1 x^2\,dx$ split up the x-axis between 0 and 1 into n intervals of length $1/n$, from 0 to $1/n$, from $1/n$ to $2/n$, from $2/n$ to $3/n, \ldots$, and from $(n - 1)/n$ to $n/n = 1$.

Consider the ith interval, between $(i - 1)/n$ and i/n. For every x in this interval, $[(i - 1)/n]^2 \leq x^2 \leq [i/n]^2$. Thus the area under the graph of $f(x) = x^2$ between $(i - 1)/n$ and i/n is greater than $[(i - 1)/n]^2(1/n)$ and less than $[i/n]^2(1/n)$. (These are the areas of the rectangles with width $1/n$ and heights $[(i - 1)/n]^2$ and $[i/n]^2$, respectively.) Since this is true for each ith interval, $i = 1, 2, \ldots, n$, the total area $\int_0^1 x^2\, dx$ is between $[0/n]^2(1/n) + [1/n]^2(1/n) + \cdots + [(n - 1)/n]^2(1/n)$ and $[1/n]^2(1/n) + [2/n]^2(1/n) + \cdots + [n/n]^2(1/n)$. Using the formula $1^2 + 2^2 + 3^2 + \cdots + n^2 = n(n + 1)(2n + 1)/6$, the first sum is $(2n^2 - 3n + 1)/6n^2$ while the second sum is $(2n^2 + 3n + 1)/6n^2$. This is true for all n, so

$$\frac{1}{3} = \lim_{n \to \infty} \frac{(2n^2 - 3n + 1)}{6n^2} \leq \int_0^1 x^2\, dx \leq \lim_{n \to \infty} \frac{(2n^2 + 3n + 1)}{6n^2} = \frac{1}{3}.$$

Thus $\int_0^1 x^2\, dx = 1/3$.

1.18 PRIMITIVES AND THE FUNDAMENTAL THEOREM OF CALCULUS

The procedure in the previous section was rather complicated, even for the simple example considered. An alternative procedure involves finding an antiderivative for the function being integrated.

DEFINITION: The function F is an *antiderivative* or *primitive* of the function f if $F'(x) = f(x)$ for all x (in some feasible region).

Note that if $F(x)$ is a primitive for $f(x)$, then so is $F(x) + c$ for any constant c.

Does the function f have a primitive? The first half of the *fundamental theorem of calculus* shows that $\int_a^x f(t)\, dt$ is a primitive for f if f is continuous. To see this suppose f is continuous and let $F(x) = \int_a^x f(t)\, dt$. Then $F(x + h) - F(x)$ is the area under f between x and $x + h$. For small h, the area $F(x + h) - F(x)$ is approximately equal to the area of the rectangle with width h and height $f(x)$, i.e., $hf(x)$. Thus

$$F'(x) = \lim_{h \to 0} \frac{F(x + h) - F(x)}{h} = f(x),$$

and F is a primitive for f. This important result is summarized in

RESULT: $d(\int_a^x f(t)\, dt)/dx = f(x)$ if f is continuous at x.

EXAMPLE: If $F(x) = \int_2^x (\ln t) e^{t^2} \, dt$, then $F'(x) = (\ln x)) e^{x^2}$; i.e., we just evaluate the integrand $(f(t))$ at $t = x$.

EXAMPLE: If $F(x) = \int_x^a e^{t^2} \, dt$, then we use the fact that $\int_x^a e^{t^2} \, dt = -\int_a^x e^{t^2} \, dt = \int_a^x - e^{t^2} \, dt$ to find $F'(x) = -e^{x^2}$.

The second half of the *fundamental theorem of calculus* provides a way to evaluate integrals (and the areas they represent). If $F(x)$ and $G(x)$ are both primitives of the function f, then $F'(x) \equiv G'(x) \equiv f(x)$, so F and G differ only by some constant, i.e., $G(x) \equiv F(x) + c$. Suppose $F(x) = \int_a^x f(t) \, dt$ and $a < b$. Then $F(a) = 0$ (the area is over a region with width zero), and $F(b) = \int_a^b f(t) \, dt$. For the primitive $G(x) \equiv F(x) + c$,

$$\int_a^b f(t) \, dt = F(b) = F(b) - F(a)$$

$$= (F(b) + c) - (F(a) + c) = G(b) - G(a).$$

This important result is summarized in

RESULT: If F is any primitive for f, then $\int_a^b f(t) \, dt = F(b) - F(a)$.

This provides a method for evaluating integrals. One often sees the notation $F(x)]_a^b$ to represent $F(b) - F(a)$.

EXAMPLE: $x^3/3$ is a primitive for x^2 [check: $d(x^3/3)/dx = x^2$], so $\int_0^1 t^2 \, dt = (1^3/3) - (0^3/3) = 1/3$.

EXAMPLE: $\ln(x + 1)$ is a primitive for $1/(x + 1)$ [check: $d(\ln(x + 1))/dx = 1/(x + 1)$], so

$$\int_1^2 \frac{dt}{t + 1} = \ln(x + 1) \Big]_1^2 = \ln(3) - \ln(2) = \ln(3/2).$$

1.19 INDEFINITE INTEGRAL

The notation $\int f(x) \, dx$ (called the *indefinite integral*) is commonly used to denote an arbitrary primitive of f. This can create some confusion because the primitive, $F(x)$, is also written as a function of x.

EXAMPLE: $\int x^2 \, dx = (x^3/3) + c$.

The constant of integration, c, is included because the indefinite integral represents an arbitrary primitive of f and all primitives of f differ only by a constant. Thus once we know one primitive, $F(x)$, all other primitives are of the form $G(x) = F(x) + c$ for some constant c.

The confusion in this notation arises because x is used both as a dummy variable in $\int f(x)\, dx$ and as the actual variable in $F(x)$. Recall that we found that one primitive of f is $F(x) = \int_a^x f(t)\, dt$. Notice that the variable x does *not* appear as the variable being integrated, which is t. The t is a dummy variable. We could have used $f(z)\, dz$ or $f(s)\, ds$ or any other dummy variable except x as a placeholder. We cannot use x in $f(t)\, dt$ because x has a specific role as the upper bound of integration, $\int_a^x$. Despite this, it is common practice to use x as both the dummy variable in $\int f(x)\, dx$ and the variable in the primitive, $F(x)$.

EXAMPLE: $\int 2x\, dx = x^2 + c$.

1.20 BASIC RULES OF INTEGRATION

Simple observations about areas along with our definitions provide some basic facts about definite integrals:

$$\int_a^a f(t)\, dt = 0,$$

$$\int_a^b f(t)\, dt = -\int_b^a f(t)\, dt,$$

$$\int_a^b f(t)\, dt + \int_b^c f(t)\, dt = \int_a^c f(t)\, dt,$$

$$\int_a^b -f(t)\, dt = -\int_a^b f(t)\, dt,$$

$$\int_a^b kf(t)\, dt = k\int_a^b f(t)\, dt,$$

$$\int_a^b [f(t) + g(t)]\, dt = \int_a^b f(t)\, dt + \int_a^b g(t)\, dt.$$

The basic rules for finding primitives follow from the basic rules of differentiation. It is important to remember that we are moving in the opposite direction from differentiation. We are asking, what is a function whose derivative is f? rather than, what is the derivative of f? We also have available a simple method to check our results: if $F(x)$ is a primitive of $f(x)$, then the derivative of F must equal f, $F'(x) = f(x)$. Basic properties of indefinite integrals include

$$\int e^x \, dx = e^x + c,$$

$$\int \frac{1}{x} \, dx = \ln|x| + c,$$

$$\int x^n \, dx = \frac{x^{n+1}}{n+1} + c \quad \text{for} \quad n \neq -1$$

$$\left(\int 1 \, dx = x + c \text{ is the case } n = 0 \right),$$

$$\int [f(x) + g(x)] \, dx = \int f(x) \, dx + \int g(x) \, dx,$$

$$\int kf(x) \, dx = k \int f(x) \, dx,$$

$$\int 0 \, dx = c.$$

1.21 INTEGRATION BY PARTS

By the product rule for differentiation,

$$\frac{d}{dx}[u(x)v(x)] = u'(x)v(x) + u(x)v'(x).$$

Integrating both sides,

$$\int_a^b [u'(x)v(x) + u(x)v'(x)] \, dx = \int_a^b \frac{d}{dx}[u(x)v(x)] \, dx.$$

The left-hand side can be broken up into $\int_a^b u'(x)v(x) \, dx + \int_a^b u(x)v'(x) \, dx$. A primitive for the right-hand side is $u(x)v(x)$, so

$$\int_a^b \frac{d}{dx}[u(x)v(x)] \, dx = u(x)v(x) \Big]_a^b.$$

Rearranging these terms, we get the formula for *integration by parts*,

$$\int_a^b u'(x)v(x) \, dx = u(x)v(x) \Big]_a^b - \int_a^b u(x)v'(x) \, dx.$$

This formula can sometimes be used to simplify complex integration problems. The difficulty is deciding what to consider $u'(x)$ and what to consider $v(x)$.

EXAMPLE: To evaluate $\int_0^1 xe^x \, dx$ let $u'(x) = e^x$ and $v(x) = x$. Then we can use $u(x) = e^x$ (we could use $u(x) = e^x + c$, but the constant would just cancel out eventually, after creating more work in the initial computation) and $v'(x) = 1$. To decide whether this is a good choice for a decomposition, we check whether $\int_0^1 u(x)v'(x) \, dx$ is simpler than the original problem. Here $\int_0^1 u(x)v'(x) \, dx = \int_0^1 e^x \, dx$, which is simpler. [If we had set $u'(x) = x$ and $v(x) = e^x$, then $u(x) = x^2/2$ and $v'(x) = e^x$, so $\int_0^1 u(x)v'(x) \, dx = \int_0^1 (x^2/2)e^x \, dx$, which is more complicated than the original problem.] From the integration-by-parts formula,

$$\int_0^1 xe^x \, dx = xe^x \bigg]_0^1 - \int_0^1 e^x \, dx = (1 \cdot e^1 - 0 \cdot e^0) - e^x \bigg]_0^1$$

$$= e - (e^1 - e^0) = e^0 = 1.$$

EXAMPLE: To evaluate $\int_1^e \ln x dx$, let $u'(x) = 1$ and $v(x) = \ln x$, so $u(x) = x$ and $v'(x) = 1/x$. Then $\int_1^e u(x)v'(x) \, dx = \int_1^e (x/x) \, dx$, which is simpler than the original problem. By the integration-by-parts formula,

$$\int_1^e \ln x \, dx = x \ln x \bigg]_1^e - \int_1^e dx = (e \ln e - \ln 1) - x \bigg]_1^e$$

$$= (e - 0) - (e - 1) = 1.$$

The integration-by-parts formula can also be used to find primitives.

EXAMPLE: To find $\int xe^x \, dx$, let $u'(x) = e^x$ and $v(x) = x$, so $u(x) = e^x$ and $v'(x) = 1$. Then $\int xe^x \, dx = xe^x - \int e^x \, dx = xe^x - e^x + c$. To check this, differentiate $xe^x - e^x + c$ to get $e^x + xe^x - e^x = xe^x$. Thus $xe^x - e^x$ is a primitive for xe^x.

EXAMPLE: To find $\int \ln x dx$, let $u'(x) = 1$ and $v(x) = \ln x$, so $u(x) = x$ and $v'(x) = 1/x$. Then $\int \ln x dx = x \ln x - \int dx = x \ln x - x + c$. To check this, differentiate $x \ln x - x + c$ to get $\ln x + x(1/x) - 1 = \ln x$. Thus $x \ln x - x$ is a primitive for $\ln x$.

1.22 CHANGE OF VARIABLE

By the chain rule for differentiation,

$$\frac{d}{dy}(h(g(y))) = h'(g(y))g'(y).$$

Integrating both sides,

$$\int_A^B \frac{d}{dy}(h(g(y)))\,dy = \int_A^B h'(g(y))g'(y)\,dy.$$

A primitive for the left-hand side is $h(g(y))$ so

$$\int_A^B \frac{d}{dy}(h(g(y)))\,dy = h(g(y))\Bigg]_A^B.$$

By the properties of the definite integral, $h(g(y))]_A^B$ is the area under the graph of $h'(x)$ between $x = g(A)$ and $x = g(B)$. If we let $a = g(A)$ and $b = g(B)$, then another notation for the same area is $\int_a^b h'(x)\,dx$. Thus

$$\int_a^b h'(x)\,dx = \int_A^B \frac{d}{dy}(h(g(y)))\,dy = \int_A^B h'(g(y))g'(y)\,dy.$$

Letting the function f be the derivative function h', we have derived the *change-of-variable* formula:

$$\int_a^b f(x)\,dx = \int_A^B f(g(y))g'(y)\,dy \quad \text{where } a = g(A) \text{ and } b = g(B).$$

This formula can sometimes be used to simplify complex integration problems. The difficulty is deciding how to decompose the original function and keeping track of the relationship between (a, b) and (A, B).

EXAMPLE: To evaluate $\int_1^4 (e^{\sqrt{x}}/\sqrt{x})\,dx$, let $f(x) = e^{\sqrt{x}}/\sqrt{x}$ and $x = g(y) = y^2$. To find A and B, solve $g(A) = 1$ to get $A = 1$ and $g(B) = 4$ to get $B = 2$. The derivative of g is $g'(y) = 2y$. By the change-of-variable formula,

$$\int_1^4 \frac{e^{\sqrt{x}}}{\sqrt{x}}\,dx = \int_1^2 \frac{e^{\sqrt{y^2}}}{\sqrt{y^2}}2y\,dy = \int_1^2 \frac{e^y}{y}2y\,dy = \int_1^2 2e^y\,dy = 2e^y\Bigg]_1^2$$

$$= 2e^2 - 2e.$$

EXAMPLE: Sometimes the integrand looks like the right-hand side of the change-of-variable formula. To evaluate $\int_1^2 2xe^{x^2+1}\,dx$, note that for $g(x) = x^2 + 1$ and $f(y) = e^y$, $g'(x) = 2x$ so $\int_1^2 2xe^{x^2+1}\,dx = \int_1^2 f(g(x))g'(x)\,dx$. For $a = g(A) = g(1) = 2$ and $b = g(B) = g(2) = 5$, by the change-of-variable formula, $\int_2^5 e^y\,dy = \int_1^2 2xe^{x^2+1}\,dx$. The left-hand side is equal to $e^y]_2^5 = e^5 - e^2$, so that is the value of the original integral.

These two examples used the change-of-variable formula in opposite directions. One must be careful to determine the direction in which the formula is being used. In particular, one must know whether the initial limits of integration are to be used as a and b (so A and B are found as solutions to $a = g(A)$ and $b = g(B)$) or as A and B (so $a = g(A)$ and $b = g(B)$).

EXAMPLE: To evaluate $\int_0^3 x^2\sqrt{x+1}\,dx$, let $x = g(y) = y^2 - 1$ and $f(x) = x^2\sqrt{x+1}$. For this approach, the original limits of integration correspond to a and b so we solve $g(A) = 0$ to find $A = 1$ and $g(B) = 3$ to find $B = 2$. Since $g'(y) = 2y$, by the change-of-variable formula,

$$\int_0^3 x^2\sqrt{x+1}\,dx = \int_1^2 (y^2 - 1)^2\left(\sqrt{y^2 - 1 + 1}\right)2y\,dy$$

$$= \int_1^2 (y^4 - 2y^2 + 1)y2y\,dy = \int_1^2 (2y^6 - 4y^4 + 2y^2)\,dy$$

$$= \left[\frac{2y^7}{7} - \frac{4y^5}{5} + \frac{2y^3}{3}\right]_1^2 = \left(\frac{256}{7} - \frac{128}{5} + \frac{16}{3}\right)$$

$$-\left(\frac{2}{7} - \frac{4}{5} + \frac{2}{3}\right) = \frac{254}{7} - \frac{124}{5} + \frac{14}{3}.$$

Notice how the change of variables, $x = y^2 - 1$, was chosen to eliminate the square root and leave only a polynomial to integrate.

1.23 IMPROPER INTEGRALS

An *improper integral* is an integral involving "infinity" either as a limit of integration [e.g., $\int_a^\infty f(t)\,dt$, or $\int_{-\infty}^b f(t)\,dt$, or $\int_{-\infty}^\infty f(t)\,dt$] or in the integrand [e.g., $f(t) = 1/t^2$ is undefined at $t = 0$; so $\int_{-1}^1 (1/t^2)\,dt$ involves "infinity"]. These integrals must be evaluated using a limiting process that avoids using "infinity" directly. The value of the improper integral is defined as follows:

$$\int_a^\infty f(t)\,dt = \lim_{b \to \infty} \int_a^b f(t)\,dt \quad \text{if the limit exists.}$$

$$\int_{-\infty}^b f(t)\,dt = \lim_{a \to -\infty} \int_a^b f(t)\,dt \quad \text{if the limit exists.}$$

$$\int_{-\infty}^\infty f(t)\,dt = \lim_{\substack{a \to -\infty \\ b \to \infty}} \int_a^b f(t)\,dt \quad \text{if the limit exists.}$$

If $f(t)$ is undefined at say $t = 1$, let the notation $B \to 1^-$ mean B approaches 1 from below and $A \to 1^+$ mean A approaches 1 from above.

Then if $a < 1 < b$,

$$\int_a^b f(t)\, dt = \lim_{B \to 1^-} \int_a^B f(t)\, dt + \lim_{A \to 1^+} \int_A^b f(t)\, dt$$

if both limits exist.

EXAMPLE:

$$\int_0^\infty e^{-rt}\, dt = \lim_{b \to \infty} \int_0^b e^{-rt}\, dt$$

$$= \lim_{b \to \infty} \left[-\frac{1}{r} e^{-rt} \right]_0^b$$

$$= \lim_{b \to \infty} \left(-\frac{1}{r} e^{-rb} + \frac{1}{r} \right)$$

$$= \frac{1}{r}.$$

EXAMPLE:

$$\int_0^4 (1/\sqrt{x})\, dx = \lim_{a \to 0^+} \int_a^4 (1/\sqrt{x})\, dx$$

$$= \lim_{a \to 0^+} \left[2\sqrt{x} \right]_a^4$$

$$= \lim_{a \to 0^+} (2\sqrt{4} - 2\sqrt{a})$$

$$= 4.$$

EXAMPLE:

$$\int_1^2 [1/(x - 1)]\, dx = \lim_{a \to 1^+} \int_a^2 [1/(x - 1)]\, dx$$

$$= \lim_{a \to 1^+} \left[\ln(x - 1) \right]_a^2$$

$$= \lim_{a \to 1^+} (\ln 1 - \ln(a - 1))$$

$$= \lim_{a \to 1^+} (-\ln(a - 1)).$$

This *diverges* (i.e., the value becomes an arbitrarily large negative number) and there is no finite limit. We say the original integral *diverges*.

EXAMPLE:

$$\int_1^\infty (1/x^2)\, dx = \lim_{b \to \infty} \int_1^b (1/x^2)\, dx$$

$$= \lim_{b \to \infty} \left[-1/x \right]_1^b$$

$$= \lim_{b \to \infty} \left[(-1/b) - (-1) \right]$$

$$= 1.$$

EXAMPLE:

$$\int_{-1}^1 (1/x)\, dx = \lim_{b \to 0^-} \int_{-1}^b (1/x)\, dx + \lim_{a \to 0^+} \int_a^1 (1/x)\, dx$$

$$= \lim_{b \to 0^-} \left[\ln|x| \right]_{-1}^b + \lim_{a \to 0^+} \left[\ln x \right]_a^1$$

$$= \lim_{b \to 0^-} (\ln|b| - \ln 1) + \lim_{a \to 0^+} (\ln 1 - \ln a).$$

Each of the limits diverges, so $\int_{-1}^1 (1/x)\, dx$ diverges. Note that we are not allowed to say "the negative values for $x < 0$ exactly balance the positive values for $x > 0$." If any limit diverges, the integral diverges. This also illustrates the importance of checking the integrand to see whether the integral is improper. If we had not done this, we would have acted as if $\int_{-1}^1 (1/x)\, dx = \ln|x|\,]_{-1}^1 = \ln 1 - \ln 1 = 0$, which is wrong.

1.24 DIFFERENTIATING INTEGRALS

By the first half of the fundamental theorem of calculus, if f is continuous at x, then

$$\frac{d}{dx} \int_a^x f(t)\, dt = f(x).$$

If the upper limit of integration is the continuously differentiable function $b(x)$ rather than x, what is

$$\frac{d}{dx} \int_a^{b(x)} f(t)\, dt?$$

To find out, let $F(x) = \int_a^{b(x)} f(t)\, dt$. Then $F(x + h) - F(x)$ is the area under f between $b(x)$ and $b(x + h)$. But $b(x + h)$ is approximately $b(x) + hb'(x)$. Thus for small h, the area $F(x + h) - F(x)$ is approximately equal to the area of the rectangle with width $hb'(x)$ and height

$f(b(x))$, i.e., $hb'(x)f(b(x))$. Thus

$$F'(x) = \lim_{h \to 0} \frac{F(x+h) - F(x)}{h} = b'(x)f(b(x)).$$

What if the lower limit of integration is a continuously differentiable function of x? If $F(x) = \int_{a(x)}^{b} f(t)\,dt$, then $F(x) = -\int_{b}^{a(x)} f(t)\,dt$, so $F'(x) = -a'(x)f(a(x))$.

If both upper and lower limits of integration are functions of x, then

$$F(x) = \int_{a(x)}^{b(x)} f(t)\,dt = \int_{a(x)}^{c} f(t)\,dt + \int_{c}^{b(x)} f(t)\,dt$$

so

$$F'(x) = -a(x)f(a(x)) + b'(x)f(b(x)).$$

What if the integrand is a function of x as well as t? If $F(x) = \int_{a}^{b} f(t, x)\,dt$ and f and $\partial f/\partial x$ are continuous, then

$$F(x + h) = \int_{a}^{b} f(t, x+h)\,dt \approx \int_{a}^{b} \left[f(t, x) + h\frac{\partial f(t, x)}{\partial x} \right] dt$$

so

$$F(x+h) - F(x) \approx \int_{a}^{b} h\frac{\partial f(t, x)}{\partial x}\,dt = h\int_{a}^{b} \frac{\partial f(t, x)}{\partial x}\,dt.$$

Thus

$$F'(x) = \lim_{h \to 0} \frac{F(x+h) - F(x)}{h} = \int_{a}^{b} \frac{\partial f(t, x)}{\partial x}\,dt.$$

If any combination of the three possibilities (integrand a function of x, upper or lower limit of integration a function of x) holds, we just add up the corresponding effects.

EXAMPLE: Let $f(t, x) = t + x$, $a(x) = x$, $b(x) = 1 + 2x$ and $F(x) = \int_{a(x)}^{b(x)} f(t, x)\,dt$. Then

$$F'(0) = -a'(0)f(a(0), 0) + b'(0)f(b(0), 0) + \int_{a(0)}^{b(0)} \frac{\partial f(t, 0)}{\partial x}\,dt$$

$$= -(1)f(0, 0) + 2f(1, 0) + \int_{0}^{1} 1\,dt = 0 + 2 + 1 = 3.$$

1.25 DIFFERENTIAL EQUATIONS

A *first-order differential equation* is an equation of the form $dy/dx = H(x, y)$. A solution to this equation is a function $f(x)$ satisfying $f'(x) \equiv H(x, f(x))$. Then $y = f(x)$ satisfies the differential equation. If we have an *initial condition*, such as $y(0) = \bar{y}$, this will further determine the function f.

EXAMPLE: For $H(x, y) \equiv 1$, the function $f(x) = x + c$ satisfies $f'(x) \equiv H(x, f(x))$ for any constant c. With initial condition $y(0) = 2$, the constant c must satisfy $2 = y(0) = f(0) = 0 + c$ or $c = 2$. Thus the only solution satisfying the initial condition is $f(x) = x + 2$.

Consider a special, simple form of differential equation in which the variables are separable, i.e., in which $H(x, y) = g(x)h(y)$. If $f(x)$ is a solution satisfying the initial condition $y^0 = f(x^0)$, then $f'(x) \equiv g(x)h(f(x))$. If $h(f(x)) \neq 0$, then $f'(x)/h(f(x)) \equiv g(x)$. Integrating both sides (using t as a dummy variable) between x^0 and an arbitrary x, $\int_{x^0}^x (f'(t)/h(f(t)))\, dt = \int_{x^0}^x g(t)\, dt$. With a change of variable on the left-hand side to $y = f(t)$, the limits of integration become $y^0 = f(x^0)$ and $f(x)$, and $\int_{y^0}^{f(x)} (1/h(y))\, dy = \int_{x^0}^x g(t)\, dt$. This defines the solution $f(x)$.

In practice, we separate the original differential equation so that all terms in y appear on one side of the equation and all terms in x appear on the other. Then we integrate both sides and solve.

EXAMPLE: To solve $dy/dx = x^3/y^2$ with initial condition $y = 1$, when $x = 0$, first separate the variables, i.e., "$y^2 dy = x^3 dx$." Note that we have acted as if dy and dx are differentials rather than the single term dy/dx. Integrating both sides, $\int y^2\, dy = \int x^3\, dx$, or $y^3/3 = x^4/4 + c$. Note that we use only a single constant of integration. Plugging in $y = 1$ and $x = 0$ we can solve for c, $1/3 = 0 + c$ or $c = 1/3$. Finally, solving for y, we get $y = [(3x^4/4) + 1]^{1/3} = f(x)$ as the solution satisfying the initial condition.

EXAMPLE: To solve $dy/dx = 3x^2$ with initial condition $y = -2$, when $x = 0$, first separate the variables, i.e., "$dy = 3x^2 dx$," then integrate both sides, $\int dy = \int 3x^2 dx$ or $y = x^3 + c$. Substituting in the initial conditions and solving for c, $c = -2$. Thus the solution satisfying the initial conditions is $y = f(x) = x^3 - 2$.

EXAMPLE: To solve $dy/dx = 10xy$ with initial condition $y = 1$, when $x = 1$, first separate the variables, i.e., "$dy/y = 10x\, dx$," then integrate both sides, $\int dy/y = \int 10x\, dx$ or $\ln|y| = 5x^2 + c$. Substituting in the initial conditions and solving for c, $c = -5$. Thus the solution satisfying the initial conditions is $y = f(x) = e^{5x^2-5}$. It is always possible to check the solution by differentiating. Here $f'(x) = (e^{5x^2-5})(10x)$ by the chain rule. But $e^{5x^2-5} = y$ so $f'(x) = 10xy$ as required.

PROBLEMS

Only problems dealing with differentiation of integrals, a topic likely to be new to most readers, are included in this chapter.

1.1 Evaluate

$$\frac{d}{dx}\left\{\int_{-1}^{2x} e^{xt^2}\, dt\right\}$$

at $x = 0$.

1.2 Evaluate

$$\frac{d}{dx}\left\{\int_{3-x}^{4} \ln(t - x)\, dt\right\}$$

at $x = 1$.

1.3 Evaluate

$$\frac{d}{dx}\left\{\int_{2x}^{ex} \ln(xt)\, dt\right\}$$

at $x = 1$.

2

LINEAR
ALGEBRA

2.1 INTRODUCTION

This chapter contains background material on some topics in linear algebra, including subspaces, hyperplanes, eigenvalues, and quadratic forms. Our later work on constrained optimization will rely on material from the sections on subspaces and hyperplanes for first-order conditions and on material from the section on eigenvalues and quadratic forms for second-order conditions. Our stability analysis will also rely on material from the eigenvalues and quadratic forms section. The reader is assumed to be familiar with basic vector and matrix operations, linear independence, rank, determinants and inverses, Cramer's rule, etc.

In this and most other chapters, our concern is understanding why results are true, so sketches of proofs or proofs for simple special cases are often given. This is to help make the results part of one's "intuition" so that it is possible to reconstruct the main tools in later chapters from intuition rather than memorization.

2.2 SUBSPACES

This section introduces subspaces and bases for subspaces.

DEFINITION: A (*linear*) *subspace* L of $\mathbb{R}^n$ is a set of vectors in $\mathbb{R}^n$ such that

1. If $\mathbf{x}, \mathbf{y} \in L$, then $\mathbf{x} + \mathbf{y} \in L$ and
2. If $\mathbf{x} \in L$ and $s \in \mathbb{R}$, then $s\mathbf{x} \in L$.

EXAMPLE: For $\mathbb{R}^2$, $\mathbb{R}^2$ itself satisfies 1 and 2, so it is a linear subspace. The set $\{(0,0)\}$ also satisfies 1 and 2, so it is a linear subspace. Finally, any line through the origin satisfies 1 and 2 since for any $\mathbf{a} \neq \mathbf{0}$ on the line, $\mathbf{x} \in L$ implies $\mathbf{x} = s_1\mathbf{a}$ for some $s_1 \in \mathbb{R}$ and $\mathbf{y} \in L$ implies $\mathbf{y} = s_2\mathbf{a}$ for some $s_2 \in \mathbb{R}$, so $\mathbf{x} + \mathbf{y} = (s_1 + s_2)\mathbf{a} \in L$ and $s\mathbf{x} = s(s_1\mathbf{a}) = (ss_1)\mathbf{a} \in L$.

EXAMPLE: For $\mathbb{R}^3$, the linear subspaces are $\{(0,0,0)\}$, the lines through the origin, the planes through the origin, and $\mathbb{R}^3$.

DEFINITION: A set of vectors $\{\mathbf{a}_1, \mathbf{a}_2, \ldots, \mathbf{a}_m\}$ in L *spans* L if every vector in L can be written as a linear combination of $\{\mathbf{a}_1, \mathbf{a}_2, \ldots, \mathbf{a}_m\}$.

DEFINITION: A set of vectors $\{\mathbf{a}_1, \mathbf{a}_2, \ldots, \mathbf{a}_m\}$ in $\mathbb{R}^n$ is a *linearly independent* set if $\lambda_1\mathbf{a}_1 + \cdots + \lambda_m\mathbf{a}_m = 0$ implies $\lambda_1 = \lambda_2 = \cdots = \lambda_m = 0$.

If we can write one vector in a set of vectors as a linear combination of the others, then the set of vectors is not linearly independent.

DEFINITION: A *basis* for the linear subspace L is a linearly independent set of vectors which spans L.

It is possible to show that every basis of L must contain the same number of vectors. This number is called the *dimension* of L. No set of linearly independent vectors in L can contain more vectors than the dimension of L.

EXAMPLE: For $\mathbb{R}^3$, $\{(0,0,0)\}$ has dimension zero, the lines through the origin have dimension one, the planes through the origin have dimension two, and $\mathbb{R}^3$ has dimension three.

Every nontrivial subspace has many different bases. For a one-dimensional subspace L, these different bases are all transparently equivalent: if $\{\mathbf{a}_1\}$ is a basis for L and $\{\mathbf{b}_1\}$ is a basis for L, then there is a nonzero scalar, $\alpha \in \mathbb{R}$, such that $\mathbf{a}_1 = \alpha\mathbf{b}_1$. When L has dimension greater than 1, the relationship between two bases $\{\mathbf{a}_1, \ldots, \mathbf{a}_m\}$ and $\{\mathbf{b}_1, \ldots, \mathbf{b}_m\}$ may not be transparent. However, there is always a nonsingular $m \times m$ matrix transforming one basis to the other.

Given a basis $\{\mathbf{a}_1, \ldots, \mathbf{a}_m\}$ for the subspace L, every vector in L has a unique representation in terms of the basis. If $\mathbf{x} \in L$ and $\mathbf{x} = \sum_{i=1}^m \lambda_i\mathbf{a}_i = \sum_{i=1}^m \mu_i\mathbf{a}_i$, then $0 = \sum_{i=1}^m (\lambda_i - \mu_i)\mathbf{a}_i$, so by independence $\lambda_i - \mu_i = 0$ for $i = 1, 2, \ldots m$.

In $\mathbb{R}^n$, there is only one subspace of dimension zero, $\{0\}$, and one subspace of dimension n, $\mathbb{R}^n$ itself. For $0 < m < n$ there are many different subspaces with dimension m. (Note the difference between this and our previous discussion of the many different bases for a single subspace.) For example, in $\mathbb{R}^3$, every line through the origin is a subspace of dimension one. Thus there is an infinity of different subspaces of dimension one. However, in a very important sense all subspaces of the same dimension, independent of their parent space ($\mathbb{R}^n$ for any n), are equivalent (technically called isomorphic). Thus every subspace of dimension m may be thought of intuitively as $\mathbb{R}^m$. Only when we ask questions concerning vectors (potentially) outside the subspace do differences arise. For example, a two-dimensional subspace of $\mathbb{R}^2$ contains all of $\mathbb{R}^2$, while most vectors in $\mathbb{R}^3$ are not contained in the two-dimensional subspace of $\mathbb{R}^3$ with basis $\{(1, 0, 0), (0, 1, 0)\}$.

2.3 SYSTEMS OF EQUATIONS

As a simple application of the intuition generated by an understanding of the idea of subspaces, consider a system of linear equations. Let A be a $k \times n$ matrix with ith column $\mathbf{a}_i$, $i = 1, \ldots, n$. Also let $\mathbf{b} \in \mathbb{R}^k$. When does there exist an $\mathbf{x} \in \mathbb{R}^n$ satisfying $A\mathbf{x} = \mathbf{b}$? When does $A\mathbf{x} = \mathbf{b}$ have a unique solution? To answer these questions, note that the system of equations can be rewritten as $\sum_{i=1}^n x_i \mathbf{a}_i = \mathbf{b}$. Thus the first question becomes "when can $\mathbf{b}$ be written as a linear combination of the $\mathbf{a}_i$'s" or equivalently "when is $\mathbf{b}$ in the subspace spanned by the columns of A?" When a solution exists, it will be unique if and only if $\{\mathbf{a}_1, \ldots, \mathbf{a}_n\}$ is linearly independent. The "if" part follows from our previous observation that a vector in a subspace has a unique representation in terms of a basis for the subspace. The "only if" part follows from the observation that if $\{\mathbf{a}_1, \ldots, \mathbf{a}_n\}$ are not independent then there is some $\boldsymbol{\lambda} \in \mathbb{R}^n$, $\boldsymbol{\lambda} \neq \mathbf{0}$ such that $\sum_{i=1}^n \lambda_i \mathbf{a}_i = \mathbf{0}$. But then if $\mathbf{x}$ is a solution, so is $\mathbf{x} + \alpha \boldsymbol{\lambda}$ for any $\alpha \in \mathbb{R}$ (since $A\boldsymbol{\lambda} = \mathbf{0}$).

DEFINITION: The *rank* of matrix A is the number of linearly independent columns of A.

Note that the rank of a matrix equals the dimension of the subspace spanned by the columns of the matrix. Thus $\text{rank}[\mathbf{a}_1, \mathbf{a}_2, \ldots, \mathbf{a}_n, \mathbf{b}] = \text{rank}[\mathbf{a}_1, \mathbf{a}_2, \ldots, \mathbf{a}_n]$ if and only if $\mathbf{b}$ is in the subspace spanned by $\{\mathbf{a}_1, \mathbf{a}_2, \ldots, \mathbf{a}_n\}$.

Our observations concerning the number of solutions to the system of equations $A\mathbf{x} = \mathbf{b}$ can be summarized in the (probably more familiar) rank conditions:

1. There is no solution if and only if $\text{rank}[\mathbf{a}_1, \mathbf{a}_2, \ldots, \mathbf{a}_n, \mathbf{b}] > \text{rank}[\mathbf{a}_1, \mathbf{a}_2, \ldots, \mathbf{a}_n]$.

2. There is a unique solution if and only if $\text{rank}[\mathbf{a}_1, \mathbf{a}_2, \ldots, \mathbf{a}_n, \mathbf{b}] = \text{rank}[\mathbf{a}_1, \mathbf{a}_2, \ldots, \mathbf{a}_n] = n$.

3. There are infinitely many solutions if and only if $\text{rank}[\mathbf{a}_1, \mathbf{a}_2, \ldots, \mathbf{a}_n, \mathbf{b}] = \text{rank}[\mathbf{a}_1, \mathbf{a}_2, \ldots, \mathbf{a}_n] < n$.

To find all solutions to $A\mathbf{x} = \mathbf{b}$, consider each of the three cases. In case 1 there is no solution. In case 2, if A is an $m \times n$ matrix, there is an $n \times n$ nonsingular submatrix A^* obtained by deleting $m - n$ appropriate rows from A. If $\mathbf{b}^*$ is obtained by deleting the same $m - n$ "rows" from the column vector $\mathbf{b}$, then $\mathbf{x}^* = (A^*)^{-1}\mathbf{b}^*$ is the unique solution. In case 3, if rank $A = k < n$, there will be an $(n - k)$-dimensional subspace of solutions to $A\mathbf{x} = \mathbf{0}$. If S is the subspace of solutions and $\mathbf{x}^*$ is any particular solution to $A\mathbf{x}^* = \mathbf{b}$, then the set of solutions to $A\mathbf{x} = \mathbf{b}$ is $\{\mathbf{x}^* + \mathbf{s} \mid \mathbf{s} \in S\}$.

EXAMPLE: If

$$A = \begin{bmatrix} 2 & 0 & 2 \\ 0 & 2 & 2 \\ 1 & 1 & 2 \end{bmatrix} \quad \text{and} \quad \mathbf{b} = \begin{pmatrix} 2 \\ 2 \\ 2 \end{pmatrix},$$

then case 3 applies. Since

$$\mathbf{x}^* = \begin{pmatrix} 1 \\ 1 \\ 0 \end{pmatrix}$$

satisfies $A\mathbf{x}^* = \mathbf{b}$ and the set of solutions to $A\mathbf{x} = \mathbf{0}$ consists of all vectors of the form

$$\begin{pmatrix} -z \\ -z \\ z \end{pmatrix}$$

for $z \in \mathbb{R}$, the set of solutions to $A\mathbf{x} = \mathbf{b}$ is

$$\left\{ \begin{pmatrix} 1 - z \\ 1 - z \\ z \end{pmatrix} \middle| z \in \mathbb{R} \right\}.$$

Note every other particular solution, for example,

$$\mathbf{x}^{**} = \begin{pmatrix} 0 \\ 0 \\ 1 \end{pmatrix},$$

yields the same set of overall solutions.

2.4 SCALAR PRODUCT AND HYPERPLANES

In this section we introduce the scalar product of two vectors and hyperplanes. Hyperplanes are objects similar to lines in $\mathbb{R}^2$ or a plane in $\mathbb{R}^3$, but in $\mathbb{R}^n$ for arbitrary n.

DEFINITION: For $\mathbf{x}, \mathbf{y} \in \mathbb{R}^n$, the *scalar product* (or *dot product*) of $\mathbf{x}$ and $\mathbf{y}$ is $\mathbf{x} \cdot \mathbf{y} := \sum_{i=1}^{n} x_i y_i$.

DEFINITION: For $\mathbf{x}, \mathbf{y} \in \mathbb{R}^n$, $\mathbf{x}$ and $\mathbf{y}$ are *orthogonal* if $\mathbf{x} \cdot \mathbf{y} = 0$.

DEFINITION: For $\mathbf{x} \in \mathbb{R}^n$, the *length* (or *norm*) of $\mathbf{x}$ is $\|\mathbf{x}\| := \sqrt{\mathbf{x} \cdot \mathbf{x}}$.

For $t = (\mathbf{x} \cdot \mathbf{y})/\|\mathbf{y}\|^2$, $(\mathbf{x} - t\mathbf{y}) \cdot \mathbf{y} = 0$. Thus we can decompose $\mathbf{x}$ into two parts, one a multiple of $\mathbf{y}$, $t\mathbf{y}$, and the other orthogonal to $\mathbf{y}$, $\mathbf{x} - t\mathbf{y}$. We call $t\mathbf{y}$ the *projection* of $\mathbf{x}$ on $\mathbf{y}$. Note that any vector $\mathbf{z}$ which has the same projection on $\mathbf{y}$, $t\mathbf{y}$, has the same scalar product with $\mathbf{y}$.

Given a vector $\mathbf{y}$, which vector $\mathbf{x}$ with norm $c > 0$ maximizes (minimizes) $\mathbf{x} \cdot \mathbf{y}$? The set of vectors with $\|\mathbf{x}\| = c$ consists of all those vectors with heads on the "sphere" with radius c. To simplify the problem assume $\|\mathbf{y}\| = 1$. Then for any $\mathbf{x}$, if the projection of $\mathbf{x}$ on $\mathbf{y}$ is $t\mathbf{y}$, then $\mathbf{x} \cdot \mathbf{y} = t\|\mathbf{y}\|^2 = t$. To maximize $\mathbf{x} \cdot \mathbf{y}$ we must make the projection on $\mathbf{y}$ as large as possible subject to $\|\mathbf{x}\| = c$. To do this we want to waste none of the length of $\mathbf{x}$ orthogonal to $\mathbf{y}$. To see this, suppose $\|\mathbf{x}\| = c$ and $\mathbf{x} \cdot \mathbf{y} = t$. By the Pythagorean theorem, $\|\mathbf{x}\|^2 = \|t\mathbf{y}\|^2 + \|\mathbf{x} - t\mathbf{y}\|^2$. But $\|\mathbf{x}\|^2 = c^2$ and $\|t\mathbf{y}\|^2 = t^2\|\mathbf{y}\|^2 = t^2$ so, rearranging, $t^2 = c^2 - \|\mathbf{x} - t\mathbf{y}\|^2$. Since the last term is nonnegative, $t \leq c$. To make t as large as possible, set $\mathbf{x} - t\mathbf{y} = \mathbf{0}$, so $t = c$. Thus to maximize $\mathbf{x} \cdot \mathbf{y}$ subject to $\|\mathbf{x}\| = c$, set $\mathbf{x} = c\mathbf{y}$. [If $\|\mathbf{y}\| \neq 1$, we must adjust the solution to $\mathbf{x} = (c/\|\mathbf{y}\|)\mathbf{y}$.] Similarly, to minimize $\mathbf{x} \cdot \mathbf{y}$ set $\mathbf{x} = -c\mathbf{y}$.

We next consider hyperplanes, starting with hyperplanes through the origin before considering general hyperplanes. For a given, nonzero $\mathbf{a} \in \mathbb{R}^n$, consider $H_{\mathbf{a}}(0) = \{\mathbf{x} \in \mathbb{R}^n | \mathbf{a} \cdot \mathbf{x} = 0\}$. This is a *hyperplane*, and $\mathbf{a}$ is called the *normal* to the hyperplane since every vector $\mathbf{x}$ in $H_{\mathbf{a}}(0)$ is orthogonal to $\mathbf{a}$. $H_{\mathbf{a}}(0)$ is a linear subspace of $\mathbb{R}^n$ with dimension $n - 1$ (the single constraint $\mathbf{a} \cdot \mathbf{x} = 0$ eliminates one dimension). $H_{\mathbf{a}}(0)$ splits $\mathbb{R}^n$ into three parts, $H_{\mathbf{a}}(0)$ itself and two half spaces, $\{\mathbf{x} \in \mathbb{R}^n | \mathbf{a} \cdot \mathbf{x} < 0\}$ and $\{\mathbf{x} \in \mathbb{R}^n | \mathbf{a} \cdot \mathbf{x} > 0\}$. Note that $H_{\mathbf{a}}$ is "thin" in $\mathbb{R}^n$ (a line in $\mathbb{R}^2$, a plane in $\mathbb{R}^3$, etc.).

For a given, nonzero $\mathbf{a} \in \mathbb{R}^n$ and $c \in \mathbb{R}$, $H_{\mathbf{a}}(c) = \{\mathbf{x} \in \mathbb{R}^n | \mathbf{a} \cdot \mathbf{x} = c\}$ is obtained by shifting $H_{\mathbf{a}}(0)$ in the direction $\mathbf{a}$ (or $-\mathbf{a}$) until it goes through $(c/\|\mathbf{a}\|^2)\mathbf{a}$ [since $\mathbf{a} \cdot (c/\|\mathbf{a}\|^2)\mathbf{a} = c$]. $H_{\mathbf{a}}(c)$ is a hyperplane but not a subspace unless $c = 0$. Note that if c is positive, then the hyperplane is shifted in the same direction as $\mathbf{a}$. For a given normal, all hyperplanes $H_{\mathbf{a}}(c)$ are parallel. Increases in c move the hyperplane in the direction $\mathbf{a}$; decreases in c move the hyperplane in the direction $-\mathbf{a}$. Equal changes in c lead to equal shifts in the hyperplane. For example, consider the budget line $\{(x, y) | p_x x + p_y y = I\}$ where $p_x(p_y)$ is the price of $x(y)$ and I is income. Of course, only those points with nonnegative x and y make economic sense. As income I increases from 1 to 2 the budget line shifts out.

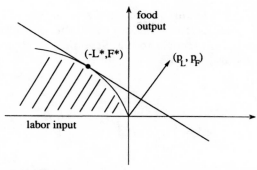

FIGURE 2.1 Profit maximization using hyperplanes.

These properties of hyperplanes can be used graphically to maximize profit. Suppose a firm produces food (gathers it) using only labor with the production possibilities shown in Figure 2.1. Any point in the shaded area is technically feasible. If p_L is the price of labor, p_F the price of food, L the amount of labor, and F the amount of food, then (assuming the firm acts competitively) profit is $p_F F - p_L L$. Labor is measured in the negative direction in the diagram, so an *isoprofit* line—a set of $(-L, F)$ pairs with equal profit level—corresponding to profit c is just $H_{(p_L, p_F)}(c)$. We seek the feasible point which attains the highest profit level. Since increases in c correspond to shifts of the hyperplane in the direction (p_L, p_F), the point $(-L^*, F^*)$ attains the highest feasible profit. Note that this solution method jointly determines the optimal food output and the optimal labor input.

2.5 BACKGROUND THEOREM FOR OPTIMIZATION

This section contains a theorem used to generate the necessary first-order conditions for constrained optimization. At this point the relationship to optimization will probably be unclear, but one should understand the theorem.

Given $\{\mathbf{a}^1, \mathbf{a}^2, \ldots, \mathbf{a}^m\}$ an independent set of vectors in $\mathbb{R}^n$ ($m \leq n$), we know that L_1, the set of vectors spanned by $\{\mathbf{a}^1, \mathbf{a}^2, \ldots, \mathbf{a}^m\}$, is a linear subspace of dimension m. Let $L_2 = \{\mathbf{x} \in \mathbb{R}^n | \mathbf{a}^i \cdot \mathbf{x} = 0,\ i = 1, 2, \ldots, m\}$. If $\mathbf{x}, \mathbf{y} \in L_2$ and $s \in \mathbb{R}$ then $\mathbf{a}^i \cdot (\mathbf{x} + \mathbf{y}) = \mathbf{a}^i \cdot \mathbf{x} + \mathbf{a}^i \cdot \mathbf{y} = 0 + 0 = 0$ for $i = 1, 2, \ldots, m$, and $\mathbf{a}^i \cdot (s\mathbf{x}) = s(\mathbf{a}^i \cdot \mathbf{x}) = (s)(0) = 0$ for $i = 1, 2, \ldots, m$. Thus L_2 is also a linear subspace. If $\mathbf{x} \in L_2$ and $\mathbf{y} \in L_1$, then $\mathbf{y} = \sum_{i=1}^m \lambda_i \mathbf{a}^i$ for some scalars $\lambda_1, \lambda_2, \ldots, \lambda_m$ since $\{\mathbf{a}^1, \mathbf{a}^2, \ldots, \mathbf{a}^m\}$ is a basis for L_1. Then $\mathbf{x} \cdot \mathbf{y} = \mathbf{x} \cdot (\sum_{i=1}^m \lambda_i \mathbf{a}^i) = \sum_{i=1}^m \lambda_i \mathbf{x} \cdot \mathbf{a}^i = 0$. Since $\mathbf{x} \cdot \mathbf{x} \neq 0$ for all $\mathbf{x} \neq 0$, if $\mathbf{x}$ is in both L_1 and L_2, then $\mathbf{x}$ must be 0. It is also possible to show that any $z \in \mathbb{R}^n$ can be written uniquely as $z = z^1 + z^2$ where $z^i \in L_i$, $i = 1, 2$. (This is done in a multistep procedure similar to our decomposition of x into $t y$ and a vector orthogonal to y in Section 2.4.) Hence L_2 must be a subspace of dimension $n - m$.

EXAMPLE: In $\mathbb{R}^3$ let

$$a^1 = \begin{pmatrix} 1 \\ 0 \\ 0 \end{pmatrix} \quad \text{and} \quad a^2 = \begin{pmatrix} 0 \\ 1 \\ 0 \end{pmatrix}.$$

Then $L_1 = \{(x_1, x_2, 0) | x_1, x_2 \in \mathbb{R}\}$ and $L_2 = \{(0, 0, x_3) | x_3 \in \mathbb{R}\}$. For any $(x_1, x_2, x_3) \in \mathbb{R}^3$, $(x_1, x_2, 0) \in L_1$ and $(0, 0, x_3) \in L_2$, and $(x_1, x_2, x_3) = (x_1, x_2, 0) + (0, 0, x_3)$ is the unique decomposition of x into the sum of one vector from L_1 and one vector from L_2.

Suppose we are given an additional vector $b \in \mathbb{R}^n$, and we want to look at $b \cdot x$ where $x \in L_2$. As we saw above, if $b \in L_1$ then $b \cdot x = 0$ for all $x \in L_2$. However, if $b \notin L_1$, then $b = b^1 + b^2$ where $b^1 \in L_1$ and $b^2 \in L_2$ with $b^2 \neq 0$. Letting

$$x = \frac{c}{\|b^2\|^2} b^2 \in L_2,$$

we see that $b \cdot x = c$, so that for any $c \in \mathbb{R}$ there is a vector $x \in L^2$ such that $b \cdot x = c$. This proves the following result, which will form the basis for the first-order conditions for optimization.

THEOREM: *Given* $\{a^1, a^2, \ldots, a^m\}$ *an independent set of vectors in* $\mathbb{R}^n$ *($m \leq n$) and* $b \in \mathbb{R}^n$, $b \cdot x = 0$ *for all* x *such that* $a^i \cdot x = 0$ $i = 1, 2, \ldots, m$ *if and only if there exist scalars* $\lambda_1, \lambda_2, \ldots, \lambda_m$ *such that* $b = \sum_{i=1}^m \lambda_i a^i$.

2.6 EIGENVALUES AND QUADRATIC FORMS

In this section we introduce eigenvalues and quadratic forms. The results are used in the second-order conditions for optimization as well as in stability theory.

DEFINITION: A nonzero vector x is an *eigenvector* of the square matrix M if there is some number λ such that $Mx = \lambda x$. Such a λ is called an *eigenvalue*.

The eigenvalues of M can be found by solving for the roots of the characteristic polynomial of the matrix M, i.e., by solving determinant

$(M - \lambda I) = 0$ for λ, where I is the identity matrix. There are n (not necessarily distinct) roots if M is $n \times n$. If M is symmetric, all roots are real; otherwise some may be complex. The number of times a root appears is called its *multiplicity*. (For example, the $n \times n$ identity matrix has root one with multiplicity n.) The sum of the multiplicities is always n.

If M is a symmetric $n \times n$ matrix, then

1. For each eigenvalue, λ, of M, the set $\{x \in \mathbb{R}^n | Mx = \lambda x\}$ is a subspace of $\mathbb{R}^n$. This set is just the eigenvectors corresponding to eigenvalue λ, along with the vector 0.

2. If λ_1 and λ_2 are distinct eigenvalues of M with corresponding eigenvectors x_1 and x_2, respectively, then $x_1 \cdot x_2 = 0$. To see this, note that $x_1' M x_2 = x_1' \lambda_2 x_2 = \lambda_2 x_1 \cdot x_2$ while $x_2' M x_1 = x_2' \lambda_1 x_1 = \lambda_1 x_2 \cdot x_1$. Since M is symmetric these two must be equal, so $(\lambda_2 - \lambda_1) x_1 \cdot x_2 = 0$. But $\lambda_2 \neq \lambda_1$ so $x_1 \cdot x_2 = 0$.

EXAMPLE: For

$$M = \begin{bmatrix} 2 & -6 \\ -6 & -7 \end{bmatrix}$$

the eigenvalues are -10 and 5. For eigenvalue -10, solving $(M + 10I)x = 0$, the corresponding subspace is

$$\left\{ \begin{pmatrix} z \\ 2z \end{pmatrix} \middle| z \in \mathbb{R} \right\}.$$

For eigenvalue 5, solving $(M - 5I)x = 0$, the corresponding subspace is

$$\left\{ \begin{pmatrix} 2z' \\ -z' \end{pmatrix} \middle| z' \in \mathbb{R} \right\}.$$

For any $z, z' \in \mathbb{R}$, $(z, 2z) \cdot (2z', -z') = 0$.

DEFINITION: A set of vectors $\{x_1, \ldots, x_n\}$ is *orthonormal* if $x_i \cdot x_j$ is 0 whenever $i \neq j$ and 1 whenever $i = j$.

Each pair of vectors in an orthonormal set is orthogonal, and each vector has length one.

DEFINITION: A square matrix M is an *orthogonal matrix* if its inverse and transpose coincide; i.e., $M'M = I$ where M' is the transpose of M and I is the identity matrix.

If M is an orthogonal matrix, then the set of vectors consisting of the columns of M (or the rows of M) is an orthonormal set.

Suppose M is a symmetric $n \times n$ matrix with n distinct, nonzero eigenvalues. For each eigenvalue, λ_i, pick an eigenvector x_i with length one [if $y \neq 0$ is an eigenvector, then so is $(1/\|y\|)y$]. Let P be the $n \times n$

matrix with $\mathbf{x}_i$ as its ith column, $i = 1, \ldots, n$. Then P is an orthogonal matrix, and $P'MP = P'[\lambda_1\mathbf{x}_1, \lambda_2\mathbf{x}_2, \ldots, \lambda_n\mathbf{x}_n] = D$ where D is the diagonal matrix with entries $d_{ij} = 0$ if $i \neq j$ and $d_{ii} = \lambda_i$. This result can be generalized to the following theorem.

THEOREM: *If M is a symmetric $n \times n$ matrix, then there is an orthogonal matrix P such that $P^{-1}MP = D$ where D is a diagonal matrix with diagonal entries the eigenvalues of M, each appearing as many times as its multiplicity.*

EXAMPLE: Let

$$M = \begin{bmatrix} 0 & -1 \\ -1 & 0 \end{bmatrix}.$$

Then $\det(M - \lambda I) = \lambda^2 - 1 = (\lambda + 1)(\lambda - 1)$ and M has eigenvalues -1 and $+1$. For

$$P = \begin{bmatrix} 1/\sqrt{2} & 1/\sqrt{2} \\ 1/\sqrt{2} & -1/\sqrt{2} \end{bmatrix}, \qquad P^{-1}MP = \begin{bmatrix} -1 & 0 \\ 0 & 1 \end{bmatrix}.$$

(Note that the columns of P are eigenvectors corresponding to -1 and 1, respectively.)

To check second-order conditions for optimization problems, we will have a particular potential solution in mind and we will be interested in what happens to the objective function as we move away from the potential solution in any feasible direction. This will come down to understanding the properties of objects of the form $\mathbf{x}'M\mathbf{x}$ where M is a matrix of second partial derivatives and $\mathbf{x}$ is a feasible direction of movement away from the potential solution. If $\mathbf{x}'M\mathbf{x} < 0$ for all nonzero feasible changes, then we are at a strict local maximizer. The problem is how to check this without trying the infinity of feasible $\mathbf{x}$ vectors. The answer requires some knowledge of *quadratic forms*, $\mathbf{x}'M\mathbf{x}$.

First consider a diagonal matrix M. Then $\mathbf{x}'M\mathbf{x} = \sum_{i=1}^{n} m_{ii}x_i^2$ where m_{ii} is the ith diagonal element of M. Clearly $\mathbf{x}'M\mathbf{x} < 0$ for all $\mathbf{x} \neq \mathbf{0}$ if and only if all the diagonal elements of M are strictly negative. Similarly, $\mathbf{x}'M\mathbf{x} > 0$ for all $\mathbf{x} \neq \mathbf{0}$ if and only if all diagonal elements of M are strictly positive.

If M is not a diagonal matrix but is symmetric (as a second-order condition matrix would be), then by the previous theorem there is an orthogonal matrix P such that $P^{-1}MP$ is the diagonal matrix D with diagonal entries equal to the eigenvalues of M. Then $\mathbf{x}'M\mathbf{x} = \mathbf{x}'PDP^{-1}\mathbf{x}$ $= \mathbf{y}'D\mathbf{y}$ where $\mathbf{y} = P^{-1}\mathbf{x} = P'\mathbf{x}$ (because P is orthogonal) and $\mathbf{y} \neq \mathbf{0}$ if and only if $\mathbf{x} \neq \mathbf{0}$. This transforms the problem into the diagonal case and

$x'Mx > 0$ for all $x \neq 0$ if and only if all the eigenvalues of M are strictly positive. Similarly, $x'Mx < 0$ requires negative eigenvalues.

DEFINITION: The symmetric matrix M is

1. Positive definite if $x'Mx > 0$ for all $x \neq 0$.
2. Negative definite if $x'Mx < 0$ for all $x \neq 0$.
3. Positive semidefinite if $x'Mx \geq 0$ for all $x \neq 0$.
4. Negative semidefinite if $x'Mx \leq 0$ for all $x \neq 0$.

We have just shown

THEOREM: *The symmetric matrix M is*

1. *Positive definite if and only if all its eigenvalues are strictly positive.*
2. *Negative definite if and only if all its eigenvalues are strictly negative.*
3. *Positive semidefinite if and only if all its eigenvalues are nonnegative.*
4. *Negative semidefinite if and only if all its eigenvalues are nonpositive.*

An alternative test for definiteness uses determinants of submatrices of the original matrix. Let A_r be the determinant of M_r, the $r \times r$ upper left submatrix of M.

THEOREM: *The symmetric $n \times n$ matrix M is*

1. *Positive definite if and only if $A_r > 0$ for $r = 1, 2, \ldots, n$.*
2. *Negative definite if and only if $(-1)^r A_r > 0$ for $r = 1, 2, \ldots, n$.*

Given the previous result concerning the eigenvalue test for definiteness, this result is obvious for diagonal matrices since A_r is just the product of the first r eigenvalues. This is the best way to remember the result. The intuition comes from diagonal matrices. To get a feeling for the general result, suppose M is positive definite. The observations below follow the proof of Theorem 35 in Chapter 2 of Murata (1977).

1. M is positive definite if and only if there is a nonsingular matrix B such that $B'B = M$ ($B = D^*P$ where $P^{-1}MP = D$ diagonalizes M and D^* is the diagonal matrix with diagonal entries the square roots of the eigenvalues).

2. If M is positive definite, then $A_r \neq 0$ for $r = 1, 2, \ldots, n$. [If $A_r = 0$, there exists a vector with r components, $x_r \neq 0$, such that $M_r x_r = 0$. For $x = (x_r, 0, 0, \ldots, 0)$, $x'Mx = 0$ contrary to M positive definite.]

3. Define

$$\begin{pmatrix} C_{1,r+1} \\ \vdots \\ C_{r,r+1} \end{pmatrix} = -M_r^{-1} \begin{pmatrix} M_{1,r+1} \\ \vdots \\ M_{r,r+1} \end{pmatrix} \quad \text{for } r = 1, 2, \ldots, n-1$$

where $[M_{ij}] = M$, and let C be the upper triangular matrix with the C_{ij}

above the diagonal, ones on the diagonal, and zeros below the diagonal. $C'MC$ is positive definite (by 1) since $C'MC = C'B'BC = (BC)'(BC)$. But $C'MC$ is a diagonal matrix with diagonal entry $d_{ii} = A_1$, if $i = 1$, and $d_{ii} = A_i/A_{i-1}$, if $i > 1$. All the diagonal entries must be positive so $A_i > 0$ for all i.

To check second-order conditions for optimization problems with constraints we will be interested in objects of the form $x'Mx$ where M is a matrix of second partial derivatives and x is a vector of feasible changes. However, the constraints limit the set of feasible x. A sketch of the proof for the constrained case is a bit too complicated for our purposes here. See Theorem 36 in Chapter 2 of Murata (1977) for a complete proof. The idea is roughly as follows. The s binding constraints mean that when we make changes in x to see whether our potential solution is really a maximizer, only $n - s$ of the components can be freely varied, with the remaining s being determined by the constraints. By "substitution" for the last s variables we reduce the problem to one with $n - s$ variables and no constraints. The idea is similar to solving the two-variable, one-constraint problem of maximizing xy subject to $x + y = 2$ by substituting for y and solving the unconstrained problem of maximizing $x(2 - x)$. The gradients for the constraints are added to the matrix to give the effective conditions needed to determine the last s variables given $n - s$ variables. With $n - s$ unconstrained variables only $n - s$ determinants need to be checked. The transformation of the s variables introduces a $(-1)^s$ term. The result is

THEOREM: *Let M be an $n \times n$ symmetric matrix and G be an $s \times n$ matrix of rank $s < n$ (with the last s columns of G independent). Let B be the $(s + n) \times (s + n)$ matrix defined by*

$$B := \left[\begin{array}{c|c} M & G' \\ \hline G & 0 \end{array}\right]$$

where 0 is the $s \times s$ matrix of zeros, and let B_r be the determinant of the $(2s + r) \times (2s + r)$ lower right submatrix of B. Then

1. $x'Mx > 0$ *for all* $x \in \mathbb{R}^n$, $x \neq 0$ *such that* $Gx = 0$ *if and only if* $(-1)^s B_r > 0$ *for* $r = 1, 2, \ldots, n - s$.
2. $x'Mx < 0$ *for all* $x \in \mathbb{R}^n$, $x \neq 0$ *such that* $Gx = 0$ *if and only if* $(-1)^{s+r} B_r > 0$ *for* $r = 1, 2, \ldots, n - s$.

2.7 SEMIDEFINITE MATRICES

Although we will be mainly concerned with positive definite (PD) and negative definite (ND) matrices, a minor difficulty with checking positive and negative semidefinite (PSD, NSD) matrices should be pointed out. For

$A_{n \times n} = [a_{ij}]$, the conditions

$$a_{11} \geq 0, \begin{vmatrix} a_{11} & a_{12} \\ a_{21} & a_{22} \end{vmatrix} \geq 0, \ldots, |A| \geq 0$$

are necessary but not sufficient for A to be PSD. The problem is that we may be testing the relevant rows and columns too late. For

$$A = \begin{bmatrix} 0 & 0 \\ 0 & -4 \end{bmatrix},$$

$a_{11} = 0 \geq 0$ and $|A| = 0 \geq 0$ but

$$(x_1, x_2) \begin{bmatrix} 0 & 0 \\ 0 & -4 \end{bmatrix} \begin{pmatrix} x_1 \\ x_2 \end{pmatrix} = -4x_2^2 \leq 0$$

so A is NSD rather than PSD.

Given $A_{n \times n}$ with rank $A = m < n$, there exist $k_1, k_2, \ldots, k_{n-m}$, all distinct elements of $\{1, 2, \ldots, n\}$, such that if A^* is the $m \times m$ matrix obtained by deleting the rows and columns $k_1, k_2, \ldots, k_{n-m}$, then rank $A^* = m$. A is PSD (NSD) if and only if A^* is PD (ND). For

$$A = \begin{bmatrix} 0 & 0 \\ 0 & -4 \end{bmatrix}, \quad A^* = [-4] \text{ is ND so } A \text{ is NSD.}$$

2.8 DOMINANT DIAGONAL MATRICES

In some economic problems it is easy to verify that a matrix has what is called dominant diagonal. In certain qualitative ways the matrix has properties similar to those of a matrix with the same diagonal entries but zero off-diagonal entries. This can be a useful observation.

DEFINITION: An $n \times n$ matrix $A = [a_{ij}]$ has a *dominant diagonal* if there exist positive numbers $d_1, d_2, \ldots, d_n$ such that $d_j|a_{jj}| > \sum_{i \neq j} d_i|a_{ij}|$ for $j = 1, 2, \ldots, n$.

THEOREM: *If A has a dominant negative diagonal (i.e., $a_{ii} < 0$ for all i, and A has a dominant diagonal), then all the eigenvalues of A have negative real parts.*

Note that A need not be symmetric so the eigenvalues of A could be complex numbers.

EXAMPLE: For $b < -8$ the matrix

$$\begin{bmatrix} b & 2 \\ -4 & -1 \end{bmatrix}$$

has a dominant negative diagonal (let $d_1 = 1$ and $d_2 = 1 - b/8$). At

$b = -1 - \sqrt{57} < -8$, the eigenvalues satisfy $(-1 - \sqrt{57} - \lambda)(-1 - \lambda) + 8 = 0$ or $\lambda^2 + \lambda(2 + \sqrt{57}) + 9 + \sqrt{57} = 0$ with solutions $\lambda = -1 - (1/2)\sqrt{57} \pm 5/2 < 0$.

PROBLEMS

2.1 Find all solutions to

$$\begin{bmatrix} -3 & 3 & -1 \\ 3 & -4 & 1 \\ -1 & 1 & -1 \end{bmatrix} \mathbf{x} = \begin{pmatrix} 1 \\ 3 \\ 1 \end{pmatrix}.$$

2.2 Given

$$x - z = 2,$$
$$3x + 2y - 3z = -2,$$
$$-x + 4y + 2z = 2,$$

use Cramer's rule to find y.

2.3 Given the set of vectors

$$\{(1, -3, 0, -5), (-2, 6, 0, 10), (1, 2, 1, -1) \ (3, 1, 2, -7)\},$$

(a) Which pairs of vectors are orthogonal?
(b) Do the vectors form an independent set?
(c) Find a basis for the subspace spanned by the vectors.
(d) Find a vector in $\mathbb{R}^4$ which is not in the subspace spanned by the vectors.

2.4 Given the set of vectors $\{(1/\sqrt{2}, 0, -1/\sqrt{2}), (0, 1, 0)\}$,

(a) Is the set an orthonormal set?
(b) Is the vector $(1, 2, 3)$ in the subspace spanned by the vectors?
(c) Find a basis for $\mathbb{R}^3$ which includes the two vectors and is an orthonormal set.
(d) Find the unique representation of $(1, 1, 1)$ in terms of the basis from (c).

2.5 Is $\{(-1, 2, 0, 1), (3, 6, 1, 0), (0, -2, 3, 4), (1, 4, 0, 3)\}$ an independent set of vectors?

2.6 (a) Find all vectors $\mathbf{y}$ in $\mathbb{R}^2$ such that $(3, -1) \cdot \mathbf{y} = 3$.
(b) Find the vector $\mathbf{y}$ that maximizes $(3, -1) \cdot \mathbf{y}$ subject to $\|\mathbf{y}\| = 1$.
(c) Graph the hyperplanes

$$H_{\begin{pmatrix} -1 \\ 2 \end{pmatrix}}(0) \quad \text{and} \quad H_{\begin{pmatrix} -1 \\ 2 \end{pmatrix}}(1).$$

(d) Graph the subspace spanned by

$$\left\{ \begin{pmatrix} -1 \\ -2 \end{pmatrix} \right\} \text{ and the subspace } \left\{ \mathbf{y} \in \mathbb{R}^2 \mid \begin{pmatrix} -1 \\ -2 \end{pmatrix} \cdot \mathbf{y} = 0 \right\}.$$

2.7 Check the following matrices for definiteness.

(a)
$$\begin{bmatrix} 1 & 2 \\ 2 & 1 \end{bmatrix}$$

(b)
$$\begin{bmatrix} -1 & 1 \\ 1 & -1 \end{bmatrix}$$

(c)
$$\begin{bmatrix} 1 & 0 & -1 \\ 0 & 3 & 0 \\ -1 & 0 & 4 \end{bmatrix}$$

(d)
$$\begin{bmatrix} 1 & 7 & 0 \\ 7 & 4 & -1 \\ 0 & -1 & 1 \end{bmatrix}$$

(e)
$$\begin{bmatrix} 1 & 3 & 2 & 3 \\ 3 & 5 & -2 & 4 \\ 2 & -2 & 2 & 1 \\ 3 & 4 & 1 & 2 \end{bmatrix}$$

2.8 (a) What is the rank of

$$A = \begin{bmatrix} 1 & 3 & 2 & 3 \\ 3 & -2 & 1 & 4 \\ 5 & -7 & 0 & 5 \\ -2 & 5 & 1 & 1 \end{bmatrix}?$$

(b) Find a basis for the subspace generated by the columns of A.

2.9 For each system of equations below,
   (i) Use the rank conditions to determine the number of solutions.
   (ii) Find the determinant of the matrix associated with the system.
   (iii) If applicable, find the matrix inverse.
   (iv) Solve the systems with a unique solution:

(a)
$$3x - 9y = 2$$
$$x - 3y = 1$$

(b)
$$3x - y = 2$$
$$-9x + 3y = -6$$

(c)
$$3x + 3y = 1$$
$$-x - 9y = -1$$

(d)
$$x - z = 0$$
$$3x + 2y - 3z = -1$$
$$-x + 4y + z = -2$$

3

BASIC
ANALYSIS

3.1 INTRODUCTION

This chapter contains basic material on closed and open sets, compact sets, and convex sets along with material on separating hyperplanes. An intuitive understanding of this background material will aid in understanding a variety of topics in optimization as well as in consumer and producer theory. For example, in consumer theory, to guarantee that we can represent preferences by a numerical function (a utility function), we impose the condition that for each bundle x, the set of bundles strictly preferred to x and the set of bundles x is strictly preferred to are both open relative to the consumption set. In producer theory, the set of technically feasible production plans (i.e., vectors listing input and output levels) is assumed to be closed. Compactness and convexity are useful in finding conditions under which local solutions to optimization problems will also be global solutions. This is discussed in Chapter 5.

3.2 CLOSED AND OPEN SETS

To talk about closed sets in $\mathbb{R}^n$ we need to understand limits of sequences of points in $\mathbb{R}^n$. We begin with the case $n = 1$. A *sequence* in $\mathbb{R}$ is a list of (not necessarily distinct) numbers, $x_1, x_2, x_3, \ldots$, written $(x_n)_{n=1}^{\infty}$.

DEFINITION: A sequence $(x_n)_{n=1}^\infty$ in $\mathbb{R}$ *converges* to $x \in \mathbb{R}$ if for every $\varepsilon > 0$ there exists an integer N such that $|x_n - x| < \varepsilon$ for all $n > N$ (i.e., for n greater than N, each x_n is within ε of x). x is called the *limit* of the sequence.

EXAMPLES:

The sequence $(1/n)_{n=1}^\infty$ converges to zero. This is often written $1/n \to 0$.

The sequence with $(-1)^n/n = x_n$ converges to zero.

The sequence with $(-1)^n = x_n$ does not converge.

Note that every increasing sequence $(x_n)_{n=1}^\infty$ which is bounded above in $\mathbb{R}$ converges to a limit. Similarly, every decreasing sequence which is bounded below converges to a limit. In order to describe these limits it is useful to introduce the notions of supremum and infimum.

For any nonempty set $S \subset \mathbb{R}$, x is an upper bound (a lower bound) for S if $x \geq s$ ($x \leq s$) for all s in S. If an upper bound (lower bound) exists for S, then the least upper bound or supremum of S, written sup(S) [the greatest lower bound or infimum of S, written inf(S)] is the smallest of the upper bounds (the largest of the lower bounds). The supremum (infimum) extends the notion of the maximum element of S (the minimum element of S) to situations in which the maximum (minimum) is not in S.

EXAMPLES:

$$\inf(\{1/n | n = 1, 2, \ldots\}) = 0,$$

$$\inf([2, 3]) = 2,$$

$$\sup(\{(1/n) | n = 1, 2, \ldots\}) = 1,$$

$$\sup((0, 1)) = 1.$$

In the first example inf(S) is not an element of S but in the second example it is. The second example had a minimum element but the first did not. Whenever a set has a minimum element, min(S), the minimum and infimum agree: min(S) = inf(S). In the third example sup(S) is an element of S but in the fourth example it is not. The third example had a maximum element but the fourth did not. Whenever a set has a maximum element, max(S), the supremum and maximum agree: max(S) = sup(S).

We now turn to the case $n > 1$. A *sequence* in $\mathbb{R}^n$ is a list of (not necessarily distinct) vectors from $\mathbb{R}^n$, $\mathbf{x}_1, \mathbf{x}_2, \mathbf{x}_3, \ldots$, written $(\mathbf{x}_j)_{j=1}^\infty$. For such a sequence we can consider each coordinate sequence individually (i.e., we can consider the sequence in $\mathbb{R}$ made up of the first coordinate of each vector, or the sequence in $\mathbb{R}$ made up of the second coordinate of each vector, etc.).

DEFINITION: A sequence $(x_j)_{j=1}^{\infty}$ in $\mathbb{R}^n$ *converges* to $x \in \mathbb{R}^n$ if each coordinate converges (view each coordinate as in $\mathbb{R}^1$). x is called the *limit* of the sequence.

EXAMPLE: If

$$x_n = \left(\frac{1}{n}, 1 + \frac{n}{2n+1} \right)$$

then x_n converges to $(0, 3/2)$.

A sequence in S (i.e., a sequence $(x_j)_{j=1}^{\infty}$ with $x_j \in S$ for $j = 1, 2, \dots$) is said to be *convergent* if it has a limit. In general, the limit need not be in S. However, for special types of sets such a limit is always in the set.

DEFINITION: A subset S of $\mathbb{R}^n$ is *closed* if the limit of every convergent sequence in S belongs to S.

To show S is closed we need to prove every convergent sequence in S has its limit in S. To show S is not closed we need only find a single sequence in S with a limit not in S.

EXAMPLES:

For $S = \{(x, y) | x^2 + y^2 \leq 1\}$ let $(x_j, y_j)_{j=1}^{\infty}$ be any sequence such that $x_j^2 + y_j^2 \leq 1$ for all j and $x_j \to x$, $y_j \to y$. Then $x^2 + y^2 \leq 1$ so $(x, y) \in S$. Since the sequence was arbitrary, S is closed.

For $S = \{(x, y) | x^2 + y^2 < 1\}$ let $(x_j, y_j) = (0, 1 - 1/j)$ for $j = 1, 2, \dots$. Then $x_j^2 + y_j^2 < 1$ for all j and $x_j \to 0$, $y_j \to 1$. Thus $(0, 1)$ is the limit of a convergent sequence in S. But $0^2 + 1^2 = 1$ so the limit is not in S, and S is not closed.

For $S = \{(x, y) | x^2 + y^2 \leq 1, x \neq 1\}$ let $(x_j, y_j) = (1 - 1/j, 0)$ for $j = 1, 2, \dots$. As in the previous example, this is a convergent sequence in S with limit $(1, 0)$, which is not in S. Thus S is not closed.

DEFINITION: The *intersection* of a family of sets S_i, $i \in I$, is

$$\bigcap_{i \in I} S_i := \{x | x \in S_i \quad \text{for all } i \in I\}.$$

DEFINITION: The *union* of a family of sets S_i, $i \in I$ is

$$\bigcup_{i \in I} S_i := \{x | x \in S_i \quad \text{for some } i \in I\}.$$

EXAMPLE: For $I = \{1, 2\}$ and $S_1 = [0, 3)$, $S_2 = [2, 4)$,

$$\bigcap_{i \in I} S_i = [2, 3) \quad \text{and} \quad \bigcup_{i \in I} S_i = [0, 4).$$

RESULTS: The following properties of closed sets will be useful.

1. The intersection of any collection of closed sets is closed.

Proof: If $x_j \in \cap_i S_i$ for all j, and x_j converges to x, then $x_j \in S_i$ for all i and j. Since each S_i is closed, $x \in S_i$ for all i and $x \in \cap_i S_i$.

2. The union of finitely many closed sets is closed.

Proof: If $x_j \in \cup_i S_i$ for all j, and x_j converges to x, then at least one of the closed sets must contain infinitely many of the x_j. Hence there exist an i and a subsequence j_k such that $x_{j_k} \in S_i$ for all k. Since S_i is closed, $x = \lim x_{j_k} \in S_i \subset \cup_i S_i$.

EXAMPLE: To see that the second result cannot be extended to infinitely many closed sets, note $\cup_{i \in I} S_i$ is not closed if $S_i = \{1/i\}$ and $I = \{1, 2, \dots\}$.

If S is not closed, we might be interested in an expanded set including not only S but also the points "missing" as limits of sequences.

DEFINITION: The *closure* of a set $S \subset \mathbb{R}^l$, denoted $\bar{S}$, is the set of limits of convergent sequences in S (or cluster points or points of closure of S); i.e., $\bar{S} = \{x \in \mathbb{R}^l |$ there exists a sequence $(x_j)_{j=1}^\infty$ with $x_j \in S$ for all j such that x_j converges to $x\}$.

For any $x \in S$, the sequence $x_j = x$ for all j is a convergent sequence in S with limit x so $S \subset \bar{S}$. If S is closed, it contains all its points of closure, so $S = \bar{S}$. Only if S is not closed could $\bar{S}$ contain points not in S. $\bar{S}$ is closed and is the smallest closed set containing S. It is also the intersection of all closed sets containing S.

EXAMPLES:

For $S = \{1\}$, the only sequence in S is $x_j = 1$ for all j, with limit 1 so $\bar{S} = \{1\}$.

For $S = \{(1/n)|n = 1, 2, \dots\}$, the sequence $x_j = 1/j \in S$ for all j has limit $0 \notin S$, so $\bar{S} = S \cup \{0\}$.

For $S = \{(x, y)|x^2 + y^2 \leq 1\}$, the limit of any convergent sequence in S is in S because S is closed. Thus $\bar{S} = S$.

For $S = \{(x, y)|x^2 + y^2 < 1\}$, any point (x, y) with $x^2 + y^2 = 1$ is the limit of a convergent sequence in S [let $(x_j, y_j) = ((j - 1)x/j, (j - 1)y/j)]$, so $\bar{S} = \{(x, y)|x^2 + y^2 \leq 1\}$.

For $S = \{(x, y)|x^2 + y^2 \leq 1, x \neq 1\}$, the point $(1, 0)$ is the limit of the convergent sequence $(1 - 1/j, 0) \in S$, so $\bar{S} = \{(x, y)|x^2 + y^2 \leq 1\}$.

The last three examples all had the same closure even though the sets differed.

We now turn to a discussion of open sets. Recall the *complement* of a set S, written $\mathbb{R}^l \setminus S$, is the set of points in $\mathbb{R}^l$ that are not in S.

DEFINITION: A subset $S \subset \mathbb{R}^l$ is *open* if its complement is closed.

EXAMPLES:

For $S = \{(x, y) | x^2 + y^2 \leq 1\}$, $\mathbb{R}^l \setminus S = \{(x, y) | x^2 + y^2 > 1\}$ is not closed so S is not open.

For $S = \{(x, y) | x^2 + y^2 < 1\}$, $\mathbb{R}^l \setminus S = \{(x, y) | x^2 + y^2 \geq 1\}$ is closed so S is open.

The set $\mathbb{R}^l$ itself is both closed and open.

Most sets are neither closed nor open. Both definitions require "global" properties of the set. A typical set such as $[0, 1) \subset \mathbb{R}$ will satisfy each condition at some spots and fail each condition at others.

RESULTS: The following properties of open sets will be useful.

1. The union of any collection of open sets is open.

Proof: If S_i is open for all i, then $\mathbb{R}^l \setminus S_i$ is closed for all i, so $\cap_i (\mathbb{R}^l \setminus S_i)$ is closed. Thus $\cup_i S_i = \mathbb{R}^l \setminus (\cap_i (\mathbb{R}^l \setminus S_i))$ is open.

2. The intersection of finitely many open sets is open.

Proof: Again look at complements of open sets and use our previous result for the union of finitely many closed sets.

3. $S \subset \mathbb{R}^l$ is open if and only if for every $x \in S$ there exists an $r > 0$ such that $\{z \in \mathbb{R}^l | \|z - x\| < r\}$ (the open ball of radius r around x) is a subset of S. (This provides an alternative method for showing a set is open.)

Proof: Let S be open. Let $x \in \mathbb{R}^l$ be such that for all $r > 0$ $\{z | \|z - x\| < r\} \not\subset S$. For each n we can pick $x_n \in \mathbb{R}^l \setminus S$ such that $\|x_n - x\| < 1/n$. Then $x_n \to x$ and, since $\mathbb{R}^l \setminus S$ is closed, $x \in \mathbb{R}^l \setminus S$. Hence for any $x \in S$ there exists an $r > 0$ such that $\{z \in \mathbb{R}^l | \|z - x\| < r\}$ is a subset of S.

For the proof in the other direction, assume a ball exists for each $x \in S$. Let $(x_n)_{n=1}^{\infty}$ be a sequence in $\mathbb{R}^l \setminus S$ such that $x_n \to x'$. Then $x' \in \mathbb{R}^l \setminus S$ (since $x' \in S$ implies $x_n \in S$ for all large n) so $\mathbb{R}^l \setminus S$ is closed. Thus S is open.

A *neighborhood* N of a point $x \in \mathbb{R}^l$ is a subset of $\mathbb{R}^l$ containing an open set T such that $x \in T$. The neighborhood itself may be closed or open or neither, but it must contain an open set that contains x.

DEFINITION: x is a *boundary point* of $S \subset \mathbb{R}^l$ if every neighborhood N of x has a nonempty intersection with both S and $\mathbb{R}^l \setminus S$. The set of boundary points is called the *boundary* of S and is denoted ∂S. x is an *interior point* of $S \subset \mathbb{R}^l$ if S is a neighborhood of x (i.e., S contains an open set containing **x**). The set of interior points of S is called the *interior of S*.

EXAMPLES:

For $S = \{(x, y)|x^2 + y^2 \leq 1\}$, for any point (x, y) with $x^2 + y^2 < 1$, for ε sufficiently small $N_\varepsilon = \{\mathbf{z}| \|\mathbf{z} - (x, y)\| < \varepsilon\} \subset S$, while for $x^2 + y^2 > 1$, for ε sufficiently small $N_\varepsilon \subset \mathbb{R}^l \setminus S$. For $x^2 + y^2 = 1$, for any neighborhood N of (x, y), for sufficiently small ε the points $((1 - \varepsilon)x, (1 - \varepsilon)y) \in S$ and $((1 + \varepsilon)x, (1 + \varepsilon)y) \in \mathbb{R}^l \setminus S$ both lie in N. Thus $\partial S = \{(x, y)|x^2 + y^2 = 1\}$, and the set of interior points of S is $\{(x, y)|x^2 + y^2 < 1\}$.

For $S = \{(x, y)|x^2 + y^2 < 1\}$, by the same argument as in the previous example, $\partial S = \{(x, y)|x^2 + y^2 = 1\}$ and all points in S are interior points.

For $S = \{1/n|n = 1, 2, \dots\}$, for any point, $1/n$, in S, every neighborhood of $1/n$ contains points in S ($1/n$ itself) and points not in S ($1/n + \varepsilon$ for ε sufficiently small) so $S \subset \partial S$. Every neighborhood of 0 contains points not in S (all $x \in N$ with $x < 0$) and points in S ($1/n$ for n sufficiently large), so $0 \in \partial S$. Thus $\partial S = S \cup \{0\}$ and S has no interior points.

As illustrated in the three examples, there is no simple general relationship between S and ∂S: S can be a strict subset of ∂S or ∂S can be a strict subset of S or S can be such that $S \cap \partial S = \varnothing$. However, ∂S is always a subset of the closure of S, so ∂S is a subset of S if S is closed. The interior of S is always a subset of S and is equal to S if S is open.

In consumer theory, when we consider the properties of the set of bundles strictly preferred to **x**, we do not necessarily find the set to be open, even for well-behaved preferences. The problem is that only bundles in the consumption set are of interest to us, while the openness condition considers all points. This is remedied by considering sets which are open relative to the consumption set.

DEFINITION: A subset S of $X \subset \mathbb{R}^l$ is *closed relative to X* if for every sequence $(\mathbf{x}_n)_{n=1}^\infty$, if $\mathbf{x}_n \in S$ for all n and $\mathbf{x}_n$ converges to $\mathbf{x} \in X$, then $\mathbf{x} \in S$.

DEFINITION: A subset S of $X \subset \mathbb{R}^l$ is *open relative to X* if the complement of S, $X \setminus S$, is closed relative to X.

EXAMPLE: Let $\mathbb{R}^l = \mathbb{R}^2$, $X = \{(x, y)|x \geq 0, y \geq 0\} = \mathbb{R}_+^2$. Then $S = \{(x, y)|x \geq 0, y \geq 0$ and $x + y > 1\}$ is open relative to X though it is not open in $\mathbb{R}^2$. This type of example often arises in consumer theory: preferred sets are open relative to the consumption set (often $\mathbb{R}_+^l$) but need not be open in the parent space $\mathbb{R}^l$.

When discussing open or closed sets it is crucial to be clear about the set X relative to which openness or closedness is to be measured.

EXAMPLES:

The set $S = \{(x, y)|y = 0,\ 0 < x < 1\}$ is neither open nor closed relative to $\mathbb{R}^2$ [no ball around $(1/2, 0) \in S$ is a subset of S, so S is not open in $\mathbb{R}^2$, while $\lambda_j = (1 - 1/(j + 1), 0) \in S$ for all j, but λ_j converges to $(1, 0) \notin S$, so S is not closed in $\mathbb{R}^2$].

Relative to $X = \{(x, y)|y = 0,\ x \in \mathbb{R}\}$ S is open since $X \setminus S$ is $\{(x, y)|y = 0,\ x \le 0\} \cup \{(x, y)|y = 0,\ x \ge 1\}$, which is closed in X (and in $\mathbb{R}^2$). The way to think about an ε-ball around, say, $(1/2, 0)$ is to intersect the set X with the ε-ball around $(1/2, 0)$ in $\mathbb{R}^2$. The result is $\{(x, y)|y = 0,\ 1/2 - \varepsilon < x < 1/2 + \varepsilon\}$.

Relative to $X' = \{(x, y)|0 < x < 1,\ y \in \mathbb{R}\}$ S is closed. For any sequence $((x_n, y_n))_{n=1}^{\infty}$ in S, if (x_n, y_n) converges to $(x, y) \in X'$, then $0 < x < 1$ by the definition of X', and $y = 0$ since y_n must be zero for all n. Thus $(x, y) \in S$.

3.3 COMPACT SETS

In this section we introduce compactness. This property is useful in optimization.

DEFINITION: $S \subset \mathbb{R}^l$ is *bounded* if there exists an $r \in \mathbb{R}$ such that $\|\mathbf{x}\| < r$ for all $\mathbf{x} \in S$.

A set is bounded if it fits within some ball around the origin with finite radius. It is important to distinguish the notions "bounded set" and "a set containing its boundary." $\{x \in \mathbb{R}|0 \le x\}$ contains its boundary [$\partial S = \{0\}$], but it is not bounded, while $\{x \in \mathbb{R}|0 < x < 1\}$ is bounded but does not contain its boundary [$\partial S = \{0, 1\}$].

EXAMPLES:

$\{(x, y)|y = 0,\ 0 < x < 1\}$ is contained in a ball of radius one around the origin, so it is bounded.

$\{(x, y, z)|x^2 + y^2 + z^2 \le 10^{2000}\}$ is contained in a ball with radius $10^{1000} + 1$, so it is bounded.

$\{(x, y)|x \ge y\}$ contains all points of the form (t, t) for $t \in \mathbb{R}$, so it is not bounded.

$\{(1/n)|n = 1, 2, \ldots\}$ is contained in a ball of radius two around the origin [this "ball" in $\mathbb{R}$ is the interval $(-2, 2)$], so it is bounded.

DEFINITION: A subset S of $\mathbb{R}^l$ is *compact* if it is closed and bounded.

EXAMPLES:

$S = \{(x, y)|x^2 + y^2 \le 1\}$ is closed, and for all $\mathbf{z} \in S$, $\|\mathbf{z}\| \le 1$, so S is bounded and thus compact.

$S = \{(x, y)|x \ge 0, y \ge 0,$ and $xy \le 1\}$ is closed in $\mathbb{R}^2$ but not bounded $((t, 0) \in S$ for all $t \ge 0)$, so it is not compact.

$S = \{(1/n)|n = 1, 2, \dots\}$ is bounded but not closed, so it is not compact.

THEOREM: *If $S \subset \mathbb{R}^l$, then it is compact if and only if every sequence in S has a subsequence converging to a point in S; i.e., if $(\mathbf{x}_n)_{n=1}^{\infty}$ is a sequence with $\mathbf{x}_n \in S$ for all n, then there are a subsequence $(\mathbf{x}_{n_q})_{q=1}^{\infty}$ and an $\mathbf{x} \in S$ such that $\mathbf{x}_{n_q}$ converges to $\mathbf{x}$.*

Proof: Assume $S \subset \mathbb{R}^l$ is compact and let $(\mathbf{x}_n)_{n=1}^{\infty}$ be a sequence in S.

1. S is bounded so we can break it into finitely many closed cubes (with overlap at the edges) with edge length 1. At least one cube contains infinitely many $\mathbf{x}_n$. Pick such a cube and a subsequence such that all $\mathbf{x}_{n_q}$ are in the cube.

2. Break the cube from step 1 into closed subcubes with edge length $1/2$. Find a sub-subsequence of the subsequence from 1 such that all $\mathbf{x}_{n_q}$ are in one subcube.

3. Repeat the procedure with subcubes of edge length 2^{-s+1} at step s to get a convergent subsequence with a limit in S (since S is closed).

The proof in the other direction is most easily done by contradiction. If S is not closed, then the sequence used to show this has no subsequence converging to a point in S. If S is not bounded, a sequence with $\|\mathbf{x}_n\| > n$ can be generated, and it clearly has no convergent subsequence.

RESULTS: The following properties of compact sets will be useful.

1. The intersection of any collection of compact sets is compact.

Proof: The intersection is clearly bounded, and the intersection of closed sets is closed.

2. The union of finitely many compact sets is compact.

Proof: The union of finitely many closed sets is closed. If $\|\mathbf{x}\| < r_i$ for all $\mathbf{x}$ in the ith set, then $\max\{r_1, r_2, \dots r_l\}$ will work as a bound for the union.

3. The union of infinitely many compact sets may fail to be compact.

Proof: The union may not be closed (e.g., if $F_i = \{1/i\}$ for $i = 1, 2, \dots,$ then $\cup_i F_i$ is not closed) or the union may not be bounded (e.g., if $F_i = \{i\}$ for $i = 1, 2, \dots,$ then $\cup_i F_i$ is not bounded).

DEFINITION: The function $f: S \to T$ is *continuous at* $\mathbf{x}^0 \in S$ if for every sequence $(\mathbf{x}_n)_{n=1}^{\infty}$ in S with $\mathbf{x}_n$ converging to $\mathbf{x}^0$, $f(\mathbf{x}_n)$ converges to $f(\mathbf{x}^0)$. f is *continuous* if it is continuous at every point $\mathbf{x}^0$ in its domain S.

THEOREM: *If* $f: S \to \mathbb{R}$ *is continuous on a compact set* $K \subset S$, *then* $f(K) = \{f(\mathbf{y}) | \mathbf{y} \in K\}$ *is compact and there exist points* $\mathbf{x}^*, \mathbf{y}^* \in K$ *at which* f *attains its minimum and maximum values on* K; *i.e.,* $f(\mathbf{x}^*) \le f(\mathbf{z}) \le f(\mathbf{y}^*)$ *for all* $\mathbf{z} \in K$.

Proof: Let $(\mathbf{x}_n)_{n=1}^{\infty}$ be a sequence in $f(K)$. Then for all n there exists a $\mathbf{y}_n \in K$ such that $f(\mathbf{y}_n) = \mathbf{x}_n$. By the previous theorem, there exists a convergent subsequence $(\mathbf{y}_{n_q})_{q=1}^{\infty}$ converging to some $\mathbf{y}^0 \in K$. By continuity, $f(\mathbf{y}_{n_q}) = \mathbf{x}_{n_q}$ converges to $\mathbf{x}^0 = f(\mathbf{y}^0) \in f(K)$. Thus $f(K)$ is compact. Since $f(K)$ is a closed and bounded subset of $\mathbb{R}$, both $\inf f(K)$ and $\sup f(K)$ are contained in $f(K)$ [and thus equal $\min f(K)$ and $\max f(K)$, respectively]. Any $\mathbf{x}^*$ in K such that $f(\mathbf{x}^*) = \min f(K)$ is a minimizer, and any $\mathbf{y}^*$ in K such that $f(\mathbf{y}^*) = \max f(K)$ is a maximizer.

3.4 CONVEX SETS

DEFINITION: A subset S of $\mathbb{R}^l$ is *convex* (*strictly convex*) if for all $\mathbf{x}, \mathbf{y} \in S$ with $\mathbf{x} \ne \mathbf{y}$ and for all $\lambda \in (0, 1)$, $\lambda \mathbf{x} + (1 - \lambda)\mathbf{y} \in S$ [$\lambda \mathbf{x} + (1 - \lambda)\mathbf{y}$ is in the interior of S].

EXAMPLES:

$\{(x, y) | x^2 + y^2 \le 1\}$ is convex.
$\{(x, y) | x^2 + y^2 \le 1, \ x \ne 1\}$ is convex.
$\{(x, y) | x \ge 0, \ y \ge 0, \ xy \le 1\}$ is not convex because it contains $(4, 0)$ and $(0, 4)$ but not $(2, 2)$.
$\{1, 2\}$ is not convex.

RESULTS: The following properties of convex sets will be useful. Let A and B be convex subsets of $\mathbb{R}^l$.

1. $A \cap B$ is convex. (This can be extended to the intersection of any family of convex sets.)

Proof: If $\mathbf{x}, \mathbf{y}$ are in $A \cap B$, then $\mathbf{x}, \mathbf{y}$ are in A and $\mathbf{x}, \mathbf{y}$ are in B. Thus for each $\lambda \in [0, 1]$, $\lambda \mathbf{x} + (1 - \lambda)\mathbf{y}$ is in A and in B.

2. $A + B := \{x + y | x \in A, \ y \in B\}$ is convex.

Proof: If $\mathbf{x}, \mathbf{y} \in A + B$, then there exist $\mathbf{x}^A, \mathbf{y}^A \in A$ and $\mathbf{x}^B, \mathbf{y}^B \in B$ such that $\mathbf{x} = \mathbf{x}^A + \mathbf{x}^B$, $\mathbf{y} = \mathbf{y}^A + \mathbf{y}^B$. Then $\lambda \mathbf{x} + (1 - \lambda)\mathbf{y} = \lambda(\mathbf{x}^A + \mathbf{x}^B) + (1 - \lambda)(\mathbf{y}^A + \mathbf{y}^B) = (\lambda \mathbf{x}^A + (1 - \lambda)\mathbf{y}^A) + (\lambda \mathbf{x}^B + (1 - \lambda)\mathbf{y}^B)$. By the convexity of A and B, the first (second) term is in A (B respectively), so the sum is in $A + B$.

3. The union of two convex sets need not be convex.

Proof: For example, $\{1\} \cup \{2\}$ is not convex.

4. The half-spaces $\{x \in \mathbb{R}^l | a \cdot x \leq c\}$, $\{x \in \mathbb{R}^l | a \cdot x < c\}$, $\{x \in \mathbb{R}^l | a \cdot x \geq c\}$, $\{x \in \mathbb{R}^l | a \cdot x > c\}$ and the hyperplanes $\{x \in \mathbb{R}^l | a \cdot x = c\}$ are convex for all $a \in \mathbb{R}^l$ and $c \in \mathbb{R}$.

Proof: Any inequality (or equality) satisfied by two vectors is satisfied by any convex combination of the two vectors.

DEFINITION: The *convex hull* of $S \subset \mathbb{R}^n$, written con S, is the intersection of all convex subsets of $\mathbb{R}^n$ containing S.

Since the intersection of convex sets is convex, con S is a convex set. Clearly $S \subset$ con S, and con $S = S$ if and only if S is convex. Con S is the smallest convex set containing S.

RESULTS: The following properties of convex hulls will be useful. They are presented without proof. However, some examples are provided to illustrate the results.

1. For $S \subset \mathbb{R}^n$, any point $x \in$ con S is the convex combination of $n + 1$ or fewer points from S (i.e., there exist numbers $\lambda_1, \ldots, \lambda_{n+1}$ with $0 \leq \lambda_i \leq 1$ for $i = 1, \ldots, n + 1$ and $\sum_{i=1}^{n+1} \lambda_i = 1$ and points $x_i \in S$ $i = 1, \ldots, n + 1$ such that $x = \sum_{i=1}^{n+1} \lambda_i x_i$).

For example, if $S = \{1, 2\} \subset \mathbb{R}^1$ then con S is the interval $[1, 2]$ and any $x \in [1, 2]$ is a convex combination of 1 and 2, e.g., $1.5 = (.5)1 + (.5)2$.

2. If $S \subset \mathbb{R}^n$ is open then so is con S. For example, if $S = \{(x, y) | 0 < x, 0 < y, xy < 1\} \subset \mathbb{R}^2$, then any point in $\mathbb{R}^2$ with strictly positive coordinates lies on a line joining two points from S and thus is in con S. Con $S = \{(x, y) | x > 0, y > 0\} = \mathbb{R}^2_{++}$.

3. If $S \subset \mathbb{R}^n$ is closed, con S need not be closed. For example, if $S = \{(x, y) | x \geq 0, 0 \leq y \leq x^2\}$, then for $j = 1, 2, \ldots$, the point $(1/(j + 1), 1)$ is in con S since $(0, 0)$ and $(j + 1, (j + 1)^2)$ are in S and $(1/(j + 1), 1) = [(j^2 + 2j)/(j + 1)^2](0, 0) + [1/(j + 1)^2](j + 1, (j + 1)^2)$. But $(1/(j + 1), 1)$ converges to $(0, 1)$ which is not in con S, so con S is not closed. Con $S = \mathbb{R}^2_{++} \cup \{(x, y) | x \geq 0, y = 0\}$.

4. If $S \subset \mathbb{R}^n$ is compact, con S is compact. Clearly, if S is bounded so is con S. The previous example with closed S but con S not closed used the fact that S was unbounded for the crucial step. With bounded S, such a construction is not possible.

The next three results concern sums of sets. Let $S_1, S_2, \ldots, S_m$ be nonempty subsets of $\mathbb{R}^n$ and let $S = \sum_{i=1}^m S_i$.

5. Con $S = \sum_{i=1}^m$ con S_i. Thus the operations of summation and taking convex hulls may be interchanged in order with no effect.

The next two results provide bounds on the nonconvexities in S when the S_i are (possibly) nonconvex. Result 6, known as the Shapley–Folkman theorem, shows that no matter how many sets are added, to reach any point in con S as a sum of points from the S_i or con S_i requires at most n (the dimension of the space, not the number of sets added) of the points be chosen from a con S_i rather than an S_i. Result 7 gives a measure of how close we can get to an arbitrary point from con S using the sum of points from the S_i themselves. Both of these results are useful for examining economic problems (e.g., if individual firm production sets are nonconvex, how bad are the nonconvexities in the aggregate production set, or, if technologies or preferences are nonconvex, how good an "approximate equilibrium" can be obtained).

6. For any $\mathbf{x} \in$ con S there exist $\mathbf{x}_i \in$ con S_i $i = 1, 2, \ldots, m$ such that $\mathbf{x} = \sum_{i=1}^m \mathbf{x}_i$ and $\mathbf{x}_i \in S_i$ for all but at most n of the sets S_i. Note n is the dimension of the overall space, not the number of sets added.

7. If $\sup_{\mathbf{x} \in \text{con } S_i} (\inf_{\mathbf{y} \in S_i} \|\mathbf{x} - \mathbf{y}\|) < c$ for $i = 1, 2, \ldots, m$, then for any $\mathbf{x} \in$ con S there exist $\mathbf{x}_i \in S_i$ for $i = 1, \ldots, m$ such that $\|\mathbf{x} - \sum_{i=1}^m \mathbf{x}_i\| < nc$. Note that for $\mathbf{x} \in$ con S_i, $\inf_{\mathbf{y} \in S_i} \|\mathbf{x} - \mathbf{y}\|$ is the distance from $\mathbf{x}$ to the closest point in S_i, so the condition essentially means that for any i, for any $\mathbf{x} \in$ con S_i there is a point $\mathbf{y} \in S_i$ within distance c from $\mathbf{x}$. Again note that the bound is in terms of n, the dimension of the space, not m, the number of sets added.

EXAMPLE: As an example of the last two results let $S_i = \{0, 1\} \subset \mathbb{R}^1$ for $i = 1, \ldots, m$. Then con S_i is the interval $[0, 1]$, $\sum_{i=1}^m S_i = \{0, 1, \ldots, m\}$, and con S is the interval $[0, m]$. The largest distance between a point in con S_i and S_i is $1/2$, so any $c > 1/2$ will work in result 7. If $x \in$ con S is an integer, then, setting $x_i = 1$ for $i = 1, 2, \ldots, x$ and $x_i = 0$ for $i = x + 1, \ldots, m$, $x_i \in S_i$ for all i and $x = \sum_{i=1}^m x_i$. In this case the nonconvexities create no problem. Suppose $x \in$ con S is not an integer, and let t be the greatest integer less than or equal to x. For result 6 set $x_i = 1$ for $i = 1, \ldots, t$, $x_i = 0$ for $i = t + 1, \ldots, m - 1$, and $x_m = x - t \in (0, 1)$. Then $\sum_{i=1}^m x_i = x$ and $x_i \in S_i$ for $i = 1, \ldots, m - 1$, with $x_m \in$ con S_m. Only one of the x_i had to be chosen from con S_i rather than S_i in order to sum exactly to x. For result 7 let $k = t$ if $x - t \le 1/2$ and $k = t + 1$ if $x - t > 1/2$ (i.e., k is the integer closest to x). Set $x_i = 1$ for $i = 1, \ldots, k$ and $x_i = 0$ for $i = k + 1, \ldots, m$. Then $x_i \in S_i$ for all i and $\|x - \sum_{i=1}^m x_i\| \le 1/2$. When required to choose x_i from S_i for all i, we can always get the sum within distance $1/2$ from the target x.

3.5 SEPARATION THEOREMS

The separation theorems are useful for proving one of the main welfare results of economics, the second welfare theorem in general equilibrium. Loosely stated, the problem is to show that there is some system of prices, $\mathbf{p} \in \mathbb{R}^l$, at which all the preferred bundles are separated from all the feasible bundles (i.e., preferred bundles are not "affordable"). These prices are then used to support a particular desired allocation as a competitive equilibrium. We first consider separation theorems for a convex set and a single point and then move on to a theorem about the separation of two convex sets.

RESULTS: The following results are known as separating hyperplane theorems. Let A be a nonempty, convex subset of $\mathbb{R}^l$.

1. If A is closed and $\mathbf{x} \notin A$ then there exists a $\mathbf{p} \neq \mathbf{0}$ such that $\mathbf{p} \cdot \mathbf{x} < \mathbf{p} \cdot \mathbf{y}$ for all $\mathbf{y} \in A$.

Proof: Pick any $\mathbf{y}^0 \in A$ and consider $f(\mathbf{y}) = \|\mathbf{x} - \mathbf{y}\|$ defined on the compact set $A \cap \{\mathbf{z} | \|\mathbf{z} - \mathbf{x}\| \leq \|\mathbf{y}^0 - \mathbf{x}\|\}$. Since f is continuous there exists a $\bar{\mathbf{y}} \in A$ that minimizes f on this set. Let $\mathbf{p} = \bar{\mathbf{y}} - \mathbf{x} \neq \mathbf{0}$. Then $\mathbf{p} \cdot \mathbf{x} = \mathbf{p} \cdot (\mathbf{x} - \bar{\mathbf{y}}) + \mathbf{p} \cdot \bar{\mathbf{y}} = -\mathbf{p} \cdot \mathbf{p} + \mathbf{p} \cdot \bar{\mathbf{y}} < \mathbf{p} \cdot \bar{\mathbf{y}}$. It remains to show $\mathbf{p} \cdot \mathbf{x} < \mathbf{p} \cdot \mathbf{y}$ for arbitrary $\mathbf{y} \in A$. Take any $\mathbf{y} \in A$. For all $\lambda \in (0, 1)$, $\lambda \mathbf{y} + (1 - \lambda)\bar{\mathbf{y}} \in A$, so $\|\mathbf{x} - (\lambda \mathbf{y} + (1 - \lambda)\bar{\mathbf{y}})\| \geq \|\mathbf{x} - \bar{\mathbf{y}}\|$. Thus

$$
\begin{aligned}
0 &\leq \|\mathbf{x} - \lambda \mathbf{y} - (1 - \lambda)\bar{\mathbf{y}}\|^2 - \|\mathbf{x} - \bar{\mathbf{y}}\|^2 \\
&= (\mathbf{x} - \lambda \mathbf{y} - (1 - \lambda)\bar{\mathbf{y}}) \cdot (\mathbf{x} - \lambda \mathbf{y} - (1 - \lambda)\bar{\mathbf{y}}) - (\mathbf{x} - \bar{\mathbf{y}}) \cdot (\mathbf{x} - \bar{\mathbf{y}}) \\
&= (\lambda(\bar{\mathbf{y}} - \mathbf{y}) - \mathbf{p}) \cdot (\lambda(\bar{\mathbf{y}} - \mathbf{y}) - \mathbf{p}) - \mathbf{p} \cdot \mathbf{p} \\
&= \lambda[-2\mathbf{p} \cdot (\bar{\mathbf{y}} - \mathbf{y}) + \lambda(\bar{\mathbf{y}} - \mathbf{y}) \cdot (\bar{\mathbf{y}} - \mathbf{y})].
\end{aligned}
$$

This must hold for all $\lambda > 0$ so for λ very near zero, this implies $0 \leq -2\mathbf{p} \cdot (\bar{\mathbf{y}} - \mathbf{y})$ or $\mathbf{p} \cdot \bar{\mathbf{y}} \leq \mathbf{p} \cdot \mathbf{y}$. Since $\mathbf{p} \cdot \mathbf{x} < \mathbf{p} \cdot \bar{\mathbf{y}}$ this completes the proof.

2. If $\mathbf{x} \notin A$ there exists a $\mathbf{p} \neq \mathbf{0}$ such that $\mathbf{p} \cdot \mathbf{x} \leq \mathbf{p} \cdot \mathbf{y}$ for all $\mathbf{y} \in A$.

Proof: If $\mathbf{x}$ is not in the closure of A, then proceed as in result 1 using the closure of A rather than A. If $\mathbf{x}$ is in the closure of A, then take a sequence of points $(\mathbf{x}_n)_{n=1}^{\infty}$ with $\mathbf{x}_n$ not in the closure of A for all n and $\mathbf{x}_n \to \mathbf{x}$. For each n find a $\bar{\mathbf{y}}_n$ as in result 1. Since $\bar{\mathbf{y}}_n - \mathbf{x}_n \neq \mathbf{0}$, $\mathbf{p}_n = (\bar{\mathbf{y}}_n - \mathbf{x}_n)/\|\bar{\mathbf{y}}_n - \mathbf{x}_n\|$ is well defined. Then $\|\mathbf{p}_n\| = 1$ for all n so the sequence $(\mathbf{p}_n)_{n=1}^{\infty}$ is contained in a compact set and hence has a convergent subsequence. Let $\mathbf{p}$ be any limit for a convergent subsequence.

3. If B is another convex set and $A \cap B = \varnothing$, then there exists a $\mathbf{p} \neq \mathbf{0}$ such that $\mathbf{p} \cdot \mathbf{x} \leq \mathbf{p} \cdot \mathbf{y}$ for all $\mathbf{x} \in A$, $\mathbf{y} \in B$.

Proof: $B + (-A)$ is convex and $\mathbf{0} \notin B - A$. By result 2, there exists a $\mathbf{p} \neq \mathbf{0}$ such that $0 \leq \mathbf{p} \cdot (\mathbf{y} - \mathbf{x})$ for all $\mathbf{y} \in B$, $\mathbf{x} \in A$. Thus $\mathbf{p} \cdot \mathbf{x} \leq \mathbf{p} \cdot \mathbf{y}$ for all $\mathbf{y} \in B$, $\mathbf{x} \in A$.

Clearly, if A is not convex, results 1–3 do not hold in general. For example, if $A = \{(x, y) | x = 0 \text{ or } y = 0\}$ then no point or (nonempty) set can be separated from A by a hyperplane. If A is not convex but $\mathbf{x} \notin \operatorname{con} A$, then $\mathbf{x}$ can be separated from con A and hence from A. Similarly, if A and B are sets and $(\operatorname{con} A) \cap (\operatorname{con} B) = \varnothing$, then A and B can be separated by a hyperplane.

In economic problems, the normal to a supporting hyperplane often provides important information about prices. For example, suppose $V(y)$ is the set of input bundles with which it is technically feasible to produce output y, and $\mathbf{x} \in V(y)$. Then $\mathbf{x}$ would be chosen as a least expensive input bundle to produce y at input prices $\mathbf{p}$ only if $\mathbf{p} \cdot \mathbf{x} \le \mathbf{p} \cdot \mathbf{z}$ for all $\mathbf{z} \in V(y)$.

PROBLEMS

3.1 For each of the following sets determine whether it is closed, open, compact, or convex:
   (a) $[-10, 1] \subset \mathbb{R}$
   (b) $(-\infty, 0] \subset \mathbb{R}$
   (c) $(-\infty, 0) \subset \mathbb{R}$
   (d) $[-10, 0) \subset \mathbb{R}$
   (e) $\{\mathbf{x} \in \mathbb{R}^2 | x_i \ge 0 \ i = 1, 2, \text{ and } x_1^2 + x_2^2 \ge 1\}$
   (f) $\{\mathbf{x} \in \mathbb{R}^2 | x_i \ge 0 \ i = 1, 2 \text{ and } x_1^2 + x_2^2 < 1\}$
   (g) $\{\mathbf{x} \in \mathbb{R}^2 | -10 \le x_1 \le 1\}$
   (h) $\{\mathbf{x} \in \mathbb{R}^2 | x_i \ge 1 \ i = 1, 2 \text{ and } x_1 x_2 \le 2\}$

3.2 For $A = \{\mathbf{x} \in \mathbb{R}^2 | 0 \le x_1 \le 1 \text{ and } 2 \le x_2 \le 3\}$ and $B = \{\mathbf{x} \in \mathbb{R}^2 | 0 \le x_1 \le 1 \text{ and } x_2 = x_1\}$:
   (a) Find $A + B$.
   (b) Find a hyperplane separating A and B.

3.3 Find a hyperplane separating the point $(2, 2)$ from the set $\{(x, y) \in \mathbb{R}^2 | x^2 + y^2 \le 1\}$.

3.4 Determine which of the following sets are open, closed, compact, and convex:
   (a) $\{(x, y) \in \mathbb{R}^2 | x^2 + y^2 = 1\}$
   (b) $\{(x, y) \in \mathbb{R}^2 | x \ge 0, \ y \ge 0, \text{ and } xy \ge 1\}$
   (c) $\{(x, y) \in \mathbb{R}^2 | -1 < x < 1 \text{ and } y = x\}$

3.5 True/False. Let $S \subset \mathbb{R}^2$ be noncompact. Then the problem of maximizing $f(x, y) = x^2 + y^2$ subject to $(x, y) \in S$ cannot have a global maximizer.

3.6 Is $\{(x, y) | 0 \le x < 1 \text{ and } y = 0\}$ open or closed relative to $\{(x, y) | x^2 + y^2 < 1\}$?

3.7 Is $\{(x, y) | 0 < x \le 10 \text{ and } 0 \le y \le \ln x\}$ compact or convex?

3.8 Is $\{(x, y) \in \mathbb{R}^2 | xy < 1\}$ open, closed, compact, or convex?

3.9 Is $\{x \in \mathbb{R} | x^2 \geq 1\}$ open, closed, compact, or convex?

3.10 For each of the following sets, decide whether it is open, closed, compact, or convex:
(a) $\{x \in \mathbb{R} | x^2 > 1\}$
(b) $\{(x, y) \in \mathbb{R}^2 | x \geq 1, \ y \geq 1, \ xy \leq 9\}$

3.11 Is $\{(x, y) \in \mathbb{R}^2 | xy < 0 \text{ and } x^2 + y^2 \leq 1\}$ open, closed, compact, or convex?

3.12 Decide whether the set

$$\{(x, y) \in \mathbb{R}^2 | x \geq 0, \ y \geq 0, \ x^2 + y^2 \geq 1, \text{ and } x + y \leq 4\}$$

is open, closed, compact, or convex and explain.

3.13 Is $\{(x, y) \in \mathbb{R}^2 | y \geq x \text{ and } xy \geq 1\}$ open, closed, compact, or convex?

4

CORRESPONDENCES

4.1 INTRODUCTION

In some problems, the usual notion of a function is not adequate. For example, what is the optimal production for a competitive firm with cost function $C(x) = x$ when the output price is $p = 1$? The firm is indifferent among all output levels so the profit maximizers are the elements of the set $\{x \in \mathbb{R} | x \geq 0\}$. A similar problem may arise if a consumer has an indifference curve, part of which is a straight line. At certain prices and incomes, the consumer will be indifferent among many different consumption bundles. In order to handle these problems we introduce the notion of a correspondence. A *correspondence* $\varphi: S \mapsto T$ is a function from S to the nonempty subsets of T. The symbol $\mapsto$ indicates that this is a correspondence rather than a function. Some authors allow $\varphi(s)$ to be the empty set. Also, many authors don't distinguish the set containing the single point x from the point x itself; strictly speaking one should write $\varphi(s) = \{x\}$ rather than $\varphi(s) = x$ when $\varphi(s)$ is a singleton set. If S is a subset of $\mathbb{R}^l$ then s is a vector. However, when S is not explicitly specified, we will write s rather than s. All the definitions and results in this chapter apply whether S is a subset of $\mathbb{R}$ or of $\mathbb{R}^l$ for $l > 1$. A familiar example of a correspondence is the budget correspondence from prices and income to the set of affordable bundles. If p is a price vector from $\mathbb{R}^l_{++}$ and I is an income from $\mathbb{R}_+$, then the budget correspondence is

$$B: \mathbb{R}^l_{++} \times \mathbb{R}_+ \mapsto \mathbb{R}^l_+, \quad \text{where } B(\mathbf{p}, I) = \left\{ \mathbf{x} \in \mathbb{R}^l_+ | \mathbf{p} \cdot \mathbf{x} \leq I \right\}.$$

We will examine some notions of continuity for correspondences and a result, the maximum theorem, that has implications for comparative statics in optimization problems. The maximum theorem, along with some results in Chapter 5, will provide conditions under which optimizers and the optimized value of the objective function will be continuous functions of the parameters of the problem. The continuity definitions provide a check of one's understanding of open sets, since continuity of correspondences is defined using open sets.

4.2 CONTINUITY OF CORRESPONDENCES

Two important notions of continuity for correspondences are upper hemicontinuity and lower hemicontinuity. In older literature one will sometimes see the words upper semicontinuity or lower semicontinuity used instead. These older terms have been replaced because of the potential for confusion with the terms upper and lower semicontinuity of functions (see Chapter 5, Section 5.13). Upper hemicontinuity requires that the set $\varphi(s)$ does not "blow up" for small changes in s, while lower hemicontinuity requires that the set $\varphi(s)$ does not "drastically shrink" for small changes in s.

DEFINITION: The correspondence $\varphi\colon S \mapsto T$ is *upper hemicontinuous at* $s \in S$ (uhc at $s \in S$) if for all open sets V such that $\varphi(s) \subset V$ there exists an open set N containing s such that $x \in N$ implies $\varphi(x) \subset V$. The correspondence φ is *upper hemicontinuous* (uhc) if it is upper hemicontinuous at all $s \in S$.

Note that if $\varphi(s)$ is a singleton set for all $s \in S$, then φ could be thought of as a regular function, φ^*. Then the correspondence φ is upper hemicontinuous if and only if the function φ^* is continuous. For singleton-valued φ, the definition of uhc is the topological version of the standard ε, δ definition of continuity of a function.

DEFINITION: The correspondence $\varphi\colon S \mapsto T$ is *lower hemicontinuous at* $s \in S$ (lhc at $s \in S$) if for all open sets V such that $V \cap \varphi(s) \neq \varnothing$, there exists an open set N containing s such that $x \in N$ implies $\varphi(x) \cap V \neq \varnothing$. The correspondence φ is *lower hemicontinuous* (lhc) if it is lower hemicontinuous at all $s \in S$.

Note that if $\varphi(s)$ is a singleton set for all $s \in S$ and φ^* is the corresponding function, then the correspondence φ is lower hemicontinuous if and only if the function φ^* is continuous.

EXAMPLE: For φ: $[0, 3] \mapsto [0, 3]$ defined by

$$\varphi(s) = \begin{cases} \{1\} & \text{if } 0 \le s < 2, \\ \{x \in \mathbb{R} | 0 \le x \le 3\} & \text{if } s = 2, \\ \{2\} & \text{if } 2 < s \le 3 \end{cases}$$

φ is upper hemicontinuous everywhere [for $s \ne 2$, φ is constant in a neighborhood of s, while for $s = 2$, V must contain $\varphi(2) = T$, so clearly $\varphi(s) \subset V$ for s near 2] but not lower hemicontinuous at 2 [for $V = \{x \in \mathbb{R} | 1.1 < x < 1.9\}$, $\varphi(2) \cap V \ne \varnothing$, but $\varphi(s) \cap V = \varnothing$ for all $s \ne 2$].

EXAMPLE: For φ: $[0, 2] \mapsto [0, 2]$ defined by

$$\varphi(s) = \begin{cases} \{1\} & \text{if } 0 \le x \le 1, \\ \{x \in \mathbb{R} | 0 \le x \le 2\} & \text{if } 1 < x \le 2 \end{cases}$$

φ is lower hemicontinuous everywhere [for $s \ne 1$, φ is constant in a neighborhood of s, while for $s = 1$, V must contain 1 to have $V \cap \varphi(1) \ne \varnothing$ and $1 \in \varphi(s)$ for all s] but not upper hemicontinuous at 1 [$V = \{x \in \mathbb{R} | .9 < x < 1.1\}$ contains $\varphi(1)$ but does not contain $\varphi(s)$ for any $s > 1$].

DEFINITION: The correspondence φ: $S \mapsto T$ is *continuous* (*continuous at s*) if φ is upper hemicontinuous and lower hemicontinuous (uhc and lhc at s).

When checking for uhc or lhc it is important to keep clear the order of steps and the space in which each step takes place. The point s is in S, and $\varphi(s)$ is a set in T. V is an open set in T that contains $\varphi(s)$ when checking for uhc [has a nonempty intersection with $\varphi(s)$ when checking for lhc]. N is an open set in S that contains s. For uhc, $\varphi(x)$ is a subset of T that should be contained in V for all x in N. [For lhc, $\varphi(x)$ is a subset of T that should have a nonempty intersection with V for all x in N.] To prove uhc (lhc) at s, for any V containing (having nonempty intersection with) $\varphi(s)$, one must be able to find an open set N containing s, such that V contains $\varphi(x)$ for all x in N [V has a nonempty intersection with $\varphi(x)$ for all x in N].

DEFINITION: The correspondence φ: $S \mapsto T$ is *open valued* (*closed valued*, *compact valued*, or *convex valued*) if $\varphi(s)$ is an open (closed, compact, or convex, respectively) subset of T for all $s \in S$.

EXAMPLE: Consider the correspondence φ: $[0, \infty) \mapsto \mathbb{R}^2$ defined by $\varphi(t) = \{(x, y) \in \mathbb{R}^2 | -1 < y < 1 \text{ and } x^2 + y^2 \le t^2\}$. For which values of t is $\varphi(t)$ open, closed, compact, or convex?

It is not open for any t: For all $t \ge 0$, $(t, 0) \in \varphi(t)$ but for any fixed t, $(t + 1/n, 0) \notin \varphi(t)$ for any integer $n \ge 1$. Since $(t + 1/n, 0) \to (t, 0)$ as $n \to \infty$, no neighborhood around $(t, 0)$ is contained in $\varphi(t)$.

It is closed for $0 \leq t < 1$: For $0 \leq t < 1$, $\varphi(t) = \{(x, y) \in \mathbb{R}^2 | x^2 + y^2 \leq t^2\}$ which is closed. For $t \geq 1$, $(0, y) \in \varphi(t)$ for $-1 < y < 1$, but $(0, 1)$ and $(0, -1)$ are not in $\varphi(t)$, so $\varphi(t)$ is not closed.

It is compact for $0 \leq t < 1$: For each t, $\varphi(t) \subset \{(x, y) \in \mathbb{R}^2 | x^2 + y^2 \leq t^2\}$, which is bounded, so $\varphi(t)$ is compact if it is closed.

It is convex for all t: $\varphi(t)$ is the intersection of convex sets, $\varphi(t) = \{(x, y) \in \mathbb{R}^2 | -1 < y\} \cap \{(x, y) \in \mathbb{R}^2 | y < 1\} \cap \{(x, y) \in \mathbb{R}^2 | x^2 + y^2 \leq t^2\}$.

4.3   THE MAXIMUM THEOREM

We are often interested in the behavior of maximizers and the maximized value of a function as some parameters change. For example, for the budget correspondence $B(\mathbf{p}, I) = \{\mathbf{x} \in \mathbb{R}_+^l | \mathbf{p} \cdot \mathbf{x} \leq I\}$ and the continuous utility function $u(\mathbf{x})$, the utility maximizers over the budget set given $(\mathbf{p}, I)$ are the elements of the demand correspondence or demand function if demand is single valued (Chapter 5, Section 5.10 examines conditions under which demand will be single valued and conditions under which it will be convex valued if it is a correspondence). The maximized value of utility is the value of the indirect utility function $V(\mathbf{p}, I)$. The following theorem guarantees that optimizers and the optimized value of the objective function are "well behaved" under certain conditions. The result is stated for maximization, but the same conclusions hold for minimization.

MAXIMUM THEOREM: *Let the correspondence B: $S \mapsto T$ be compact valued and continuous and let the function f: $S \times T \to \mathbb{R}$ be continuous. Then*

1. The function m: $S \to \mathbb{R}$ defined by $m(x) := \max\{f(x, y) | y \in B(x)\}$ is well defined and continuous.

2. The correspondence d: $S \mapsto T$ defined by $d(x) := \{y \in B(x) | f(x, y) = m(x)\}$ is nonempty and compact valued and upper hemicontinuous.

The theorem is more general than our demand problem. To translate to the demand setting, $S = \mathbb{R}_{++}^l \times \mathbb{R}_+$ is the set of price–income pairs, $T = \mathbb{R}_+^l$ is the consumption set, B is the budget correspondence, $f(\mathbf{p}, I, \mathbf{x}) = u(\mathbf{x})$ is the utility function, $d(\mathbf{p}, I)$ is the demand correspondence, and $m(\mathbf{p}, I)$ is the indirect utility function. The theorem shows that if the budget correspondence is compact valued and the budget correspondence and utility function are continuous, then the indirect utility function is continuous and the demand correspondence is uhc and compact valued. If demand is single valued, uhc implies continuity of the demand function.

EXAMPLE: Consider a consumer with consumption set $\mathbb{R}_+^2$ and utility function $u(x, y) = x + y$ who initially owns one unit of the first good. If the price of y is fixed at one and p is the price of x, then for each $p \geq 0$

the consumer's demand is the solution to: maximize $x + y$ subject to $x \geq 0$, $y \geq 0$, and $px + y \leq p$ (note the consumer's wealth depends on the value of her initial endowment, p). The budget correspondence $B(p) = \{(x, y) \in \mathbb{R}^2 | x \geq 0, y \geq 0, px + y \leq p\}$ is compact valued and continuous for $p > 0$ and the utility function is continuous. By the maximum theorem, for $p > 0$ the demand correspondence is uhc and compact valued and the indirect utility function is continuous. Solving the problem for $p > 0$, the demand correspondence is

$$(x^*(p), y^*(p)) = \begin{cases} \{(1, 0)\} & \text{if } 0 < p < 1, \\ \{(z, 1 - z) | 0 \leq z \leq 1\} & \text{if } p = 1, \\ \{(0, p)\} & \text{if } 1 < p \end{cases}$$

and the indirect utility function is

$$V(p) = u(x^*(p), y^*(p)) = \begin{cases} 1 & \text{if } 0 < p \leq 1, \\ p & \text{if } 1 < p, \end{cases}$$

both satisfying the required properties. Except when $p = 1$, there is a unique bundle that maximizes utility. Note that at $p = 0$ the budget correspondence is not continuous [it is not lhc since $B(0) = \{(x, y) \in \mathbb{R}^2 | y = 0, x \geq 0\}$], and neither demand nor indirect utility is well defined.

PROBLEMS

4.1 Consider the correspondence $\varphi: [-1, 1] \mapsto [-1, 1]$ defined by $\varphi(x) = \{y \in [-1, 1] | -x^2 < y < x^2\} \cup \{0\}$. Decide whether φ is uhc or lhc at $x = 0$ and at $x = 1$. Explain.

4.2 Define the correspondence $\varphi: [0, 1] \mapsto [0, 1]$ by

$$\varphi(x) = \begin{cases} \{y | x < y \leq x + 1/2\} & \text{if } 0 \leq x < 1/2, \\ \{y | y = x\} & \text{if } 1/2 \leq x \leq 1. \end{cases}$$

(a) At which values of x is φ upper hemicontinuous? Explain.
(b) At which values of x is φ lower hemicontinuous? Explain.

4.3 For each correspondence below, determine whether it is (i) upper hemicontinuous (ii) lower hemicontinuous, (iii) convex valued, and (iv) compact valued.

(a) $\varphi: [0, 1] \mapsto [0, 2]$, $\varphi(x) = \{y | y > x\} \cap [0, 2]$
(b) $\varphi: [0, 1] \mapsto [0, 2]$, $\varphi(x) = \{2 - 2x, 2x\} \cap [0, 2]$
(c) $\varphi: [0, 1] \mapsto [0, 2]$, $\varphi(x) = \{2 - 2x, 3x\} \cap [0, 2]$
(d) $\varphi: [0, 1] \mapsto \mathbb{R}^2$, $\varphi(p) = \{(x, y) \in \mathbb{R}^2 | x \geq 0, y \geq 0, \text{ and } px + (1 - p)y \leq p\}$

4.4 Determine which of the following correspondences are upper hemicontinuous and which are lower hemicontinuous.

(a) $\varphi: [0, 1] \mapsto [0, 2]$, $\varphi(x) = \{y \,|\, x < y < x + 1\} \cap [0, 2]$

(b) $\varphi: \mathbb{R} \mapsto \mathbb{R}$, $\varphi(x) = \begin{cases} \left\{ \dfrac{1}{x - 1} \right\} & \text{if } x \neq 1 \\ \{0\} & \text{if } x = 1 \end{cases}$

(c) $\varphi: [0, 1] \mapsto [0, 2]$, $\varphi(x) = \{y \,|\, xy = 0\} \cap [0, 2]$

4.5 Let $\varphi: [0, 1] \mapsto [0, 1]$ be defined by

$$\varphi(x) = \begin{cases} \{y \,|\, 0 \leq y < 1\} & \text{if } x = 0, \\ \{y \,|\, 0 \leq y \leq x\} & \text{if } 0 < x \leq 1/2, \\ \{y \,|\, 0 \leq y < 1 - x \text{ or } y = x\} & \text{if } 1/2 < x \leq 1. \end{cases}$$

(a) Draw the graph of φ.
(b) At which values of x is φ upper hemicontinuous?
(c) At which values of x is φ lower hemicontinuous?

5

CALCULUS
OF SEVERAL
VARIABLES

5.1 INTRODUCTION

This chapter covers a wide variety of topics. It begins with an examination of level surfaces, gradients, and their relationship, in Sections 5.2 and 5.3. The results (such as the derivation of marginal rates of substitution) are very useful in economics. The next topic is the chain rule for functions of several variables in Section 5.4. This is a vital tool for comparative statics and many other economic problems.

The bulk of this chapter examines necessary and sufficient conditions for optimization. Optimization problems for calculus of several variables follow the same pattern as for one variable: use first-order conditions to find all potential solutions, use second-order conditions to check whether each potential solution is a local maximizer or local minimizer, and check for the global solution. The results are based on an understanding of level curves (Sections 5.2 and 5.3) and two Taylor expansions derived in Section 5.5. Sections 5.6 and 5.7 examine optimization without constraints and optimization with equality constraints, respectively. These two topics are special cases of the general results on first-order conditions and second-order conditions for arbitrary optimization problems contained in Sections 5.8 and 5.9. Section 5.8 provides the most important analysis of first-order conditions. In many ways it is the easiest to understand, since it presents all the cases in a unified framework. It should be the center of the reader's attention, with Sections 5.6 and 5.7 viewed as the special cases which they are. Section 5.9 considers the second-order conditions for the general case. Up to this point, the analysis concerns local maximizers and minimizers. Section 5.10 introduces concave, convex, and quasiconcave functions and examines procedures for finding global solutions.

The final sections contain several short topics. Section 5.11 contains a brief introduction to one aspect of duality theory. This will be useful in Section 7.7 of Chapter 7, when we consider an application of our results to consumer theory. Section 5.12 introduces homogeneous and homothetic functions, which are important in producer and consumer theory. Section 5.13 considers semicontinuous functions. They are useful in some specialized topics such as the integrability problem in consumer theory (starting from a "demand function," how can we determine whether the "demand" could have been generated by utility-maximizing behavior?).

We begin with some notation. In order to specify clearly the domain and range spaces of the functions we deal with, we will sometimes use the notation $f: S \to T$ to specify that the function f maps elements of S to elements of T [for example, $f: \mathbb{R}^2 \to \mathbb{R}$ defined by $f(x, y) = x + y$]. For every element of S, $s \in S$, $f(s)$ must be well defined, and $f(s) \in T$. The notation does not mean that for every $t \in T$, for some $s \in S$, $f(s) = t$. The notation allows vector-valued functions, $\mathbf{f}: \mathbb{R}^n \to \mathbb{R}^m$ where $m > 1$. Then $\mathbf{f}$ can be thought of as being made up of m component functions, $f^i: \mathbb{R}^n \to \mathbb{R}^1$, $i = 1, 2, \ldots, n$. For example, $f: \mathbb{R}^1 \to \mathbb{R}^2$ defined by

$$\mathbf{f}(x) = \begin{pmatrix} x \\ x^2 \end{pmatrix}$$

has component functions $f^1(x) = x$ and $f^2(x) = x^2$. The notion of continuity is easily extended to functions of several variables.

DEFINITION: A function $\mathbf{f}: \mathbb{R}^n \to \mathbb{R}^m$ is *continuous at* $\mathbf{c} \in \mathbb{R}^n$ if f is defined at $\mathbf{c}$ and $\mathbf{f}(x) \to \mathbf{f}(c)$ as $x \to c$. If $\mathbf{f}$ is continuous at each point in its domain, we say $\mathbf{f}$ is *continuous*.

5.2 LEVEL SURFACES

The first difference between one and more than one variable is that there are now at least two different kinds of graphs that would be of interest. For example, consider a three-dimensional map of a national park and the corresponding topographic map. If we think of the function $z = f(x, y)$ where z is elevation, x is longitude, and y is latitude, then the three-dimensional map is a graph of this function over the domain corresponding to the park. We need three dimensions because we need to specify our position east–west (x), north–south (y), and up–down (z). Although three-dimensional maps (especially maps of mountainous areas) are great fun to look at, most maps are drawn on flat paper. The information about

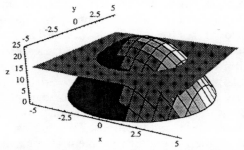

FIGURE 5.1 Graph of the function and a plane at height 16.

elevation can be captured by drawing in a set of contour lines, with each contour line representing all points with a specific elevation. The contour lines are not graphs of the function but are instead what are called *level curves* (level surfaces in higher dimensions). Level curves are so commonly used in economics that they often have special names. An indifference curve for a consumer is a level curve containing all bundles of goods that attain a certain level of utility. An isoquant in production theory is a level curve containing all bundles of inputs that attain a certain output level.

To see the difference between the graph of a function and the graph of a level curve, consider the function $z = f(x, y) = 25 - x^2 - y^2$. To find a level curve corresponding to $z = 16$, we take a plane at height 16 and intersect it with the graph and then project the intersection down to the x–y plane. See Figure 5.1. The level curve is shown in Figure 5.2, which looks only at the x–y plane. A level curve is always in a figure with dimension one less than the graph (a two-dimensional plane versus three-dimensional space in the example).

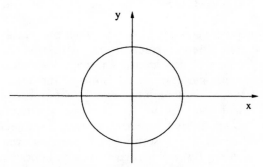

FIGURE 5.2 Graph of the level curve.

It is very important to be able to determine when we should be dealing with the graph of a function and when we should be dealing with the graph of a level curve.

DEFINITION: The *graph* of the function $f: \mathbb{R}^n \to \mathbb{R}^1$ is the set of points in $\mathbb{R}^{n+1}$ given by $\{(\mathbf{x}, f(\mathbf{x})) | \mathbf{x} \in \mathbb{R}^n\}$. The *level surface* corresponding to $f \equiv c$ (for some $c \in \mathbb{R}$) is $\{\mathbf{x} \in \mathbb{R}^n | f(\mathbf{x}) = c\}$.

The level curve corresponding to c is found by intersecting the hyperplane $H_{(0,0,\ldots,0,1)}(c) = \{\mathbf{x} \in \mathbb{R}^{n+1} | x_{n+1} = c\}$ with the graph of f, projecting down to the hyperplane $H_{(0,0,\ldots,0,1)}(0) = \{\mathbf{x} \in \mathbb{R}^{n+1} | x_{n+1} = 0\}$, and ignoring the last component. Note that for $f: \mathbb{R}^n \to \mathbb{R}$ the graph of f is a set of points in $\mathbb{R}^{n+1}$, while the level surfaces of f (one for each value of c) are sets of points in $\mathbb{R}^n$.

5.3 GRADIENTS AND TANGENT PLANES

Much of the intuition for properties of functions of several variables comes from linear approximations to the functions. (Recall the tangent line approximation to the graph of a function of one variable.) The linear approximation at a point depends on the derivatives of the function at that point. With functions of several variables, we can take linear approximations to the graph of the function and linear approximations to level curves. These and related topics are covered in this section.

For a function of several varibles, if we hold all but one variable constant, we can define the *partial derivative* with respect to the remaining variable just as we defined the derivative for functions of one variable. For example, for the function $f(x, y, z)$, if we hold x and z fixed at x^0 and z^0, respectively, then the partial derivative of f with respect to y at the point (x^0, y^0, z^0) is

$$\frac{\partial f(x^0, y^0, z^0)}{\partial y} = \lim_{\Delta y \to 0} \left(\frac{f(x^0, y^0 + \Delta y, z^0) - f(x^0, y^0, z^0)}{\Delta y} \right).$$

Note the notation (∂) used to distinguish a partial derivative from a derivative of a function of one variable.

If this partial derivative exists for all (x, y, z) triples, then we have the partial derivative function $\partial f(x, y, z)/\partial y$. We similarly define $\partial f(x, y, z)/\partial x$ and $\partial f(x, y, z)/\partial z$, each time holding all but one of the variables fixed when taking the limit. We treat as constants those variables which we are not differentiating with respect to. For example, if $f(x, y) = x^2 y + y$, then differentiating with respect to x, we treat y as a constant, so $\partial f(x, y)/\partial x = 2xy$; when differentiating with respect to y, we treat x as a constant, so $\partial f(x, y)/\partial y = x^2 + 1$. As an alternative notation, $f_1(x, y)$ is used to represent the partial derivative with respect to the first variable (here x) and $f_2(x, y)$ is used to represent the partial derivative with respect to the second variable. A third alternative is $f_x(x, y), f_y(x, y)$.

Partial derivatives have the same interpretation as regular derivatives for functions of one variable: if only x changes, then $\partial f(x, y)/\partial x$ gives the best linear approximation to the effect on f [i.e., if $z = f(x, y)$ then $\Delta z = \partial f(x, y)/\partial x \, \Delta x$ is the tangent line approximation for the effect of a change in x].

What if x and y change simultaneously? If the function f is *differentiable*, we will be able to add up the effects of a change in x and a change in y. Differentiability is a "smoothness" condition and is not implied by the existence of partial derivatives at a point.

Recall that for $f: \mathbb{R}^1 \to \mathbb{R}^1$ to be differentiable at x^0, a tangent line to the graph of the function at the point $(x^0, f(x^0))$ must exist and provide a good approximation to the graph near $(x^0, f(x^0))$. The derivative $f'(x^0)$ is the slope of the tangent line, and the notion of a good approximation is captured by

$$f(x^0 + h) = f(x^0) + f'(x^0)h + hE(h, x^0)$$

where

$$E(h, x^0) = \frac{f(x^0 + h) - f(x^0)}{h} - f'(x^0) \to 0 \quad \text{as } h \to 0.$$

The total error from using the tangent line approximation is $hE(h, x^0)$, which is small relative to h or "of smaller order than h as $h \to 0$." One can think of $hE(h, x^0)$ as h^2, which is negligible relative to h when h is small. Using the tangent line approximation, we "estimate" $y = f(x^0) + f'(x^0)(x - x^0)$.

EXAMPLE: For $f: \mathbb{R}^1 \to \mathbb{R}^1$ defined by $f(x) = x^2$, at $x^0 = 1$ the tangent line approximation is $y = 1 + 2(x - 1) = 2x - 1$. This is a good approximation for x near 1 and a not very good approximation for x far from 1.

For several variables, the function $f: \mathbb{R}^n \to \mathbb{R}^1$ is differentiable at x^0 if there is a tangent plane (hyperplane if $n > 2$) to the graph of the function at the point $(\mathbf{x}^0, f(\mathbf{x}^0))$ which provides a good approximation to the graph near $(\mathbf{x}^0, f(\mathbf{x}^0))$. The tangent plane must give a good approximation everywhere near $(\mathbf{x}^0, f(\mathbf{x}^0))$, not just for changes in some directions.

DEFINITION: The function $f: \mathbb{R}^n \to \mathbb{R}^1$ is *differentiable at* $\mathbf{x}^0$ if there exists a vector $\nabla f(\mathbf{x}^0)$ (called the *gradient* vector) such that

$$f(\mathbf{x}^0 + \mathbf{v}) = f(\mathbf{x}^0) + \nabla f(\mathbf{x}^0) \cdot \mathbf{v} + \|\mathbf{v}\| E(\mathbf{v}, \mathbf{x}^0) \tag{1}$$

where $E(\mathbf{v}, \mathbf{x}^0) \to 0$ as $\mathbf{v} \to 0$. The function is *differentiable* if it is differentiable at every **x**. It is *continuously differentiable* if it is differentiable and $\nabla f(\mathbf{x})$ is continuous.

Compare this definition with the definition for the single-variable case. It is identical except for changes to vector notation: x^0 becomes $\mathbf{x}^0$, h becomes $\mathbf{v}$, scalar product is used in $\nabla f(\mathbf{x}^0) \cdot \mathbf{v}$ rather than the product of scalars in $f'(x^0)h$, and $\|\mathbf{v}\|$ is used to reduce $\mathbf{v}$ to a scalar for the error term. Notice that it requires the tangent hyperplane to be a good approximation everywhere near $(\mathbf{x}^0, f(\mathbf{x}^0))$, not just in certain directions.

When a function f of one variable is differentiable at a point x^0, there is a tangent line to the graph of f at x^0 that provides a good approximation to the graph near x^0. The equation of the tangent line is $y = f(x^0) + (x - x^0)f'(x^0)$. When a function f of several variables is differentiable at a point x^0, there is a tangent plane (hyperplane in higher dimensions) to the graph of f at $\mathbf{x}^0$ that provides a good approximation to the graph near $\mathbf{x}^0$. The equation of the tangent plane is $y = f(\mathbf{x}^0) + (\mathbf{x} - \mathbf{x}^0) \cdot \nabla f(\mathbf{x}^0)$. Note the similarity to the one-variable case. The terms are the vector equivalents of the terms for the one-variable case; e.g., the gradient $\nabla f(\mathbf{x}^0)$ replaces the derivative $f'(x^0)$. The tangent plane equation can be rewritten as $y - f(\mathbf{x}^0) = \nabla f(\mathbf{x}^0) \cdot (\mathbf{x} - \mathbf{x}^0)$ or $\Delta y = \nabla(\mathbf{x}^0) \cdot \Delta \mathbf{x}$. Thus the effects of changes in several variables x_i can just be added up to get the overall effect.

EXAMPLE: If output, Y, is a function of capital, K, labor, L, and a raw material, M, given by $Y = f(K, L, M) = K^{1/2}L^{1/4}M^{1/4}$ and we start at $(K, L, M) = (400, 16, 810000)$, we can use the tangent plane approximation to estimate the effect of an increase of 5 units of capital and 2 units of labor. The partial derivatives with respect to K and L (i.e., the marginal products of capital and labor, respectively) are $f_1(K, L, M) = (1/2)K^{-1/2}L^{1/4}M^{1/4}$ and $f_2(K, L, M) = (1/4)K^{1/2}L^{-3/4}M^{1/4}$. Evaluated at $(K, L, M) = (400, 16, 810000)$, the marginal products are $f_1(400, 16, 810000) = 3/2$ and $f_2(400, 16, 810000) = 75/4$. The tangent plane approximation to the effect of an increase of 5 units of capital is $5f_1(400, 16, 810000) = 15/2$ while the tangent plane approximation to the effect of an increase of 2 units of labor is $2f_2(400, 16, 810000) = 75/2$. The tangent plane approximation to the overall effect of a simultaneous change $(\Delta K, \Delta L) = (5, 2)$ is just the sum of the individual effects, $15/2 + 75/2 = 45$. Thus the tangent plane estimate for the total effect is that output will increase by 45 units.

The reason the ability to sum the individual effects to find the total impact is useful is that in real economic problems we almost never know the actual function, $f(\mathbf{x})$, but we may know estimates of its partial derivatives at a point, $f_i(\mathbf{x}^0)$. These can be used as in the preceding example.

It is important to note that even the existence of all directional derivatives at a point does not imply differentiability or continuity. Differentiability requires additional "smoothness." For example, all directional derivatives exist at $(0, 0)$ for

$$g(x, y) = \begin{cases} xy^2/(x^2 + y^2) & \text{if } x \neq 0, \\ 0 & \text{if } x = 0, \end{cases}$$

while g is neither differentiable nor continuous at $(0, 0)$.

We now derive several important properties of the gradient from Eq. (1) in the definition of differentiability. The properties have important uses in economics and optimization.

RESULTS: Assume that $f: \mathbb{R}^n \to \mathbb{R}^1$ is differentiable at $\mathbf{x}^0$ with gradient vector $\nabla f(\mathbf{x}^0)$. The following properties are consequences of differentiability.

1. f is continuous at x^0.

Proof: As $\mathbf{v} \to \mathbf{0}$, $\nabla f(\mathbf{x}^0) \cdot \mathbf{v} \to 0$ and $\|\mathbf{v}\| E(\mathbf{v}, \mathbf{x}^0) \to 0$ so $f(\mathbf{x}^0 + \mathbf{v}) \to f(\mathbf{x}^0)$ as $\mathbf{v} \to \mathbf{0}$.

2. For all vectors $\mathbf{u}$ with length 1, the directional derivative in the direction $\mathbf{u}$ is $f_\mathbf{u}(\mathbf{x}^0) = \nabla f(\mathbf{x}^0) \cdot \mathbf{u}$.

Proof: Plugging $\mathbf{v} = h\mathbf{u}$ into Eq. (1) from the definition of differentiability and rearranging,

$$\frac{f(\mathbf{x}^0 + h\mathbf{u}) - f(\mathbf{x}^0)}{\|h\mathbf{u}\|} - \frac{\nabla f(\mathbf{x}^0) \cdot (h\mathbf{u})}{\|h\mathbf{u}\|} = E(h\mathbf{u}, \mathbf{x}^0).$$

But $\|h\mathbf{u}\| = h$ and $E(h\mathbf{u}, \mathbf{x}^0) \to 0$ as $h \to 0$, so

$$f_\mathbf{u}(\mathbf{x}^0) = \lim_{h \to 0} \frac{f(\mathbf{x}^0 + h\mathbf{u}) - f(\mathbf{x}^0)}{h} = \nabla f(\mathbf{x}^0) \cdot \mathbf{u}.$$

3. For all i, the ith component of $\nabla f(\mathbf{x}^0)$ is $\partial f(\mathbf{x}^0)/\partial x_i$.

Proof: Setting $\mathbf{u} = \mathbf{e}_i$ in result 2, where $\mathbf{e}_i$ is the vector with 1 in the ith component and zeros elsewhere, $\partial f(\mathbf{x}^0)/\partial x_i = \nabla f(\mathbf{x}^0) \cdot \mathbf{e}_i = i$th component of $\nabla f(\mathbf{x}^0)$.

Thus if $f: \mathbb{R}^n \to \mathbb{R}^1$ is differentiable at $\mathbf{x}^0$, then the gradient vector is the vector of partial derivatives. Combined with result 2, this means that the directional derivative in the direction $\mathbf{u}$ is given by

$$f_\mathbf{u}(\mathbf{x}^0) = \sum_{i=1}^{n} \frac{\partial f}{\partial x_i}(\mathbf{x}^0) u_i.$$

EXAMPLE: For $f(x, y) = x^2 y$, $f_u(x, y) = 2xyu_1 + x^2u_2$. The partial derivatives are $f_x(x, y) = 2xy$ and $f_y(x, y) = x^2$, so

$$f_u(x, y) = 2xyu_1 + x^2u_2 = f_x(x, y)u_1 + f_y(x, y)u_2.$$

For the next three properties, let $\mathbf{v}$ be the vector of changes in $\mathbf{x}$, i.e., $\Delta\mathbf{x} = (\mathbf{x}^0 + \mathbf{v}) - \mathbf{x}^0 = \mathbf{v}$. Rearranging Eq. (1) from the definition of differentiability, $f(\mathbf{x}^0 + \mathbf{v}) - f(\mathbf{x}^0) = \nabla f(\mathbf{x}^0) \cdot \mathbf{v} + \|\mathbf{v}\|E(\mathbf{v}, \mathbf{x}^0)$ or $\Delta f = \nabla f(\mathbf{x}^0) \cdot \Delta\mathbf{x} + \|\Delta\mathbf{x}\|E(\Delta\mathbf{x}, \mathbf{x}^0)$.

4. The equation of the *tangent plane to the graph* of f at $(\mathbf{x}^0, f(\mathbf{x}^0))$ is given by ignoring the error term in Eq. (1). That is, for any $\mathbf{v} \in \mathbb{R}^n$, $(\mathbf{x}^0 + \mathbf{v}, f^*(\mathbf{x}^0 + \mathbf{v}))$ lies on the tangent plane to the graph if and only if

$$f^*(\mathbf{x}^0 + \mathbf{v}) - f(\mathbf{x}^0) = \nabla f(\mathbf{x}^0) \cdot \mathbf{v}. \tag{2}$$

Note that for small $\mathbf{v}$, $f^*(\mathbf{x}^0 + \mathbf{v}) - f(\mathbf{x}^0) \approx f(\mathbf{x}^0 + \mathbf{v}) - f(\mathbf{x}^0) = \Delta f$.

To put Eq. (2) in the usual form for the equation of a hyperplane, note that it is a hyperplane in $\mathbb{R}^{n+1}$, while $\mathbf{v} = \Delta\mathbf{x} \in \mathbb{R}^n$. Creating vectors in $\mathbb{R}^{n+1}$ by adding new $(n + 1)$st component -1 to the gradient and $f^* - f(\mathbf{x}^0)$ to $\Delta\mathbf{x}$, Eq. (2) can be rewritten

$$0 = \nabla f(\mathbf{x}^0) \cdot \Delta\mathbf{x} - (f^*(\mathbf{x}^0 + \Delta\mathbf{x}) - f(\mathbf{x}^0)) \quad \text{or}$$

$$0 = (\nabla f(\mathbf{x}^0), -1) \cdot (\Delta\mathbf{x}, f^*(\mathbf{x}^0 + \Delta\mathbf{x}) - f(\mathbf{x}^0)).$$

5. The equation of the *tangent plane to the level curve* corresponding to $f(\mathbf{x}) \equiv f(\mathbf{x}^0)$ at the point $\mathbf{x}^0$ is given by ignoring the error term in Eq. (1) and recognizing that to stay on the level curve, we must maintain $f(\mathbf{x}^0 + \mathbf{v}) \equiv f(\mathbf{x}^0)$. For any $\mathbf{v} \in \mathbb{R}^n$, $(\mathbf{x}^0 + \mathbf{v})$ lies on the tangent plane to the level curve $f(\mathbf{x}) \equiv f(\mathbf{x}^0)$ if and only if $0 = \nabla f(\mathbf{x}^0) \cdot \mathbf{v}$. No rearrangement is needed here since $\mathbf{v} \in \mathbb{R}^n$, and the hyperplane and level curve are also in $\mathbb{R}^n$.

6. The marginal rate of substitution of x_i for x_j along the level curve corresponding to $f(\mathbf{x}) \equiv f(\mathbf{x}^0)$ at the point $\mathbf{x}^0$ is the number of units of x_j which must be removed in order to maintain a constant "output" f when a unit of x_i is added and all other "inputs" are unchanged. The change in input j (i) is v_j (v_i) and all other inputs are unchanged, so $v_k = 0$ for $k \neq i, j$. Substituting this $\mathbf{v}$ and the values of the components of $\nabla f(\mathbf{x}^0)$ into the equation in result 5,

$$0 = \frac{\partial f}{\partial x_i}(\mathbf{x}^0)v_i + \frac{\partial f}{\partial x_j}(\mathbf{x}^0)v_j \quad \text{or}$$

$$\left.\frac{\partial x_j}{\partial x_i}\right|_{\substack{\mathbf{x}=\mathbf{x}^0 \\ f^*(\mathbf{x})=f(\mathbf{x}^0)}} = \frac{\text{change in input } j}{\text{change in input } i} = \frac{v_j}{v_i} = -\frac{\partial f(\mathbf{x}^0)/\partial x_i}{\partial f(\mathbf{x}^0)/\partial x_j}$$

The notation for the first term on the left indicates that the partial derivative is to be evaluated at the point $\mathbf{x}^0$ and for changes that maintain f at the level $f(\mathbf{x}^0)$.

Note that in general x_j is not a function of x_i, but here it is, since we are discussing changes along a level curve and the compensating changes in x_i and x_j that will maintain the given output level.

7. The direction of change in inputs $\mathbf{x}$ which most increases output $f(\mathbf{x})$ starting at $\mathbf{x}^0$ is the direction $\nabla f(\mathbf{x}^0)$. This if of course for marginal changes only.

Proof: If it is possible to add any $\mathbf{v}$ with $\|\mathbf{v}\| = \varepsilon$, the increase in output is $f(\mathbf{x}^0 + \mathbf{v}) - f(\mathbf{x}^0) = \nabla f(\mathbf{x}^0) \cdot \mathbf{v} + \|\mathbf{v}\| E(\mathbf{v}, \mathbf{x}^0)$. As $\varepsilon \to 0$, we can ignore the error term and work with the tangent plane, $f^*(\mathbf{x}^0 + \mathbf{v}) - f(\mathbf{x}^0) = \nabla f(\mathbf{x}^0) \cdot \mathbf{v}$. Recall from Chapter 2 that for a fixed vector $\mathbf{a}$, the vector $\mathbf{b}$ of length c which maximizes $\mathbf{a} \cdot \mathbf{b}$ is $\mathbf{b} = (c/\|\mathbf{a}\|)\mathbf{a}$. Thus $f^*(\mathbf{x}^0 + \mathbf{v}) - f(\mathbf{x}^0)$ is maximized if $\mathbf{v} = (\varepsilon/\|\nabla f(\mathbf{x}^0)\|)\nabla f(\mathbf{x}^0)$. This tangent plane approximation "becomes correct" as $\varepsilon \to 0$.

EXAMPLE: $u(x, y, z) = x + y + z^2$ is differentiable at $(1, 1, 1)$.

1. To find $\nabla u(1, 1, 1)$, $\nabla u(x, y, z) = \begin{pmatrix} 1 \\ 1 \\ 2z \end{pmatrix}$, so $\nabla u(1, 1, 1) = \begin{pmatrix} 1 \\ 1 \\ 2 \end{pmatrix}$.

2. To find the equation of the tangent plane to the graph of u at $(1, 1, 1)$, $u(1, 1, 1) = 3$, so

$$(u^* - 3) = \nabla u(1, 1, 1) \cdot \begin{pmatrix} x - 1 \\ y - 1 \\ z - 1 \end{pmatrix} = (x - 1) + (y - 1) + 2(z - 1).$$

3. To find the equation of the tangent plane to the level curve corresponding to $u \equiv 3$ at $(1, 1, 1)$,

$$0 = \nabla u(1, 1, 1) \cdot \begin{pmatrix} x - 1 \\ y - 1 \\ z - 1 \end{pmatrix} = (x - 1) + (y - 1) + 2(z - 1).$$

4. To find the marginal rate of substitution of x for z along the level curve $u \equiv 3$ at the point $(1, 1, 1)$,

$$0 = \frac{\partial u}{\partial x}(1, 1, 1)\Delta x + \frac{\partial u}{\partial z}(1, 1, 1)\Delta z,$$

so

$$\frac{\partial z}{\partial x}\bigg|_{\substack{(x, y, z) = (1, 1, 1) \\ u = 3}} = -\frac{\partial u(1, 1, 1)/\partial x}{\partial u(1, 1, 1)/\partial z} = -1/2$$

5. To find the direction of change in inputs which yields the largest increase in output u (for marginal input changes) at $(1, 1, 1)$, the direction is

$$\frac{1}{\| \nabla u(1, 1, 1) \|} \nabla u(1, 1, 1) = \frac{1}{\sqrt{6}} \begin{pmatrix} 1 \\ 1 \\ 2 \end{pmatrix}.$$

EXAMPLE: For $a \in \mathbb{R}^1$ and $\mathbf{b} \in \mathbb{R}^n$, let $f: \mathbb{R}^n \to \mathbb{R}^1$ be defined by $f(\mathbf{x}) = a + \mathbf{b} \cdot \mathbf{x}$. Then $\nabla f(\mathbf{x}) = \mathbf{b}$ for all $\mathbf{x}$. The graph of f in $\mathbb{R}^{n+1}$ is the hyperplane $H_{(b, -1)}(-a)$. [To see this, rearrange the equation of f to get $-a = \mathbf{b} \cdot \mathbf{x} - f(\mathbf{x}) = (\mathbf{b}, -1) \cdot (\mathbf{x}, f(\mathbf{x}))$.] The level curve $f(\mathbf{x}) \equiv c$ in $\mathbb{R}^n$ is the hyperplane $H_b(c - a)$. [To see this, rearrange $f(\mathbf{x}) = a + \mathbf{b} \cdot \mathbf{x} \equiv c$ to get $c - a \equiv \mathbf{b} \cdot \mathbf{x}$.]

Given $\mathbf{x}^0$ and $\nabla f(\mathbf{x}^0)$, we can use the results of the example to find approximate level curves for f by picking a level (a y value) and solving the tangent plane equation. The approximate level curve for level $f(\mathbf{x}^0) + c$ is given by solving $f(\mathbf{x}^0) + c = f(\mathbf{x}^0) + \nabla f(\mathbf{x}^0) \cdot (\mathbf{x} - \mathbf{x}^0)$ or $c = \nabla f(\mathbf{x}^0) \cdot (\mathbf{x} - \mathbf{x}^0)$ for $\mathbf{x}$. This can be done for any c.

EXAMPLE: For $\mathbf{x}^0 = (1, 2)$ and $\nabla f(\mathbf{x}^0) = (1, 1)$ the approximate level curve for level $f(\mathbf{x}^0) + K$ is given implicitly by $K = (1, 1) \cdot (\mathbf{x} - (1, 2))$. See Figure 5.3.

The approximate level curves are parallel, equally spaced (for equal increments in K) hyperplanes with normal $\nabla f(\mathbf{x}^0)$. Higher levels of K correspond to movements in the direction $\nabla f(\mathbf{x}^0)$. Lower (more negative) levels of K correspond to movements in the direction $-\nabla f(\mathbf{x}^0)$. These are general results.

These approximations are based on the particular base point $\mathbf{x}^0$ and the gradient at the base point, $\nabla f(\mathbf{x}^0)$. For a different base point we would

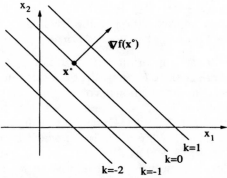

FIGURE 5.3 Approximate level curves for f.

likely get a very different set of approximations (just as for calculus of one variable, the tangent line approximation to the graph of a function depended on a base point).

EXAMPLE: For $f(x_1, x_2) = x_1^2 x_2$, $\nabla f(\mathbf{x}) = (2x_1 x_2, x_1^2)$. At base point $\mathbf{x}^0 = (1, 2)$, $f(\mathbf{x}^0) = 2$ and $\nabla f(\mathbf{x}^0) = (4, 1)$, so the approximate level curve for level $2 + K$ is $K = (4, 1) \cdot (\mathbf{x} - (1, 2))$, or $x_2 = -4x_1 + K + 6$. If we start from base point $\mathbf{x}^1 = (2, 1)$, $\nabla f(2, 1) = (4, 4)$ and the approximate level curve for level $f(\mathbf{x}^1) + K^1$ is given by $K^1 = (4, 4) \cdot (\mathbf{x} - (2, 1))$ or $x_2 = -x_1 + 3 + K^1/4$. Since $f(\mathbf{x}^1) = 4$, the level $K^1 = -2$ corresponds to the level $K = 0$ from the original base point. Note that the estimates based at $(2, 1)$ are very different from the estimates based at $(1, 2)$.

Each set of estimated level curves gives very good estimates near its base point. Since we are usually interested in tiny changes from the base point, good estimates locally are all that we need. The key point is that near the base point, the level curves of the function are essentially parallel, equally spaced (for equal increments in the function) hyperplanes with normal the gradient, $\nabla f(\mathbf{x}^0)$. Higher levels of the function correspond to movement in the direction of the gradient, lower levels to movements in the direction $-\nabla f(\mathbf{x}^0)$.

EXAMPLE: For $f(x, y) = y - x^2$, with $(1, 1)$ as a base point, let us compare the true level curves of f with their linear approximations.

1. True level curves: $f(1, 1) = 0$ so the level curve through $(1, 1)$ is given by $y - x^2 = 0$ or $y = x^2$. For any K, the level curve $f = K$ is given by $y = x^2 + K$.

2. Linear approximations to the level curves: For the linear approximation we need a base point to start from, $(1, 1)$, and the gradient evaluated at the base point, $\nabla f(1, 1) = (-2, 1)$. The linear approximations for level $f(1, 1) + K$ are given by $K = \nabla f(1, 1) \cdot (\mathbf{x} - (1, 1))$. The linear approximation to the level curve $f = 0$ based at $(1, 1)$ is thus given by the solution to $0 = -2(x - 1) + 1(y - 1)$ or $y = 2x - 1$. From the base point $(1, 1)$, the linear approximation to the level curve $f = K$ is given by the solution to $K = -2(x - 1) + 1(y - 1)$ or $y = 2x - 1 + K$.

Clearly these linear approximations are not good approximations when x is a very large positive (or negative) number. However, when x is near 1, they are good approximations. To see this, compare the true and approximate level curves for $f = 0$ when $x = 1 + \delta$. On the true level curve $y = (1 + \delta)^2 = 1 + 2\delta + \delta^2$. On the approximate level curve $y = 2(1 + \delta) - 1 = 1 + 2\delta$. The difference is δ^2, which is small relative to δ when δ is small (i.e., $\delta^2/\delta \to 0$ as $\delta \to 0$). Thus the error from using the linear approximation is arbitrarily small relative to dx when dx is small.

One final observation concerns the case $\nabla f(\mathbf{x}^0) = \mathbf{0}$ (the vector of zeros). The equation for the approximate level curve with level $f(\mathbf{x}^0) + K$ is $K = \mathbf{0} \cdot (\mathbf{x} - \mathbf{x}^0) = 0$. Thus every x is on the approximate level curve for $K = 0$ and no $\mathbf{x}$ is on the approximate level curve for any $K \neq 0$.

Finally, consider differentials. For functions of one variable, the differentials dx and dy are changes in x and y, starting from $(x, f(x))$, such that the new point remains on the tangent line approximation to the graph of f at x. Thus $dy = f'(x) dx$. For functions of several variables, the differentials $dx_1, dx_2, \ldots, dx_n$, dy are changes in the x_i and y, starting from $(\mathbf{x}, f(\mathbf{x}))$, such that the new point remains on the tangent plane approximation to the graph of f at $\mathbf{x}$. Thus

$$dy = \nabla f(\mathbf{x}) \cdot (dx_1, dx_2, \ldots, dx_n) = \nabla f(\mathbf{x}) \cdot d\mathbf{x}.$$

This is called the *total differential* because we keep track of all the changes in y caused by changes in $x_1, x_2, \ldots, x_n$. From Eq. (1), $f(\mathbf{x}^0 + \mathbf{v}) - f(\mathbf{x}^0) = \nabla f(\mathbf{x}^0) \cdot \mathbf{v} + \|\mathbf{v}\| E(\mathbf{v}, \mathbf{x}^0)$ where $E(\mathbf{v}, \mathbf{x}^0) \to 0$ as $\mathbf{v} \to \mathbf{0}$. Ignoring the error term (i.e., looking at the tangent plane) $\Delta y = \nabla f(\mathbf{x}^0) \cdot \Delta \mathbf{x}$ or $dy = \nabla f(\mathbf{x}^0) \cdot d\mathbf{x}$.

5.4 CHAIN RULE

The *chain rule* has many applications in economics. It is a necessary tool for comparative statics. For $f: \mathbb{R}^1 \to \mathbb{R}^1$ and $g: \mathbb{R}^1 \to \mathbb{R}^1$ both differentiable, with $y = f(x)$ and $x = g(t)$, by the chain rule for one variable,

$$\frac{dy}{dt} = \frac{df}{dx}(g(t)) \frac{dg}{dt}(t).$$

For $f: \mathbb{R}^n \to \mathbb{R}^1$, differentiable with $y = f(\mathbf{x})$ and, for $i = 1, 2, \ldots, n$, $g^i: \mathbb{R}^m \to \mathbb{R}^1$ differentiable with $x_i = g^i(\mathbf{t})$, how does y change as t_k changes? As t_k changes, each x_i changes according to

$$\frac{\partial x_i}{\partial t_k}(\mathbf{t}) = \frac{\partial g^i}{\partial t_k}(\mathbf{t}).$$

When any x_i changes, y changes according to

$$\frac{\partial y}{\partial x_i}(\mathbf{x}) = \frac{\partial f}{\partial x_i}(\mathbf{x}).$$

The total change accumulates in the same manner as the total differential:

$$\frac{\partial y}{\partial t_k}(\mathbf{g}(t)) = \sum_{i=1}^{n} \frac{\partial f}{\partial x_i}(\mathbf{g}(t)) \frac{\partial g^i}{\partial t_k}(t) = \nabla f(\mathbf{g}(t)) \cdot \begin{pmatrix} \dfrac{\partial g^1(t)}{\partial t_k} \\ \vdots \\ \dfrac{\partial g^n(t)}{\partial t_k} \end{pmatrix}$$

$$= \nabla f(\mathbf{g}(t)) \cdot \left(\frac{\partial \mathbf{g}(t)}{\partial t_k} \right).$$

EXAMPLE:

$$x_1 = t_1 + t_2,$$

$$x_2 = t_1 t_2,$$

$$y = x_1 + x_1 x_2.$$

Then

$$\frac{\partial y}{\partial t_1} = \frac{\partial y_1}{\partial x_1} \frac{\partial x_1}{\partial t_1} + \frac{\partial y}{\partial x_2} \frac{\partial x_2}{\partial t_1} = (1 + x_2)(1) + (x_1)(t_2).$$

At $(t_1, t_2) = (1, 1)$, $x_1 = 2$, $x_2 = 1$, and $\partial y / \partial t_1 = 4$.

EXAMPLE:

$$g(x, y, z) = x + y + z,$$

$$x = h(t, q) = t^2 + q,$$

$$y = f(t, q) = t + 2 - q^2,$$

$$z = e(s) = s^2,$$

$$q = v(s) = 2s,$$

$$t = r(s, a) = 3s^2 + a - 1.$$

What is $\partial g/\partial s$? This example requires repeated application of the chain rule. No matter how complicated the problem, a step-by-step approach will obtain the proper decomposition. The decomposition below is explained in the following three steps.

$$\underset{(1)\ (2)\ (3)}{\frac{\partial g}{\partial s}} = \underset{(1)}{\frac{\partial g}{\partial x}}\left[\underset{(2)\ (3)}{\frac{\partial x}{\partial t}\frac{\partial t}{\partial s}} + \underset{(2)\ (3)}{\frac{\partial x}{\partial q}\frac{dq}{ds}}\right] + \underset{(1)}{\frac{\partial g}{\partial y}}\left[\underset{(2)\ (3)}{\frac{\partial y}{\partial t}\frac{\partial t}{\partial s}} + \underset{(2)\ (3)}{\frac{\partial y}{\partial q}\frac{dq}{ds}}\right] + \underset{(1)}{\frac{\partial g}{\partial z}}\left[\underset{(2)}{\frac{dz}{ds}}\right]$$

1. g is a function of x, y, and z, so take all partials. The complete solution will be a sum of these partials, each multiplied by the appropriate coefficient to be determined in subsequent steps.

2. x is a function of t and q, so take both partials. Again, there will be appropriate coefficients to be determined later. y is a function of t and q, so take both partials. z is a function of s alone, so we take the regular derivative for a function of one variable, and there will be no further terms since we have reached the final s term.

3. t is a function of s and a, but a is not a function of s, so the only term is $\partial t/\partial s$. [If we had $a = c(s)$ we would have an additional term da/ds. Here one may think of putting in the term $da/ds = 0$.] q is a function of s alone so the appropriate term is dq/ds. Note that every string of derivatives ends in a $\partial/\partial s$ or d/ds term.

Thus

$$\frac{\partial g}{\partial s} = 1[(2t)(6s) + (1)(2)] + 1[(1)(6s) + (-2q)(2)] + 1[(2s)]$$

$$= 12ts + 2 + 8s - 4q.$$

At $a = 1$ and $s = 0$, $t = q = 0$, so $\partial g/\partial s = 2 - 4q = 2$.

Each example had several stages in its solution. The first stage is abstract, with an equation in terms of $\partial g/\partial x$, $\partial x/\partial t$, etc. In the second stage we substitute in the actual derivative function (e.g., $\partial x/\partial t = 2t$). In the final stage these derivative functions are evaluated at a particular point. In some problems, we will need to complete only one or two stages.

EXAMPLE: $z = 6x^2 - 3xy + 2y^2$ and $x = 1/y$. How does z change when y changes? In this type of problem we must be careful to determine whether the appropriate concept to use is the partial derivative, $\partial z/\partial y$, or the *total derivative*, sometimes written dz/dy. The partial derivative looks only at $z = 6x^2 - 3xy + 2y^2$ to get $\partial z/\partial y = -3x + 4y$. The total derivative takes account of the effect of y on x, $dx/dy = -1/y^2$, to get

$$\frac{dz}{dy} = 12x\frac{dx}{dy} - 3y\frac{dx}{dy} - 3x + 4y$$

$$= 12x(-1/y^2) - 3y(-1/y^2) - 3x + 4y$$

$$= -12x/y^2 + 3/y - 3x + 4y.$$

This could be further simplified by substituting $x = 1/y$ to get $dz/dy = -12y^3 + 3/y - 3/y + 4y = -12/y^3 + 4y$. If we had substituted $x = 1/y$ into the original equation for z to get $z = 6/y^2 - 3 + 2y^2$, the regular derivative for a function of one variable would yield $dz/dy = -12/y^3 + 4y$.

This type of problem, where a variable (y) enters both directly and indirectly (through $x = 1/y$), can create confusion. One kind of confusion is notational. There is no standard notation for such total derivatives. (This notational problem is more severe for an example such as $w = x + y + z$, where $x = 1/y$ but z is independent of y. Then $w = 1/y + y + z$ so we should not use the notation dw/dy for the total derivative because w also depends on z. On the other hand, we cannot use $\partial w/\partial y$ to represent the total derivative because it is likely to be confused with the regular partial derivative of the original function.) Another type of confusion is caused by inexperience. It often takes a significant amount of practice before one can confidently determine whether to use the partial derivative or the total derivative. This problem is particularly acute in many economics applications. One should always be aware of this decision problem.

5.5 TAYLOR'S THEOREM

Taylor's theorem will play an important role in some of our discussion about optimization. In particular, for optimization without constraints, the first- and second-order conditions for optimization will be derived directly from two Taylor expansions at the end of this section. We start by introducing higher-order derivatives.

Higher-order derivatives are derivatives of derivatives. They are obtained by treating other variables as constants and following the usual rules for differentiating functions of several variables:

$$\frac{\partial(\partial f/\partial x_i)}{\partial x_i} = \frac{\partial^2 f}{\partial x_i^2} = f_{ii}; \qquad \frac{\partial(\partial f/\partial x_j)}{\partial x_i} = \frac{\partial^2 f}{\partial x_i \partial x_j} = f_{ji} \quad \text{etc.}$$

Note the order of i and j in each expression.

As was the case with the first partial derivatives, existence of these higher-order partials does not imply the lower-order partials are well behaved; i.e., existence of second partials is not the same as f being twice differentiable. However, most functions used in economics are well behaved.

EXAMPLE:

$$f(x_1, x_2) = x_1^3 + x_1^2 x_2 + x_2^2,$$

$$f_1 = 3x_1^2 + 2x_1 x_2, \qquad f_2 = x_1^2 + 2x_2,$$

$$f_{11} = 6x_1 + 2x_2, \qquad f_{21} = 2x_1,$$

$$f_{12} = 2x_1, \qquad f_{22} = 2.$$

Note that $f_{12} = f_{21}$. This is a useful property:

YOUNG'S THEOREM: *If for $f: \mathbb{R}^n \to \mathbb{R}^1$, f_i and f_j exist everywhere and f_{ij} and f_{ji} are continuous at $\mathbf{x}^0$, then $f_{ij}(\mathbf{x}^0) = f_{ji}(\mathbf{x}^0)$.*

We now turn to Taylor's theorem. Recall Taylor's theorem for functions of one variable: If $f: \mathbb{R}^1 \to \mathbb{R}^1$ is $m + 1$ times differentiable, then

$$f(x) = f(a) + \frac{D^1 f(a)(x-a)^1}{1!} + \frac{D^2 f(a)(x-a)^2}{2!}$$

$$+ \cdots + \frac{D^m f(a)(x-a)^m}{m!} + \frac{D^{m+1} f(b)(x-a)^{m+1}}{(m+1)!}$$

for some b between x and a.

We will use a similar result for functions of several variables to derive necessary conditions and sufficient conditions for an optimum using the first and second derivatives. A formal statement of Taylor's theorem is provided for reference, but the important results of this section are the expansions we will derive using the theorem.

TAYLOR'S THEOREM: *Assume that $f: \mathbb{R}^n \to \mathbb{R}^1$ and all its partial derivatives of order less than or equal to m are differentiable. Then there is a* *point* **b** *on the line segment between* **a** *and* **x** *such that*

$$f(\mathbf{x}) = f(\mathbf{a}) + \sum_{i=1}^{n} \frac{\partial f(\mathbf{a})}{\partial x_i}(x_i - a_i)$$

$$+ \frac{1}{2!} \sum_{i_1=1}^{n} \sum_{i_2=1}^{n} \frac{\partial^2 f(\mathbf{a})}{\partial x_{i_1} \partial x_{i_2}}(x_{i_1} - a_{i_1})(x_{i_2} - a_{i_2})$$

$$+ \cdots + \frac{1}{m!} \sum_{i_1=1}^{n} \sum_{i_2=1}^{n} \cdots \sum_{i_m=1}^{n} \frac{\partial^m f(\mathbf{a})}{\partial x_{i_1} \partial x_{i_2} \cdots \partial x_{i_m}}$$

$$\times (x_{i_1} - a_{i_1})(x_{i_2} - a_{i_2}) \cdots (x_{i_m} - a_{i_m})$$

$$+ \frac{1}{(m+1)!} \sum_{i_1=1}^{n} \sum_{i_2=1}^{n} \cdots \sum_{i_{m+1}=1}^{n} \frac{\partial^{m+1} f(\mathbf{b})}{\partial x_{i_1} \partial x_{i_2} \cdots \partial x_{i_{m+1}}}$$

$$\times (x_{i_1} - a_{i_1})(x_{i_2} - a_{i_2}) \cdots (x_{i_{m+1}} - a_{i_{m+1}}).$$

Note the similarity to Taylor's theorem for one variable (which is just a special case of this version.) For our optimization results, we are interested in the first three terms of the Taylor expansion. Note that

1. $\displaystyle\sum_{i=1}^{n} \frac{\partial f(\mathbf{a})}{\partial x_i}(x_i - a_i) = \nabla f(\mathbf{a}) \cdot (\mathbf{x} - \mathbf{a})$ and

2. $\displaystyle\sum_{i_1=1}^{n} \sum_{i_2=1}^{n} \frac{\partial^2 f(\mathbf{a})}{\partial x_{i_1} \partial x_{i_2}}(x_{i_1} - a_{i_1})(x_{i_2} - a_{i_2}) = (\mathbf{x} - \mathbf{a})' \left[\frac{\partial^2 f(\mathbf{a})}{\partial x_i \partial x_j} \right] (\mathbf{x} - \mathbf{a});$

i.e., the second term is the scalar product of the gradient of f at **a** and the vector of deviations from **a**, $(\mathbf{x} - \mathbf{a})$, and the third term is a quadratic form in the deviations from **a**, with matrix $[f_{ij}(\mathbf{a})]$. Under appropriate conditions this matrix is symmetric by Young's theorem.

Thus if $f: \mathbb{R}^n \to \mathbb{R}^1$ and all its (first) partial derivatives are continuously differentiable, by Taylor's theorem, given $\mathbf{a} \in \mathbb{R}^n$, for any $\mathbf{x} \in \mathbb{R}^n$ there are points $\mathbf{b}(\mathbf{x})$ and $\overline{\mathbf{b}}(\mathbf{x})$ on the line segment between **a** and **x** such that

1. $f(\mathbf{x}) = f(\mathbf{a}) + \nabla f(\mathbf{b}(\mathbf{x})) \cdot (\mathbf{x} - \mathbf{a})$ and
2. $f(\mathbf{x}) = f(\mathbf{a}) + \nabla f(\mathbf{a}) \cdot (\mathbf{x} - \mathbf{a}) + \frac{1}{2}(\mathbf{x} - \mathbf{a})'[f_{ij}(\overline{\mathbf{b}}(\mathbf{x}))](\mathbf{x} - \mathbf{a}).$

We will use these two expressions to find necessary conditions for optima and sufficient conditions for optima of functions which are twice continuously differentiable.

5.6 OPTIMIZATION WITHOUT CONSTRAINTS

This section and the three following sections examine the properties of local optimizers. They develop necessary conditions for optimization, which every local optimizer must satisfy, and sufficient conditions for optimization, which, if satisfied at a point, guarantee the point is a local optimizer. This section examines the simplest case, optimization with no constraints. The results follow directly from the two expansions generated at the end of the previous section. Section 5.7 examines optimization subject to equality constraints. Sections 5.8 and 5.9 consider general optimization problems, which include unconstrained and equality-constrained optimization as special cases. Section 5.8 provides the most important analysis of first-order conditions. In many ways it is the easiest to understand, since it presents all the cases in a simple unified framework. It should be the center of the reader's attention, with Sections 5.6 and 5.7 viewed as the special cases which they are. Section 5.9 considers the second-order conditions for the general case.

DEFINITION: f attains a *local maximum* (*local minimum*) at $\mathbf{a}$ if there exists an $\varepsilon > 0$ such that $f(\mathbf{x}) \leq f(\mathbf{a})(f(\mathbf{x}) \geq f(\mathbf{a}))$ for all $\mathbf{x}$ with $\|\mathbf{x} - \mathbf{a}\| < \varepsilon$. The maximum (minimum) is *strict* if $f(\mathbf{x}) < f(\mathbf{a})$ ($f(\mathbf{x}) > f(\mathbf{a})$) for all $\mathbf{x}$ with $0 < \|\mathbf{x} - \mathbf{a}\| < \varepsilon$.

We will derive necessary conditions and sufficient conditions for optima using the (vector of) first and (matrix of) second derivatives of f at a point $\mathbf{a}$, $\nabla f(\mathbf{a})$ and $[f_{ij}(\mathbf{a})]$, respectively. The results are similar to those for a single variable and are summarized in:

THEOREM: *If f: $\mathbb{R}^n \to \mathbb{R}$ and all its first partial derivatives are continuously differentiable on a set which contains $\mathbf{a}$ in its interior, then*

1. (*Necessary conditions*) *f has a local maximum (minimum) at $\mathbf{a}$ only if $\nabla f(\mathbf{a}) = \mathbf{0}$ and $[f_{ij}(\mathbf{a})]_{n \times n}$ is negative (positive) semidefinite.*

2. (*Sufficient conditions*) *f has a strict local maximum (minimum) at $\mathbf{a}$ if $\nabla f(\mathbf{a}) = \mathbf{0}$ and $[f_{ij}(\mathbf{a})]_{n \times n}$ is negative (positive) definite.*

Note the similarity to the theorem for one variable. $f' = 0$ is replaced by $\nabla f = \mathbf{0}$, and $f'' \leq (\geq, <, >) 0$ is replaced by $[f_{ij}(\mathbf{a})]_{n \times n}$ NSD (PSD, ND, and PD, respectively) where $[f_{ij}(\mathbf{a})]_{n \times n}$ is the $n \times n$ matrix of second partial derivatives of f evaluated at $\mathbf{a}$. As with the theorem for one variable, the necessary conditions are not sufficient and the sufficient conditions are not necessary. Before sketching the proof of the theorem we consider some examples.

EXAMPLE: $f(x, y) = -3x^2 + xy - 2x + y - y^2 + 1$,

$$\nabla f = \begin{pmatrix} -6x + y - 2 \\ x + 1 - 2y \end{pmatrix}; \quad [f_{ij}] = \begin{bmatrix} -6 & 1 \\ 1 & -2 \end{bmatrix}.$$

$$f_{11} = -6 < 0 \quad \text{and} \quad \begin{vmatrix} -6 & 1 \\ 1 & -2 \end{vmatrix} = 11 > 0,$$

so $[f_{ij}]$ is negative definite.

$$\nabla f = \begin{bmatrix} -6 & 1 \\ 1 & -2 \end{bmatrix} \begin{pmatrix} x \\ y \end{pmatrix} + \begin{pmatrix} -2 \\ 1 \end{pmatrix},$$

so $\nabla f(x, y) = \mathbf{0}$ if

$$\begin{bmatrix} -6 & 1 \\ 1 & -2 \end{bmatrix} \begin{pmatrix} x \\ y \end{pmatrix} + \begin{pmatrix} -2 \\ 1 \end{pmatrix} = \mathbf{0}$$

or

$$\begin{pmatrix} x \\ y \end{pmatrix} = \begin{bmatrix} -6 & 1 \\ 1 & -2 \end{bmatrix}^{-1} \begin{pmatrix} 2 \\ -1 \end{pmatrix} = \frac{1}{11} \begin{bmatrix} -2 & -1 \\ -1 & -6 \end{bmatrix} \begin{pmatrix} 2 \\ -1 \end{pmatrix} = \begin{pmatrix} -3/11 \\ 4/11 \end{pmatrix}.$$

Thus f has a strict local maximum at

$$\begin{pmatrix} -3/11 \\ 4/11 \end{pmatrix}.$$

EXAMPLE: For $\mathbf{a} \in \mathbb{R}^1$, $\mathbf{b} \in \mathbb{R}^n$, and D an $n \times n$ symmetric matrix, let $f: \mathbb{R}^n \to \mathbb{R}^1$ be defined by $f(\mathbf{x}) = a + \mathbf{b} \cdot \mathbf{x} + \mathbf{x}'D\mathbf{x}$. Then $\nabla f(\mathbf{x}) = \mathbf{b} + 2D\mathbf{x}$ and $[f_{ij}] = 2D$ (note the similarity to $f: \mathbb{R}^1 \to \mathbb{R}^1$ defined by $f(x) = a + bx + dx^2$). If $f(\mathbf{x}) \le f(0)$ for all $\mathbf{x}$, then $\mathbf{b}$ must be the zero vector and D must be NSD. If $\mathbf{b} = \mathbf{0}$ and D is ND, then for all $\mathbf{x} \ne 0$, $f(\mathbf{x}) = a + \mathbf{0} \cdot \mathbf{x} + \mathbf{x}'D\mathbf{x} = a + \mathbf{x}'D\mathbf{x} < a = f(0)$, so f has a strict local maximum at $\mathbf{0}$.

EXAMPLE: There are more possible cases for the matrix of second partials than NSD, PSD, ND, and PD. Let $f(x, y) = x^2 - y^2$. Then

$$\nabla f = \begin{pmatrix} 2x \\ -2y \end{pmatrix} \quad \text{and} \quad [f_{ij}] = \begin{bmatrix} 2 & 0 \\ 0 & -2 \end{bmatrix}.$$

$$(1, 0)[f_{ij}] \begin{pmatrix} 1 \\ 0 \end{pmatrix} = 2 \quad \text{and} \quad (0, 1)[f_{ij}] \begin{pmatrix} 0 \\ 1 \end{pmatrix} = -2,$$

so $(0, 0)$ (where $\nabla f = 0$) is a *saddle point* of the function, and it is neither a local maximizer nor a local minimizer. In some directions (x changing and y fixed) f seems to be minimized at $(0,0)$, whereas in other directions (y changing and x fixed) f seems to be maximized at $(0,0)$.

EXAMPLE: Let $f(x, y) = x^3 + x^2 y + 2y^2$. Then

$$\nabla f = \begin{pmatrix} 3x^2 + 2xy \\ x^2 + 4y \end{pmatrix} \quad \text{and} \quad [f_{ij}] = \begin{bmatrix} 6x + 2y & 2x \\ 2x & 4 \end{bmatrix}.$$

Here $[f_{ij}]$ depends on the (x, y) at which it is evaluated. $\nabla f(x, y) = \mathbf{0}$ if $3x^2 + 2xy = 0$ and $x^2 + 4y = 0$. From the last equation $y = -x^2/4$. Substituting this value into the previous equation, $0 = 3x^2 + 2x(-x^2/4) = 3x^2 - x^3/2 = (x^2/2)(6 - x)$. Thus $x = 0$ (and $y = -0/4 = 0$) or $x = 6$ (and $y = -36/4 = -9$).

$$[f_{ij}(0,0)] = \begin{bmatrix} 0 & 0 \\ 0 & 4 \end{bmatrix},$$

which is PSD.

$$[f_{ij}(6, -9)] = \begin{bmatrix} 18 & 12 \\ 12 & 4 \end{bmatrix},$$

and its determinants are

$$18 > 0 \quad \text{and} \quad \begin{vmatrix} 18 & 12 \\ 12 & 4 \end{vmatrix} = -72 < 0.$$

Thus $(6, -9)$ is a saddle point for the function. $(0, 0)$ satisfies the necessary conditions for a local minimum, but not the sufficient conditions. In fact, $f(x, 0) = x^3$, so f cannot attain either a local maximum or a local minimum at $(0,0)$. This function has no local maxima or local minima.

We now turn to a sketch of the proof of the theorem. The proof follows exactly the same outline as for one variable, with generalization to $\mathbb{R}^n$.

If $f : \mathbb{R}^n \to \mathbb{R}^1$ and all its (first) partial derivatives are continuously differentiable, then given $\mathbf{a} \in \mathbb{R}^n$, for any $\mathbf{x} \in \mathbb{R}^n$ there are points $\mathbf{b(x)}$ and $\overline{\mathbf{b}}(\mathbf{x})$ on the line segment between $\mathbf{a}$ and $\mathbf{x}$ such that

1. $f(\mathbf{x}) = f(\mathbf{a}) + \nabla f(\mathbf{b(x)}) \cdot (\mathbf{x} - \mathbf{a})$.
2. $f(\mathbf{x}) = f(\mathbf{a}) + \nabla f(\mathbf{a}) \cdot (\mathbf{x} - \mathbf{a}) + \frac{1}{2}(\mathbf{x} - \mathbf{a})'[f_{ij}(\overline{\mathbf{b}}(\mathbf{x}))](\mathbf{x} - \mathbf{a})$.

We will use these two expansions to find necessary conditions for optima and sufficient conditions for optima of functions which are twice continuously differentiable.

Using the first expansion, let $\mathbf{x}(\lambda) = \mathbf{a} + \lambda \nabla f(\mathbf{a})$ for $\lambda \in R^1$, $\lambda \neq 0$. Then $f(\mathbf{x}(\lambda)) - f(\mathbf{a}) = \nabla f(\mathbf{b}(\lambda)) \cdot (\lambda \nabla f(\mathbf{a}))$ for some $\mathbf{b}(\lambda)$ on the line segment between $\mathbf{a}$ and $\mathbf{a} + \lambda \nabla f(\mathbf{a})$. Thus

$$\frac{f(\mathbf{a} + \lambda \nabla f(\mathbf{a})) - f(\mathbf{a})}{\lambda} = \nabla f(\mathbf{b}(\lambda)) \cdot \nabla f(\mathbf{a}).$$

As $\lambda \to 0$, $\mathbf{b}(\lambda) \to \mathbf{a}$ (the line segment shrinks to the point $\mathbf{a}$), and ∇f is continuous so $\nabla f(\mathbf{b}(\lambda)) \to \nabla f(\mathbf{a})$. If $\nabla f(\mathbf{a}) \neq \mathbf{0}$, then for λ sufficiently close to 0 and positive (negative), $\nabla f(\mathbf{b}(\lambda)) \cdot \nabla f(\mathbf{a}) > 0$ and $f(\mathbf{a} + \lambda \nabla f(\mathbf{a})) > f(\mathbf{a})$ ($f(\mathbf{a} + \lambda \nabla f(\mathbf{a})) < f(\mathbf{a})$). Thus a necessary condition for a local maximum (minimum) is $\nabla f(\mathbf{a}) = \mathbf{0}$.

We now use the necessary condition just derived in the second expansion. If f attains a local maximum (minimum) at $\mathbf{a}$, then $\nabla f(\mathbf{a}) = \mathbf{0}$, so for $\mathbf{x} \in \mathbb{R}^n$,

$$f(\mathbf{x}) - f(\mathbf{a}) = \mathbf{0} \cdot (\mathbf{x} - \mathbf{a}) + (1/2)(\mathbf{x} - \mathbf{a})' \big[f_{ij}(\overline{\mathbf{b}}(\mathbf{x})) \big] (\mathbf{x} - \mathbf{a})$$

for some $\overline{\mathbf{b}}(\mathbf{x})$ on the line segment between $\mathbf{x}$ and $\mathbf{a}$. If $[f_{ij}(\mathbf{a})]$ is not negative semidefinite (positive semidefinite), then there exists a vector $\mathbf{v}$ such that $\mathbf{v}'[f_{ij}(\mathbf{a})]\mathbf{v} > 0$ ($\mathbf{v}'[f_{ij}(\mathbf{a})]\mathbf{v} < 0$). Let $\mathbf{x}(\lambda) = \mathbf{a} + \lambda \mathbf{v}$ for $\lambda \neq 0$. Then

$$f(\mathbf{a} + \lambda \mathbf{v}) - f(\mathbf{a}) = (1/2)\lambda \mathbf{v}' \big[f_{ij}(\overline{\mathbf{b}}(\mathbf{x}(\lambda))) \big] \lambda \mathbf{v}$$

$$= (\lambda^2/2)\mathbf{v}' \big[f_{ij}(\overline{\mathbf{b}}(\mathbf{x}(\lambda))) \big] \mathbf{v}.$$

As $\lambda \to 0$, $\overline{\mathbf{b}}(\mathbf{x}(\lambda)) \to \mathbf{a}$ and each entry in the matrix $[f_{ij}(\overline{\mathbf{b}}(\mathbf{x}(\lambda)))]$ converges to the corresponding entry in $[f_{ij}(\mathbf{a})]$, so $\mathbf{v}'[f_{ij}(\overline{\mathbf{b}}(\mathbf{x}(\lambda)))]\mathbf{v} \to \mathbf{v}'[f_{ij}(\mathbf{a})]\mathbf{v} > 0$ $[\mathbf{v}'[f_{ij}(\overline{\mathbf{b}}(\mathbf{x}(\lambda)))]\mathbf{v} \to \mathbf{v}'[f_{ij}(\mathbf{a})]\mathbf{v} < 0]$. But then for sufficiently small λ, $f(\mathbf{a} + \lambda \mathbf{v}) - f(\mathbf{a}) > 0$ ($f(\mathbf{a} + \lambda \mathbf{v}) - f(\mathbf{a}) < 0$). Thus a necessary condition for attaining a local maximum (minimum) at $\mathbf{a}$ is $\nabla f(\mathbf{a}) = \mathbf{0}$ and $[f_{ij}(\mathbf{a})]$ is negative semidefinite (positive semidefinite). This completes the proof of the necessary conditions.

For the sufficient conditions, if $\nabla f(\mathbf{a}) = \mathbf{0}$ and $[f_{ij}(\mathbf{a})]$ is negative definite, then for $\mathbf{x} \in \mathbb{R}^n$, $f(\mathbf{x}) - f(\mathbf{a}) = \mathbf{0} \cdot (\mathbf{x} - \mathbf{a}) + \frac{1}{2}(\mathbf{x} - \mathbf{a})'[f_{ij}(\overline{\mathbf{b}}(\mathbf{x}))](\mathbf{x} - \mathbf{a})$ where $\overline{\mathbf{b}}(\mathbf{x})$ is some point on the line segment between $\mathbf{a}$ and $\mathbf{x}$. As $\mathbf{x} \to \mathbf{a}$, $\overline{\mathbf{b}}(\mathbf{x}) \to \mathbf{a}$, and each entry in the matrix $[f_{ij}(\overline{\mathbf{b}}(\mathbf{x}))]$ converges to the corresponding entry in $[f_{ij}(\mathbf{a})]$, so for $\mathbf{x}$ sufficiently close to $\mathbf{a}$, $[f_{ij}(\overline{\mathbf{b}}(\mathbf{x}))]$ is negative definite. [The conditions for ND are strict inequalities. Since $[f_{ij}(\overline{\mathbf{b}}(\mathbf{x}))] \to [f_{ij}(\mathbf{a})]$, eventually $[f_{ij}(\overline{\mathbf{b}}(\mathbf{x}))]$ will also satisfy the strict inequalities.] Thus there exists an $\varepsilon > 0$ such that for all $\mathbf{x}$ with $0 < \|\mathbf{x} - \mathbf{a}\| < \varepsilon$, $f(\mathbf{x}) - f(\mathbf{a}) = \frac{1}{2}(\mathbf{x} - \mathbf{a})'[f_{ij}(\overline{\mathbf{b}}(\mathbf{x}))](\mathbf{x} - \mathbf{a}) < 0$, and f attains a strict local maximum at $\mathbf{a}$.

Similarly, $\nabla f(\mathbf{a}) = \mathbf{0}$ and $[f_{ij}(\mathbf{a})]$ positive definite implies f attains a strict local minimum at $\mathbf{a}$. This completes the proof of the sufficient conditions.

5.7 OPTIMIZATION SUBJECT TO EQUALITY CONSTRAINTS

This section considers the special case of optimization subject to equality constraints. Many optimization problems in economics involve constraints, e.g., maximization of utility subject to a budget constraint or minimization of cost subject to attaining a certain level of output. One method for solving optimization problems subject to a single equality constraint is the method of substitution. When the equality constraint is sufficiently simple, we can solve for one choice variable, say x_n, as a function f, of the other choice variables $(x_1, x_2, \ldots, x_{n-1})$ by use of the equality constraint. Then we can optimize a function of $n - 1$ variables (the original function with x_n replaced by $f(x_1, x_2, \ldots, x_{n-1})$) without any constraint on the $(x_1, x_2, \ldots, x_{n-1})$, to find optimal values $x_1^*, x_2^*, \ldots, x_{n-1}^*$. Finally $x_n^* = f(x_1^*, x_2^*, \ldots, x_{n-1}^*)$. An alternative is the method of Lagrange multipliers, which is often simpler to use and provides additional economic insight.

Given the problem maximize $f(\mathbf{x})$ subject to $g(\mathbf{x}) = 0$, where f: $\mathbb{R}^n \to \mathbb{R}^1$ and $g: \mathbb{R}^n \to \mathbb{R}^1$ are differentiable, we can apply our knowledge of gradients to determine a necessary condition for $\mathbf{x}^0$ to be a maximizer of f subject to the equality constraint. The set $\{\mathbf{x} \in \mathbb{R}^n | g(\mathbf{x}) = 0\}$ is just a level surface for the function g. Suppose we seek to maximize f over those points (x_1, x_2) which lie on the level curve $g(x_1, x_2) \equiv 0$. If $\overline{\mathbf{x}}$ satisfies the constraint, the tangent line approximation to $g(\mathbf{x}) = 0$ at $\overline{\mathbf{x}}$ is $0 = \nabla g(\overline{\mathbf{x}}) \cdot (\mathbf{x} - \overline{\mathbf{x}})$. Suppose $\nabla g(\overline{\mathbf{x}}) \neq \mathbf{0}$. If $\nabla f(\overline{\mathbf{x}})$ is not a multiple of $\nabla g(\overline{\mathbf{x}})$, then the level curve of f, $\{\mathbf{x} \in \mathbb{R}^n | f(\mathbf{x}) = f(\overline{\mathbf{x}})\}$, intersects the level curve of g at $\overline{\mathbf{x}}$ in such a manner that an obvious direction of movement along the constraint (in Figure 5.4, down and to the left) will increase f.

Whenever $\nabla f(\mathbf{x})$ is not a multiple of $\nabla g(\mathbf{x})$ (and $\nabla g(\mathbf{x}) \neq 0$), there will be some direction to move along the constraint so that f will increase (also, there will be a direction to move along the constraint so that f will decrease). f is maximized subject to $g(\mathbf{x}) \equiv 0$ at $\mathbf{x}^0$ only if the level curve of f, $\{\mathbf{x} | f(\mathbf{x}) \equiv f(\mathbf{x}^0)\}$, is tangent to the feasible set $\{\mathbf{x} | g(\mathbf{x}) \equiv 0\}$ at $\mathbf{x}^0$, in which case $\nabla f(\mathbf{x}^0)$ is a multiple of $\nabla g(\mathbf{x}^0)$. This can be generalized to more than one constraint. The number of independent constraints should be less than the number of variables or there will be "no" choice to be made.

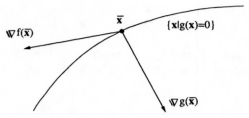

FIGURE 5.4   Gradients of the objective and constraint functions at $\bar{x}$.

(If $g^2(\mathbf{x}) \equiv 2g^1(\mathbf{x})$, then $g^1(\mathbf{x}) \equiv 0$ and $g^2(\mathbf{x}) \equiv 0$ are not independent constraints.)

A key to understanding the ideas for optimization subject to constraint is to recall our previous work in linear algebra concerning hyperplanes. If $h(\mathbf{x}) = a + \mathbf{b} \cdot \mathbf{x}$ where a is a fixed scalar and $\mathbf{b}$ is a fixed vector in $\mathbb{R}^n$, then $\nabla h(\mathbf{x}) \equiv \mathbf{b}$ and the level curves of h, $\{\mathbf{x} \mid h(\mathbf{x}) = c\}$, are just hyperplanes $H_{\mathbf{b}}(c - a) = \{\mathbf{x} \mid c - a = \mathbf{b} \cdot \mathbf{x}\}$ with normal $\mathbf{b}$. Our previous work on hyperplanes can be applied to arbitrary differentiable functions f: $\mathbb{R}^n \to \mathbb{R}^1$, $g^i: \mathbb{R}^n \to \mathbb{R}^1$, $i = 1, 2, \ldots, m < n$ by recalling that differentiability implies that the tangent hyperplanes are good approximations, locally, to the level curves. Thus at a point $\mathbf{x}^0 \in \mathbb{R}^n$ we can consider the linear approximation functions:

$$\hat{f}(\mathbf{x}) := f(\mathbf{x}^0) + \nabla f(\mathbf{x}^0) \cdot (\mathbf{x} - \mathbf{x}^0)$$

$$= \left(f(\mathbf{x}^0) - \nabla f(\mathbf{x}^0) \cdot \mathbf{x}^0 \right) + \nabla f(\mathbf{x}^0) \cdot \mathbf{x}$$

and, for $i = 1, 2, \ldots, m$,

$$\hat{g}^i(\mathbf{x}) := g^i(\mathbf{x}^0) + \nabla g^i(\mathbf{x}^0) \cdot (\mathbf{x} - \mathbf{x}^0)$$

$$= \left(g^i(\mathbf{x}^0) - \nabla g^i(\mathbf{x}^0) \cdot \mathbf{x}^0 \right) + \nabla g^i(\mathbf{x}^0) \cdot \mathbf{x}.$$

These functions are in the same form as h above. We will use a property of hyperplanes to derive a necessary condition for local optimization of f subject to the m constraints $g^i(\mathbf{x}) = 0$, $i = 1, 2, \ldots, m$. f is optimized at $\mathbf{x}^0$ only if $\hat{f}(\mathbf{x}) - \hat{f}(\mathbf{x}^0) = \nabla f(\mathbf{x}^0) \cdot (\mathbf{x} - \mathbf{x}^0) = 0$ for all $(\mathbf{x} - \mathbf{x}^0)$ such that $\hat{g}^i(\mathbf{x}) - \hat{g}^i(\mathbf{x}^0) = \nabla g^i(\mathbf{x}^0) \cdot (\mathbf{x} - \mathbf{x}^0) = 0$ for $i = 1, 2, \ldots, m$. If for some $\bar{x}$, $\hat{g}^i(\bar{x}) - \hat{g}^i(\mathbf{x}^0) = 0$ for $i = 1, 2, \ldots, m$, but $\hat{f}(\bar{x}) - \hat{f}(\mathbf{x}^0) = c \neq 0$, then we use the fact that the linear functions $\hat{f}$ and $\hat{g}^i$ are good approximations locally to find an $\mathbf{x}^1(\lambda) \approx \mathbf{x}^0 + \lambda(\bar{x} - \mathbf{x}^0)$ and an $\mathbf{x}^2(\lambda) \approx \mathbf{x}^0 - \lambda(\bar{x} - \mathbf{x}^0)$

for all λ near zero such that $\mathbf{x}^1(\lambda)$ and $\mathbf{x}^2(\lambda)$ satisfy all constraints and $f(\mathbf{x}^1(\lambda)) > f(\mathbf{x}^0) > f(\mathbf{x}^2(\lambda))$, so $\mathbf{x}^0$ cannot be a local optimizer.

THEOREM: *Let $f, g^1, g^2, \ldots, g^m$ $(m < n)$ be continuously differentiable functions from $\mathbb{R}^n \to \mathbb{R}^1$. If $\mathbf{x}^0$ is a point such that there exists an $\varepsilon > 0$ and*

1. $g^i(\mathbf{x}^0) = 0$, $i = 1, 2, \ldots, m$ *and*
2. $f(\mathbf{x}^0) \geq f(\mathbf{x})$ *(or $f(\mathbf{x}^0) \leq f(\mathbf{x})$) for all $\mathbf{x}$ such that*

$$\|\mathbf{x} - \mathbf{x}^0\| < \varepsilon \quad \text{and} \quad g^i(\mathbf{x}) = 0, i = 1, 2, \ldots, m$$

(i.e., $\mathbf{x}^0$ is a local optimizer of f subject to the m constraints), then there exist $\lambda_0, \lambda_1, \lambda_2, \ldots, \lambda_m$, not all zero, such that $\lambda_0 \nabla f(\mathbf{x}^0) = \sum_{i=1}^m \lambda_i \nabla g^i(\mathbf{x}^0)$. If rank $[\nabla g^1(\mathbf{x}^0), \nabla g^2(\mathbf{x}^0), \ldots, \nabla g^m(\mathbf{x}^0)] = m$ then we can choose $\lambda_0 = 1$.

Proof: If the rank is less than m, the gradient vectors $\nabla g^i(\mathbf{x}^0)$ are linearly dependent, so there exist $\lambda_1, \lambda_2, \ldots, \lambda_m$ not all zero such that $\sum_{i=1}^m \lambda_i \nabla g^i(\mathbf{x}^0) = \mathbf{0}$. Then just set $\lambda_0 = 0$.

If the rank is equal to m, then the proof is just a generalization of the idea for $m = 1$ (using the theorem from Section 2.5 in Chapter 2). Divide $\nabla f(\mathbf{x}^0)$ into two parts, $\nabla f(\mathbf{x}^0) = \mathbf{v}^1 + \mathbf{v}^2$, where $\mathbf{v}^1$ is in the subspace spanned by the gradient vectors $\nabla g^i(\mathbf{x}^0)$ and $\mathbf{v}^2$ is orthogonal to each gradient vector $\nabla g^i(\mathbf{x}^0)$. For small, nonzero λ,

$$\frac{f(\mathbf{x} + \lambda \mathbf{v}^2) - f(\mathbf{x}^0)}{\lambda} \approx \frac{\nabla f(\mathbf{x}^0) \cdot (\lambda \mathbf{v}^2)}{\lambda} = (\mathbf{v}^1 + \mathbf{v}^2) \cdot \mathbf{v}^2 = \mathbf{v}^2 \cdot \mathbf{v}^2.$$

For small λ, $\mathbf{x}^0 + \lambda \mathbf{v}^2$ "approximately" lies on each constraint level curve (it is on the tangent plane to each constraint level curve since $\nabla g^i(\mathbf{x}^0) \cdot \mathbf{v}^2 = 0$ for all i). If $\mathbf{v}^2 \neq \mathbf{0}$, then for small positive (negative) λ, $f(\mathbf{x}^0 + \lambda \mathbf{v}^2) > f(\mathbf{x}^0) [< f(\mathbf{x}^0)]$ and $\mathbf{x}^0 + \lambda \mathbf{v}^2$ approximately satisfies all constraints. It is then possible to find $\mathbf{x}(\lambda)$ near $\mathbf{x}^0 + \lambda \mathbf{v}^2$ which satisfies all the constraints and has $f(\mathbf{x}(\lambda)) > f(\mathbf{x}^0) [< f(\mathbf{x}^0)]$ for λ small. Since $\mathbf{x}^0$ is a local maximizer (minimizer), $\mathbf{v}^2$ must be $\mathbf{0}$. Hence $\nabla f(\mathbf{x}^0) = \mathbf{v}^1 = \sum_{i=1}^m \lambda_i \nabla g^i(\mathbf{x}^0)$ (i.e., $\mathbf{v}^1$ is in the subspace generated by the $\nabla g^i(\mathbf{x}^0)$). When the $\nabla g^i(\mathbf{x}^0)$ are independent (i.e., rank $[\nabla g^1(\mathbf{x}^0), \nabla g^2(\mathbf{x}^0), \ldots, \nabla g^m(\mathbf{x}^0)] = m$), $(\lambda_1, \lambda_2, \ldots, \lambda_m)$ is unique given $\lambda_0 = 1$.

EXAMPLE: For $f(x_1, x_2) = (10 - x_1^2 - x_2^2)/4$ and

$$g(x_1, x_2) = \begin{cases} (x_1^2 - x_2^2 - 1)/4 & \text{if } x_1 \geq 0, \\ 10 & \text{if } x_1 < 0, \end{cases}$$

the constrained optimum is attained at $\mathbf{x}^0 = (1, 0)$.

$$\nabla f(1,0) = \begin{pmatrix} -1/2 \\ 0 \end{pmatrix}, \quad \nabla g(1,0) = \begin{pmatrix} 1/2 \\ 0 \end{pmatrix}, \quad \text{and}$$

$$\nabla f(1,0) = (-1)\nabla g(1,0).$$

EXAMPLE: This example illustrates why the rank $= m$ condition is needed to guarantee we can set $\lambda_0 = 1$. (The rank $= m$ condition is one example of a *constraint qualification condition*.)

$$f(x, y, z) = x,$$

$$g^1(x, y, z) = (x - 1)^2 - z + 1,$$

$$g^2(x, y, z) = (x - 1)^2 + z - 1,$$

$$\nabla f = \begin{pmatrix} 1 \\ 0 \\ 0 \end{pmatrix}, \quad \nabla g^1 = \begin{pmatrix} 2(x - 1) \\ 0 \\ -1 \end{pmatrix}, \quad \text{and} \quad \nabla g^2 = \begin{pmatrix} 2(x - 1) \\ 0 \\ 1 \end{pmatrix}.$$

The set of points satisfying both constraints is $\{(1, y, 1)|y \in \mathbb{R}^1\}$, and y is essentially irrelevant. The only possible λ_i's satisfying the theorem have $\lambda_0 = 0$ and $\lambda_1 = \lambda_2$ [the set of optimizers is $\{(1, y, 1)|y \in \mathbb{R}^1\}$].

EXAMPLE: As usual, the first-order condition is a necessary condition for interior optima, but it is not sufficient. For $f(x, y) = y$ and $g(x, y) = y - x^3$

$$\nabla f = \begin{pmatrix} 0 \\ 1 \end{pmatrix}, \quad \nabla g = \begin{pmatrix} -3x^2 \\ 1 \end{pmatrix}.$$

Thus

$$\nabla f(0,0) = \begin{pmatrix} 0 \\ 1 \end{pmatrix} = 1 \cdot \begin{pmatrix} 0 \\ 1 \end{pmatrix} = 1 \nabla g(0,0).$$

Also, $g(0,0) = 0$. However, it is obvious that $(0,0)$ is neither a local maximizer nor a local minimizer.

The second-order conditions can also be derived using Taylor's theorem. If $\nabla f(\mathbf{x}^0) = \lambda \nabla g(\mathbf{x}^0)$ for some λ and f is twice continuously differentiable, then $\mathbf{x}^0$ is a local maximizer (minimizer) of f:

1. Only if

$$\mathbf{v}'\left[\frac{\partial^2 f}{\partial x_i \partial x_j}(\mathbf{x}^0)\right]\mathbf{v} \leq 0 \qquad \left(\mathbf{v}'\left[\frac{\partial^2 f}{\partial x_i \partial x_j}(\mathbf{x}^0)\right]\mathbf{v} \geq 0\right)$$

for all $\mathbf{v}$ such that $\nabla g(\mathbf{x}^0) \cdot \mathbf{v} = 0$;

2. If

$$\mathbf{v}'\left[\frac{\partial^2 f}{\partial x_i \, \partial x_j}\right]\mathbf{v} < 0 \qquad \left(\mathbf{v}'\left[\frac{\partial^2 f}{\partial x_i \, \partial x_j}\right]\mathbf{v} > 0\right)$$

for all $\mathbf{v} \neq \mathbf{0}$ such that $\nabla g(\mathbf{x}^0) \cdot \mathbf{v} = 0$.

These conditions correspond to our previous necessary conditions 1 and sufficient conditions 2 for maximizers (minimizers) of unconstrained functions except that only deviations $\mathbf{v}$ ($\mathbf{x} = \mathbf{x}^0 + \mathbf{v}$) that keep $\mathbf{x}^0 + \mathbf{v}$ on the tangent plane to the constraint level curve $g(\mathbf{x}) \equiv 0$ must be checked in the quadratic form $\mathbf{v}'[\partial^2 f(\mathbf{x}^0)/\partial x_i \, \partial x_j]\mathbf{v}$. That is, $[f_{ij}(\mathbf{x}^0)]$, the matrix of second partial derivatives evaluated at $\mathbf{x}^0$, must be "negative (positive) (semi) definite for $\mathbf{v}$'s that are orthogonal to the gradient vector $\nabla g(\mathbf{x}^0)$," or, the second-order conditions need only be checked in directions which do not violate the constraint.

If there are several constraints, then only directions $\mathbf{v}$ that violate none of the constraints need to be checked: $\mathbf{v}'[f_{ij}(\mathbf{x}^0)]\mathbf{v} < 0 \, (\leq 0, > 0, \geq 0)$ for all $\mathbf{v}$ such that $\nabla g^i(\mathbf{x}^0) \cdot \mathbf{v} = 0$, $i = 1, 2, \ldots, m$. Writing the set of conditions $\nabla g^1(\mathbf{x}^0) \cdot \mathbf{v} = 0$, $i = 1, 2, \ldots, m$, as a matrix condition,

$$\left[\frac{\partial g^i}{\partial x_j}(\mathbf{a})\right]_{m \times n} \mathbf{v} = \mathbf{0},$$

we get

THEOREM: *Let $f, g^1, g^2, \ldots, g^m$ ($m < n$) be functions from $\mathbb{R}^n \rightarrow \mathbb{R}^1$ which are twice continuously differentiable on a set containing $\mathbf{a}$ in its interior and such that $rank[\nabla g^1(\mathbf{a}), \nabla g^2(\mathbf{a}), \ldots, \nabla g^m(\mathbf{a})] = m$. Then if $g^i(\mathbf{a}) = 0$ for $i = 1, 2, \ldots, m$,*

1. (*Necessary conditions*) *f has a local maximum (minimum) at $\mathbf{a}$ subject to $g^i(\mathbf{x}) = 0$, $i = 1, 2, \ldots, m$, only if there exist scalars $\lambda_1, \lambda_2, \ldots, \lambda_m$ such that $\nabla f(\mathbf{a}) = \sum_{i=1}^{m} \lambda_i \nabla g^i(\mathbf{a})$ and $\mathbf{v}'[f_{ij}(\mathbf{a})]\mathbf{v} \leq 0 \, (\geq 0)$ for all $\mathbf{v}$ such that $[\partial g^i(\mathbf{a})/\partial x_j]\mathbf{v} = \mathbf{0}$;*

2. (*Sufficient conditions*) *f has a strict local maximum (minimum) at $\mathbf{a}$ subject to the constraints $g^i(\mathbf{x}) = 0$, $i = 1, 2, \ldots, m$, if there exist scalars $\lambda_1, \lambda_2, \ldots, \lambda_m$ such that $\nabla f(\mathbf{a}) = \sum_{i=1}^{m} \lambda_i \nabla g^i(\mathbf{a})$ and $\mathbf{v}'[f_{ij}(\mathbf{a})]\mathbf{v} < 0 \, (> 0)$ for all $\mathbf{v} \neq \mathbf{0}$ such that $[\partial g^i(\mathbf{a})/\partial x_j]\mathbf{v} = \mathbf{0}$.*

Note the similarity to our previous theorem for unconstrained optima. When there are constraints, only movements along the (tangent planes to the) level curves $g^i(\mathbf{x}) \equiv 0$ must be checked for the second-order conditions. All other directions are not feasible changes in $\mathbf{x}$. There may be other directions in which f increases, but these directions violate the constraint [and do not lie on the tangent plane to the level curve $g(\mathbf{x}) \equiv 0$].

The second-order conditions listed in the preceding theorem can be checked using the conditions on determinants given in the final theorem of Section 2.6 of Chapter 2.

5.8 FIRST-ORDER CONDITIONS FOR CONSTRAINED OPTIMIZATION

The previous sections considered the special cases of unconstrained and equality-constrained optimization. We now consider general optimization problems. This is the most important section on first-order conditions because it covers all cases in a unified framework. The first-order conditions follow from the properties of the hyperplanes used to approximate the level curves of the functions.

If f is a real-valued smooth function of n variables $x_1, x_2, \ldots, x_n$, then the linear approximation to f at a point $\mathbf{x}^0 = (x_1^0, \ldots, x_n^0)$ is determined by the gradient of f at $\mathbf{x}^0$, $\nabla f(\mathbf{x}^0) = (\partial f(\mathbf{x}^0)/\partial x_1, \ldots, \partial f(\mathbf{x}^0)/\partial x_n)$:

$$f(\mathbf{x}) \approx f(\mathbf{x}^0) + (\mathbf{x} - \mathbf{x}^0) \cdot \nabla f(\mathbf{x}^0)$$

$$= f(\mathbf{x}^0) + \left(x_1 - x_1^0 \right)\frac{\partial f(\mathbf{x}^0)}{\partial x_1} + \cdots + \left(x_n - x_n^0 \right)\frac{\partial f(\mathbf{x}^0)}{\partial x_n}.$$

[This is the same idea as expressed in the total differential, $df = \nabla f(\mathbf{x}^0) \cdot d\mathbf{x}$.] The linear approximations to the level curves of f are parallel, "perpendicular" to $\nabla f(\mathbf{x}^0)$, equally spaced for equal increments in the value of f, and with higher values of f as we move in the direction given by the gradient. See Figure 5.5.

For an optimization problem without constraints, whenever $\nabla f(\mathbf{x}^0)$ is not the zero vector Figure 5.5 applies, so $\mathbf{x}^0$ cannot be an optimizer. Thus

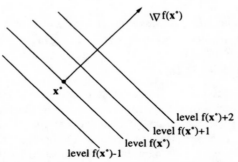

FIGURE 5.5 Approximate level curves for f.

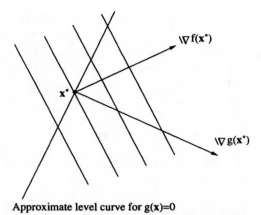

Approximate level curve for g(x)=0

FIGURE 5.6 Approximate level curves for the objective and constraint functions.

a necessary condition for $\mathbf{x}^0$ to be an optimizer of f without constraints is $\nabla f(\mathbf{x}^0) = \mathbf{0}$.

For an optimization problem with equality constraints, whenever $\nabla f(\mathbf{x}^0)$ is not the zero vector Figure 5.5 applies, but it is now not possible to move in all directions. Given the constraint $g(\mathbf{x}) = 0$, if $g(\mathbf{x}^0) = 0$, then starting at $\mathbf{x}^0$, we can move only in directions $d\mathbf{x}$ satisfying $0 = dg = \nabla g(\mathbf{x}^0) \cdot d\mathbf{x}$. For $\nabla g(\mathbf{x}^0)$ not equal to the zero vector, if $\nabla f(\mathbf{x}^0)$ is not a multiple of $\nabla g(\mathbf{x}^0)$, then the approximate level curve of g corresponding to the constraint crosses the level curves of f, and a value of f greater than $f(\mathbf{x}^0)$ is attainable. See Figure 5.6. Thus a necessary condition for $\mathbf{x}^0$ to be an optimizer of f subject to $g(\mathbf{x}) = 0$ is $\nabla f(\mathbf{x}^0) = \lambda \nabla g(\mathbf{x}^0)$ for some number λ [given $g(\mathbf{x}^0) = 0$ and $\nabla g(\mathbf{x}^0)$ is not the zero vector].

For an optimization problem with inequality constraints, whenever $\nabla f(\mathbf{x}^0)$ is not the zero vector, Figure 5.5 applies, but it is not possible to move in all directions. Given the constraint $g(\mathbf{x}) \le 0$, there are two possibilities.

1. If $g(\mathbf{x}^0) < 0$, then the constraint is not binding at $\mathbf{x}^0$, and any direction $d\mathbf{x}$ is feasible. Thus the unconstrained case applies, and $\nabla f(\mathbf{x}^0) = \mathbf{0}$ is a necessary condition.

2. If $g(\mathbf{x}^0) = 0$, then the constraint is binding at $\mathbf{x}^0$. First consider changes $d\mathbf{x}$ that maintain $g(\mathbf{x}) = 0$. This is exactly the case of an equality constraint so [given $\nabla g(\mathbf{x}^0)$ is not the zero vector] a necessary condition is $\nabla f(\mathbf{x}^0) = \lambda \nabla g(\mathbf{x}^0)$ for some number λ. However, we can be more specific about λ. The approximate level curves of f and g are parallel when $\nabla f(\mathbf{x}^0) = \lambda \nabla g(\mathbf{x}^0)$, but if $\lambda < 0$, then moving in the direction given by $\nabla f(\mathbf{x}^0)$ increases f but decreases g. This is a feasible move since the constraint $g(x) \le 0$ only prevents increasing g. Hence if we are maximiz-

ing f subject to $g(\mathbf{x}) \leq 0$, then $\lambda \geq 0$. (If we are minimizing f subject to $g(\mathbf{x}) \leq 0$, then $\lambda \leq 0$.)

Cases 1 and 2 can be combined in a single condition: [given $\nabla g(\mathbf{x}^0)$ is not the zero vector] a necessary condition for $\mathbf{x}^0$ to be an optimizer of f subject to $g(\mathbf{x}) \leq 0$ is that there is a number λ such that

$$g(\mathbf{x}^0) \leq 0,$$

$$\nabla f(\mathbf{x}^0) - \lambda \nabla g(\mathbf{x}^0) = \mathbf{0},$$

$\lambda \geq 0$ for maximization ($\lambda \leq 0$ for minimization), and

$$\lambda g(\mathbf{x}^0) = 0.$$

The last condition arises because either the constraint is satisfied as an equality, $g(\mathbf{x}^0) = 0$, so $\lambda g(\mathbf{x}^0) = 0$, or the constraint is satisfied as a strict inequality, $g(\mathbf{x}^0) < 0$, in which case the second condition should be $\nabla f(\mathbf{x}^0) = \mathbf{0}$, requiring $\lambda = 0$. In either case $\lambda g(\mathbf{x}^0) = 0$.

For a general statement of the *Kuhn–Tucker conditions*, consider the problem of maximizing $f(\mathbf{x})$ subject to $g^i(\mathbf{x}) \leq b^i$ for $i = 1, 2, \ldots, m$ and $h^j(\mathbf{x}) = c^j$ for $j = 1, 2, \ldots, k$. Necessary conditions for $\mathbf{x}^0$ to be a solution are

$$g^i(\mathbf{x}^0) \leq b^i \quad \text{for } i = 1, 2, \ldots, m,$$

$$h^j(\mathbf{x}^0) = c^j \quad \text{for } j = 1, 2, \ldots, k,$$

and there exist numbers $\lambda_0, \lambda_1, \ldots, \lambda_{m+k}$ not all zero such that

$$\lambda_0 \nabla f(\mathbf{x}^0) - \sum_{i=1}^{m} \lambda_i \nabla g^i(\mathbf{x}^0) - \sum_{j=1}^{k} \lambda_{m+j} \nabla h^j(\mathbf{x}^0) = \mathbf{0},$$

$$\lambda_i \geq 0 \quad \text{for } i = 1, 2, \ldots, m,$$

$$\lambda_i (b^i - g^i(\mathbf{x}^0)) = 0 \quad \text{for } i = 1, 2, \ldots, m.$$

When a *constraint qualification condition* [e.g., those of

$$\nabla g^1(\mathbf{x}^0), \nabla g^2(\mathbf{x}^0), \ldots, \nabla g^m(\mathbf{x}^0), \nabla h^1(\mathbf{x}^0), \nabla h^2(\mathbf{x}^0), \ldots, \nabla h^k(\mathbf{x}^0)$$

corresponding to binding constraints are independent vectors] holds, then we can set $\lambda_0 = 1$. The conditions are remembered by forming the Lagrangian

$$L(\mathbf{x}, \boldsymbol{\lambda}) = \lambda_0 f(\mathbf{x}) + \sum_{i=1}^{m} \lambda_i (b^i - g^i(\mathbf{x})) + \sum_{j=1}^{k} \lambda_{m+j} (c^j - h^j(\mathbf{x}))$$

and taking partial derivatives with respect to all variables.

The sign condition on the Lagrange multiplier, λ, for each inequality constraint depends on three factors: whether the problem is maximization or minimization, whether the constraint is $g^i(\mathbf{x}) \leq b$ or $g^i(\mathbf{x}) \geq b$, and whether the term $\lambda_i g^i(\mathbf{x})$ appears in the Lagrangian as $-\lambda_i g^i(\mathbf{x})$ or $+\lambda_i g^i(\mathbf{x})$. The condition $\lambda_i \geq 0$ is based on maximization with $g^i \leq b$ and the term appearing as $-\lambda_i g^i$. Each time one of these three choices is changed, the sign condition switches. Thus minimization with $g^i \leq b$ and term $-\lambda_i g^i(\mathbf{x})$ has condition $\lambda_i \leq 0$. Maximization with $g^i \geq b$ and term $+\lambda_i g^i$ has condition $\lambda_i \geq 0$ because there are two switches. Minimization with $g^i \geq b$ and term $+\lambda_i g^i$ has an odd number (3) of switches, so the condition is $\lambda_i \leq 0$. The appropriate sign condition can always be reconstructed by recalling that the approximate level curve of f must separate the feasible directions of movement from the desirable directions of movement. The feasible directions, $d\mathbf{x}$, must satisfy all constraints so $\nabla h^j(\mathbf{x}^0) \cdot d\mathbf{x} = 0$ for all j and $\nabla g^i(\mathbf{x}^0) \cdot d\mathbf{x} \leq 0$ (≥ 0) if inequality constraint i is binding at $\mathbf{x}^0$ and is of the form $g^i(\mathbf{x}) \leq b^i$ $[g^i(\mathbf{x}) \geq b^i]$. The desirable directions increase f for a maximization problem $[\nabla f(\mathbf{x}^0) \cdot d\mathbf{x} > 0]$ and decrease f for a minimization problem $[\nabla f(\mathbf{x}^0) \cdot d\mathbf{x} < 0]$.

EXAMPLES: To see that a constraint qualification condition is necessary before we can set $\lambda_0 = 1$, consider the problem: maximize $f(x, y) = x$ subject to $g^1(x, y) = -y \leq 0$ and $g^2(x, y) = (x - 1)^3 + y \leq 0$. The feasible set is shown in Figure 5.7 and the obvious solution is the point $(1, 0)$. However, $\nabla f(1, 0) = (1, 0)$, $\nabla g^1(1, 0) = (0, -1)$ and $\nabla g^2(1, 0) = (0, 1)$. The only $\lambda_0, \lambda_1, \lambda_2$ satisfying the conditions are $\lambda_0 = 0$ and $\lambda_1 = \lambda_2 > 0$. As a second example, consider the problem: maximize $f(x, y) = -(x - 1)^2 - (y - 1)^2$ subject to $g(x, y) = y^2 \leq 0$. The constraint is equivalent to $y = 0$ so the obvious solution is $(x^*, y^*) = (1, 0)$. However, $\nabla f(1, 0) = (0, 2)$ and $\nabla g(1, 0) = (0, 0)$ so the only λ_0, λ_1 satisfying the conditions are $\lambda_0 = 0$ and $\lambda_1 > 0$.

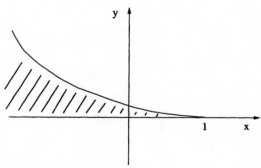

FIGURE 5.7 The feasible set.

There are various constraint qualification conditions, but each one can be used to guarantee we can set $\lambda_0 = 1$ at a solution. The independence assumption we use is a relatively easy-to-check constraint qualification condition.

Sometimes nonnegativity constraints are handled in a slightly different way. Consider the problem maximize $f(\mathbf{x})$ subject to $x_i \geq 0$, $i = 1, 2, \ldots, n$, and $g(\mathbf{x}) \leq 0$. Suppose that a constraint qualification condition holds at $\mathbf{x}^0$. Then writing the nonnegativity constraints as $-x_i \leq 0$ for $i = 1, 2, \ldots, n$, the Kuhn–Tucker conditions become (for $\mathbf{e}_i$ the vector with 1 in the ith component and zeros elsewhere).

$$-x_i \leq 0 \quad \text{for } i = 1, 2, \ldots, n,$$

$$g(\mathbf{x}) \leq 0,$$

and there exist numbers $\lambda_1, \lambda_2, \ldots, \lambda_{n+1}$ such that

$$\nabla f(\mathbf{x}^0) - \sum_{i=1}^{n} \lambda_i(-\mathbf{e}_i) - \lambda_{n+1}\nabla g(\mathbf{x}^0) = \mathbf{0},$$

$$\lambda_i \geq 0 \quad \text{for } i = 1, 2, \ldots, n + 1,$$

$$\lambda_i x_i^0 = 0 \quad \text{for } i = 1, 2, \ldots, n, \quad \text{and}$$

$$\lambda_{n+1} g(\mathbf{x}^0) = 0.$$

Notice that $\nabla f(\mathbf{x}^0) - \lambda_{n+1}\nabla g(\mathbf{x}^0) = (-\lambda_1, -\lambda_2, \ldots, -\lambda_n)$, so each component is nonpositive. Also notice that $(\nabla f(\mathbf{x}^0) - \lambda_{n+1}\nabla g(\mathbf{x}^0)) \cdot \mathbf{x}^0 = (-\lambda_1, \ldots, -\lambda_n) \cdot \mathbf{x}^0 = 0$. With these observations, we see that there is an alternative, equivalent set of necessary conditions for this problem: there is a number, λ, such that

$$\mathbf{x}^0 \geq \mathbf{0},$$

$$\nabla f(\mathbf{x}^0) - \lambda\nabla g(\mathbf{x}^0) \leq \mathbf{0},$$

$$(\nabla f(\mathbf{x}^0) - \lambda\nabla g(\mathbf{x}^0)) \cdot \mathbf{x}^0 = 0,$$

$$\lambda \geq 0,$$

$$g(\mathbf{x}^0) \leq 0, \quad \text{and}$$

$$\lambda g(\mathbf{x}^0) = 0.$$

EXAMPLE: Consider the problem of maximizing f subject to $y \leq 2x - 1$, $y \geq 0$, and $x \geq 0$. There are two ways to treat the nonnegativity constraints.

1. Including all constraints in the Lagrangian we get

$$L(x, y, \lambda_1, \lambda_2, \lambda_3) = y - x^2 + \lambda_1(-1 + 2x - y) + \lambda_2(x) + \lambda_3(y)$$

The necessary conditions are

$$\frac{\partial L}{\partial x} = -2x + 2\lambda_1 + \lambda_2 = 0,$$

$$\frac{\partial L}{\partial y} = 1 - \lambda_1 + \lambda_3 = 0,$$

$$\frac{\partial L}{\partial \lambda_1} = -1 + 2x - y \geq 0,$$

$$\frac{\partial L}{\partial \lambda_2} = x \geq 0,$$

$$\frac{\partial L}{\partial \lambda_3} = y \geq 0,$$

$$\lambda_1 \geq 0,$$

$$\lambda_2 \geq 0,$$

$$\lambda_3 \geq 0,$$

$$\lambda_1(-1 + 2x - y) = 0,$$

$$\lambda_2(x) = 0,$$

$$\lambda_3(y) = 0.$$

To solve this, note that the second condition plus $\lambda_3 \geq 0$ implies $\lambda_1 > 0$ (so $-1 + 2x - y = 0$), which, along with the first condition and $\lambda_2 \geq 0$, implies $x > 0$ (so $\lambda_2 = 0$). To see $\lambda_3 = 0$, suppose λ_3 was strictly positive. Then y would be zero, and $x = \lambda_1 = \frac{1}{2}$, so $\lambda_3 = -\frac{1}{2}$, a contradiction. Thus $\lambda_3 = 0$. From the second condition $\lambda_1 = 1$, so $x = 1$ and $y = 1$. The only solution to the conditions is $(x^*, y^*, \lambda_1^*, \lambda_2^*, \lambda_3^*) = (1, 1, 1, 0, 0)$.

2. Using the alternative method for dealing with nonnegativity constraints, the Lagrangian is $L(x, y, \lambda) = y - x^2 + \lambda(-1 + 2x - y)$ and the

necessary conditions are

$$\frac{\partial L}{\partial x} = -2x + 2\lambda \leq 0,$$

$$\frac{\partial L}{\partial y} = 1 - \lambda \leq 0,$$

$$\left(\frac{\partial L}{\partial x}, \frac{\partial L}{\partial y}\right) \cdot (x, y) = 0,$$

$$x \geq 0,$$

$$y \geq 0,$$

$$\frac{\partial L}{\partial \lambda} = -1 + 2x - y \geq 0,$$

$$\lambda(-1 + 2x - y) = 0,$$

$$\lambda \geq 0.$$

From the second condition $\lambda > 0$, so $-1 + 2x - y = 0$ and, from the first condition, $x > 0$. By the third condition (and the inequalities) this implies $\partial L/\partial x = -2x + 2\lambda = 0$. To see that $y > 0$, suppose $y = 0$. Then $x = \frac{1}{2} = \lambda$ and $\partial L/\partial y = \frac{1}{2}$, contrary to the second condition. Thus $y > 0$, and by the third condition $\partial L/\partial y = 1 - \lambda = 0$. Thus $1 = \lambda = x$, and $y = 1$. The only solution to the necessary conditions is $(x^*, y^*, \lambda^*) = (1, 1, 1)$. The two approaches produce the same results.

5.9 SECOND-ORDER CONDITIONS FOR OPTIMIZATION

For the first-order necessary conditions for optimization we used the fact that $f(x) \approx f(x^0) + (x - x^0) \cdot \nabla f(x^0)$ and used the right-hand side as a linear approximation to f. For the second-order conditions we need to look at the curvature of f, so we consider the quadratic terms and a closer approximation. Let $[f_{ij}(x)]$ be the matrix with element $\partial^2 f(x)/\partial x_i \partial x_j$ in row i and column j. Then $f(x) \approx f(x^0) + (x - x^0) \cdot \nabla f(x^0) + \frac{1}{2}(x - x^0)'[f_{ij}(x^0)](x - x^0)$.

Consider the function of a single variable, $f(x) = x^2$. Then

$$\nabla f(x) = \frac{df(x)}{dx} = 2x \quad \text{and} \quad [f_{ij}(x)] = \frac{d^2 f(x)}{dx^2} = 2$$

so the approximation (at $x^0 = 1$) becomes $f(x) \approx 1 + (x - 1)2 + \frac{1}{2}(x - 1)2(x - 1) = x^2$. Just as the linear approximation is exact when the original function is linear, this approximation is exact when the function is quadratic.

Consider the function $f(x, y) = x^2 + y^2$. Then

$$\nabla f(x, y) = (2x, 2y) \quad \text{and} \quad [f_{ij}(\mathbf{x})] = \begin{bmatrix} 2 & 0 \\ 0 & 2 \end{bmatrix}.$$

The optimizers of f (without constraint) must satisfy $\nabla f(x^0, y^0) = (2x^0, 2y^0) = (0, 0)$, so the only potential optimizer is $(x^0, y^0) = (0, 0)$. At this point our second-order "approximation" is

$$f(x, y) \approx f(0, 0) + (x - 0, y - 0) \cdot \nabla f(0, 0)$$

$$+ \left(\frac{1}{2}\right)(x - 0, y - 0)[f_{ij}(0, 0)]\begin{pmatrix} x - 0 \\ y - 0 \end{pmatrix},$$

or

$$f(x, y) \approx \left(\frac{1}{2}\right)(x, y)\begin{bmatrix} 2 & 0 \\ 0 & 2 \end{bmatrix}\begin{pmatrix} x \\ y \end{pmatrix}.$$

To be a maximum (minimum) without constraint it must be the case that

$$(x, y)\begin{bmatrix} 2 & 0 \\ 0 & 2 \end{bmatrix}\begin{pmatrix} x \\ y \end{pmatrix} \leq 0 \ (\geq 0)$$

for any (x, y). On the other hand, if

$$(x, y)\begin{bmatrix} 2 & 0 \\ 0 & 2 \end{bmatrix}\begin{pmatrix} x \\ y \end{pmatrix} < 0 \ (> 0)$$

for all $(x, y) \neq (0, 0)$ then any small deviation from $(0, 0)$ leads to a decrease (increase) in f, so $(0, 0)$ is a strict local maximizer (minimizer). In this example,

$$\frac{1}{2}(x, y)\begin{bmatrix} 2 & 0 \\ 0 & 2 \end{bmatrix}\begin{pmatrix} x \\ y \end{pmatrix} = x^2 + y^2,$$

so for all nonzero deviations f increases, and $(0, 0)$ is a strict local minimizer of f.

Again consider the function $f(x, y) = x^2 + y^2$, but subject to the constraint $g(x, y) = x + y = 0$. To find potential optimizers form the Lagrangian $L(x, y, \lambda) = x^2 + y^2 + \lambda(2 - x - y)$. First-order conditions are

$$\frac{\partial L}{\partial x} = 2x - \lambda = 0,$$

$$\frac{\partial L}{\partial y} = 2y - \lambda = 0,$$

$$\frac{\partial L}{\partial \lambda} = 2 - x - y = 0.$$

The only solution to these necessary conditions is $(x^*, y^*, \lambda^*) = (1, 1, 2)$. The quadratic approximation at $(1, 1)$ is

$$f(x, y) \approx f(1, 1) + (x - 1, y - 1) \cdot \nabla f(1, 1)$$

$$+ \left(\frac{1}{2}\right)(x - 1, y - 1)[f_{ij}(1, 1)]\binom{x - 1}{y - 1}$$

$$= 2 + (x - 1, y - 1) \cdot (2, 2) + \left(\frac{1}{2}\right)(x - 1, y - 1)\begin{bmatrix} 2 & 0 \\ 0 & 2 \end{bmatrix}\binom{x - 1}{y - 1}.$$

From the previous necessary conditions we know that for any feasible $(dx, dy) = (x - 1, y - 1)$, $(dx, dy) \cdot (2, 2) = 0$. Thus for a maximum (minimum) subject to the constraint it must be the case that for any feasible (dx, dy),

$$(dx, dy)\begin{bmatrix} 2 & 0 \\ 0 & 2 \end{bmatrix}\binom{dx}{dy} \leq 0 \, (\geq 0).$$

On the other hand, if

$$(dx, dy)\begin{bmatrix} 2 & 0 \\ 0 & 2 \end{bmatrix}\binom{dx}{dy} < 0 \, (> 0) \quad \text{for all feasible}(dx, dy) \neq (0, 0),$$

then any feasible deviation from $(1, 1)$ leads to a decrease (increase) in f, so $(1, 1)$ is a strict local maximizer (minimizer) of f subject to the constraint. In this example, to be feasible $(dx, dy) \cdot \nabla g(1, 1) = 0$ or $dy = -dx$. Thus

$$(dx, dy)\begin{bmatrix} 2 & 0 \\ 0 & 2 \end{bmatrix}\binom{dx}{dy} = 2(dx)^2 + 2(-dx)^2 > 0$$

$$\text{for all feasible}(dx, dy) \neq (0, 0),$$

and $(1, 1)$ is a strict local minimizer of f subject to the constraint.

The general second-order conditions are similar to those of the examples. What we need are conditions on $[f_{ij}(\mathbf{x}^0)]$ that imply

$d\mathbf{x}'[f_{ij}(\mathbf{x}^0)]\,d\mathbf{x} < 0$ (or > 0, or ≤ 0, or ≥ 0) for all feasible $d\mathbf{x}$. For the unconstrained case, the condition is that $[f_{ij}(\mathbf{x}^0)]$ be a negative definite matrix (or positive definite for > 0, or negative semidefinite for ≤ 0, or positive semidefinite for ≥ 0). For the constrained case it is possible to use a transformation of variables to show that the conditions are equivalent to the conditions given below. (See Chapter 2, Section 2.6.)

In what follows we consider only those constraints that are binding at the potential solution $\mathbf{x}^0$, with corresponding Lagrange multipliers λ_i^0. We use the previously derived necessary first-order conditions to find a potential solution $\mathbf{x}^0$ and ignore all inequality constraints that are not binding at $\mathbf{x}^0$. Thus the Lagrangian below includes only those constraints that are binding at $\mathbf{x}^0$. We also assume that the remaining constraints are independent and the variables are arranged so that, with binding constraints $i = 1, 2, \ldots, s$ at $\mathbf{x}^0$, the last s rows of the $n \times s$ matrix $[\nabla g^1(\mathbf{x}^0), \nabla g^2(\mathbf{x}^0), \ldots, \nabla g^s(\mathbf{x}^0)]$ are independent. This guarantees that the "informative" rows of the constraint matrix are in the appropriate position to be used in the conditions below. Finally, we assume *strict complementary slackness*; i.e., all binding inequality constraints have strictly positive multipliers. When this condition fails, we may have trouble deciding whether to include a constraint in the Lagrangian used to generate the second-order condition matrix (see Section 6.4.4 of Chapter 6)

$$L(\mathbf{x}, \boldsymbol{\lambda}) = f(\mathbf{x}) + \sum_{k=1}^{s} \lambda_k (b^k - g^k(\mathbf{x})).$$

Consider the $(s + n) \times (s + n)$ matrix of second partial derivatives of L.

$$[L_{ij}(\mathbf{x}, \boldsymbol{\lambda})] = \left[\begin{array}{c|c} [f_{ij}(\mathbf{x})] - \sum_{k=1}^{s} \lambda_k [g_{ij}(\mathbf{x})] & [-\nabla g^1(\mathbf{x}), \ldots, -\nabla g^s(\mathbf{x})] \\ \hline \begin{array}{c} -\nabla g^1(\mathbf{x})' \\ \vdots \\ -\nabla g^s(\mathbf{x})' \end{array} & [0] \end{array} \right].$$

Let D_i be the $(2s + i) \times (2s + i)$ lower right-hand corner submatrix of $[L_{ij}(\mathbf{x}^0, \boldsymbol{\lambda}^0)]$.

For n components of $\mathbf{x}$ and s binding constraints, there are $n - s$ inequalities to check. (We include the case of no constraints, $s = 0$.) In what follows, recall $(-1)^0 = 1$. Assume that the first-order necessary conditions hold at $\mathbf{x}^0$. Then denoting the determinant of D_r by $|D_r|$:

1. A sufficient condition for $\mathbf{x}^0$ to be a strict local minimizer of f subject to the constraints is $(-1)^s |D_r| > 0$ for $r = 1, 2, \ldots, n - s$;

2. A necessary condition for x^0 to be a local minimizer of f subject to the constraints is $(-1)^s |D_r| \geq 0$ for $r = 1, 2, \ldots, n - s$;

3. A sufficient condition for x^0 to be a strict local maximizer of f subject to the constraints is $(-1)^{r+s} |D_r| > 0$ for $r = 1, 2, \ldots, n - s$;

4. A necessary condition for x^0 to be a local maximizer of f subject to the constraints is $(-1)^{r+s} |D_r| \geq 0$ for $r = 1, 2, \ldots, n - s$.

When the first-order conditions hold at x^0, the second-order sufficient conditions can be summarized as follows (the necessary conditions just replace $>$ with $\geq$ and $<$ with $\leq$):

1. For no constraints: $|D_r| > 0$ for all r for a minimum; $|D_1| < 0$ and the determinants alternate in sign as r increases for a maximum.

2. For a single constraint: $|D_r| < 0$ for all r for a minimum; $|D_1| > 0$ and the determinants alternate in sign as r increases for a maximum.

3. For two constraints: $|D_r| > 0$ for all r for a minimum; $|D_1| < 0$ and the determinants alternate in sign as r increases for a maximum.

The second-order conditions depend on whether the problem is maximization or minimization. They do not depend on whether the inequality constraints are of the form $g^i(x) \leq b^i$ or $g^i(x) \geq b$ or on whether the term $\lambda_i g^i(x)$ enters the Lagrangian as $-\lambda_i g^i(x)$ or $+\lambda_i g^i(x)$. This is because each of these two choices already counterbalances itself, entering once via a row of the matrix and once via a column. (Recall the first-order conditions did depend on these choices.)

EXAMPLE: Consider the problem of minimizing $f(x, y) = x^2 + y^2$ subject to $x + y - 2 = 0$. Form the Lagrangian $L(x, y, \lambda) = x^2 + y^2 + \lambda(2 - x - y)$. The first-order conditions are

$$\frac{\partial L}{\partial x} = 2x - \lambda = 0, \qquad \frac{\partial L}{\partial y} = 2y - \lambda = 0, \quad \text{and} \quad \frac{\partial L}{\partial \lambda} = 2 - x - y = 0.$$

The only solution to these necessary conditions is $(x^*, y^*, \lambda^*) = (1, 1, 2)$. The matrix of second partials is

$$[L_{ij}] = \begin{bmatrix} 2 & 0 & -1 \\ 0 & 2 & -1 \\ -1 & -1 & 0 \end{bmatrix}.$$

[Note that in order to compute $[L_{ij}]$ one must differentiate again in the same order as was done originally. The first partials were taken in order with respect to x, y, then λ. Thus the first row of $[L_{ij}]$ must be the partials of $\partial L / \partial x$ with respect to x, y, and then λ, the second row must be the partials of $\partial L / \partial y$ with respect to x, y and then λ, etc.

For a minimum with one constraint, we need to check $n - s = 2 - 1 = 1$ determinant only. $|D_1| = -4 < 0$ so $(1, 1)$ is a strict local minimizer of f subject to the constraint.

EXAMPLE: Consider the problem of maximizing $f(x, y, z) = x + y + z$ subject to $x^2 + y^2 + z^2 = 3$. Form the Lagrangian: $L(x, y, z, \lambda) = x + y + z + \lambda(3 - x^2 - y^2 - z^2)$. The first-order conditions are

$$\frac{\partial L}{\partial x} = 1 - 2\lambda x = 0, \qquad \frac{\partial L}{\partial y} = 1 - 2\lambda y = 0,$$

$$\frac{\partial L}{\partial z} = 1 - 2\lambda z = 0, \quad \text{and} \quad \frac{\partial L}{\partial \lambda} = 3 - x^2 - y^2 - z^2 = 0.$$

There are two solutions to these equations:

$$x = y = z = -1 \quad \text{and} \quad \lambda = -\tfrac{1}{2} \quad \text{and} \quad x = y = z = 1 \quad \text{and} \quad \lambda = \tfrac{1}{2}.$$

The matrix of second partials is

$$[L_{ij}] = \begin{bmatrix} -2\lambda & 0 & 0 & -2x \\ 0 & -2\lambda & 0 & -2y \\ 0 & 0 & -2\lambda & -2z \\ -2x & -2y & -2z & 0 \end{bmatrix}.$$

We must check $n - s = 3 - 1 = 2$ determinants, $|D_1|$ and $|D_2|$, at each of the potential solutions.

At $x = y = z = -1$ and $\lambda = -\tfrac{1}{2}$,

$$|D_1| = \begin{vmatrix} 1 & 0 & 2 \\ 0 & 1 & 2 \\ 2 & 2 & 0 \end{vmatrix} = -8 \quad \text{and} \quad |D_2| = \begin{vmatrix} 1 & 0 & 0 & 2 \\ 0 & 1 & 0 & 2 \\ 0 & 0 & 1 & 2 \\ 2 & 2 & 2 & 0 \end{vmatrix} = -12,$$

so this is a strict local minimum.

At $x = y = z = 1$ and $\lambda = \tfrac{1}{2}$

$$|D_1| = \begin{vmatrix} -1 & 0 & -2 \\ 0 & -1 & -2 \\ -2 & -2 & 0 \end{vmatrix} = 8 \quad \text{and}$$

$$|D_2| = \begin{vmatrix} -1 & 0 & 0 & -2 \\ 0 & -1 & 0 & -2 \\ 0 & 0 & -1 & -2 \\ -2 & -2 & -2 & 0 \end{vmatrix} = -12,$$

so this is a strict local maximum.

EXAMPLE: Consider the problem of maximizing $f(x, y) = y - x^2$ subject to $y \leq 2x - 1$, $x \geq 0$ and $y \geq 0$. We have previously solved the first-order necessary conditions for this problem to find the only potential solution is $x = y = 1$. At this potential solution, only the $y \leq 2x - 1$ constraint is binding. Thus for our check of second-order conditions, we should use the Lagrangian $L(x, y, \lambda) = y - x^2 + \lambda(-1 + 2x - y)$. The matrix of second partials is

$$[L_{ij}] = \begin{bmatrix} -2 & 0 & -2 \\ 0 & 0 & 1 \\ -2 & 1 & 0 \end{bmatrix}.$$

With one binding constraint we must check $n - s = 2 - 1 = 1$ determinant. $|D_1| = 2$ so $(1, 1)$ is a strict local maximizer of f subject to the constraints.

EXAMPLE: Consider the problem of maximizing $f(x, y) = (x + 1)y$ subject to $x \geq 0$, $y \geq 0$, and $x + y \leq \frac{1}{2}$. Setting up the Lagrangian and solving the first-order necessary conditions yields the potential solution $x^* = 0$, $y^* = \frac{1}{2}$, $\lambda_1 = \frac{1}{2}$, $\lambda_2 = 0$, $\lambda_3 = 1$. At this point, there are two binding inequality constraints. With two variables and two independent constraints there is only a single point satisfying both constraints as equalities, and the second-order conditions disappear (we need to check $n - s = 2 - 2 = 0$ determinants). As inequalities there are still directions $d\mathbf{x}$ to check for the second-order conditions. However, the fact that λ_1 and λ_3 are strictly positive at this potential solution (i.e., strict complementary slackness holds) guarantees that any feasible $d\mathbf{x}$ decreases the value of the objective.

To see this, note that $g^1(x, y) = -x$ and $g^3(x, y) = x + y$, to put the Lagrangian in the form

$$f(x, y) + \lambda_1(0 - g^1(x, y)) + \lambda_2(0 - g^2(x, y)) + \lambda_3(\tfrac{1}{2} - g^3(x, y)).$$

Then $\partial L/\partial x = 0$ and $\partial L/\partial y = 0$ (and $\lambda_2 = 0$) imply $\nabla f(0, \frac{1}{2}) = \lambda_1 \nabla g^1(0, \frac{1}{2}) + \lambda_3 \nabla g^3(0, \frac{1}{2})$. To be a feasible direction of change, $d\mathbf{x}$ must satisfy $d\mathbf{x} \cdot \nabla g^1(0, \frac{1}{2}) \leq 0$ and $d\mathbf{x} \cdot \nabla g^3(0, \frac{1}{2}) \leq 0$. For $d\mathbf{x} \neq 0$, at least one of these inequalities must be strict. (∇g^1 and ∇g^3 are independent so the only vector in $\mathbb{R}^2$ orthogonal to both of them is $\mathbf{0}$.) But then for $d\mathbf{x} \neq \mathbf{0}$, $d\mathbf{x} \cdot \nabla f(0, \frac{1}{2}) = \lambda_1 d\mathbf{x} \cdot \nabla g^1(0, \frac{1}{2}) + \lambda_3 d\mathbf{x} \cdot \nabla g^3(0, \frac{1}{2})$, which is strictly negative because both λ_1 and λ_3 are strictly positive. There is no need to check any second-order conditions because there is already a (dominating) first-order decrease in value. Similar results hold whenever the number of binding constraints equals the number of variables as long as our linear independence and strict complementary slackness conditions hold.

5.10 CONCAVE FUNCTIONS, CONVEX FUNCTIONS, AND GLOBAL SOLUTIONS

So far, we have developed conditions to find local optimizers. What about global optimizers? For a general problem, if the feasible set is not bounded, we must consider any sequence of feasible points, $(\mathbf{x}^t)_{t=1}^{\infty}$, such that $\|\mathbf{x}^t\| \to \infty$ as $t \to \infty$ and check what happens to $f(\mathbf{x}^t)$. This must be compared to the best of the local solutions. In general, this may be difficult to do because of the infinity of directions to check with $\|\mathbf{x}^t\| \to \infty$. In practice, many shortcuts are often apparent.

In many economic problems, the properties of the objective and constraint functions will guarantee that local solutions are also global solutions, eliminating the need for the complicated check of directions. This section develops these properties and then summarizes what we know about finding global solutions.

DEFINITION: Let f be defined over an open convex set $X \subset \mathbb{R}^m$. f is a *concave* (*convex*) *function* over X if for all $\mathbf{x}, \mathbf{y} \in X$ and $\lambda \in [0, 1]$, $f(\lambda \mathbf{x} + (1 - \lambda)\mathbf{y}) \geq (\leq)\lambda f(\mathbf{x}) + (1 - \lambda)f(\mathbf{y})$. f is *strictly concave* (*strictly convex*) if strict inequality holds when $0 < \lambda < 1$ and $\mathbf{x} \neq \mathbf{y}$.

It is important to distinguish between convex sets and convex functions. A set S is convex if for every pair of points in S, the line segment joining the points is also in S; i.e., $\mathbf{x}, \mathbf{y} \in S$ implies $\lambda \mathbf{x} + (1 - \lambda)\mathbf{y} \in S$ for all $\lambda \in [0, 1]$. The concepts are related in that if $f: \mathbb{R}^n \to \mathbb{R}$ is a convex function, then for any $c \in \mathbb{R}$, $\{x \in \mathbb{R} | f(x) \leq c\}$ is a convex subset of $\mathbb{R}^n$ and $\{(x, y) \in \mathbb{R}^{n+1} | f(x) \leq y\}$ is a convex subset of $\mathbb{R}^{n+1}$. Similar results (with switches in the inequalities) hold for concave functions, since f is concave if and only if $-f$ is convex.

The following theorem has important implications for optimization.

THEOREM: *Suppose f is a concave* (*convex*) *continuously differentiable function on the open convex set $X \subset \mathbb{R}^m$. Then for any $\mathbf{x}, \mathbf{y} \in X$, $f(\mathbf{x}) \leq (\geq)f(\mathbf{y}) + \nabla f(\mathbf{y}) \cdot (\mathbf{x} - \mathbf{y})$; i.e., the graph of f lies everywhere on or below* (*above*) *any tangent plane.*

Proof: $f(\lambda \mathbf{x} + (1 - \lambda)\mathbf{y}) \geq \lambda f(\mathbf{x}) + (1 - \lambda)f(\mathbf{y})$ for all $\lambda \in [0, 1]$ by concavity. $f(\lambda \mathbf{x} + (1 - \lambda)\mathbf{y}) = f(\mathbf{y} + \lambda(\mathbf{x} - \mathbf{y})) = f(\mathbf{y}) + \lambda \nabla f(\mathbf{y} + \theta \lambda(\mathbf{x} - \mathbf{y})) \cdot (\mathbf{x} - \mathbf{y})$ for some $\theta \in [0, 1]$ by Taylor's theorem. Therefore

$$\lambda f(\mathbf{x}) + (1 - \lambda)f(\mathbf{y}) \leq f(\mathbf{y}) + \lambda \nabla f(\mathbf{y} + \theta \lambda(\mathbf{x} - \mathbf{y})) \cdot (\mathbf{x} - \mathbf{y}) \quad \text{or}$$

$$\lambda f(\mathbf{x}) \leq \lambda f(\mathbf{y}) + \lambda \nabla f(\mathbf{y} + \theta \lambda(\mathbf{x} - \mathbf{y})) \cdot (\mathbf{x} - \mathbf{y})$$

or, for $\lambda \neq 0$,

$$f(\mathbf{x}) \leq f(\mathbf{y}) + \nabla f(\mathbf{y} + \theta \lambda(\mathbf{x} - \mathbf{y})) \cdot (\mathbf{x} - \mathbf{y}).$$

Letting $\lambda \to 0^+$ and using the fact that f is continuously differentiable, we get $f(\mathbf{x}) \le f(\mathbf{y}) + \nabla f(\mathbf{y}) \cdot (\mathbf{x} - \mathbf{y})$. A similar proof applies for a convex function.

The functions used in economic problems are frequently assumed to be either convex or concave as appropriate for the situation at hand. Note the implications for optimization which follow from the theorem.

1. If f is concave and $\nabla f(\mathbf{a}) = \mathbf{0}$, then $\mathbf{a}$ is a global maximizer of f. $[f(\mathbf{x}) \le f(\mathbf{a}) + \nabla f(\mathbf{a}) \cdot (\mathbf{x} - \mathbf{a}) = f(\mathbf{a})$ for all $\mathbf{x} \in X$.]

2. If f is strictly concave and $\nabla f(\mathbf{a}) = \mathbf{0}$, then $\mathbf{a}$ is the unique global maximizer of f. [$\mathbf{a}$ is a global maximizer as above, and if $\mathbf{b} \ne \mathbf{a}$ is another global maximizer, then $f((1/2)\mathbf{a} + (1/2)\mathbf{b}) > (1/2)f(\mathbf{a}) + (1/2)f(\mathbf{b}) = f(\mathbf{a}) = f(\mathbf{b})$, contrary to $\mathbf{a}$ being a global maximizer.]

3. If f is concave and the feasible set is convex, then if $\mathbf{a}$ satisfies the first-order conditions it is a global maximizer of f. [The hyperplane through $\mathbf{a}$ with normal $\nabla f(\mathbf{a})$ separates the convex feasible set from the "preferred set" $\{\mathbf{x}|f(\mathbf{x}) > f(\mathbf{a})\}$.]

Note that if $g^i(\mathbf{x})$ is a convex function, then the set $\{\mathbf{x} \in \mathbb{R}^n | g^i(\mathbf{x}) \le 0\}$ is a convex set. Also note that hyperplanes are convex sets. Finally, recall that the intersection of convex sets is convex. Thus if all inequality constraints are specified by convex functions ($g^i(\mathbf{x}) \le 0$ with g^i convex) and all equality constraints are given by *affine functions* (functions of the form $y - \mathbf{p} \cdot \mathbf{x} = 0$), then the feasible set is convex.

4. If f is strictly concave and the feasible set is convex, then if $\mathbf{a}$ satisfies the first-order conditions it is the unique global maximizer of f subject to the constraints.

Results similar to 1–4 hold for convex functions and minimization.

The next theorem and its corollary show the relationship between concavity (convexity) of a function $f: \mathbb{R}^m \to \mathbb{R}$ and the Hessian matrix of second partials $[f_{ij}]$.

THEOREM: *Suppose f is twice continuously differentiable on the open convex set $X \subset \mathbb{R}^m$. Then f is a concave (convex) function over X if and only if the Hessian matrix $H = [f_{ij}]$ for f is negative semidefinite (positive semidefinite) at each point in X.*

COROLLARY: *Under the conditions of the theorem, if H is negative definite (positive definite) at each point in X, then f is strictly concave (strictly convex) over X.*

Note that the corollary is not an if-and-only-if statement.

EXAMPLE: $f: \mathbb{R}^1 \to \mathbb{R}^1$ given by $f(x) = -x^4$ is strictly concave over $\mathbb{R}^1$, but $H(x) = -12x^2$, so $H(0) = 0$, and H is not negative definite at 0.

Proof of the theorem: The proof for convexity of f is similar to the following proof for concavity.

1. Suppose f is concave. By Taylor's theorem

$$f(\mathbf{x}) = f(\mathbf{y}) + \nabla f(\mathbf{y}) \cdot (\mathbf{x} - \mathbf{y}) + (1/2)(\mathbf{x} - \mathbf{y})' H(\mathbf{y} + \theta(\mathbf{x} - \mathbf{y}))(\mathbf{x} - \mathbf{y})$$

for some $\theta \in [0, 1]$. By the first theorem of this section, $f(\mathbf{x}) \le f(\mathbf{y}) + \nabla f(\mathbf{y}) \cdot (\mathbf{x} - \mathbf{y})$. Therefore $(\mathbf{x} - \mathbf{y})' H(\mathbf{y} + \theta(\mathbf{x} - \mathbf{y}))(\mathbf{x} - \mathbf{y}) \le 0$ for all $\mathbf{x}, \mathbf{y} \in X$. Fix $\mathbf{y}$ and let $\mathbf{x} = \mathbf{y} + \varepsilon \mathbf{v}$ for a fixed (but arbitrary) $\mathbf{v}$. Then $\varepsilon^2 \mathbf{v}' H(\mathbf{y} + \theta(\varepsilon \mathbf{v})\varepsilon \mathbf{v})\mathbf{v} \le 0$, and letting $\varepsilon \to 0$, $\mathbf{v}' H(\mathbf{y})\mathbf{v} \le 0$. Since $\mathbf{v}$ is arbitrary, $H(\mathbf{y})$ is negative semidefinite. This holds for all $\mathbf{y} \in X$.

2. Suppose H is negative semidefinite over X. Let $\mathbf{x}, \mathbf{y} \in X$, and $\lambda \in [0, 1]$. Let $\mathbf{z} = \mathbf{y} + \lambda(\mathbf{x} - \mathbf{y})$ and $\mathbf{w} = \mathbf{x} - \mathbf{y}$, so $\mathbf{y} = \mathbf{z} - \lambda \mathbf{w}$ and $\mathbf{x} = \mathbf{y} + (1 - \lambda)\mathbf{w}$. By Taylor's theorem,

$$f(\mathbf{y}) = f(\mathbf{z}) - \lambda \nabla f(\mathbf{z}) \cdot \mathbf{w} + (1/2)\lambda^2 \mathbf{w}' H(\mathbf{z} - \theta_1 \lambda \mathbf{w})\mathbf{w}, \quad \text{and}$$

$$f(\mathbf{x}) = f(\mathbf{z}) + (1 - \lambda) \nabla f(\mathbf{z}) \cdot \mathbf{w} + (1/2)(1 - \lambda)^2 \mathbf{w}' H(\mathbf{z} + \theta_2(1 - \lambda)\mathbf{w})\mathbf{w}.$$

Taking a weighted sum of these expressions yields

$$\lambda f(\mathbf{x}) + (1 - \lambda)f(\mathbf{y}) = f(\mathbf{z}) + (1/2)\lambda(1 - \lambda)^2 \mathbf{w}' H(\mathbf{z} + \theta_2(1 - \lambda)\mathbf{w})\mathbf{w}$$

$$+ (1/2)\lambda^2(1 - \lambda)\mathbf{w}' H(\mathbf{z} - \theta_1 \lambda \mathbf{w})\mathbf{w}$$

$$\le f(\mathbf{z}) = f(\lambda \mathbf{x} + (1 - \lambda)\mathbf{y})$$

by H NSD.

Proof of the corollary: Follow the argument in (2) of the proof of the theorem, noting $\mathbf{w} \ne \mathbf{0}$ and $\lambda \in (0, 1)$, so H negative definite implies strict inequality in the last line of part 2.

Some additional useful facts about convex and concave functions are listed below.

1. *Jensen's inequality*: Let $f: \mathbb{R}^n \to \mathbb{R}$. Then f is convex if and only if for all integers $m \ge 1$, for all nonnegative $\lambda_1, \lambda_2, \ldots, \lambda_m$ that satisfy $\sum_{i=1}^m \lambda_i = 1$, for all $\mathbf{x}_1, \ldots, \mathbf{x}_m \in \mathbb{R}^n$,

$$f\left(\sum_{i=1}^m \lambda_i \mathbf{x}_i\right) \le \sum_{i=1}^m \lambda_i f(\mathbf{x}_i).$$

In words, the value of the function at a convex combination of points is less than or equal to the the convex combination of the values at the points.

A similar result with the inequality reversed holds for concave functions.

2. If $X \subset \mathbb{R}^n$ is convex and $f: X \to \mathbb{R}$ is concave (or convex) then f is continuous on the interior of X. Note f need not be continuous on the boundary of X. For example $f: [0, 1] \to \mathbb{R}$ defined by $f(x) = 1$ if $x \neq 0, 1$ and $f(0) = f(1) = 0$ is concave but not continuous at 0 or 1.

Concavity is often too strong an assumption. A weaker assumption is quasiconcavity.

DEFINITION: f is *quasiconcave* if for all $c \in \mathbb{R}$, $\{x | f(x) \geq c\}$ is convex, or equivalently, $f(\lambda x + (1 - \lambda)y) \geq$ minimum $\{f(x), f(y)\}$ for all $\lambda \in (0, 1)$. f is *strictly quasiconcave* if for all $x \neq y$, $f(\lambda x + (1 - \lambda)y) >$ minimum $\{f(x), f(y)\}$ for all $\lambda \in (0, 1)$.

Note that objective functions are often quasiconcave (e.g., a utility function). Also note that concavity implies quasiconcavity but not vice versa.

EXAMPLE: $f(x) = x^3 + x$ is quasiconcave (f is strictly increasing) but not concave ($f''(x) = 6x$, which is sometimes positive and sometimes negative).

DEFINITION: The *bordered Hessian* for the function f, evaluated at x, is

$$B(\mathbf{x}) = \begin{bmatrix} 0 & \dfrac{\partial f(\mathbf{x})}{\partial x_1} & \cdots & \dfrac{\partial f(\mathbf{x})}{\partial x_n} \\ \dfrac{\partial f(\mathbf{x})}{\partial x_1} & \dfrac{\partial^2 f(\mathbf{x})}{\partial x_1 \, \partial x_1} & \cdots & \dfrac{\partial^2 f(\mathbf{x})}{\partial x_1 \, \partial x_n} \\ \vdots & \vdots & & \vdots \\ \dfrac{\partial f(\mathbf{x})}{\partial x_n} & \dfrac{\partial^2 f(\mathbf{x})}{\partial x_n \, \partial x_1} & \cdots & \dfrac{\partial^2 f(\mathbf{x})}{\partial x_n \, \partial x_n} \end{bmatrix}.$$

The bordered Hessian is the regular Hessian (the matrix of second partials) with a "border" of first partials. Let $M_r(\mathbf{x})$ be the $r \times r$ upper left submatrix of the bordered Hessian $B(\mathbf{x})$.

PROPERTIES: The following properties of quasiconcave and concave functions will be useful.

1. f is quasiconcave if and only if $f(\mathbf{x}) - f(\mathbf{y}) \geq 0$ implies $\nabla f(\mathbf{y}) \cdot (\mathbf{x} - \mathbf{y}) \geq 0$. This property means that the *upper contour set* at $\mathbf{y}$, $\{\mathbf{x} | f(\mathbf{x}) \geq f(\mathbf{y})\}$, lies "above" the tangent plane to the level curve at $\mathbf{y}$, $\{\mathbf{x} | \nabla f(\mathbf{y}) \cdot (\mathbf{x} - \mathbf{y}) = 0\}$, where "above" means "in the direction $\nabla f(\mathbf{y})$."

2a. If the determinants of $M_r(\mathbf{x})$ satisfy $(-1)^{r+1} |M_r(\mathbf{x})| > 0$ for $r = 2, 3, \ldots, n + 1$, for all $\mathbf{x}$, then f is strictly quasiconcave.

2b. If f is quasiconcave on $\mathbb{R}^n_+$, then $(-1)^{r+1}|M_r(\mathbf{x})| \geq 0$ for $r = 2, 3, \ldots, n + 1$, for all $\mathbf{x} \in \mathbb{R}^n_+$.

3. If $f_1, \ldots, f_m$ are concave functions defined on the same convex domain, it is easy to see that for any nonnegative numbers $t_1, \ldots, t_m$ the sum $\Sigma t_i f_i$ is also a concave function. Quasiconcavity does not hold up under such addition of functions. For example, $f_1(x) = -2x$ and $f_2(x) = x^3 + x$ are both quasiconcave but their sum is not.

EXAMPLE: The function $f(x, y) = (x + 1)y$ is quasiconcave in the region $x \geq 0$, $y \geq 0$. The potential maximizer subject to the constraints $x \geq 0$, $y \geq 0$, and $x + y \leq \frac{1}{2}$ is $x^* = 0$, $y^* = \frac{1}{2}$. Thus the set of nonnegative (x, y) with $f(x, y) \geq \frac{1}{2}$ lies "above" the tangent plane $\nabla f(0, \frac{1}{2}) \cdot ((x, y) - (0, \frac{1}{2})) = 0$. This means that the solution to the first-order conditions is the unique global maximizer of f subject to the constraints.

In general, suppose the feasible set is convex and $\mathbf{x}^0$ satisfies the first-order conditions for maximizing f subject to the inequality constraints. If f is quasiconcave and $\nabla f(\mathbf{x}^0) \neq \mathbf{0}$, with f twice continuously differentiable near $\mathbf{x}^0$, then $\mathbf{x}^0$ is a global maximizer of f subject to the constraints.

When using the sign conditions on determinants to check for quasiconcavity (property 2a above), it is important to note that strict inequality is needed. For example, $f(x) = x^2$ is not quasiconcave ($\{x \in \mathbb{R} | f(x) \geq 1\} = (-\infty, -1] \cup [1, \infty)$, which is not a convex set), but

$$B(x) = \begin{bmatrix} 0 & 2x \\ 2x & 2 \end{bmatrix},$$

so $(-1)^{2+1}|M_r(x)| = 4x^2 \geq 0$ for all x with strict inequality everywhere except at $x = 0$. Failure of the strict inequality condition at just one point was enough to prevent quasiconcavity. For a continuously differentiable function $f: \mathbb{R} \to \mathbb{R}$, the sufficient condition (2a) is equivalent to $f'(x) \neq 0$ for all x. This guarantees f is either always decreasing or always increasing, so upper contour sets are always intervals.

To get a feeling for the relationship between quasiconcavity and convexity of upper contour sets, consider a production function $F: \mathbb{R}^2_+ \to \mathbb{R}$, $Y = F(K, L)$, with strictly positive marginal products everywhere ($F_K > 0$ and $F_L > 0$). For a fixed output level Y^0, we are interested in the function $L(K)$ specifying the amount of labor needed to get output Y^0 given capital level K, $Y^0 \equiv F(K, L(K))$. Differentiating the identity with respect to K,

$$0 \equiv F_K(K, L(K)) + F_L(K, L(K))L'(K), \tag{1}$$

or $L' = -F_K/F_L < 0$. Differentiating the identity in (1) with respect to K,

$$0 \equiv F_{KK} + F_{KL}L' + (F_{LK} + F_{LL}L')L' + F_L L''. \tag{2}$$

Substituting the value for L' determined in (1) into (2) and solving for L'',

$$L'' = (1/F_L)^3 \left(-F_L^2 F_{KK} + F_L F_K F_{KL} + F_L F_K F_{LK} - F_K^2 F_{LL} \right)$$

$$= (1/F_L)^3 \det \begin{bmatrix} 0 & F_K & F_L \\ F_K & F_{KK} & F_{KL} \\ F_L & F_{LK} & F_{LL} \end{bmatrix}$$

Thus $L'' > 0$ if and only if the determinant of the bordered Hessian is strictly positive or $L(K)$ is (differentiably) strictly convex if and only if F is (differentiably) strictly quasiconcave. The term "differentiably strictly convex (or quasiconcave)" means the appropriate determinants are nonzero, so the strict convexity (or quasiconcavity) can be determined from the Hessian (or bordered Hessian).

It is common in economic problems to impose concavity or quasiconcavity assumptions on the objective function (e.g., a utility function) and convexity assumptions on the feasible set [via concavity or quasiconcavity assumptions on the negative of the function g used in the constraint $g(\mathbf{x}) \leq 0$, e.g., the budget constraint]. However, the second-order conditions for optimization do not require quasiconcavity of the objective function, f, or convexity of the feasible set. The second-order conditions impose constraints on the curvature of level sets for f relative to the curvature of level sets for g. The absolute properties of $[f_{ij}(\mathbf{x})]$ (positive definite, negative definite, corresponding to a saddle pint, etc.) are unimportant. The properties of $[f_{ij}(\mathbf{x})]$ relative to $[g_j^i(\mathbf{x})]$ are important. Recall that $[f_{ij}(\mathbf{x})] - \lambda[g_j^i(\mathbf{x})]$ is a submatrix of the matrix used to check second-order conditions. The next two examples demonstrate that it is the relative curvature that matters.

EXAMPLE: $f(x, y) = -xy$ is not quasiconcave, but $(x, y) = (1, 1)$ maximizes $-xy$ subject to $(x - 1.1)^2 + (y - 1.1)^2 \leq 0.02$, because the feasible set is sharply curved relative to the level sets for f. See Figure 5.8, in which the feasible set is the shaded region.

EXAMPLE: The feasible set $\{(x, y)|xy \leq 1\}$ is not convex, but $(1, 1)$ maximizes $-(x - 1.1)^2 - (y - 1.1)^2$ subject to $xy \leq 1$, because the objective function level curves are sharply curved relative to the feasible set. See Figure 5.9, in which the feasible set is the shaded region.

Let us summarize our procedure for finding global solutions to optimization problems. We use first-order conditions (with $\lambda_0 = 1$ if constraint qualification conditions hold at all feasible points, otherwise with general λ_0) to find all possible finite solutions. At each potential solution, if strict complementary slackness holds and all determinants are nonzero in the check of second-order conditions, the potential solutions can be classified

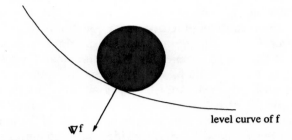

FIGURE 5.8   A maximum with a nonquasiconcave objective function.

as strict local maximizers, strict local minimizers, or neither maximizers nor minimizers. (If strict complementary slackness fails we must be more careful in determining binding constraints. If some determinants are zero, we may need to do additional work to determine whether the potential solution is a local optimizer.) To summarize what we know about finding global solutions:

1. If the feasible set is compact and the objective function is continuous, then the best of the local solutions is the global solution.

2. If the feasible set is convex and the objective function is concave, then any point satisfying the first-order conditions is a global maximizer. (If more than one point is a maximizer, then the set of maximizers is convex. For example, if we have a demand correspondence rather than a demand function, with concave utility the demand correspondence will be convex valued.) If the feasible set is convex and the objective function is strictly concave, then any point satisfying the first-order conditions is the unique global maximizer. (Similar conclusions hold for convex objective functions and minimizers.)

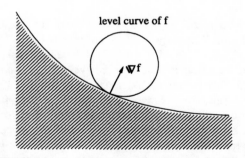

FIGURE 5.9   A maximum from a nonconvex feasible set.

3. If the feasible set is convex and the objective function is quasiconcave, then any point satisfying the first-order conditions [with $\nabla f \neq \mathbf{0}$] is a global maximizer. (If more than one point is a maximizer, then the set of maximizers is convex. For example, if we have a demand correspondence rather than a demand function, with quasiconcave utility the demand correspondence will be convex valued.) If, in addition, the feasible set is strictly convex or the objective function is strictly quasiconcave, then any point satisfying the first-order conditions (with $\nabla f \neq \mathbf{0}$) is the unique global maximizer. [To see we need $\nabla f \neq \mathbf{0}$, consider the problem of maximizing $f(x, y) = xy$ subject to $x \geq 0$, $y \geq 0$, and $x + y \leq 2$. The feasible set is convex and f is quasiconcave on $\mathbb{R}^2_+$. The first-order conditions hold at $(0, 0)$ with $\nabla f(0, 0) = \mathbf{0}$ but $(0, 0)$ is clearly not even a local maximizer.]

4. When the feasible set is closed but not bounded, if neither 2 nor 3 applies, we must consider sequences of feasible points. This is illustrated in the following two examples. Our procedure has identified all local optimizers but there may be a sequence of feasible points $(\mathbf{x}^t)$ such that for large t, $f(\mathbf{x}^t)$ exceeds the value at any local optimizer. Then there is no global optimizer. (Most economists never see a problem in which the feasible set is not closed. In such a problem it is sometimes possible to optimize over the closure of the feasible set and then compare feasible points to points outside the set, but in the closure.)

EXAMPLE: Maximize $-y + 1/x$ subject to $x \geq 3$ and $y \geq 1/x^2$. The only local maximizer is $(x^*, y^*) = (3, \frac{1}{9})$ with $-y^* + 1/x^* = 2/9$. The feasible set is convex, but the objective function is neither concave nor quasiconcave. To check whether $(3, \frac{1}{9})$ is the global maximizer we must check every unbounded feasible sequence. The objective function helps us decide which sequences are crucial to check. Note that for any fixed x, the y value yielding both a feasible point (x, y) and the largest possible value of the objective function is $y = 1/x^2$. This suggests the crucial sequence $(x^t, y^t) = (t, 1/t^2)$. Since $\lim_{t \to \infty} f(t, 1/t^2) = \lim_{t \to \infty}(1/t - 1/t^2) = 0 < f(3, \frac{1}{9})$, no sequence can lead to values exceeding $f(3, \frac{1}{9})$, and $(3, \frac{1}{9})$ is the unique global maximizer.

EXAMPLE: Maximize $-y + 1/x^2$ subject to $x \geq \frac{3}{2}$ and $-y + 25/(16(x^2 + 1)) \leq 0$. The only local maximizer is $(x^*, y^*) = (3/2, 25/52)$ with $-y^* + 1/x^{*2} = -(25/52) + (4/9) < 0$. The feasible set is convex, but the objective function is neither concave nor quasiconcave. To check whether $(3/2, 25/52)$ is the global maximizer we must check every unbounded feasible sequence. Once again the objective function helps us decide which sequences are crucial to check. Note that for any fixed x, the y value yielding both a feasible point (x, y) and the largest possible value of the objective function is $y = 25/(16(x^2 + 1))$. This suggests the crucial sequence $(x', y') = (t, 25/16(t^2 + 1))$. Since

$$\lim_{t \to \infty} f(t, 25/(16(x^2 + 1))) = \lim_{t \to \infty} \{(1/t^2) - 25/(16(t^2 + 1))\}$$

$$= 0 > f(3/2, 25/52),$$

this sequence dominates $(3/2, 25/52)$. Note that none of the (x', y') are local maximizers, since it is always better to increase x and adjust y accordingly. No finite point is the global maximizer, and there is no global solution for this problem.

5.11 DUALITY

Duality theory encompasses a wide variety of topics in optimization theory. Duality can be used to show, for example, that econometric estimation of production relationships can proceed via cost functions, because of the relationship between the class of production functions satisfying certain basic properties and the class of cost functions satisfying certain other basic properties. We will be interested here in only one simple example of a dual relationship, that between a certain pair of optimization problems. We will use this result in Chapter 7 (Section 7.7) to develop further relationships among functions derived in a consumer's problem. For a more in depth look at duality in consumer and producer theory, see, for example, Cornes (1992).

Let $f: \mathbb{R}^n \to \mathbb{R}$ and $g: \mathbb{R}^n \to \mathbb{R}$ be continuously differentiable functions with $\nabla f(\mathbf{x}) \neq \mathbf{0} \neq \nabla g(\mathbf{x})$ for all $\mathbf{x}$. Consider two optimization problems:

Maximize $f(\mathbf{x})$ subject to $g(\mathbf{x}) \leq c$, and (1)
Minimize $g(\mathbf{x})$ subject to $f(\mathbf{x}) \geq b$. (2)

THEOREM: (1) *has solution* $\mathbf{x}^*$ *with* $f(\mathbf{x}^*) = b^*$ *if and only if problem* (2) *with* $b = b^*$ *has solution* $\mathbf{x}^*$ *with* $g(\mathbf{x}^*) = c$.

Proof: Suppose (1) has solution $\mathbf{x}^*$ with $f(\mathbf{x}^*) = b^*$. Since $\nabla f(\mathbf{x}^*) \neq \mathbf{0}$, the constraint must be binding at $\mathbf{x}^*$, so $g(\mathbf{x}^*) = c$, and for any $\mathbf{x}'$ such that $g(\mathbf{x}') < c$, $f(\mathbf{x}') < b^*$. But this implies that $\mathbf{x}^*$ minimizes g subject to $f(\mathbf{x}) \geq b^*$.

By a similar argument, if $\mathbf{x}^*$ minimizes g subject to $f(\mathbf{x}) \geq b^*$ and $g(\mathbf{x}^*) = c$, then $f(\mathbf{x}^*) = b^*$ and $\mathbf{x}^*$ maximizes f subject to $g(\mathbf{x}) \leq c$.

EXAMPLE:

1. Maximize $x + y$ subject to $x^2 + y^2 \leq 2$. The solution is $x^* = y^* = 1$, with Lagrange multiplier $\lambda^* = 1/2$ and $x^* + y^* = 2$.

2. Minimize $x^2 + y^2$ subject to $x + y \geq 2$. The solution is $x^{**} = y^{**} = 1$, with Lagrange multiplier $\lambda^{**} = 2 = 1/\lambda^*$ ($\lambda^{**} = 1/\lambda^*$ is a general result) and $(x^{**})^2 + (y^{**})^2 = 2$.

5.12 HOMOGENEOUS AND HOMOTHETIC FUNCTIONS

In producer and consumer theory, production and utility functions are sometimes assumed to be homogeneous or homothetic. Many derived economic functions, such as demand or cost, must be homogeneous.

DEFINITION: Let f be defined on a set $S \subset \mathbb{R}^n$. Then f is *homogeneous of degree k* over S if $f(\lambda x) = \lambda^k f(x)$ for all $x \in S$ and $\lambda \in \mathbb{R}$ such that $\lambda x \in S$.

In economics, S is commonly $\mathbb{R}^n_+$ or $\mathbb{R}^n_{++}$. Derived economic functions are often homogeneous. For example, a consumer's demand functions are homogeneous of degree 0 in prices and income, while a competitive firm's cost function is homogeneous of degree 1 in input prices. The following theorems indicate some consequences of homogeneity.

EULER'S THEOREM: *If f is homogeneous of degree k over S and differentiable at* $x \in S$, *then* $x \cdot \nabla f(x) = kf(x)$.

Proof: Since $f(\lambda x) \equiv \lambda^k f(x)$, differentiating with respect to λ, $x \cdot \nabla f(\lambda x) = k\lambda^{k-1} f(x)$. Setting $\lambda = 1$ yields the desired result.

THEOREM: *If f is homogeneous of degree k over S, then the partials of f are homogeneous of degree k − 1 over S.*

Proof: Differentiating $f(\lambda x) \equiv \lambda^k f(x)$ with respect to x_i, $\lambda f_i(\lambda x) \equiv \lambda^k f_i(x)$. Dividing both sides by λ yields the desired result.

Note that if f is homogeneous of degree k, then $f_i(x)/f_j(x) = f_i(\lambda x)/f_j(\lambda x)$; i.e., the marginal rate of substitution is constant along any ray through the origin. Other nonhomogeneous functions also have constant marginal rates of substitution along all rays through the origin. A function with constant marginal rates of substitution along all rays through the origin is called a *homothetic* function. If h is a homothetic function, then $h(x) = h(y)$ if and only if $h(\lambda x) = h(\lambda y)$ for all $\lambda > 0$. The function h is homothetic if and only if it can be written as $h(x) = g(f(x))$, where f is homogeneous and g is a function from $\mathbb{R}$ to $\mathbb{R}$ (many definitions require f to be homogeneous of degree $k > 0$ and g to be monotonically increasing, since these conditions hold in economic problems).

EXAMPLE: Is $u(x, y) = xy + x^2y^2$ homogeneous or homothetic on $\mathbb{R}^2_{++}$? Since $u(\lambda x, \lambda y) = \lambda^2 xy + \lambda^4 x^2 y^2$, u is not homogeneous. Since

$$\frac{u_2(x, y)}{u_1(x, y)} = \frac{x + 2x^2y}{y + 2xy^2} = \frac{x(1 + 2xy)}{y(1 + 2xy)} = \frac{x}{y}$$

is constant along any ray through the origin, u is homothetic.

5.13 SEMICONTINUOUS FUNCTIONS

In some economic problems it is natural to deal with functions that are not continuous, but for which the discontinuities have particular properties. For example, a technology with an avoidable setup cost would yield a cost function that is discontinuous at output 0. The concepts of semicontinuity are often useful in such contexts. Let $\lim_{\varepsilon \downarrow 0}$ be the limit as ε approaches zero from above (i.e., ε is always positive).

DEFINITION: A function $f: X \to \mathbb{R}$ where $X \subset \mathbb{R}^n$ is *lower semicontinuous at* $\mathbf{x} \in X$ if $f(\mathbf{x}) = \lim_{\varepsilon \downarrow 0}(\inf\{f(\mathbf{y})|\ |\mathbf{x} - \mathbf{y}| \le \varepsilon\})$. If f is lower semicontinuous at each $\mathbf{x} \in X$, we say f is *lower semicontinuous*.

This means that for any sequence of points $\mathbf{x}_t$ converging to $\mathbf{x}$, $f(\mathbf{x}) \le \lim_{t \to \infty} f(\mathbf{x}_t)$. The preceding cost function example is lower semicontinuous at 0, since the cost of zero output is less than the cost of any positive output.

DEFINITION: A function $f: X \to \mathbb{R}$ where $X \subset \mathbb{R}^n$ is *upper semicontinuous at* $\mathbf{x} \in X$ if $f(\mathbf{x}) = \lim_{\varepsilon \downarrow 0}(\sup\{f(\mathbf{y})|\ |\mathbf{x} - \mathbf{y}| \le \varepsilon\})$. If f is upper semicontinuous at each $\mathbf{x} \in X$, we say f is *upper semicontinuous*.

This means that for any sequence of points $\mathbf{x}_t$ converging to $\mathbf{x}$, $f(\mathbf{x}) \ge \lim_{t \to \infty} f(\mathbf{x}_t)$. For example, $f: \mathbb{R} \to \mathbb{R}$ defined by $f(x) = 0$ for $x \ne 0$ and $f(0) = 1$ is upper semicontinuous at 0. An economically useful characterization of upper semicontinuity is that f is upper semicontinuous on the closed set X if and only if the upper contour set, $\{\mathbf{x} \in X | f(\mathbf{x}) \ge c\}$, is closed for all $c \in \mathbb{R}$. This definition is useful in consumer theory. If f is upper semicontinuous and S is a compact set, then there is an s in S such that $f(s) \ge f(x)$ for all x in S. (Upper semicontinuous functions attain a maximum, though not necessarily a minimum, on any compact set.) Thus upper semicontinuous utility functions can be used to do consumer theory. For some issues in consumer theory, such as the integrability problem (starting from a "demand function," how can we determine whether the "demand" could have been generated by utility maximizing behavior), upper semicontinuous rather than continuous utility functions are appropriate.

Note the different types of discontinuity allowed in lower and upper semicontinuity. Lower semicontinuity allows f to jump up discontinuously as we move from the point, while upper semicontinuity allows f to jump down discontinuously as we move from the point. Each type of semicontinuity prohibits the other type of jump. If a function is both upper and lower semicontinuous, then both types of jump are ruled out and the function is continuous.

Be careful to distinguish semicontinuity of functions from hemicontinuity of correspondences. This is especially tricky in older work, where "semicontinuity" is also used as the term for correspondences and some authors refer to correspondences as "multivalued functions."

PROBLEMS

5.1 Output (Y) is produced using two inputs (K and L) according to $Y = f(K, L) = 1 + (KL - 1)^{1/3}$.
   (a) What is the equation of the tangent plane to the production surface at the point corresponding to $K = 1$ and $L = 2$?
   (b) What is the equation of the tangent plane to the isoquant (level curve) corresponding to $Y \equiv 3$ at $(K, L) = (1, 9)$?
   (c) What is the marginal rate of substitution of L for K along the isoquant corresponding to $Y \equiv f(2, 1)$ at $(K, L) = (2, 1)$?
   (d) If, starting at $(K, L) = (2, 1)$, a tiny (marginal) amount of inputs could be added in any proportions [with $\|(\Delta K, \Delta L)\| = \varepsilon$], how many extra units of L should be added for each extra unit of K added in order to maximize the increase in output (i.e., what should the ratio $\Delta L/\Delta K$ be)?

5.2 Given $z = f(x, y, t) = ye^x + t^2$ where $x = g(y, t) = \ln(y + t)$ and $y = h(t) = t^3 - 9$ use the chain rule to find the total effect of a change in t on z, "dz/dt", at $t = 2$.

5.3 Output, Y, is produced using two inputs, K and L, according to $Y = f(K, L) = K^{1/4}L^{1/2}$.
   (a) What is the equation of the tangent plane to the production surface at $K = 16$ and $L = 9$?
   (b) What is the equation of the tangent plane to the level curve $Y \equiv f(1, 4)$ at $K = 1$ and $L = 4$?
   (c) What is the marginal rate of substitution of K for L along the isoquant $Y \equiv 3$ at $K = 1$ and $L = 9$?

5.4 A firm uses capital, K, and labor, L, to produce output, Y, according to $Y = K^\alpha L^\beta$ where α and β are positive constants.
   (a) What is the equation of the level curve corresponding to output one?
   (b) What is the equation of the tangent plane to the production surface at $K = L = Y = 1$?

   (c) What is the equation of the tangent "plane" to the level curve corresponding to $Y = 1$ at $K = L = 1$?

   (d) For small changes along the level curve, starting at $K = L = 1$, how many units of labor are needed to replace each unit of capital?

   (e) If it were possible to increase K and L slightly in any proportion so that $\|(\Delta K, \Delta L)\| = c$ where c is a very small positive number, what change in K and L would lead to the greatest increase in output?

5.5 s and t are independent variables and

$$r = m(s, t) = st,$$

$$y = h(s, t) = t + s(t - 1),$$

$$x = g(r, s) = rs + s^2,$$

$$z = g(x, y) = x^2 + y(x + 1).$$

Use the chain rule to find out how z changes when s changes at $s = t = 0$.

5.6 x and y are independent variables and

$$r = f(x, y) = x^2 + y^2,$$

$$s = g(x, y) = x - y,$$

$$t = h(x, r) = 2x + r^2,$$

$$z = m(s, t) = (s - 1)(t + 1).$$

Use the chain rule to find out how z changes when x changes at $x = y = 1$.

5.7 q and s are independent variables and

$$z = f(x, y) = xy,$$

$$x = g(s, t) = s^2 - t,$$

$$y = h(r, s) = sr^3,$$

$$t = m(r) = \frac{r^2}{2},$$

$$r = n(s, q) = \frac{s}{q}.$$

Use the chain rule to find out how z changes when s changes at $s = 2$ and $q = 1$.

5.8 For the region with $x > 0$ and $-x < y < x$ define f by $f(x, y) = x^2 - y^2$.
(a) Is f concave where defined?
(b) Is f quasiconcave where defined?

5.9 Given the utility function $u(x_1, x_2) = \sqrt{x_1} + \sqrt{x_2}$,
(a) Is it quasiconcave for $x_1 > 0$, $x_2 > 0$?
(b) Is it concave for $x_1 > 0$, $x_2 > 0$?

5.10 Show $f: \{(x, y) \in \mathbb{R}^2 | x \geq 0, y \geq 0\} \to \mathbb{R}$ defined by $f(x, y) = \sqrt{xy}$ is concave.

5.11 Is $f(x, y) = x^2 y^2$ concave and/or quasiconcave on $\{(x, y) \in \mathbb{R}^2 | x \geq 0, y \geq 0\}$? Is f concave and/or quasiconcave on $\mathbb{R}^2$?

5.12 In each of the following questions an optimization problem max or min $f(\mathbf{x})$ with inequality constraints $g^i(\mathbf{x}) \leq 0$ has been set up with Lagrangian $f(\mathbf{x}) - \sum \lambda_i g^i(\mathbf{x})$ and the first-order conditions have been solved to find the listed potential solution. Then the appropriate matrix of terms to check the second-order conditions (but evaluated at a general $(\mathbf{x}, \boldsymbol{\lambda})$ rather than $(\mathbf{x}^*, \boldsymbol{\lambda}^*)$) has been listed. In each case, given the potential solution and the second-order condition (SOC) matrix, what can be said about the optimality of the solution?
(a) $(\mathbf{x}^*, \lambda_1^*, \lambda_2^*) = (1, -1, -2, -2)$,

$$\left[L_{ij}^*(\mathbf{x}, \lambda_I) \right] = \begin{bmatrix} -1 & 0 & 1 & 0 \\ 0 & 2 & 0 & 1 \\ 1 & 0 & 0 & 0 \\ 0 & 1 & 0 & 0 \end{bmatrix}.$$

(b) $(\mathbf{x}^*, \lambda_1^*, \lambda_2^*) = (-4, 0, 1, 0, -2)$,

$$\left[L_{ij}^*(\mathbf{x}, \lambda_I) \right] = \begin{bmatrix} 3 & 0 & 0 & 0 \\ 0 & -x_1 & 0 & 1 \\ 0 & 0 & x_3 & -2 \\ 0 & 1 & -2 & 0 \end{bmatrix}.$$

(c) $(\mathbf{x}^*, \lambda_1^*, \lambda_2^*) = (4, -7, 0, 0)$,

$$\left[L_{ij}^*(\mathbf{x}, \lambda_I) \right] = \begin{bmatrix} 2 & 1 + x_1 \\ 1 + x_1 & (1 + x_1)^2 \end{bmatrix}.$$

5.13 Is $f(x, y) = e^{x+y}$ concave?

5.14 Is $f(x, y) = \ln(x + y)$ quasiconcave on the set of strictly positive x and y values?

5.15 (a) Is the function $f(x) = e^{-x^2}$ quasiconcave on $\mathbb{R}$?
(b) What is the largest interval on which f is concave?

5.16 True/False. If the function $f(x, y)$ is defined on $\mathbb{R}^2$ and quasiconcave on $\{(x, y) | x \geq 0\}$ and also quasiconcave on $\{(x, y) | x \leq 0\}$ then f is quasiconcave on $\mathbb{R}^2$.

5.17 True/False. If f is a strictly convex function, then f cannot be quasiconcave.

5.18 True/False. If $S \subset \mathbb{R}^2$ is an open set then $f(x, y) = x + y$ cannot have a global maximizer subject to $(x, y) \in S$.

5.19 True/False. If $S \subset \mathbb{R}^2$ is an open set and $f(x, y)$ is a continuous function then f cannot have a global maximizer subject to $(x, y) \in S$.

5.20 (a) Find all local maximizers for $-\sqrt{x + y}$ subject to $x \geq 0$ and $x^2 y \geq 108$.

(b) Find all global maximizers for the problem in (a) or show none exist. Explain.

5.21 Is $f(x, y, z) = \sqrt{x} + \sqrt{y} + z^2$ concave and/or quasiconcave on $\mathbb{R}^3_{++}$?

5.22 In each of the following questions, an optimization problem max or min $f(\mathbf{x})$ with inequality constraints $g^i(\mathbf{x}) \leq 0$ has been set up with Lagrangian $f(\mathbf{x}) - \Sigma \lambda_i g^i(\mathbf{x})$ and the first-order conditions have been solved to find the listed potential solution. Then the appropriate matrix of terms to check the second-order conditions [but evaluated at a general $(\mathbf{x}, \boldsymbol{\lambda})$, not $(\mathbf{x}^*, \boldsymbol{\lambda}^*)$] has been listed. In each case, given the potential solution and the SOC matrix, what can be said about the optimality of the potential solution?

(a) $(\mathbf{x}^*, \lambda_1^*, \lambda_2^*) = (2, 4, -1, 1, 0)$,

$$[L_{ij}^*(\mathbf{x}, \lambda_I)] = \begin{bmatrix} 2 & 0 & 0 & 0 \\ 0 & 2 & 0 & -1 \\ 0 & 0 & 1 & 0 \\ 0 & -1 & 0 & 0 \end{bmatrix}.$$

(b) $(\mathbf{x}^*, \lambda_1^*, \lambda_2^*) = (-2, 1, -3, -2, -1)$,

$$[L_{ij}^*(\mathbf{x}, \lambda_I)] = \begin{bmatrix} -x_1 & 0 & 0 & 0 & 0 \\ 0 & 2 & 0 & 0 & 1 \\ 0 & 0 & -1 & -1 & 0 \\ 0 & 0 & -1 & 0 & 0 \\ 0 & 1 & 0 & 0 & 0 \end{bmatrix}.$$

(c) $(\mathbf{x}^*, \lambda_1^*, \lambda_2^*) = (1, 1, 2, 0, 1)$,

$$[L_{ij}^*(\mathbf{x}, \lambda_I)] = \begin{bmatrix} x_1 & 0 & 0 & 0 \\ 0 & 2 & 0 & 1 \\ 0 & 0 & 1 & 0 \\ 0 & 1 & 0 & 0 \end{bmatrix}.$$

(d) $(\mathbf{x}^*, \lambda_1^*, \lambda_2^*) = (1, 1, 2, 0, 0)$,

$$[L_{ij}^*(\mathbf{x}, \lambda_I)] = \begin{bmatrix} 1 & 0 & 0 \\ 0 & 2 & 0 \\ 0 & 0 & (1 + x_1)^2 \end{bmatrix}.$$

(e) $(\mathbf{x}^*, \lambda_1^*, \lambda_2^*) = (1, 1, 2, 1, 0)$,

$$[L_{ij}^*(\mathbf{x}, \lambda_I)] = \begin{bmatrix} -1 & 0 & 0 & 0 \\ 0 & 2 & 0 & 1 \\ 0 & 0 & -1 & 0 \\ 0 & 1 & 0 & 0 \end{bmatrix}.$$

(f) $(\mathbf{x}^*, \lambda_1^*, \lambda_2^*) = (1, 1, 2, -1, -2)$,

$$[L_{ij}^*(\mathbf{x}, \lambda_I)] = \begin{bmatrix} -1 & 0 & 0 & 0 & 0 \\ 0 & 2 & 0 & 0 & 1 \\ 0 & 0 & -1 & 1 & 0 \\ 0 & 0 & 1 & 0 & 0 \\ 0 & 1 & 0 & 0 & 0 \end{bmatrix}.$$

(g) $(\mathbf{x}^*, \lambda_1^*, \lambda_2^*) = (1, 1, 2, 2)$,

$$[L_{ij}^*(\mathbf{x}, \lambda_I)] = \begin{bmatrix} 2 & 0 & 1 & 0 \\ 0 & 2 & 0 & 1 \\ 1 & 0 & 0 & 0 \\ 0 & 1 & 0 & 0 \end{bmatrix}.$$

5.23 True/False/Explain:
   (a) If the feasible set is bounded then any local maximizer is a global maximizer.
   (b) If the objective function is not quasiconcave and the feasible set is not convex, then no local maximizer can exist.
   (c) If the objective and constraint functions are all affine (i.e., of the form $a + \mathbf{b} \cdot \mathbf{x}$ for some a and $\mathbf{b}$) then any solution to the first-order conditions is a global optimizer.

5.24 Is $f(x, y) = x^2 y$ concave and/or quasiconcave on $\mathbb{R}_{++}^2$? Explain.

5.25 Let S be the feasible set for a maximization problem with objective function f. Decide whether the following statements are true or false and explain.
   (a) If f is concave and $\mathbf{x}^*$ satisfies all first-order conditions then $\mathbf{x}^*$ is a global maximizer of f.
   (b) If S is bounded then one of the local maximizers of f is the global maximizer.
   (c) If f is not quasiconcave then a solution to the first-order conditions cannot be a global maximizer.
   (d) If $S = \mathbb{R}_+^l$ and f is not concave we must check "directions toward ∞" to determine whether the best local maximizer is a global maximizer.

5.26 Minimize $x^2 + y^2 + z^2$ subject to $y \geq x + 4$ and $z \leq 2x + 5$.

5.27 Is $f(x, y, z) = x^2 + \ln(yz)$ concave or quasiconcave on $\mathbb{R}_{++}^3$?

6

NONLINEAR
PROGRAMMING
SUMMARY

6.1 INTRODUCTION

This chapter summarizes our results concerning constrained optimization problems by setting out a step-by-step solution procedure. The chapter can also be read as a "cookbook" introduction to nonlinear programming before reading the background material contained in previous chapters.

In order to make the procedure as simple as possible, we will transform all problems into a single format. It is important to realize that the problems may be set up in other formats (as minimization rather than maximization problems, with inequalities written as "≥ 0" rather than "≤ 0," with "$+\lambda$" rather than "$-\lambda$") but different formats may lead to different conditions on the signs of various terms. Until one is quite comfortable with these different (but equivalent) approaches, sign errors are common. Thus for the purposes of this summary we will consider only a single format into which any problem can be transformed.

The basic problem is to maximize or minimize the function $f(\mathbf{x})$ where $\mathbf{x} = (x_1, \ldots, x_n)$, subject to the inequality constraints $r^i(\mathbf{x}) \leq b^i$ (or $r^i(\mathbf{x}) \geq b^i$) for $i = 1, 2, \ldots, m$ and the equality constraints $s^j(\mathbf{x}) = c^j$ for $j = 1, 2, \ldots, k$. The values of m and/or k could be zero, in which case there would be no inequality and/or equality constraints. All functions are assumed differentiable as many times as needed.

Rather than dealing with the most general results, the procedure outlined in this chapter will focus on the results needed for the type of problems faced by 99% of economists. The second section of this chapter contains a step-by-step procedure for solving these problems. The third section contains solved examples to illustrate the procedure. A reader who has not yet read the previous chapters will probably find it useful to read through one or more of the solved examples in Section 6.3 along with the solution procedure of Section 6.2. The discussion of global solutions will probably not be understandable without having read Chapter 5. The final section contains a discussion of two alternative approaches to parts of the procedure. It also contains a discussion of three important (unstated) assumptions used in the standard procedure. These assumptions concern constraint qualification conditions, strict complementary slackness, and second-order condition matrices and are discussed more fully in Chapters 2 and 5.

6.2 SOLUTION PROCEDURE

Step A: Put the problem in standard form and set up the Lagrangian.

1. If the problem is one of minimizing $f(\mathbf{x})$, the equivalent problem of maximizing $-f(\mathbf{x})$ should be solved. Let $f^*(\mathbf{x})$ be the function to be maximized [i.e., $f^*(\mathbf{x}) \equiv f(\mathbf{x})$ if the original problem was maximization, while $f^*(\mathbf{x}) \equiv -f(\mathbf{x})$ if the original was minimization].

2. All inequality constraints should be written as $g^i(\mathbf{x}) \le 0$ [i.e., if the original constraint was $r^i(\mathbf{x}) \le b^i$, then $g^i(\mathbf{x}) = r^i(\mathbf{x}) - b^i$, while if the original was $r^i(\mathbf{x}) \ge b^i$, then $g^i(\mathbf{x}) = b^i - r^i(\mathbf{x})$]. The form " ≤ 0" is important. Inequality constraints of the form $b^{*i} \le r^i(\mathbf{x}) \le b^i$ should be treated as two constraints, $b^{*i} \le r^i(\mathbf{x})$ and $r^i(\mathbf{x}) \le b^i$, and transformed into $b^{*i} - r^i(\mathbf{x}) \le 0$ and $r^i(\mathbf{x}) - b^i \le 0$ (e.g., $0 \le x_i \le 1$ becomes $-x_i \le 0$ and $x_i - 1 \le 0$).

3. All equality constraints should be written as $h^j(\mathbf{x}) = 0$ [i.e., if the original constraint was $s^j(\mathbf{x}) = c^j$, then $h^j(\mathbf{x}) = c^j - s^j(\mathbf{x})$ or $h^j(\mathbf{x}) = s^j(\mathbf{x}) - c^j$].

4. For $\boldsymbol{\lambda} = (\lambda_1, \ldots, \lambda_m)$ and $\boldsymbol{\mu} = (\mu_1, \ldots, \mu_k)$ the Lagrangian is the function

$$L(\mathbf{x}, \boldsymbol{\lambda}, \boldsymbol{\mu}) = f^*(\mathbf{x}) - \sum_{i=1}^{m} \lambda_i g^i(\mathbf{x}) - \sum_{j=1}^{k} \mu_j h^j(\mathbf{x}).$$

The λ_i and μ_j are called multipliers or Lagrange multipliers. By construction, the $h^j(\mathbf{x})$ are equal to zero when the corresponding equality constraint holds, and the $g^i(\mathbf{x})$ are nonpositive when the corresponding inequality constraint holds.

Step B: Set up the first-order conditions.

(1) $$\frac{\partial L(\mathbf{x}, \boldsymbol{\lambda}, \boldsymbol{\mu})}{\partial x_t} = 0 \qquad\qquad \text{for } t = 1, 2, \ldots, n,$$

(2) $$\frac{\partial L(\mathbf{x}, \boldsymbol{\lambda}, \boldsymbol{\mu})}{\partial \lambda_i} \geq 0, \ \lambda_i \geq 0, \text{ and } \lambda_i \frac{\partial L(\mathbf{x}, \boldsymbol{\lambda}, \boldsymbol{\mu})}{\partial \lambda_i} = 0$$

$$\text{for } i = 1, 2, \ldots, m,$$

(3) $$\frac{\partial L(\mathbf{x}, \boldsymbol{\lambda}, \boldsymbol{\mu})}{\partial \mu_j} = 0 \qquad\qquad \text{for } j = 1, 2, \ldots, k.$$

These conditions are often called the Kuhn–Tucker conditions or the Karush–Kuhn–Tucker conditions.

Step C: Find all potential solutions.

We are looking for $(\mathbf{x}, \boldsymbol{\lambda}, \boldsymbol{\mu})$ at which all the conditions in step B are satisfied simultaneously. Because of the inequality conditions it is usually easiest to divide the problem up into the 2^m cases corresponding to $\lambda_i > 0$ or $\lambda_i = 0$ for each i. For example, with two inequality constraints we need to consider $2^2 = 4$ cases: $\lambda_1 = \lambda_2 = 0$; $\lambda_1 = 0$, $\lambda_2 > 0$; $\lambda_1 > 0$, $\lambda_2 = 0$; and $\lambda_1 > 0$, $\lambda_2 > 0$. For each case we need to find all solutions to the conditions in step B.

Note that $\lambda_i = 0$ does not imply $\partial L / \partial \lambda_i \neq 0$.

Step D: Check second-order conditions.

For each potential solution $(\mathbf{x}^*, \boldsymbol{\lambda}^*, \boldsymbol{\mu}^*)$ found in step C:

1. Find the active inequality constraints. Constraint i is active at $(\mathbf{x}^*, \boldsymbol{\lambda}^*, \boldsymbol{\mu}^*)$ if $g^i(\mathbf{x}^*) = 0$. Let I be the set of active constraints and $\boldsymbol{\lambda}_I$ be a vector with one component for each active constraint. For example, if there are three inequality constraints with only the first and third constraints active, if $\boldsymbol{\lambda}^* = (1, 0, 2)$, then $\boldsymbol{\lambda}_I = (1, 2)$. Note that inactive constraints must have a zero multiplier.

2. Rewrite the Lagrangian ignoring inactive constraints:

$$L^*(\mathbf{x}, \boldsymbol{\lambda}_I, \boldsymbol{\mu}) = f^*(\mathbf{x}) - \sum_{i \in I} \lambda_i g^i(\mathbf{x}) - \sum_{j=1}^{k} \mu_j h^j(\mathbf{x}).$$

3. Form the matrix of second partials of L^* where only the $\mathbf{x}, \lambda_I, \boldsymbol{\mu}$ variables are used. Let $s = k + \#\{i \in I\}$; i.e., s is the number of constraints written in L^*. Be sure to form the matrix consistently in terms of the order in which variables are listed in the rows and columns; i.e., $\partial^2 L^*/\partial x_t \, \partial \mu_j$ and $\partial^2 L^*/\partial \mu_j \, \partial x_t$ should appear symmetrically. To do this, first differentiate L^* in turn with respect to x_t, $t = 1, 2, \ldots, n$, λ_i, $i \in I$, and μ_j, $j = 1, 2, \ldots, k$ to form the gradient ∇L^*. Then differentiate each entry in the gradient with respect to the same $n + s$ variables, in the same order, to get an $(n + s) \times (n + s)$ matrix of second partials of L^*. Evaluate this matrix at $(\mathbf{x}^*, \lambda_I^*, \boldsymbol{\mu}^*)$ to get matrix H.

4. With H set up so that cross partials with respect to the λ_i and μ_j terms appear in the lower right of H, as described in step 3, let D_i be the determinant of the $(2s + i) \times (2s + i)$ lower right-hand submatrix of H for $i = 1, 2, \ldots, n - s$.

5. Check second-order conditions for a maximization problem: $(-1)^{s+i} D_i > 0$ for $i = 1, 2, \ldots, n - s$. Note that if $s = n$ there is no second-order condition to check. All potential solutions satisfying the second-order conditions are strict local maximizers of f^* subject to the constraints.

Step E: Find the global solution.

1. Is the objective function concave or quasiconcave with a convex feasible set? If so, a local maximizer is a global maximizer and we are done. If not, go on to the next steps.

2. Compare the values of $f^*(\mathbf{x})$ at all the potential solutions $\mathbf{x}^*$ satisfying the second-order conditions. If the feasible set is bounded (i.e., if there is some number K such that every $\mathbf{x}$ satisfying all the constraints has $\|\mathbf{x}\| < K$) and closed, then the best local maximizer is the global solution. If the feasible set is not closed and bounded, go on to the next step.

3. Check whether "∞" dominates the other potential solutions. [For example, $f(x) = x^3 - x^2$ has a local maximizer at $x = 0$, but $f(x) \to \infty$ as $x \to \infty$.] In order to do this we must check $f^*(\mathbf{x}')$ for any feasible sequence $(\mathbf{x}')_{t=1}^{\infty}$ such that the norm, $\|\mathbf{x}'\| = [\sum_{i=1}^{n} (x_i')^2]^{1/2} \to \infty$ as $t \to \infty$. If some feasible sequence with unbounded norm has (for large t) $f^*(\mathbf{x}')$ greater than the value $f^*(\mathbf{x}^*)$ at the best local maximizer, then f^* has no global maximizer subject to the constraints. [A similar step is necessary if the feasible set is not closed even if it is bounded. For example, $f(x) = x^3 - 3x$ has no global maximizer on the interval $[-3, 3)$.]

This solution procedure almost always works but it does use some (unstated) assumptions to rule out exceptional cases. This is discussed further in Section 6.4.

First-order conditions are

$$\frac{\partial L}{\partial x} = -2x + \lambda = 0, \tag{1C}$$

$$\frac{\partial L}{\partial y} = -2y + \lambda = 0, \tag{2C}$$

$$\frac{\partial L}{\partial z} = -2z + \lambda = 0, \tag{3C}$$

$$\frac{\partial L}{\partial \lambda} = x + y + z - 3 \geq 0, \qquad \lambda \geq 0, \lambda(x + y + z - 3) = 0. \tag{4C}$$

We need to check two cases corresponding to $\lambda = 0$ and $\lambda > 0$. When $\lambda = 0$, from (1C), (2C), and (3C), $x = y = z = 0$. But then $x + y + z - 3 < 0$, contrary to (4C). Thus there are no potential solutions for this case. When $\lambda > 0$, by (4C) $x + y + z + 3 = 0$. From (1C), (2C), and (3C) $x = y = z = \lambda/2$, so $3(\lambda/2) - 3 = 0$, or $\lambda = 2$ and $x = y = z = 1$. This is the only potential solution, $(1, 1, 1, 2)$.

The inequality constraint is binding at $(1, 1, 1, 2)$ so the relevant matrix of second partials is

$$\begin{bmatrix} -2 & 0 & 0 & 1 \\ 0 & -2 & 0 & 1 \\ 0 & 0 & -2 & 1 \\ 1 & 1 & 1 & 0 \end{bmatrix}.$$

$D_1 = 4$ and $D_2 = -12$, so $(-1)^{1+1}D_1 > 0$ and $(-1)^{1+2}D_2 > 0$, satisfying the second-order conditions. To find the global maximizer of f^*, first note that it is possible to find a sequence of feasible points with unbounded norm. For example, $x^t = (t, 1, 1)$ is feasible for $t = 2, \ldots$, and $\|x^t\| \to \infty$ as $t \to \infty$. However, $f^*(x) = -(\|x\|)^2$, so if $\|x\|$ is large, $f^*(x)$ is very negative and thus less than $f^*(1, 1, 1) = -3$. Hence the global maximizer is $(1, 1, 1)$. Returning to the original problem, $(1, 1, 1)$ is the global minimizer with value $f(1, 1, 1) = 3$.

(D) Maximize $y - x^2$ subject to $x \geq 0$, $y \geq 0$, and $y \leq 2x - 1$. Rewriting the last constraint as $1 - 2x + y \leq 0$, the Lagrangian is $L(x, y, \lambda_1, \lambda_2, \lambda_3) = y - x^2 - \lambda_1(-x) - \lambda_2(-y) - \lambda_3(1 - 2x + y)$.

First-order conditions are

$$\frac{\partial L}{\partial x} = -2x + \lambda_1 + 2\lambda_3 = 0, \tag{1D}$$

$$\frac{\partial L}{\partial y} = 1 + \lambda_2 - \lambda_3 = 0, \tag{2D}$$

$$\frac{\partial L}{\partial \lambda_1} = x \geq 0, \qquad \lambda_1 \geq 0, \lambda_1 x = 0, \tag{3D}$$

$$\frac{\partial L}{\partial \lambda_2} = y \geq 0, \qquad \lambda_2 \geq 0, \lambda_2 y = 0, \cdot \tag{4D}$$

$$\frac{\partial L}{\partial \lambda_3} = -1 + 2x - y \geq 0, \qquad \lambda_3 \geq 0, \lambda_3(-1 + 2x - y) = 0. \tag{5D}$$

There are $2^3 = 8$ cases to consider. However, some preliminary observations will eliminate several of the cases. From (2D) and $\lambda_2 \geq 0$ we see $\lambda_3 > 0$ (so by (5D), $-1 + 2x - y = 0$). Then from (1D) and $\lambda_1 \geq 0$ we see $x > 0$, so by (3D), $\lambda_1 = 0$. By (1D) and $\lambda_1 = 0$, $\lambda_3 = x = (1 + y)/2$. By (2D), $\lambda_2 = \lambda_3 - 1 = (y - 1)/2$. Thus $\lambda_2 = 0$ [if $\lambda_2 > 0$, then $y = 0$ by (4D), so $\lambda_2 = -1/2 < 0$, a contradiction]. The only potential solution has $\lambda_1 = \lambda_2 = 0$ and $\lambda_3 = x = 1$, so $y = 1$.

At $(1, 1, 0, 0, 1)$ the only active constraint is $-1 + 2x - y \geq 0$, so the appropriate Lagrangian for setting up second-order conditions is $L^*(x, y, \lambda_3) = y - x^2 - \lambda_3(1 - 2x + y)$. The corresponding matrix of second partials is

$$\begin{bmatrix} -2 & 0 & 2 \\ 0 & 0 & -1 \\ 2 & -1 & 0 \end{bmatrix}.$$

Here $n = 2$ and $s = 1$, so we need only check whether $(-1)^{1+1}D_1 > 0$. $D_1 = 2$, so the second-order condition is satisfied.

The feasible set is not bounded, but any feasible point satisfies $y \leq 2x - 1$, so y cannot be large unless x is also. But when x is large, $2x - 1 < x^2$; so whenever x or y is large, $y - x^2 < 0$. Thus $(1, 1)$ is the global maximizer with value 0.

(E) Maximize $x^2 + y^2$ subject to $x \geq 0$, $y \geq 0$, and $2x + y \leq 4$. Writing the constraints as $-x \leq 0$, $-y \leq 0$, and $-4 + 2x + y \leq 0$, the Lagrangian is $L(x, y, \lambda_1, \lambda_2, \lambda_3) = x^2 + y^2 - \lambda_1(-x) - \lambda_2(-y) - \lambda_3(-4 + 2x + y)$.

First-order conditions are

$$\frac{\partial L}{\partial x} = 2x + \lambda_1 - 2\lambda_3 = 0, \tag{1E}$$

$$\frac{\partial L}{\partial y} = 2y + \lambda_2 - \lambda_3 = 0, \tag{2E}$$

$$\frac{\partial L}{\partial \lambda_1} = x \geq 0, \qquad \lambda_1 \geq 0, \lambda_1 x = 0, \tag{3E}$$

$$\frac{\partial L}{\partial \lambda_2} = y \geq 0, \qquad \lambda_2 \geq 0, \lambda_2 y = 0, \tag{4E}$$

$$\frac{\partial L}{\partial \lambda_3} = 4 - 2x - y \geq 0, \qquad \lambda_3 \geq 0, \lambda_3(4 - 2x - y) = 0. \tag{5E}$$

There are $2^3 = 8$ cases to consider when looking for potential solutions.

Case 1: $\lambda_1 > 0$, $\lambda_2 = \lambda_3 = 0$. By (3E), $x = 0$. But then (1E) implies $\lambda_1 = 0$ contrary to $\lambda_1 > 0$, so there is no potential solution for this case.

Case 2: $\lambda_1 > 0$, $\lambda_2 > 0$, $\lambda_3 = 0$. By reasoning identical to that in case 1, there is no potential solution for this case.

Case 3: $\lambda_1 > 0$, $\lambda_2 = 0$, $\lambda_3 > 0$. By (3E) $x = 0$. By (1E), $\lambda_1 = 2\lambda_3$. By (5E), $y = 4$. By (2E), $\lambda_3 = 8$, so $\lambda_1 = 16$. $(x, y, \lambda_1, \lambda_2, \lambda_3) = (0, 4, 16, 0, 8)$ satisfies all first-order conditions and is a potential solution.

Case 4: $\lambda_1 > 0$, $\lambda_2 > 0$, $\lambda_3 > 0$. By (3E), $x = 0$, By (5E), $y = 4$. Then by (4E), $\lambda_2 = 0$, contrary to $\lambda_2 > 0$. Thus there are no potential solutions for this case.

Case 5: $\lambda_1 = \lambda_2 = \lambda_3 = 0$. By (1E), $x = 0$. By (2E), $y = 0$. $(0, 0, 0, 0, 0)$ is a potential solution.

Case 6: $\lambda_1 = 0$, $\lambda_2 > 0$, $\lambda_3 = 0$. By (4E), $y = 0$. By (2E), $\lambda_3 = \lambda_2 > 0$ contrary to $\lambda_3 = 0$. Thus there is no potential solution for this case.

Case 7: $\lambda_1 = \lambda_2 = 0$, $\lambda_3 > 0$. We have three equations

$$2x - 2\lambda_3 = 0, \tag{1E'}$$

$$2y - \lambda_3 = 0, \tag{2E'}$$

$$4 - 2x - y = 0. \tag{5E'}$$

Solving, we get $(8/5, 4/5, 0, 0, 8/5)$ as a potential solution.

Case 8: $\lambda_1 = 0$, $\lambda_2 > 0$, $\lambda_3 > 0$. By (4E), $y = 0$. By (5E), $x = 2$. By (1E), $\lambda_3 = 2$. By (2E), $\lambda_2 = 2$. Another potential solution is $(2, 0, 0, 2, 2)$.

We have four potential solutions to check. Start with $(0, 4, 16, 0, 8)$. Here the $y \geq 0$ constraint is not binding, so the appropriate Lagrangian is $L^*(x, y, \lambda_1, \lambda_3) = x^2 + y^2 - \lambda_1(-x) - \lambda_3(-4 + 2x + y)$ and the matrix of second partials is

$$\begin{bmatrix} 2 & 0 & 1 & -2 \\ 0 & 2 & 0 & -1 \\ 1 & 0 & 0 & 0 \\ -2 & -1 & 0 & 0 \end{bmatrix}.$$

However, with $n = 2$ and $s = 2$ there are no determinants to check, so this is a local maximizer.

Another potential solution is $(2, 0, 0, 2, 2)$. The appropriate Lagrangian here is $L^*(x, y, \lambda_2, \lambda_3) = x^2 + y^2 - \lambda_2(-y) - \lambda_3(-4 + 2x + y)$, but again $n = s$, and there are no determinants to check. This is a local maximizer.

For the third potential solution, $(8/5, 4/5, 0, 0, 8/5)$ the appropriate Lagrangian is $L^*(x, y, \lambda_3) = x^2 + y^2 - \lambda_3(-4 + 2x + y)$, and the matrix of second partials is

$$\begin{bmatrix} 2 & 0 & -2 \\ 0 & 2 & -1 \\ -2 & -1 & 0 \end{bmatrix}.$$

$D_1 = -10$, so $(-1)^{1+1}D_1 < 0$, and this point fails the second-order condition.

[The last potential solution, $(0, 0, 0, 0, 0)$, has two active constraints: $x = 0$ and $y = 0$. However, the corresponding multipliers are also zero. This fails one of our unstated assumptions. It is clearly not a maximizer even though $n = s$. This will be discussed further in Section 6.4.]

To find the global solution, observe that the feasible set is bounded so "∞" is not feasible. Comparing the value of $x^2 + y^2$ at the two local maximizers, we see $(0, 4)$ is the global maximizer with value 16.

(F) Maximize $6x + y$ subject to $y \geq 0$ and $y \leq x^3 - 3x$. Rewriting the constraints as $-y \leq 0$ and $y - x^3 + 3x \leq 0$, the Lagrangian is $L(x, y, \lambda_1, \lambda_2) = 6x + y - \lambda_1(-y) - \lambda_2(y - x^3 + 3x)$.

First-order conditions are

$$\frac{\partial L}{\partial x} = 6 - \lambda_2(-3x^2 + 3) = 0, \tag{1F}$$

$$\frac{\partial L}{\partial y} = 1 + \lambda_1 - \lambda_2 = 0, \tag{2F}$$

$$\frac{\partial L}{\partial \lambda_1} = y \geq 0, \qquad \lambda_1 \geq 0, \lambda_1 y = 0, \tag{3F}$$

$$\frac{\partial L}{\partial \lambda_2} = -y + x^3 - 3x \geq 0, \qquad \lambda_2 \geq 0, \lambda_2(-y + x^3 - 3x) = 0. \tag{4F}$$

By (1F), λ_2 cannot be zero. If $\lambda_1 = 0$, then $\lambda_2 = 1$ (by (2F)) so $x = \pm\sqrt{-1}$, which is not feasible in our domain. Thus both multipliers must be strictly positive. By (3F), $y = 0$ and thus by (4F), $x^3 - 3x = 0$, with potential values $x = 0, \pm\sqrt{3}$. The values $\pm\sqrt{3}$ are not consistent with (1F) and $\lambda_2 \geq 0$. Solving (1F) and (2F) for $x = 0$, the only potential solution has $x = 0$, $y = 0$, $\lambda_1 = 1$, and $\lambda_2 = 2$.

At $(0, 0, 1, 2)$ both constraints are active, so the appropriate Lagrangian for setting up second-order conditions is the original Lagrangian. With $n = 2 = s$ there are no second-order conditions to check, so $(0, 0)$ is a strict local maximizer.

To check for the global maximizer, note that the feasible region is not bounded. Any (x, y) with $\sqrt{3} \leq x$ and $0 \leq y \leq x^3 - 3x$ is feasible. In particular, $(x', y') = (t\sqrt{3}, 0)$ is feasible for $t = 1, 2, \ldots$ and $f(x', y') = 6t\sqrt{3} \to \infty$ as $t \to \infty$. Arbitrarily large values of f can be obtained at feasible points, and there is no global maximizer for f.

This example has a local maximizer but not a global maximizer. It is also possible to have examples with no local or global maximizers. For the problem of maximizing $f(x, y) = x$ subject to $y \geq 0$, $y \leq x$, and $xy \leq 1$, for any feasible point (x^0, y^0), for any $\varepsilon > 0$ the point $(x^0 + \varepsilon, x^0 y^0 / (x^0 + \varepsilon))$ is also feasible and attains a higher value for f. Thus there is no local or global maximizer.

(G) When solving problems with inequality constraints, it is important to check both the second-order conditions and the sign condition on λ. When maximizing xy subject to $2 - x - y \leq 0$, $(x, y, \lambda) = (1, 1, -1)$ satisfies the second-order condition and all first-order conditions except the sign condition on λ. The sign condition on λ fails and $x = y = 1$ is not even a local maximizer subject to the constraint: for any $\varepsilon > 0$, $x = y = 1 + \varepsilon$ is feasible and better than $x = y = 1$.

6.4 ALTERNATIVE PROCEDURES AND TACIT ASSUMPTIONS

In this section we discuss two alternative approaches to parts of the optimization procedure and three important tacit assumptions made in the standard procedure. The alternative approaches involve the arrangement of the second-order condition matrix and the handling of nonnegativity constraints in the Lagrangian and first-order conditions. They are examined in Sections 6.4.1 and 6.4.2, respectively.

Our procedure makes three important (unstated) assumptions concerning constraint qualification conditions, strict complementary slackness, and second-order condition matrices. These issues are discussed in Sections 6.4.3, 6.4.4, and 6.4.5, respectively. They are also discussed more completely in Chapters 2 and 5. Most economists rarely encounter these issues, but one should at least be aware of the potential problems.

6.4.1 Second-Order Condition Matrices

In some texts the order of differentiation in part 3 of step D of the procedure is reversed. The only crucial features are the following.

1. The order of variables with respect to which the partial derivatives are taken must be the same in the first step (getting ∇L^*) as in the second step (getting H). This guarantees that $\partial^2 L^* / \partial(z) \partial(w)$ and $\partial^2 L^* / \partial(w) \partial(z)$ appear symmetrically in H where (z) and (w) represent any of the x_i, λ_i, or μ_j terms.

2. The partials with respect to the x_i should all be taken either first or last. This guarantees that second partials of the form $\partial^2 L^* / \partial x_i \partial x_r$ all appear together as an $n \times n$ submatrix in the upper left or lower right corner of H.

3. The D_i should be taken as the determinant of the $(2s + i) \times (2s + i)$ submatrix "opposite" the matrix described in 2. Thus if $[\partial^2 L^* / \partial x_i \partial x_r]$ is in the upper left of the matrix, D_i should be taken using the lower right of the matrix, and vice versa.

6.4.2 Nonnegativity Constraints

Sometimes nonnegativity constraints ($x_i \geq 0$) are handled differently in terms of the way the first-order conditions are written. We will first examine this alternative approach in a simple problem with nonnegativity constraints only. Then we will examine a general optimization problem including nonnegativity constraints.

Consider the problem: Maximize $f(\mathbf{x})$ subject to $x_i \geq 0$, $i = 1, 2, \ldots, n$. Our procedure is to write the Lagrangian $L(\mathbf{x}, \boldsymbol{\lambda}) = f(\mathbf{x}) - \sum_{i=1}^{n} \lambda_i(-x_i)$ and set up the first-order conditions:

$$\frac{\partial L}{\partial x_t} = \frac{\partial f}{\partial x_t} + \lambda_t = 0, \qquad t = 1, \ldots, n,$$

$$\frac{\partial L}{\partial \lambda_i} = x_i \geq 0, \qquad \lambda_i \geq 0, \lambda_i x_i = 0, \quad i = 1, 2, \ldots, n.$$

Each λ_i is nonnegative, so $\partial f / \partial x_t \leq 0$. Each $\partial f / \partial x_t = -\lambda_t$, so $x_t \, \partial f / \partial x_t = -x_t \lambda_t = 0$. Using these results, the first-order conditions are sometimes written as $\partial f / \partial x_t \leq 0$, $t = 1, 2, \ldots, n$; $x_t \geq 0$, $t = 1, 2, \ldots, n$, and $\sum_{t=1}^{n} x_t \, \partial f / \partial x_t = 0$. In order to remember these first-order conditions, the Lagrangian is written as $\overline{L}(\mathbf{x}) = f(\mathbf{x})$, ignoring the nonnegativity constraints. The first-order conditions are then written as

$$\frac{\partial \overline{L}}{\partial x_t} \leq 0, \qquad t = 1, 2, \ldots, n,$$

$$x_t \geq 0, \qquad t = 1, \ldots, n,$$

$$\sum_{t=1}^{n} x_t \frac{\partial \overline{L}}{\partial x_t} = 0.$$

For the general problem of maximizing $f(\mathbf{x})$ subject to $g^i(\mathbf{x}) \leq 0$, $i = 1, \ldots, m$, $h^j(\mathbf{x}) = 0$, $j = 1, \ldots, k$, and $x_t \geq 0$, $t = 1, \ldots, n$, this alternative procedure writes the Lagrangian as

$$\overline{L}(\mathbf{x}, \boldsymbol{\lambda}, \boldsymbol{\mu}) = f(\mathbf{x}) - \sum_{i=1}^{m} \lambda_i g^i(\mathbf{x}) - \sum_{j=1}^{k} \mu_j h^j(\mathbf{x})$$

without including any terms for the nonnegativity constraints. The first-order conditions are (a), (b), and (c) listed below.

(a)
$$\frac{\partial \overline{L}}{\partial x_t} \leq 0, \qquad t = 1, \ldots, n,$$

$$x_t \geq 0, \qquad t = 1, \ldots, n,$$

$$x_t \frac{\partial \overline{L}}{\partial x_t} = 0, \qquad t = 1, \ldots, n.$$

The last set of conditions is sometimes written $\sum_{t=1}^{n} x_t \, \partial L / \partial x_t = 0$.

(b) $\quad \dfrac{\partial \overline{L}}{\partial \lambda_i} \geq 0, \; \lambda_i \geq 0 \quad$ and $\quad \lambda_i \dfrac{\partial \overline{L}}{\partial \lambda_i} = 0, \qquad i = 1, \ldots, m,$

(c) $\quad \dfrac{\partial \overline{L}}{\partial \mu_j} = 0, \qquad\qquad\qquad\qquad j = 1, \ldots, k.$

These differ from the first-order conditions in step B of the standard procedure in exactly the same manner as the previous example. Compared to the Lagrangian, L, for our original procedure, $\overline{L}$ does not list the constraint for $x_t \geq 0$ while L does, so $\partial \overline{L} / \partial x_t \leq 0$ while $\partial L / \partial x_t = 0$. The difference between $\partial L / \partial x_t$ and $\partial \overline{L} / \partial x_t$ is exactly the multiplier corresponding to the $x_t \geq 0$ constraint. All other first-order conditions are identical in the two procedures.

The only crucial issues here are

1. When reading a solution, be sure to check the Lagrangian to see if all nonnegativity constraints have been included. This will determine whether $\partial L / \partial x_t \leq 0$ or $\partial L / \partial x_t = 0$ is the appropriate condition.

2. When setting up a problem, be sure to do it consistently, using the same procedure to set up the Lagrangian as to find the first-order conditions.

3. To check second-order conditions, active nonnegativity constraints must be put back into the Lagrangian to form L^*.

For example, to maximize $-(x + 1)(y + 1)$ subject to $x \geq 0$ and $y \geq 0$ the alternative procedure has Lagrangian $\overline{L}(x, y) = -(x + 1)(y + 1)$ and first order-conditions

$$\frac{\partial \overline{L}}{\partial x} = -y - 1 \leq 0, \qquad x \geq 0, \; x(-y - 1) = 0,$$

$$\frac{\partial \overline{L}}{\partial y} = -x - 1 \leq 0, \qquad y \geq 0, \; y(-x - 1) = 0.$$

Checking all four cases (two variables, each either zero or strictly positive), there is only one potential solution, $(0, 0)$. To check the second-order conditions, if we do not put the nonnegativity constraints into L^*, we set $L^* = \overline{L}$, and the second-order condition matrix is

$$\begin{bmatrix} 0 & -1 \\ -1 & 0 \end{bmatrix}.$$

Then $(-1)^{0+2} D_2 = -1 < 0$ and the second-order condition seems to fail.

However, to complete the procedure correctly, we add in the constraints. Then $n = 2$ and $s = 2$, so no determinants need to be checked, and the potential solution is a local maximizer. (Note there would be a different L^* and second-order condition matrix with the two constraints added.) It is the global maximizer since $f \to -\infty$ as either x or $y \to \infty$.

6.4.3 Constraint Qualification Conditions

Consider the problem: maximize $10x + y$ subject to $x \geq 0$, $y \geq 0$, and $(x - 1)^3 + y \leq 0$. The Lagrangian is

$$L(x, y, \lambda_1, \lambda_2, \lambda_3) = 10x + y - \lambda_1(-x) - \lambda_2(-y) - \lambda_3\big((x - 1)^3 + y\big).$$

First-order conditions are

$$\frac{\partial L}{\partial x} = 10 + \lambda_1 - \lambda_3 3(x - 1)^2 = 0, \tag{1}$$

$$\frac{\partial L}{\partial y} = 1 + \lambda_2 - \lambda_3 = 0, \tag{2}$$

$$\frac{\partial L}{\partial \lambda_1} = x \geq 0, \qquad\qquad \lambda_1 \geq 0, \lambda_1 x = 0, \tag{3}$$

$$\frac{\partial L}{\partial \lambda_2} = y \geq 0, \qquad\qquad \lambda_2 \geq 0, \lambda_2 y = 0, \tag{4}$$

$$\frac{\partial L}{\partial \lambda_3} = -(x - 1)^3 - y \geq 0, \qquad \lambda_3 \geq 0, \lambda_3\big(-(x - 1)^3 - y\big) = 0. \tag{5}$$

By (2), $\lambda_3 = 1 + \lambda_2 > 0$, so $y = -(x - 1)^3$ by (5). If $\lambda_1 > 0$, then $x = 0$ by (3), so $y = 1$, and $\lambda_2 = 0$ by (4), so $\lambda_3 = 1$ by (2). But then (1) cannot hold, so λ_1 cannot be strictly positive. If $\lambda_2 > 0$, then $y = 0$ by (4), so $x = 1$ and (1) cannot hold. The only remaining case is $\lambda_1 = \lambda_2 = 0$, $\lambda_3 > 0$. By (2), $\lambda_3 = 1$, so by (1), $x = 1 \pm \sqrt{10/3}$. Neither of these values is feasible since either $x < 0$ or $y = -(x - 1)^3 < 0$. We have tried all cases and found no potential solutions.

Inspection of the feasible set reveals that there is a global maximizer at $(1, 0)$. Why did our procedure fail to find it? The problem is a failure of constraint qualification conditions. The simplest, easiest to check, but far from most general constraint qualification condition is the linear independence condition. This requires that at each feasible point, the gradients of the active constraint functions at that point are linearly independent. In our example this condition fails at the maximizer. The active constraints at

$(1,0)$ are $-y \leq 0$ and $(x - 1)^3 + y \leq 0$. The constraint functions are $g^1(x, y) = -y$ and $g^2(x, y) = (x - 1)^3 + y$ with gradients $(0, -1)$ and $(0, 1)$, respectively, evaluated at $(1,0)$. The gradients are not linearly independent.

In the procedure outlined in this chapter, we have tacitly been making a constraint qualification assumption such as "at each feasible point, the gradients of the active constraint functions at that point are linearly independent."

The procedure can be modified to remove this assumption. This is done by adding an additional multiplier, λ_0, to the objective function to make the first term in the Lagrangian $\lambda_0 f(x)$. For any maximizer $\mathbf{x}^*$ there are $\lambda_0^*, \ldots, \lambda_m^*$, and $\mu_1^*, \ldots, \mu_k^*$, not all zero, such that

$$\lambda_0^* \, \nabla f(\mathbf{x}^*) - \sum_{i=1}^{m} \lambda_i^* \, \nabla g^i(\mathbf{x}^*) - \sum_{j=1}^{k} \mu_j^* \, \nabla h^j(\mathbf{x}^*) = 0$$

(i.e., the first n first-order conditions hold) and the other conditions are satisfied. With this set of modified first-order conditions, in step C, when we find all potential solutions, we will identify all feasible points at which our linear independence assumption fails, as well as all potential solutions our original procedure would find. At any one of these points where our linear independence assumption holds, λ_0 may be set equal to one. At any one of these points where our linear independence assumption fails, we may be unable to find any λ_0 other than zero (so the first-order conditions of our original procedure do not hold).

6.4.4 Strict Complementary Slackness

The complementary slackness conditions for an inequality constraint $[\lambda_i \, \partial L(\mathbf{x}, \boldsymbol{\lambda}, \boldsymbol{\mu})/\partial \lambda_i = \lambda_i g^i(\mathbf{x}) = 0$ for $i = 1, 2, \ldots, m]$ require that either the constraint be satisfied as an equality or the corresponding multiplier be zero. The possibility that both conditions hold simultaneously is allowed. When both conditions hold for one of the constraints at a potential solution, our second-order condition procedure may need to be modified. The problem is in deciding whether to include the constraint in the modified Lagrangian, L^*. In the sense used in our procedure $[g^i(\mathbf{x}) = 0]$ the constraint is active. In another sense not used in our procedure $(\lambda_i = 0)$ it is inactive. Additional work is necessary to decide whether it should be included in L^*. This problem does not arise if a potential solution satisfies strict complementary slackness, which requires that exactly one of the two conditions holds for each inequality constraint.

In example E of Section 6.3, one potential solution, $(0, 0, 0, 0, 0)$, seemed to be a local maximizer based on our procedure but clearly was not when we looked back at the problem. The difficulty here is that the two active constraints, $x \geq 0$ and $y \geq 0$, both have zero as multipliers, so strict complementary slackness fails. When this happens, our procedure of including all active constraints when defining L^* to form the second-order condition matrix may be in error. More careful scrutiny is needed. In example E of Section 6.3 neither constraint should have been included. On the other hand, for the problem of maximizing $x^2 - y^2$ subject to $y \geq 2x$ and $y \geq -2x$, the only potential solution, $(0, 0, 0, 0)$, fails the strict complementary slackness condition but is a global maximizer, and the constraints cannot be dropped from L^* without yielding an incorrect conclusion from the second-order condition test. This difficulty may arise whenever any of the active constraints has a multiplier equal to zero.

In checking strict complementary slackness we must be careful to check each multiplier with the correct corresponding constraint. Strict complementary slackness can be satisfied with $\lambda_1 = 0 = x$ if $x \geq 0$ ($x \leq 0$) is not the constraint corresponding to λ_1. When strict complementary slackness fails, we must do additional work not specified in the original procedure in order to determine the proper L^* for checking second-order conditions.

6.4.5 Semidefinite Matrices

Our second-order conditions required nonzero determinants. A potential solution might be a maximizer even though some of the determinants are zero. This is discussed in more detail in the quadratic form section of Chapter 2. In any case, if D_i has the wrong sign (e.g., $D_i < 0$ when it should be $D_i > 0$), the potential solution is not a maximizer. If our second-order conditions (and strict complementary slackness) hold at a potential solution, then that potential solution is a strict local maximizer; i.e., no nearby feasible point is better or even as good.

PROBLEMS

There are two types of problems in this chapter. Problems 6.1–6.26 require solution of an entire optimization problem. Problems 6.27–6.36 involve individual steps in the standard procedure developed in this chapter. Readers who have not yet covered the previous chapters may want to try Problems 6.27–6.36 first.

6.1 Find all local maxima and minima of $f(x, y, z) = x^2 + x(z - 2) + 3(y - 1)^2 + z^2$.

6.2 Find all local and global maxima and minima of $f(x) = x^3 - 6x^2 + 9x + 1$ subject to $x \geq -1$.

6.3 Maximize xy subject to $x + y = 1$.

6.4 Minimize $x^2 + y^2$ subject to $x + 2y = 3$.

6.5 Minimize $x^2 + y^2 + z^2$ subject to $2x + 2y + 2z = 1$.

6.6 Maximize $x + y$ subject to $2x^2 + y^2 \leq 54$.

6.7 Maximize $x - y$ subject to $3x^2 + 2y^2 \leq 30$.

6.8 Maximize $2x + y$ subject to $x \geq 0$, $y \geq 0$, and $(x + 1)(y + 1) = 9/2$.

6.9 Maximize $x - y$ subject to $3x^2 + 2y^2 = 1$.

6.10 Maximize $(x + 1)^2 + (y - 1)^2$ subject to $x \geq 0$, $y \geq 0$ and $2x + y \leq 4$.

6.11 Minimize $x + y$ subject to $x \geq 0$, $y \geq 0$, and $(x + 1)(y + 1) \geq 2$.

6.12 Minimize $4K + 2L$ subject to $KL = 1$, $K \geq 0$.

6.13 Minimize $(x + 1)^2 + (y - 1)^2$ subject to $x \geq 0$, $y \geq 0$ and $2x + y \leq 4$.

6.14 Minimize $2x + y$ subject to $x \geq 0$, $y \geq 0$, and $(x + 1)(y + 1) \geq 2$.

6.15 Minimize $x^2 + y^2$ subject to $x + 2y = 3$.

6.16 Maximize xy subject to $x \geq 0$, $y \geq 0$, and $2x + y \leq 4$.

6.17 Minimize $3x + y$ subject to $x \geq 0$, $y \geq 0$, $(x + 1)(y + 1) = 2$.

6.18 Minimize $(x - 1)^2 + (y - 1)^2 + (z - 2)^2$ subject to $x + y + z = 2$.

6.19 Maximize $(3 - x)(5 - y)$ subject to $x \geq 0$, $y \geq 0$, and $2x + y \leq 4$.

6.20 Minimize $(x - 2)^2 + (y - 2)^2 + (z - 2)^2$ subject to $x + y + z = 2$ and $x \geq 0$, $y \geq 0$, $z \geq 0$.

6.21 Minimize $x^2 + (y - 5)^2$ subject to $x \geq 0$, $y \geq 0$, and $2x + y \leq 4$.

6.22 Maximize $x - y + z$ subject to $x^2 + y^2 + z^2 = 2$ and $x \geq 0$, $y \geq 0$, and $z \geq 0$.

6.23 Maximize $x^2 + (y - 5)^2$ subject to $x \geq 0$, $y \geq 0$, and $2x + y \leq 4$.

6.24 Minimize $f(x, y) = y$ subject to $x \geq 2$ and $(x^3)/3 - x = y$.

6.25 Minimize $x^2 + 2y^2 + 3z^2$ subject to $3x + 2y + z \geq 17$.

6.26 Minimize $x^2 + y^2$ subject to $x + y \leq -2$ and $x \geq -3$.

6.27 For the problem of maximizing $3x^2 + y^2 + 8z^2$ subject to $x \geq 0$, $y \geq 0$, $z \geq 0$ and $2x + y + 3z \leq 1$, with Lagrangian in standard form and λ_i corresponding to the ith constraint, $(x^*, y^*, z^*, \lambda_1^*, \lambda_2^*, \lambda_3^*, \lambda_4^*) = (0, 1, 0, 4, 0, 6, 2)$ is a potential solution (i.e., satisfies all first-order conditions). What is the appropriate matrix of terms to check the second-order conditions at this potential solution?

6.28 For the problem of minimizing $x^2y - 2yz$ subject to $x \geq 0$, $y \leq 0$, $x + 2y \leq z - 2$, and $xyz = 6x + 2z$, write the Lagrangian in standard form and write the first-order conditions.

6.29 For the problem of maximizing $2y - 4x^2$ subject to $x \geq 0$, $y \geq 0$, and $2y \leq 4x - 1$, with Lagrangian in standard form and λ_i corresponding to the ith constraint, $(x^*, y^*, \lambda_1^*, \lambda_2^*, \lambda_3^*) = (\frac{1}{2}, \frac{1}{2}, 0, 0, 1)$ is a potential solution (i.e., satisfies all first-order conditions). What is the appropriate matrix of terms to check the second-order conditions at this potential solution?

6.30 For the problem of minimizing $x^2 + (y - 5)^2$ subject to $x \geq 0$, $y = 3.5 - x^2$, and $2x + y \leq 4$, write the Lagrangian in standard form and write the first-order conditions.

6.31 After a certain problem has been set up in standard form, the first-order conditions are as listed below. Find all potential solutions.

$$-2x + 2 + \lambda_1 = 0,$$

$$-2y + \lambda_2 = 0,$$

$$-3 + x \geq 0, \qquad \lambda_1 \geq 0, \lambda_1(-3 + x) = 0,$$

$$-2 + y \geq 0, \qquad \lambda_2 \geq 0, \lambda_2(-2 + y) = 0.$$

6.32 For the problem of maximizing $x - y + z$ subject to $x \geq 0$, $y \geq 0$, $z \geq 0$, and $x^2 + y^2 + z^2 - 2 = 0$, with the Lagrangian in standard form and λ_i corresponding to the ith inequality constraint, $(x^*, y^*, z^*, \lambda_1^*, \lambda_2^*, \lambda_3^*, \mu^*) = (1, 0, 1, 0, 1, 0, 1/2)$ is a potential solution. What is the appropriate matrix to check the second-order conditions at this potential solution?

6.33 In each of the following questions, an optimization problem with inequality constraints has been set up in standard form and the first-order conditions have been solved to find the listed potential solution. Then the appropriate matrix of terms to check the second-order conditions (but evaluated at a general $(\mathbf{x}, \boldsymbol{\lambda})$ rather than $(\mathbf{x}^*, \boldsymbol{\lambda}^*)$) has been listed. In each case, given the potential solution and the SOC matrix, what can be said about the optimality of the solution?

(a) $(x^*, \lambda_1^*, \lambda_2^*) = (-2, 0, 0)$

$$L_{ij}^*(x, \lambda_I) = [-6]$$

(b) $(\mathbf{x}^*, \lambda_1^*, \lambda_2^*) = (1, -1, 2, 2)$

$$[L_{ij}^*(\mathbf{x}, \lambda_I)] = \begin{bmatrix} -1 & 0 & 1 & 0 \\ 0 & 2 & 0 & 1 \\ 1 & 0 & 0 & 0 \\ 0 & 1 & 0 & 0 \end{bmatrix}$$

(c) $(\mathbf{x}^*, \lambda_1^*, \lambda_2^*) = (0, 1, 1, 0)$

$$[L_{ij}^*(\mathbf{x}, \lambda_I)] = \begin{bmatrix} 0 & 0 & 1 \\ 0 & 2 & 0 \\ 1 & 0 & 0 \end{bmatrix}$$

(d) $(\mathbf{x}^*, \lambda_1^*, \lambda_2^*) = (-4, 0, 1, 0, 2)$

$$[L_{ij}^*(\mathbf{x}, \lambda_I)] = \begin{bmatrix} 1 & 0 & 0 & -1 \\ 0 & -1 & 0 & 1 \\ 0 & 0 & x_1 & 0 \\ -1 & 1 & 0 & 0 \end{bmatrix}$$

(e) $(\mathbf{x}^*, \lambda_1^*, \lambda_2^*) = (4, -7, 0, 0)$

$$[L_{ij}^*(\mathbf{x}, \lambda_I)] = \begin{bmatrix} -3 & x_1 \\ x_1 & x_2 \end{bmatrix}$$

6.34   For the problem of minimizing $xy - zy^2$ subject to $x^2 + y^2 + z^2 = 1$, $x \geq 0$, and $y + z \leq 0$, write the Lagrangian in standard form and write the first-order conditions.

6.35   For the problem of minimizing $(x - 2)^2 + (y - 2)^2 + (z - 2)^2$ subject to $x \geq 0$, $y \geq 0$, $z \geq 0$, and $x + y + z - 2 = 0$ with the Lagrangian in standard form and λ_i corresponding to the ith inequality constraint, $(x^*, y^*, z^*, \lambda_1^*, \lambda_2^*, \lambda_3^*, \mu^*) = (2/3, 2/3, 2/3, 0, 0, 0, 8/3)$ is a potential solution. What is the appropriate matrix to check the second-order conditions at this potential solution?

6.36   In each of the following questions, an optimization problem with inequality constraints has been set up in standard form and the first-order conditions have been solved to find the listed potential solution. Then the appropriate matrix of terms to check the second-order conditions, but evaluated at a general $(\mathbf{x}, \lambda)$ rather than $(\mathbf{x}^*, \lambda^*)$, has been listed. In each case, given the potential solution and the SOC matrix, what can be said about the optimality of the solution?
(a) $(\mathbf{x}^*, \lambda_1^*, \lambda_2^*) = (0, 0, 0, 0, 1)$,

$$[L_{ij}^*(\mathbf{x}, \lambda_I)] = \begin{bmatrix} -1 & 0 & 1 & 0 \\ 0 & 2 & 0 & 1 \\ 1 & 0 & 0 & 0 \\ 0 & 1 & 0 & 0 \end{bmatrix}.$$

(b) $(\mathbf{x}^*, \lambda_1^*, \lambda_2^*) = (-3, 0, 0, 4)$,

$$\left[L_{ij}^*(\mathbf{x}, \lambda_I) \right] = \begin{bmatrix} 0 & 0 & 1 \\ 0 & x_1 & 0 \\ 1 & 0 & 0 \end{bmatrix}.$$

(c) $(\mathbf{x}^*, \lambda_1^*, \lambda_2^*) = (3, 5, 2, 7)$,

$$\left[L_{ij}^*(\mathbf{x}, \lambda_I) \right] = \begin{bmatrix} 1 & 0 & 0 & -1 \\ 0 & -1 & 2 & 1 \\ 0 & 2 & 0 & 0 \\ -1 & 1 & 0 & 0 \end{bmatrix}.$$

7

COMPARATIVE
STATICS

7.1 INTRODUCTION

In many economic problems we need to know how an optimal solution or an equilibrium solution will change when a parameter in the problem changes. For example, how does the utility-maximizing bundle for a competitive consumer change when a price changes, or how does a market equilibrium price change when a tax on the good changes? These are examples of comparative statics questions. In each case we are interested in how the endogenous variables (those determined within the model) are affected by changes in the exogenous variables (the parameters determined outside the model). For the consumer choice problem, the endogenous variables are the quantities demanded (chosen by the consumer), while the exogenous variables are prices (outside the control of the competitive consumer). For the market example, the endogenous variable is the market equilibrium price (determined by supply and demand in the market), while the exogenous variable is the tax rate (determined outside the market in some political process).

For very simple examples it is possible to solve for the endogenous variables as functions of the exogenous variables (e.g., a consumer's demand as a function of prices) to answer directly the comparative statics questions. For the typical problem this is impossible, so we use a mathematical tool, the implicit function theorem (IFT), to determine the comparative statics effects. The mathematical technique is identical for optimization and equilibrium problems, but there are substantial differences in the economic requirements.

132

For optimization problems, most of the work will already have been done in the original optimization problem, and the fact that it is an optimization problem will give insights into the mathematical conditions used. Throughout this chapter we assume the constraint qualification condition holds for every optimization problem unless noted otherwise.

For equilibrium problems, the comparative statics exercise is meaningless unless the equilibrium is stable under some dynamic adjustment process (see Chapter 10). If the equilibrium is unstable, when the exogenous parameter changes the market will not converge to the new equilibrium identified by the mathematical procedure, so our comparative statics results will be meaningless for the economy. The need for a stable dynamic adjustment process is crucial in equilibrium problems, but, unfortunately, it is often ignored in practice.

One final point is that the technique is a typical calculus technique, so the answers (like a tangent line approximation to a graph of a function) give good approximations for small changes in the parameters but not necessarily good approximations for large changes. See the last example of Section 7.2 for a discussion of "how small small is."

7.2 SIMPLE IMPLICIT FUNCTION THEOREM

To understand the IFT we will start with the simplest case, one endogenous and one exogenous variable. The IFT gives sufficient conditions for the existence of an explicit relationship, $y = f(x)$, between variables implicitly related by $F(x, y) \equiv 0$.

In the simplest form, F is linear [i.e., $F(x, y) = ax + by$], and we want to known whether we can solve $F(x, y) \equiv 0$ explicitly for $y = f(x)$. For $F(x, y) = ax + by$, an explicit solution exists if and only if $b \neq 0$. If $b \neq 0$, $y = -(a/b)x$. Because F is linear, this solution is correct for every x. Also note $dy/dx = -(a/b)$ along $F(x, y) \equiv 0$.

Now consider a case where F is not necessarily linear but is continuously differentiable. When can we explicitly solve $F(x, y) \equiv 0$ for $y = f(x)$? In fact we are interested in a weaker requirement: if we have some (x^0, y^0) such that $F(x^0, y^0) = 0$, when can we find a differentiable function f such that $y^0 = f(x^0)$ and, for x near x^0, $F(x, f(x)) \equiv 0$? This corresponds to our comparative static questions. The original equilibrium is (x^0, y^0), where x is the parameter and y is the endogenous variable. We seek a value for the endogenous variable, $y = f(x)$, which satisfies the equilibrium condition when the parameter is x [i.e., $F(x, f(x)) = 0$]. Finally, we want to know how the equilibrium y changes when x changes, so we want f to be differentiable.

For the nonlinear case, we proceed by using linear approximations and the results for the linear case. Since $F(x^0, y^0) = 0$ and $F(x, y) \equiv 0$, if we change from (x^0, y^0) to $(x^0 + dx, y^0 + dy)$, the changes must satisfy

$$\frac{\partial F(x^0, y^0)}{\partial x} \, dx + \frac{\partial F(x^0, y^0)}{\partial y} \, dy = 0.$$

(This is using the tangent plane approximation to the level surface of the function.) We are now in the linear case, with $a = \partial F(x^0, y^0)/\partial x$ and $b = \partial F(x^0, y^0)/\partial y$. We can solve for dy explicitly in terms of dx if $b \neq 0$, and in that case $dy = -(a/b) \, dx$ or $dy/dx = -(a/b)$. This is of course an approximation, using the tangent plane. It is very accurate for small changes, dx, but need not be accurate for large changes. The implicit function theorem guarantees that an exact explicit function, f, exists near x^0 and satisfies $df(x^0)/dx = -(a/b)$. In terms of differentials,

$$dy = \frac{df(x^0)}{dx} \, dx = -(a/b) \, dx.$$

SIMPLE IMPLICIT FUNCTION THEOREM: *Let F: $\mathbb{R}^2 \to \mathbb{R}$ be a continuously differentiable function such that $F(x^0, y^0) = 0$ and $\partial F(x^0, y^0)/\partial y \neq 0$. Then there exist $\varepsilon > 0$ and a unique function f: $(x^0 - \varepsilon, x^0 + \varepsilon) \to \mathbb{R}$ such that*

1. *f is continuously differentiable*
2. *$f(x^0) = y^0$*
3. *$F(x, f(x)) \equiv 0$ for $x \in (x^0 - \varepsilon, x^0 + \varepsilon)$*

To find the comparative static effect of a change in x on y, starting from (x^0, y^0), differentiate $F(x, f(x)) \equiv 0$ with respect to x and evaluate the result at (x^0, y^0) to get

$$\frac{\partial F(x^0, y^0)}{\partial x} + \frac{\partial F(x^0, y^0)}{\partial y} \frac{df(x^0)}{dx} = 0,$$

or

$$\frac{df(x^0)}{dx} = -\left(\frac{\partial F(x^0, y^0)}{\partial x} \middle/ \frac{\partial F(x^0, y^0)}{\partial y} \right).$$

In summary, the IFT is a tool to help us determine when the endogenous variable can be written as a function of the exogenous variable (at least near the original equilibrium). The procedure for performing comparative statics is (1) find an appropriate function F, (2) check the conditions of the IFT [F differentiable, $F(x^0, y^0) = 0$, and the partial of F with respect to the endogenous variable nonzero], and (3) differentiate $F(x, f(x)) \equiv 0$ and evaluate at (x^0, y^0) to determine $df(x^0)/dx$.

EXAMPLE: Consider a competitive market with aggregate demand $D(p) = 242 + p - (p + 1)^5$ and aggregate supply $S(p) = p$. There is a tax of t per unit, so the price consumers pay, p^c, exceeds the price firms receive, p^f, by t; i.e., $p^c = p^f + t$. Market equilibrium obtains when supply equals demand, i.e., when $D(p^c) = S(p^f)$. Writing p^f in terms of p^c, the equilibrium condition is $242 + p^c - (p^c + 1)^5 = p^c - t$. When $t^0 = 1$ the equilibrium (consumer) price is $p^0 = 2$.

We now want to know how the equilibrium (consumer) price changes as t changes (from which we can compute the change in p^f). A natural, stable, dynamic process (price increases when demand exceeds supply) exists for this model, so the comparative statics are meaningful. To solve the problem, we (1) transform the problem into a form in which the IFT can be applied, (2) check the conditions of the IFT, and (3) use the existence and differentiability of $p^c(t)$ for t near 1 (guaranteed by the IFT) to determine $dp^c(1)/dt$.

1. An obvious choice for the function F is demand minus supply: $F(p^c, t) = 242 + p^c - (p^c + 1)^5 - p^c + t = 242 - (p^c + 1)^5 + t$. (Note we have written the endogenous variable as the first argument of F.)

2. F is continuously differentiable, $F(2, 1) = 0$, and $\partial F(2, 1)/\partial p^c = -405 \neq 0$, so by the IFT, there exists a continuously differentiable "equilibrium consumer price" function $p^c(t)$ for t near 1.

3. Differentiating $242 - (p^c(t) + 1)^5 + t \equiv 0$ with respect to t, rearranging, and evaluating the results at $t = 1$ and $p^c(1) = 2$, we get $dp^c(1)/dt = 1/405$. To find $dp^f(1)/dt$, note $p^f(t) \equiv p^c(t) - t$, so

$$\frac{dp^f(1)}{dt} = \frac{dp^c(1)}{dt} - 1 = -\frac{404}{405}.$$

EXAMPLE: A profit-maximizing monpolist produces a single output to be sold in a single market. The cost to produce q units is $C(q) = q + (1/2)q^2$, and the market demand is such that the average revenue for selling q units is $D^{-1}(q) = 4 - (q^5)/6$. The monopolist must also pay a tax of $1 per unit sold. The monopolist's profit for producing and selling q units is

$$\pi(q) = pq - C(q) - q = \left[4 - (q^5)/6\right]q - \left[q + (1/2)q^2\right] - q$$

$$= 2q - (q^2)/2 - (q^6)/6.$$

$\pi''(q) = -1 - 5q^4 < 0$, so the profit function is concave, and any solution to $\pi'(q) = 0$ is the unique, global, profit maximizer. $\pi'(1) = 0$ so output 1 is profit maximizing.

We now want to know how the profit-maximizing output changes as the tax rate changes. The procedure is identical to that used for an equilibrium problem, but as we will see, the original optimization problem has already included many of the steps. When the tax rate is t per unit, the monopolist's profit for producing and selling q units is

$$\pi(q;t) = pq - C(q) - tq = (3 - t)q - (q^2)/2 - (q^6)/6.$$

1. Since $q^0 = 1$ was the unique, global, profit maximizer for $t^0 = 1$, for small changes in t the new global maximizer will also satisfy the first-order conditions. Thus the natural choice for the function F is the first partial of the profit function with respect to q:

$$F(q,t) = \partial\pi(q,t)/\partial q = 3 - t - q - q^5.$$

2. F is continuously differentiable (note this involves second partials of the profit function), $q^0 = 1$ satisfied the first-order conditions when $t^0 = 1$, so $F(1,1) = 0$, and the (strict) second-order condition held at $q^0 = 1$ when $t^0 = 1$, so $\partial F(1,1)/\partial q = \partial^2\pi(1,1)/\partial q^2 \neq 0$. By the IFT there exists a continuously differentiable optimal output function, $q(t)$, for t near 1.

3. Substituting $q(t)$ into the first-order condition, we get the identity $F(q(t); t) \equiv 3 - t - q(t) - [q(t)]^5 \equiv 0$. Differentiating with respect to t, $-1 - [1 + 5(q(t))^4] dq(t)/dt \equiv 0$. Rearranging and evaluating at $t = 1$ and $q(1) = 1$, $dq(1)/dt = -1/6$.

EXAMPLE: For an optimization problem it is important to start with a unique global maximizer. With nonunique maximizers we do not know which "branch" of the level curve $F(q; t) = 0$ to follow. For example, consider the problem of maximizing $\pi(q; t) = -q^4 + 2q^2 + tq$. At $t^0 = 0$ there are two global maximizers, $q^0 = 1$ and $q^0 = -1$. The natural F is $F(q; t) = \partial\pi(q; t)/\partial q = -4q^3 + 4q + t$. Starting from $q^0 = 1$, the conditions of the IFT hold, and we get $dq(0)/dt = 1/8$. This means that for t near zero, the optimizer is $q^1(t) \approx 1 + t/8$. On the other hand, starting from $q^0 = -1$, the conditions of the IFT hold, and we get $dq(0)/dt = 1/8$. This means that for t near zero, the optimizer is $q^2(t) \approx -1 + t/8$.

Do both $q^1(t)$ and $q^2(t)$ represent global optimizers? No, for $t \neq 0$ only one is a global maximizer, while the other is a local, but not global, maximizer. However, the global solution switches between the branches, with $q^1(t)$ optimal for $t > 0$ and $q^2(t)$ optimal for $t < 0$. To see, this, let $\pi^i(t)$ be the maximal profit possible by following branch $q^i(t)$, i.e., $\pi^i(t) := \pi(q^i(t); t)$. Differentiating the right-hand side with respect to t (totally), simplifying, and evaluating at $t = 0$, $q^i(0)$, we get $d\pi^1(0)/dt = 1$ and $d\pi^2(0)/dt = -1$. This means that as t increases from zero, the profit on branch one increases while profit on branch two decreases. Similarly, as t decreases from zero, branch two does better than branch one.

EXAMPLE: Consider a competitive firm with cost function $C(x) = x^3/3$. For price p greater than zero, profit is $\pi(x; p) = px - x^3/3$ where output, x, is a choice variable and price, p, is a parameter (since the firm acts competitively). Maximizing profit,

$$\frac{\partial \pi}{\partial x}(x;p) = p - x^2, \qquad \frac{\partial^2 \pi}{\partial x^2}(x;p) = -2x$$

and the optimal output (given p) is $x^*(p) = \sqrt{p}$. At $p = p^0 = 1$, $x^* = x^0 = 1$ is the optimal solution. How does $x^*(p)$ change as p changes near p^0? (Note that x^*, the optimal output, is a function of p, while x, an arbitrary output, is not.) By direct computation $dx^*(1)/dp = 1/(2)(1) = \frac{1}{2}$. However, it is not always possible to solve directly like this, so we consider an application of the method just derived. For optimization problems such as this, the IFT method uses the first- and second-order conditions of profit maximization. Checking the conditions of the IFT

$\partial \pi(x^0; p^0)/\partial x = 0$ i.e., $x^0 = x^*(p^0)$
$\partial \pi(x; p)/\partial x$ is differentiable as a function of x and p near $(x^0; p^0)$
$\partial^2 \pi(x^0; p^0)/\partial x^2 \neq 0$.

Thus by the IFT, with $F(x; p) = \partial \pi(x; p)/\partial x$, there exists a function $x^*(p)$ which is differentiable, has $x^*(p^0) = x^0$, and satisfies $\partial \pi(x^*(p); p)/\partial x \equiv 0$ for p near p^0; i.e., $x^*(p)$ satisfies the first-order condition when price is p.

Since $\partial^2 \pi(x^0; p^0)/\partial x^2 < 0$ and x^0 is the unique global maximizer when $p = p^0$, if $\pi(x, p)$ changes smoothly as p changes, then for p near p^0, $x^*(p)$ satisfies the second-order condition with strict inequality and is the unique global maximizer for price p; i.e., if π changes smoothly as p changes, then $x^*(p)$ is the unique global maximizer for p near p^0. Note that we need not have solved analytically for $x^*(p)$ to know it exists and is differentiable.

By the chain rule applied to $\partial \pi(x^*(p); p)/\partial x \equiv 0$,

$$\frac{\partial^2 \pi}{\partial x^2}(x^*(p); p)\frac{dx^*(p)}{dp} + \frac{\partial^2 \pi}{\partial p \, \partial x}(x^*(p); p) \equiv 0.$$

Then, evaluated at p^0 (since the second-order condition holds strictly at p^0 the inverse exists)

$$\frac{dx^*(p^0)}{dp} = -\left(\frac{\partial^2 \pi}{\partial x^2}(x^*(p^0); p^0)\right)^{-1}\left(\frac{\partial^2 \pi}{\partial p \, \partial x}(x^*(p^0); p^0)\right).$$

Recapping this example

1. Start with a solution x^0 to an optimization problem (when the parameter is p^0) at which the first-order condition holds, the second-order condition holds with strict inequality, and such that x^0 is the unqiue global optimizer when the parameter is p^0.

2. We assume the objective function (π) is twice continuously differentiable as a function of x and p. (We need twice continuously differentiable since we apply the IFT using $F(x; p) = \partial\pi(x; p)/\partial x$, the first partial derivative of π.]

3. By the IFT, $x^*(p)$ exists for p near p^0, and, by reasoning as above, $x^*(p)$ is the unique global optimizer given p near p^*.

4. Finally,

$$\frac{dx^*(p^0)}{dp} = -\left(\frac{\partial^2\pi}{\partial x^2}(x^0; p^0)\right)^{-1}\left(\frac{\partial^2\pi}{\partial p\,\partial x}(x^0; p^0)\right).$$

What happens if there are several exogenous variables? As long as there is only one endogenous variable, the procedure can be undertaken separately for each exogenous variable. If $F(x, y, z) = 0$ implicitly defines z as a function of x and y, $z^*(x, y)$, then

$$\frac{\partial z^*(x^0, y^0)}{\partial x} = -\left[\frac{\partial F(x^0, y^0, z^0)}{\partial z}\right]^{-1}\frac{\partial F(x^0, y^0, z^0)}{\partial x} \quad \text{and}$$

$$\frac{\partial z^*(x^0, y^0)}{\partial y} = -\left[\frac{\partial F(x^0, y^0, z^0)}{\partial z}\right]^{-1}\frac{\partial F(x^0, y^0, z^0)}{\partial y}$$

or, in vector notation,

$$\left[\frac{\partial z^*(x^0, y^0)}{\partial x}\quad\frac{\partial z^*(x^0, y^0)}{\partial y}\right] = -\left[\frac{\partial F(x^0, y^0, z^0)}{\partial z}\right]^{-1}$$

$$\times\left[\frac{\partial F(x^0, y^0, z^0)}{\partial x}\quad\frac{\partial F(x^0, y^0, z^0)}{\partial y}\right].$$

The procedure using differentials uses a linear approximation to the true functions to obtain the results. If the exogeneous changes dx are infinitesimal, the endogenous changes dy are exactly correct. If the changes dx are not infinitesimal, the solutions for dy are only approximations to the true changes. Since the functions are differentiable, the percentage relative error is small for small dx. Unfortunately, it is not possible to determine how small dx must be in order to guarantee no more than (say) 5% relative error without examining the specific problem.

EXAMPLE: Suppose the endogenous variable r and the exogenous variable t are related by $r - kt^2 \equiv 0$ where k is a positive constant. At starting point $(r^0, t^0) = (0, 0)$, the procedure yields $dr = 0\, dt$. Given $dt > 0$, the percentage relative error is the absolute value of 100% times the difference between the estimated value of dr, $0\, dt = 0$, and the true change in r, $k(dt)^2$, all divided by the change in t, dt. This equals $(k\, dt)$ 100%. To get less than 5% relative error requires $dt < 1/(20k)$, which depends on the constant k. The absolute error is $|0\, dt - k(dt)^2| = k(dt)^2$. For any fixed $dt > 0$, no matter how small, the relative and absolute errors could still be very large if k was sufficiently large. We only know that for any fixed k, the absolute and relative errors go to zero as dt does.

7.3 GENERAL COMPARATIVE STATICS PROCEDURE

With more than one endogenous variable, the ideas stay the same but their execution becomes more complicated. Suppose there are n endogenous variables $\mathbf{y} = (y_1, \ldots, y_n)$ and one exogenous variable, x. We then need n equations $F^i(x, \mathbf{y}) = 0$, $i = 1, \ldots, n$. Rather than a single term $\partial F/\partial y$ we now have an $n \times n$ matrix with entry $(\partial F^i(x^0, \mathbf{y}^0)/\partial y_j$ in row i and column j. The corresponding IFT conditions are (1) each F^i is continuously differentiable, (2) $F^i(x^0, \mathbf{y}^0) = 0$ for $i = 1, \ldots, n$ (i.e., the starting point satisfies all equations), and (3) $\det[\partial F^i(x^0, \mathbf{y}^0)/\partial y_j] \neq 0$. When these conditions are satisfied, the IFT guarantees that differentiable functions $y_i = g^i(x)$ exist for $i = 1, \ldots, n$ (i.e., the endogenous variables can all be written as functions of the exogenous variable).

To determine how the endogenous y_i change as the exogenous x changes, we substitute $g^i(x)$ for y_i, $i = 1, \ldots, n$, into each of the n equations (now identities) and differentiate with respect to x to get a system of n equations in the n unknowns $dg^1(x^0)/dx, \ldots, dg^n(x^0)/dx$. This system is then solved for the desired terms. To determine any single term $dg^i(x^0)/dx$, we must differentiate all n identities.

EXAMPLE: The point $(1, -1, 2)$ lies on both of the surfaces described by the equations $x^2(y^2 + z^2) = 5$ and $(x - z)^2 + y^2 = 2$. We will show that in a neighborhood of $(1, -1, 2)$, the intersection of the two surfaces can be described by equations $y = g^1(x)$ and $z = g^2(x)$.

Here x is the parameter and (y, z) are the "choice variables." With two choice variables we need two functions. Let

$$F^1(y, z; x) = x^2(y^2 + z^2) - 5 \text{ and } F^2(y, z; x) = (x - z)^2 + y^2 - 2.$$

Both F^1 and F^2 are continuously differentiable in a neighborhood of

$(y, z; x) = (-1, 2; 1)$, and $F^1(-1, 2; 1) = 0 = F^2(-1, 2; 1)$ and

$$\begin{bmatrix} \dfrac{\partial F^1}{\partial y} & \dfrac{\partial F^1}{\partial z} \\[3mm] \dfrac{\partial F^2}{\partial y} & \dfrac{\partial F^2}{\partial z} \end{bmatrix} = \begin{bmatrix} 2x^2 y & 2x^2 z \\[2mm] 2y & -2(x - z) \end{bmatrix}.$$

Evaluated at $(y, z; x)$ equal to $(-1, 2; 1)$, the matrix is

$$\begin{bmatrix} -2 & 4 \\ -2 & 2 \end{bmatrix} \quad \text{with} \quad \det\begin{bmatrix} -2 & 4 \\ -2 & 2 \end{bmatrix} = 4 \neq 0.$$

The IFT applies and the desired functions $g^1(x)$ and $g^2(x)$ exist for x near 1.

To find the comparative static effects we form the two identities

$$x^2\left(\left[g^1(x)\right]^2 + \left[g^2(x)\right]^2\right) - 5 \equiv 0 \quad \text{and}$$

$$\left[x - g^2(x)\right]^2 + \left[g^1(x)\right]^2 - 2 \equiv 0$$

and differentiate with respect to x to obtain

$$2x\left(\left[g^1(x)\right]^2 + \left[g^2(x)\right]^2\right) + x^2\left(2g^1(x)\frac{dg^1(x)}{dx} + 2g^2(x)\frac{dg^2(x)}{dx}\right) \equiv 0$$

and

$$2\left[x - g^2(x)\right]\left[1 - \frac{dg^2(x)}{dx}\right] + 2g^1(x)\frac{dg^1(x)}{dx} \equiv 0.$$

Evaluated at $x = 1$, $g^1(1) = -1$, and $g^2(1) = 2$, this system becomes

$$10 - 2\frac{dg^1(1)}{dx} + 4\frac{dg^2(1)}{dx} = 0 \quad \text{and} \quad -2 - 2\frac{dg^1(1)}{dx} + 2\frac{dg^2(1)}{dx} = 0.$$

Solving, we obtain $dg^1(1)/dx = -7$ and $dg^2(1)/dx = -6$.

The general comparative statics problem proceeds as follows. There are n equations in n unknowns, $\mathbf{x}$, and k parameters, $\mathbf{p}$: $F^i(\mathbf{x}; \mathbf{p}) = 0$ $i = 1, 2, \ldots, n$. These equations are often the n first-order conditions which arise when an agent (consumer, producer, etc.) maximizes some objective function (utilty, profit, etc.) by choosing $\mathbf{x}$ with parameters $\mathbf{p}$ fixed and not under the agent's control. (Alternatively, the equations may represent the equilibrium conditions in a set of interrelated markets given the exogenous parameters $\mathbf{p}$.) Note the $\mathbf{x}$ are the endogenous variables and the **p** are the exogenous variables. In writing each F^i, we separate the endogenous variables from the exogenous variables with a semicolon, $F^i(\mathbf{x}; \mathbf{p})$.

In the general problem, a particular solution is known; i.e., when the parameters are $\mathbf{p}^0$, the choice $\mathbf{x}^0$ is such that $F^i(\mathbf{x}^0; \mathbf{p}^0) = 0$, $i = 1, 2, \ldots, n$. The question is whether it is possible to find a function $\mathbf{x}^*(\mathbf{p})$ for which the first-order conditions continue to hold, i.e., $F^i(\mathbf{x}^*(\mathbf{p}); \mathbf{p}) \equiv 0$, $i = 1, 2, \ldots, n$, for all $\mathbf{p}$ near $\mathbf{p}^0$. For an optimization problem, subject to suitable second-order conditions and $\mathbf{x}^0$ being the unique global optimizer when parameters are $\mathbf{p}^0$, this means that $\mathbf{x}^*(\mathbf{p})$ is the unique global optimizer when the parameters are $\mathbf{p}$.

If a particular solution $\mathbf{x}^0$ is known when the parameters are $\mathbf{p}^0$ and $\mathbf{x}^*(\mathbf{p})$ is differentiable near $\mathbf{p}^0$, then it is possible to determine how the optimal choice $\mathbf{x}^*(\mathbf{p})$ varies as $\mathbf{p}$ varies near $\mathbf{p}^0$, without actually explicitly solving for $\mathbf{x}^0(\mathbf{p})$. [It may be difficult or even "generally impossible" to solve the system of first-order conditions for $\mathbf{x}^*(\mathbf{p})$.] This is done as follows. Let $S_1 \subset \mathbb{R}^n$ be an open neighborhood of $\mathbf{x}^0$ (e.g., $\{\mathbf{x} | \|\mathbf{x} - \mathbf{x}^0\| < \varepsilon\}$ for some $\varepsilon > 0$) and $S_2 \subset \mathbb{R}^k$ be an open neighborhood of $\mathbf{p}^0$ such that $F^i: S_1 \times S_2 \to \mathbb{R}$ is r times continuously differentiable for $i = 1, 2, \ldots, n$. If $\mathbf{x}^*(\mathbf{p})$ exists and is differentiable, then $F^i(\mathbf{x}^*(\mathbf{p}); \mathbf{p}) \equiv 0$ for all $\mathbf{p}$ near $\mathbf{p}^0$, $i = 1, 2, \ldots, n$. Using the chain rule, when p_l changes

$$\sum_{j=1}^{n} \frac{\partial F^i}{\partial x_j} \frac{\partial x_j^*}{\partial p_l} + \frac{\partial F^i}{\partial p_l} = 0 \quad \text{for } i = 1, 2, \ldots, n. \tag{1}$$

Note that we include not only those changes that come about directly, $\partial F^i / \partial p_l$, but also the indirect changes that come about since x_j^*, the optimal choice, depends on p_l, and F^i depends on x_j^*. (1) can be rewritten in the form

$$\left(\frac{\partial F^i}{\partial \mathbf{x}} \right) \cdot \left(\frac{\partial \mathbf{x}}{\partial p_l} \right) + \frac{\partial F^i}{\partial p_l} = 0, \qquad i = 1, 2, \ldots, n, l = 1, 2, \ldots, k,$$

where $\partial F^i / \partial \mathbf{x}$ is the n-vector of partials of F^i with respect to the endogenous variables and $\partial \mathbf{x} / \partial p_l$ is the n-vector of partials of the (optimized) endogenous variables with respect to p_l. We will now combined all nk ($i = 1, 2, \ldots, n$, $l = 1, 2, \ldots, k$) equations into one matrix equation. First, writing a separate row for each $i = 1, 2, \ldots, n$, we get an equation

$$\left[\frac{\partial F^i}{\partial x_j} \right] \frac{\partial \mathbf{x}^*}{\partial p_l} + \frac{\partial \mathbf{F}}{\partial p_l} = \mathbf{0}$$

for each $l = 1, 2, \ldots, k$. Second, writing a separate column for each $l = 1, 2, \ldots, k$,

$$\left[\frac{\partial F^i}{\partial x_j}\right]_{n \times n} \left[\frac{\partial x_i^*}{\partial p_j}\right]_{n \times k} + \left[\frac{\partial F^i}{\partial p_j}\right]_{n \times k} = [0]_{n \times k}, \qquad (2)$$

or in words, the matrix of derivatives of the F^i functions with respect to the endogenous variables x_j, times the matrix of derivatives of the optimal choices x_i^* with respect to the parameters p_j, plus the matrix of derivatives of the F^i functions with respect to the parameters p_j, equals the matrix of zeros. In all three matrices, i indicates row, j indicates column. The entries in the first and third matrices (partial derivatives of F^i with respect to choice variables and parameters, respectively) are evaluated at $(\mathbf{x}^*(\mathbf{p}^0); \mathbf{p}^0) = (\mathbf{x}^0; \mathbf{p}^0)$. The entries in the second matrix (partial derivatives of the optimal choices x_i^* with respect to parameters) are evaluated at $\mathbf{p}^0$. If the inverse of the $n \times n$ matrix $[\partial F^i(\mathbf{x}^0; \mathbf{p}^0)/\partial x_i]$ exists, then solving (2) for $[\partial x_i^*/\partial p_j]$,

$$\left[\frac{\partial x_i^*}{\partial p_j}(\mathbf{p}^0)\right]_{n \times k} = -\left[\frac{\partial F^i}{\partial x_j}(\mathbf{x}^0; \mathbf{p}^0)\right]_{n \times n}^{-1} \left[\frac{\partial F^i}{\partial p_j}(\mathbf{x}^0; \mathbf{p}^0)\right]_{n \times k}. \qquad (3)$$

This is the basis for comparative statics changes in optimal (or equilibrium) values $\mathbf{x}^*$ as parameters $\mathbf{p}$ change.

The IFT gives a sufficient condition (but not a necessary condition) for the existence of an explicit solution of a system of implicit equations in $\mathbf{x}$ and $\mathbf{p}$ locally, near $\mathbf{p}^0, \mathbf{x}^0$. When the conditions of the IFT hold, the $\mathbf{x}$ can be written as differentiable functions of the $\mathbf{p}$ for $\mathbf{p}$ near $\mathbf{p}^0$.

IMPLICIT FUNCTION THEOREM (IFT): *Let S_1 (S_2) be an open subset of $\mathbb{R}^n$ ($\mathbb{R}^k$) containing $\mathbf{x}^0$ ($\mathbf{p}^0$) and such that $F^i: S_1 \times S_2 \to \mathbb{R}$ ($F^i(\mathbf{x}; \mathbf{p})$) is r times continuously differentiable for $i = 1, 2, \ldots, n$.*

If $F^i(\mathbf{x}^0; \mathbf{p}^0) = 0$ for all i and $\det[\partial F^i(\mathbf{x}^0; \mathbf{p}^0)/\partial x_j]_{n \times n} \neq 0$, then there exist an $\varepsilon > 0$ and unique functions g^i, $i = 1, 2, \ldots, n$, such that for each i

1. *$g^i: \{\mathbf{p} \in R^k | \|\mathbf{p} - \mathbf{p}^0\| < \varepsilon\} \to \mathbb{R}$ is r times continuously differentiable.*
2. *$g^i(\mathbf{p}^0) = x_i^0$.*
3. *For*

$$\mathbf{g}(\mathbf{p}) = \begin{pmatrix} g^1(\mathbf{p}) \\ \vdots \\ g^n(\mathbf{p}) \end{pmatrix},$$

$F^i(\mathbf{g}(\mathbf{p}); \mathbf{p}) \equiv 0$ *for all $\mathbf{p}$ with $\|\mathbf{p} - \mathbf{p}^0\| < \varepsilon$.*

If the conditions of the IFT hold, then locally, for $\mathbf{p}$ near $\mathbf{p}^0$, $\mathbf{x}^*(\mathbf{p})$ exists and is r times continuously differentiable. Then we can use the method outlined above to find out how (the optimal or equilibrium) $\mathbf{x}^*$ changes when the parameters change, without explicitly solving for $\mathbf{x}^*(\mathbf{p})$.

EXAMPLE: Can the surface with equation $xy - z(\ln y) + e^{xz} = 1$ be represented in the form $y = g(x, z)$ in a neighborhood of $(x, y, z) = (0, 1, 1)$? The point is on the surface since $0 \cdot 1 - 1(-\ln y 1) + e^{0 \cdot 1} = 1$. The question asks for y as a function of x and z, so the parameters are x and z and the "choice variable" is y. With one choice variable we need one function F^i, so let $F^1(y; x, z) = xy - z(\ln y) + e^{xz} - 1$. F^1 is continuously differentiable in a neighborhood of $(y; x, z) = (1; 0, 1)$, and $\partial F^1/\partial y = x - z/y$, so

$$\frac{\partial F^1}{\partial y}(1; 0, 1) = 0 - 1 \neq 0.$$

By the IFT, there exists a continuously differentiable function $g(x, z)$ which is defined on a neighborhood of $(0, 1)$, such that the surface near $(0, 1, 1)$ can be represented as $y = g(x, z)$. [If the question asked for $z = h(x, y)$, the fact that $\partial F/\partial z = -\ln y + xe^{xz}$ and $\partial F(1, 0, 1)/\partial z = 0$ means the IFT does not apply since $\det[\partial F/\partial z] = 0$, and we cannot answer the question without further work.] Since g is continuously differentiable near $(x, z) = (0, 1)$, we can use implicit differentiation to find

$$\left[\frac{\partial g}{\partial x}(0, 1) \quad \frac{\partial g}{\partial z}(0, 1)\right] = -\left(\frac{\partial F}{\partial y}(1; 0, 1)\right)^{-1}\left[\frac{\partial F}{\partial x}(1; 0, 1) \quad \frac{\partial F}{\partial z}(1; 0, 1)\right]$$

$$= -(1/-1)[2 \quad 0] = [2 \quad 0].$$

Notice that explicit solution of the original equation to find $y = g(x, z)$ appears difficult, so the implicit differentiation method is advantageous.

EXAMPLE: Consider the intersection of the surfaces $e^y - xyz = e$ and $x^2 + y^2 - z = 2$. Can the intersection be written in the form of differentiable functions $x^*(y)$ and $z^*(y)$ near $(0, 1, -1)$? If so, what are $dx^*(1)/dy$ and $dz^*(1)/dy$? The endogenous variables are x and z and the exogenous variable is y. Checking the conditions of the implicit function theorem, $e^1 - (0)(1)(-1) = e$ and $(0)^2 + (1)^2 - (-1) = 2$, so $(0, 1, -1)$ lies on both surfaces; $F^1(x, z; y) = e^y - xyz - e$ and $F^2(x, z; y) = x^2 + y^2 - z - 2$ are both differentiable functions, and

$$\det\begin{bmatrix}\dfrac{\partial F^1}{\partial x}(0, -1; 1) & \dfrac{\partial F^1}{\partial z}(0, -1; 1) \\[2mm] \dfrac{\partial F^2}{\partial x}(0, -1; 1) & \dfrac{\partial F^2}{\partial z}(0, -1; 1)\end{bmatrix} = \det\begin{bmatrix}1 & 0 \\ 0 & -1\end{bmatrix} \neq 0.$$

The conditions hold, so the intersection be written in the form of differentiable functions $x^*(y)$ and $z^*(y)$ near $(0, 1, -1)$. Then

$$\begin{pmatrix} \dfrac{dx^*(1)}{dy} \\[2ex] \dfrac{dz^*(1)}{dy} \end{pmatrix} = -\begin{bmatrix} 1 & 0 \\ 0 & -1 \end{bmatrix}^{-1} \begin{pmatrix} \dfrac{\partial F^1}{\partial y}(0, -1; 1) \\[2ex] \dfrac{\partial F^2}{\partial y}(0, -1; 1) \end{pmatrix}$$

$$= -\begin{bmatrix} 1 & 0 \\ 0 & -1 \end{bmatrix}\begin{pmatrix} e \\ 2 \end{pmatrix} = \begin{pmatrix} -e \\ 2 \end{pmatrix}.$$

Notes on the IFT: The following points should be kept in mind when using the IFT.

1. x^0 and p^0 are interior points in the sense that no constraints are at the borderline between active and inactive.

2. The *Jacobian*,

$$\det\left[\frac{\partial F^i}{\partial x_j}(x^0; p^0)\right],$$

must be nonzero. This is a Jacobian determinant. Notice that only derivatives with respect to the choice variables, x_j, are used. No derivatives with respect to parameters appear in the matrix. All partial derivatives in the matrix are evaluated at the known solution $(x^0; p^0)$. In optimization problems, this matrix is just the matrix of second partials of the Lagrangian, which is used in checking the second-order conditions for an optimum.

3. The solution $x^*(p) = g(p)$ is well defined and well behaved (r times continuously differentiable) if the conditions of the IFT are satisfied.

4. The solution is locally unique.

5. There may be other local solutions, but no other solution can have $\bar{g}(p^0) = x^0$, because of the local uniqueness of solutions. This occurs at p^0 in Figure 7.1.

6. When the determinant is zero, it may not be possible to solve for $g(p)$; i.e., for some p near p^0, no x near x^0 may satisfy $F(x; p) = 0$. This occurs at the larger of the two values of x at which $F(x; p^1) = 0$ in Figure 7.1.

7. Even if the determinant is zero, it may be possible to solve for $g(p)$ near the point (p^0, x^0). However, the IFT does not apply, and $g(p)$ is not differentiable. This occurs at p^2 in Figure 7.1.

EXAMPLE: Consider a general unconstrained maximization problem. (The procedure for a minimization problem is virtually identical.) Start

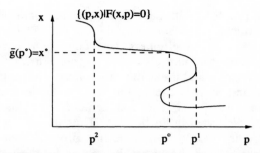

FIGURE 7.1   Good and bad points for comparative statics.

with the problem: maximize $H(\mathbf{x}; \mathbf{p})$ with respect to $\mathbf{x}$ (i.e.; $\mathbf{x}$ are choice variables and $\mathbf{p}$ are parameters). A necessary condition for interior maximization is $H_\mathbf{x}(\mathbf{x}; \mathbf{p}) = \mathbf{0}$ where $H_\mathbf{x}$ is the vector of partial derivatives with respect to choice variables. Let $\mathbf{F}(\mathbf{x}; \mathbf{p}) = H_\mathbf{x}(\mathbf{x}; \mathbf{p})$. If $\mathbf{x}^0$ is the unique global maximizer when $\mathbf{p} = \mathbf{p}^0$, then (1) $\mathbf{F}(\mathbf{x}^0; \mathbf{p}^0) = \mathbf{0}$, (2) $\mathbf{F}(\mathbf{x}; \mathbf{p})$ is continuously differentiable near $(\mathbf{x}^0; \mathbf{p}^0)$ if H is twice continuously differentiable, and (3) $\det[\partial F^i(\mathbf{x}^0; \mathbf{p}^0)/\partial x_j] \neq 0$ if the second-order condition for maximization holds strictly at $\mathbf{x}^0$ when $\mathbf{p} = \mathbf{p}^0$, i.e., $[\partial F^i(\mathbf{x}^0; \mathbf{p}^0)/\partial x_j]$ is negative definite. If (1)–(3) hold, then there exists a continuously differentiable function $\mathbf{g}(\mathbf{p})$ such that $\mathbf{g}(\mathbf{p}^0) = \mathbf{x}^0$, and for $\mathbf{p}$ near $\mathbf{p}^0$, $\mathbf{F}(\mathbf{g}(\mathbf{p}); \mathbf{p}) = H_\mathbf{x}(\mathbf{g}(\mathbf{p}); \mathbf{p}) = \mathbf{0}$ and $[\partial F^i(\mathbf{g}(\mathbf{p}); \mathbf{p})/\partial x_j]$ is negative definite, so $\mathbf{g}(\mathbf{p})$ is a local maximizer given $\mathbf{p}$. The fact that $\mathbf{x}^0$ is the unique global maximizer given $\mathbf{p}^0$ implies that for $\mathbf{p}$ sufficiently close to $\mathbf{p}^0$, $\mathbf{g}(\mathbf{p})$ is the unique global maximizer given $\mathbf{p}$.
Then

$$\left[\frac{\partial g^i}{\partial p_j}(\mathbf{p}^0) \right] = - \left[\frac{\partial F^i}{\partial x_j}(\mathbf{x}^0; \mathbf{p}^0) \right]^{-1} \left[\frac{\partial F^i}{\partial p_j}(\mathbf{x}^0; \mathbf{p}^0) \right]$$

or

$$\left[\frac{\partial x_i^*}{\partial p_j}(\mathbf{p}^0) \right] = - \left[\frac{\partial^2 H}{\partial x_j \, \partial x_i}(\mathbf{x}^0; \mathbf{p}^0) \right]^{-1} \left[\frac{\partial^2 H}{\partial p_j \, \partial x_i}(\mathbf{x}^0; \mathbf{p}^0) \right].$$

This was all based on H being twice continuously differentiable and $\mathbf{x}^0$ being the unique global maximizer given parameter $\mathbf{p}^0$, with the sufficient conditions for an interior maximum satisfied at $\mathbf{x}^0$, i.e.,

$$H_\mathbf{x}(\mathbf{x}^0; \mathbf{p}^0) = \mathbf{0} \quad \text{and} \quad \left[\frac{\partial^2 H}{\partial x_j \, \partial x_i}(\mathbf{x}^0; \mathbf{p}^0) \right] \text{ is negative definite.}$$

For optimization problems with equality and/or inequality constraints the procedure is identical. The choice variables $\mathbf{x}$ include both true choice variables and the Lagrange multipliers corresponding to active constraints. H_x corresponds to the first partials of the Lagrangian L^* with respect to the true choice variables and the active multipliers. The matrix is precisely the matrix of second partials checked as part of the second-order conditions. A problem arises if our strict complementary slackness assumption fails. This will be discussed in Section 7.6. Thus the IFT typically can be used with no further work in an optimization problem. The conditions of the IFT have already been checked while solving for the unique optimum $\mathbf{x}^0$ given $\mathbf{p}^0$.

EXAMPLE: Minimize $(x - a)^2 + (y - b)^2$ where $a = 1$ and $b = 2$. $H(x, y; 1, 2) = (x - 1)^2 + (y - 2)^2$. First-order conditions are $H_x = 2(x - 1) = 0$ and $H_y = 2(y - 2) = 0$, with unique solution $x = 1$, $y = 2$. The matrix of second partials is

$$\begin{bmatrix} 2 & 0 \\ 0 & 2 \end{bmatrix}$$

which is positive definite, so $(1, 2)$ is the unique global minimizer. How does the optimal (x, y) change as (a, b) changes? By the original optimization we know the conditions for the IFT hold, so there exist differentiable functions $x^*(a, b)$ and $y^*(a, b)$ giving the optimal (x, y) for (a, b) near $(1, 2)$. Then

$$\begin{bmatrix} \dfrac{\partial x^*(1, 2)}{\partial a} & \dfrac{\partial x^*(1, 2)}{\partial b} \\ \dfrac{\partial y^*(1, 2)}{\partial a} & \dfrac{\partial y^*(1, 2)}{\partial b} \end{bmatrix} = -\begin{bmatrix} \dfrac{\partial^2 H(1, 2; 1, 2)}{\text{``}\partial x_j\,\partial x_i\text{''}} \end{bmatrix}^{-1} \begin{bmatrix} \dfrac{\partial^2 H(1, 2; 1, 2)}{\text{``}\partial p_j\,\partial x_i\text{''}} \end{bmatrix}$$

$$= -\begin{bmatrix} 2 & 0 \\ 0 & 2 \end{bmatrix}^{-1} \begin{bmatrix} -2 & 0 \\ 0 & -2 \end{bmatrix} = \begin{bmatrix} 1 & 0 \\ 0 & 1 \end{bmatrix}.$$

7.4 INTERPRETATION OF LAGRANGE MULTIPLIERS

For the problem maximize (minimize) $f(\mathbf{x})$ subject to $g^i(\mathbf{x}) = 0$ $i = 1, 2, \ldots, m$, the Lagrange multiplier, λ_i, associated with the ith constraint has an important economic interpretation as a *shadow price*, i.e., the value (in terms of f) of loosening the ith constraint. For example, for utility maximization subject to a budget constraint [maximize $u(x)$ subject to $\mathbf{p} \cdot \mathbf{x} = I$], forming the Lagrangian $L(\mathbf{x}, \lambda) = u(\mathbf{x}) + \lambda(I - \mathbf{p} \cdot \mathbf{x})$, if

$(\mathbf{x}^*, \lambda^*)$ is a solution which satisfies the first- and second-order conditions (and is the global maximizer), then λ^* is the marginal utility of income.

EXAMPLE: Minimize the cost of producing $Y^0 > 0$ where the production function is $Y = KL$ and input prices are $r^0 > 0$ and $w^0 > 0$.

The problem is to minimize $r^0 K + w^0 L$ subject to $KL = Y^0$. Since we are using L for labor input, write the Lagrangian as $M(K, L, \lambda) = r^0 K + w^0 L + \lambda(Y^0 - KL)$. The first-order conditions are

$$M_\lambda = Y^0 - KL = 0,$$

$$M_K = r^0 - \lambda L = 0,$$

$$M_L = w^0 - \lambda K = 0.$$

Solving for K, L, and λ, $r^0/w^0 = L/K$ or $L = (r^0/w^0)K$, so $Y^0 = (r^0/w^0)K^2$ and

$$K^* = \left(\frac{w^0 Y^0}{r^0}\right)^{1/2}, \quad L^* = \left(\frac{r^0 Y^0}{w^0}\right)^{1/2}, \quad \text{and} \quad \lambda^* = \left(\frac{r^0 w^0}{Y^0}\right)^{1/2}.$$

Checking the second-order conditions,

$$\begin{bmatrix} M_{\lambda\lambda} & M_{\lambda K} & M_{\lambda L} \\ M_{K\lambda} & M_{KK} & M_{KL} \\ M_{L\lambda} & M_{LK} & M_{LL} \end{bmatrix} = \begin{bmatrix} 0 & -L & -K \\ -L & 0 & -\lambda \\ -K & -\lambda & 0 \end{bmatrix}.$$

Evaluated at K^*, L^*, and λ^*,

$$(-1)^s |D_1| = (-1) \begin{vmatrix} 0 & -\left(\dfrac{r^0 Y^0}{w^0}\right)^{1/2} & -\left(\dfrac{w^0 Y^0}{r^0}\right)^{1/2} \\ -\left(\dfrac{r^0 Y^0}{w^0}\right)^{1/2} & 0 & -\left(\dfrac{r^0 w^0}{Y^0}\right)^{1/2} \\ -\left(\dfrac{w^0 Y^0}{r^0}\right)^{1/2} & -\left(\dfrac{r^0 w^0}{Y^0}\right)^{1/2} & 0 \end{vmatrix}$$

$$= 2(r^0 w^0 Y^0)^{1/2} > 0$$

so (K^*, L^*) is a strict local (and global) minimizer. By the IFT, there exist functions $K^*(Y, r, w)$, $L^*(Y, r, w)$, and $\lambda^*(Y, r, w)$ for (Y, r, w) near (Y^0, r^0, w^0), such that the firm's cost function is $C(Y, r, w) = $ minimum $\{rK + wL | KL = Y\} = rK^*(Y, r, w) + wL^*(Y, r, w) = 2\sqrt{rwY}$. The marginal cost of producing extra output (in the most efficient manner given factor prices r and w) is $\partial C / \partial Y = (rw/Y)^{1/2}$, and

$$\frac{\partial C}{\partial Y}(Y^0, r^0, w^0) = \lambda^*(Y^0, r^0, w^0) = \lambda^*.$$

Thus for the cost minimization problem along isoquants, the Lagrange multiplier $\lambda^*(Y, r, w)$ gives the marginal cost of production (the "value" in terms of the objective function, cost, of a change in the constraint, amount of output).

This property holds in general. Suppose we have the problem maximize $f(\mathbf{x})$ subject to $g(\mathbf{x}) = c$, with associated Lagrangian $L(\mathbf{x}, \lambda; c) = f(\mathbf{x}) + \lambda(c - g(\mathbf{x}))$ (so the constraint is in the same form as $I - \mathbf{p} \cdot \mathbf{x}$ in a utility maximization subject to a budget constraint) and that $(\mathbf{x}^*, \lambda^*)$ is such that $\mathbf{x}^*$ is a maximizer of $f(\mathbf{x})$ subject to $g(\mathbf{x}) = c^0$ (i.e., when $c = c^0$) at which the Lagrangian sufficient conditions for a strick local maximum hold with multiplier λ^*. In the Lagrangian, we write c after a semicolon to indicate it is a fixed parameter in the optimization problem. By the IFT, for c near c^0 we can find a solution $(\mathbf{x}^*(c), \lambda^*(c))$ which satisfies the Lagrangian sufficient conditions for a strict local maximizer of $f(\mathbf{x})$ subject to $g(\mathbf{x}) = c$. To show that $\lambda^* = \lambda^*(c^0)$ is the value, in terms of f, of loosening the constraint, we need to show that $df(\mathbf{x}^*(c^0))/dc = \lambda^*$. Using the chain rule,

$$\frac{df(\mathbf{x}^*(c^0))}{dc} = \nabla f(\mathbf{x}^*(c^0)) \cdot \frac{d\mathbf{x}^*(c^0)}{dc}$$

$$= \lambda^* \nabla g(\mathbf{x}^*(c^0)) \cdot \frac{d\mathbf{x}^*(c^0)}{dc} \quad \text{by the first-order conditions}$$

$$= \lambda^* \quad \text{since } g(\mathbf{x}^*(c)) \equiv c \text{ implies } \nabla g(\mathbf{x}^*(c)) \cdot \frac{d\mathbf{x}^*(c)}{dc} = 1.$$

When there are several constraints, this proof can be used to show $\partial f(\mathbf{x}^*(c^0))/\partial c_i = \lambda_i$. (Clearly the proof also applies to minimization problems.)

We can illustrate the proof of this principle in two ways using our previous cost minimization example. By the IFT, there exist $K^*(Y, r, w)$, $L^*(Y, r, w)$, and $\lambda^*(Y, r, w)$ for (Y, r, w) near the original (Y^0, r^0, w^0), and the firm's cost function is $C(Y, r, w) = rK^*(Y, r, w) + wL^*(Y, r, w)$. The first illustration is exactly as in the method used above for f.

$$C(Y, r, w) = rK^*(Y, r, w) + wL^*(Y, r, w);$$

$$\frac{\partial C}{\partial Y}(Y^0, r^0, w^0) = r\frac{\partial K^*}{\partial Y}(Y^0, r^0, w^0) + w\frac{\partial L^*}{\partial Y}(Y^0, r^0, w^0)$$

$$= \lambda^* L^* \frac{\partial K^*}{\partial Y} + \lambda^* K^* \frac{\partial L^*}{\partial Y} \quad \text{by the first-order conditions}$$

$$= \lambda^* \left(L^* \frac{\partial K^*}{\partial Y} + K^* \frac{\partial L^*}{\partial Y} \right)$$

$$= \lambda^* \left(\frac{dL^* K^*}{dY} \right)$$

$$= \lambda^* \frac{dY}{dY}$$

$$= \lambda^* \quad \text{since } Y \equiv K^*(Y, r, w) L^*(Y, r, w).$$

The second method will be used in the next section to derive even more results, but here we use it to show $\partial C / \partial Y = \lambda^*$. Since $Y \equiv K^*(Y, r, w)L^*(Y, r, w)$,

$$C(Y, r, w) \equiv rK^*(Y, r, w) + wL^*(Y, r, w)$$
$$+ \lambda^*(Y, r, w)[Y - K^*(Y, r, w)L^*(Y, r, w)].$$

Thus, with all terms evaluated at (Y^0, r^0, w^0),

$$\frac{\partial C}{\partial Y} = r\frac{\partial K^*}{\partial Y} + w\frac{\partial L^*}{\partial Y} + \frac{\partial \lambda^*}{\partial Y}[Y - K^*L^*] + \lambda^*\left[1 - \frac{\partial K^*}{\partial Y}L^* - K^*\frac{\partial L^*}{\partial Y}\right]$$

$$= [r - \lambda^* L^*]\frac{\partial K^*}{\partial Y} + [w - \lambda^* K^*]\frac{\partial L^*}{\partial Y}$$

$$+ [Y - K^*L^*]\frac{\partial \lambda^*}{\partial Y} + \lambda^* \quad \text{by rearranging terms}$$

$$= \lambda^*$$

since each expression in brackets is zero by the first order conditions.

7.5 THE ENVELOPE THEOREM

The envelope theorem deals with changes in the optimal value of the objective function ($f(\mathbf{x}^*)$) as any parameter changes. This can be illustrated in terms of the previous example of cost minimization. Let $C(Y, r, w)$ be the indirect cost function, $C(Y, r, w) = $ minimum $\{rK + wL \,|\, KL = Y\}$, the lowest feasible cost for producing Y when factor prices are r and w. Again, by the IFT there exist $K^*(Y, r, w)$, $L^*(Y, r, w)$, and $\lambda^*(Y, r, w)$ for (Y, r, w) near (Y^0, r^0, w^0), and

$$
\begin{aligned}
C(Y, r, w) &= rK^*(Y, r, w) + wL^*(Y, r, w) \\
&= rK^*(Y, r, w) + wL^*(Y, r, w) \\
&\quad + \lambda^*(Y, r, w)[Y - K^*(Y, r, w)L^*(Y, r, w)]
\end{aligned}
$$

since $Y \equiv K^*(Y, r, w)L^*(Y, r, w)$. In addition to the regular Lagrangian function $M(K, L, \lambda; Y, r, w) = rK + wL + \lambda(Y - KL)$ (recall we are using L for labor so M is the Lagrangian), also consider the function M^* defined by

$$
\begin{aligned}
M^*(Y, r, w) &= rK^*(Y, r, w) + wL^*(Y, r, w) \\
&\quad + \lambda^*(Y, r, w)[Y - K^*(Y, r, w)L^*(Y, r, w)],
\end{aligned}
$$

which is equal to $C(Y, r, w)$.

Using the first-order conditions for optimization,

$$
\begin{aligned}
\frac{\partial C}{\partial r}(Y, r, w) &= \frac{\partial M^*}{\partial r}(Y, r, w) \\
&= \frac{\partial M}{\partial r}(K^*(Y, r, w), L^*(Y, r, w), \lambda^*(Y, r, w); Y, r, w).
\end{aligned}
$$

To see this, use $C(Y, r, w) \equiv M^*(Y, r, w)$ to get

$$
\begin{aligned}
\frac{\partial C}{\partial r} = \frac{\partial M^*}{\partial r} &= K^* + r\frac{\partial K^*}{\partial r} + w\frac{\partial L^*}{\partial r} + \frac{\partial \lambda^*}{\partial r}[Y - K^*L^*] \\
&\quad + \lambda^*\left[-\frac{\partial K^*}{\partial r}L^* - K^*\frac{\partial L^*}{\partial r} \right] \\
&= K^* + [r - \lambda^*L^*]\frac{\partial K^*}{\partial r} + [w - \lambda^*K^*]\frac{\partial L^*}{\partial r} \\
&\quad + [Y - K^*L^*]\frac{\partial \lambda^*}{\partial r} = K^*
\end{aligned}
$$

since all terms in brackets are zero by the first-order conditions. But this is equal to

$$
\frac{\partial M}{\partial r}(K^*, L^*, \lambda^*; Y, r, w).
$$

Similarly

$$\frac{\partial C}{\partial w} = L^* = \frac{\partial M}{\partial w}(K^*, L^*, \lambda^*; Y, r, w).$$

To see why these results hold, consider a simple example. A monopolist maximizes profit, π, by choosing output q when facing a per unit tax of $t \in (0, 1)$. The cost function is $C(q) = q + q^2$ and the average revenue function is $D^{-1}(q) = 2 - q$, so profit is $\pi(q; t) = (1 - t)q - 2q^2$. At $t = 1/2$, $q^* = 1/8$ and all the conditions of the IFT are satisfied (and $1/8$ is the unique global maximizer given $t = 1/2$), so the differentiable function $q^*(t)$ gives the monopolist's optimal output given t, for t near $t^0 = 1/2$. The envelope theorem shows that for $\pi^*(t) := \pi(q^*(t); t)$,

$$\frac{d\pi^*(t)}{dt} = \frac{\partial \pi}{\partial t}(q^*(t); t).$$

When t changes, q^* also changes so that the firm continues to maximize its profit given the current t. For a change Δt, there is a corresponding change Δq^*. By differentiability, for infinitesimal changes in t, the effect of $(\Delta t, \Delta q)$ on profits, $\pi(q; t)$, can be computed as a single, combined effect of a change in the direction $(\Delta t, \Delta q^*)$, or as the sum of two separate effects, $(\Delta t, 0)$ and $(0, \Delta q^*)$. (This just means that directional derivatives can be computed using partial derivatives.) But $\pi(q^*(t); t)$ is along the ridge that corresponds to a peak of $\pi(q; t)$ relative to q, so the effect of the infinitesimal change $(0, \Delta q)$ is zero. Thus the only change in $\pi^*(t)$ comes from the change $(\Delta t, 0)$. Formally

$$\begin{aligned}\frac{d\pi^*(t)}{dt} &= \frac{d(\pi(q^*(t); t))}{dt}\\[2mm] &= \frac{\partial \pi(q^*(t); t)}{\partial q}\frac{dq^*(t)}{dt} + \frac{\partial \pi(q^*(t); t)}{\partial t}\\[2mm] &= \frac{\partial \pi(q^*(t); t)}{\partial t}\end{aligned}$$

since $\partial \pi(q^*(t); t)/\partial q$ is zero by profit maximization at $q^*(t)$ given t. Thus it is unnecessary to compute $dq^*(t)/dt$ to find $d\pi^*(t)/dt$.

For each t^0, define $H(t; t^0) := \pi(q^*(t^0); t)$. As a function of t with fixed parameter t^0, since $q^*(t)$ is optimal for t, $H(t; t^0) = \pi(q^*(t^0); t) \leq \pi(q^*(t); t) = \pi^*(t)$. Thus for each t^0, the graph of $H(t; t^0) = \pi(q^*(t^0); t)$ (as a function of t) lies on or below the graph of $\pi^*(t)$, and $\pi^*(t)$ is the upper envelope of this family of graphs. This motivates the use of the name *envelope theorem* to identify the general result.

In general, the change in the optimized objective function (C or π^*) as a parameter changes is equal to the change in the corresponding Lagrangian, L, as the same parameter changes, evaluated at the optimal solution ($K^*(Y, r, w)$, $L^*(Y, r, w)$, $\lambda^*(Y, r, w)$ or $q^*(t)$). The fact that optimal solutions always satisfy the corresponding constraints and the first-order conditions for optimization allows us to ignore all complicating terms ($\partial K^*/\partial r$, $\partial L^*/\partial r$, and $\partial \lambda^*/\partial r$, or dq^*/dt) since all these terms drop out.

ENVELOPE THEOREM:

1. (*Without constraints*) *If* $f: \mathbb{R}^{n+k} \to \mathbb{R}$ *is a continuously differentiable function, and for parameters* $\mathbf{p} \in \mathbb{R}^k$, $\mathbf{x}^*(\mathbf{p}) \in \mathbb{R}^n$ *is the unique optimizer of* $f(\mathbf{x}; \mathbf{p})$ *[and* $\mathbf{x}^*(\mathbf{p})$ *is continuously differentiable], and we define* $f^*(\mathbf{p}) := f(\mathbf{x}^*(\mathbf{p}); \mathbf{p})$, *then*

$$\frac{\partial f^*(\mathbf{p})}{\partial p_i} = \frac{\partial f}{\partial p_i}(\mathbf{x}^*(\mathbf{p}); \mathbf{p}) \quad \text{for } i = 1, 2, \ldots, k.$$

2. (*With constraints*) *If* $f: \mathbb{R}^{n+k} \to \mathbb{R}$ *and* $g^i: \mathbb{R}^{n+k} \to \mathbb{R}$ $i = 1, 2, \ldots, m$ ($m < n$) *are continuously differentiable functions, and for parameters* $\mathbf{p} \in R^k$, $\mathbf{x}^*(\mathbf{p}) \in \mathbb{R}^n$ *and* $\boldsymbol{\lambda}^*(\mathbf{p}) \in \mathbb{R}^m$ *are such that* $\mathbf{x}^*(\mathbf{p})$ *is the unique optimizer of* $f(\mathbf{x}; \mathbf{p})$ *subject to* $g^i(\mathbf{x}, \mathbf{p}) = 0$, $i = 1, 2, \ldots, m$, *such that the Lagrangian first-order conditions hold with multipliers* $\lambda_i^*(\mathbf{p})$, $i = 1, 2, \ldots, m$, *[and* $\mathbf{x}^*(\mathbf{p})$, $\lambda_i^*(\mathbf{p})$, $i = 1, \ldots, m$, *are continuously differentiable] and we define* $f^*(\mathbf{p}) := f(\mathbf{x}^*(\mathbf{p}); \mathbf{p})$, *then for* $i = 1, 2, \ldots, k$,

$$\frac{\partial f^*(\mathbf{p})}{\partial p_i} = \frac{\partial f}{\partial p_i}(\mathbf{x}^*(\mathbf{p}); \mathbf{p}) + \sum_{j=1}^{m} \lambda_j^*(\mathbf{p}) \frac{\partial g^j}{\partial p_i}(\mathbf{x}^*(\mathbf{p}); \mathbf{p})$$

$$= \frac{\partial L}{\partial p_i}(\mathbf{x}^*(\mathbf{p}), \boldsymbol{\lambda}^*(\mathbf{p}); \mathbf{p}).$$

Proof:

1. $f^*(\mathbf{p}) \equiv f(\mathbf{x}^*(\mathbf{p}); \mathbf{p})$ so, using the chain rule,

$$\frac{\partial f^*(\mathbf{p})}{\partial p_i} = \left(\sum_{j=1}^{n} \frac{\partial f}{\partial x_j}(\mathbf{x}^*(\mathbf{p}); \mathbf{p}) \frac{\partial x_j^*(\mathbf{p})}{\partial p_i} \right)$$

$$+ \frac{\partial f}{\partial p_i}(\mathbf{x}^*(\mathbf{p}); \mathbf{p}) = \frac{\partial f}{\partial p_i}(\mathbf{x}^*(\mathbf{p}); \mathbf{p})$$

since the term in brackets is zero by the first-order conditions.

2. Since $g^j(\mathbf{x}(\mathbf{p}); \mathbf{p}) \equiv 0$, $j = 1, 2, \ldots, m$,

$$f^*(\mathbf{p}) := f(\mathbf{x}^*(\mathbf{p}); \mathbf{p}) \equiv f(\mathbf{x}^*(\mathbf{p}); \mathbf{p}) + \sum_{j=1}^{m} \lambda_j^*(\mathbf{p}) g^j(\mathbf{x}^*(\mathbf{p}); \mathbf{p}).$$

Using the chain rule,

$$\frac{\partial f^*(\mathbf{p})}{\partial p_i} = \left(\sum_{t=1}^{n} \frac{\partial f}{\partial x_t}(\mathbf{x}^*(\mathbf{p}); \mathbf{p}) \frac{\partial x_t^*(\mathbf{p})}{\partial p_i} \right) + \frac{\partial f}{\partial p_i}(\mathbf{x}^*(\mathbf{p}); \mathbf{p})$$

$$+ \sum_{j=1}^{m} \left(\frac{\partial \lambda_j^*}{\partial p_i}(\mathbf{p}) g^j(\mathbf{x}^*(\mathbf{p}); \mathbf{p}) + \lambda_j^*(\mathbf{p}) \right.$$

$$\left. \times \left[\left(\sum_{t=1}^{n} \frac{\partial g^j}{\partial x_t}(\mathbf{x}^*(\mathbf{p}); \mathbf{p}) \frac{\partial x_t^*(\mathbf{p})}{\partial p_i} \right) + \frac{\partial g^j}{\partial p_i}(\mathbf{x}^*(\mathbf{p}), \mathbf{p}) \right] \right)$$

$$= \sum_{t=1}^{n} \left[\frac{\partial f}{\partial x_t}(\mathbf{x}^*(\mathbf{p}); \mathbf{p}) + \sum_{j=1}^{m} \lambda_j^*(\mathbf{p}) \frac{\partial g^j}{\partial x_t}(\mathbf{x}^*(\mathbf{p}); \mathbf{p}) \right] \frac{\partial x_t^*(\mathbf{p})}{\partial p_i}$$

$$+ \sum_{j=1}^{m} \frac{\partial \lambda_j^*(\mathbf{p})}{\partial p_i} \left[g^j(\mathbf{x}^*(\mathbf{p}); \mathbf{p}) \right]$$

$$+ \frac{\partial f}{\partial p_i}(\mathbf{x}^*(\mathbf{p}); \mathbf{p}) + \sum_{j=1}^{m} \lambda_j^*(\mathbf{p}) \frac{\partial g^j}{\partial p_i}(x^*(\mathbf{p}); \mathbf{p})$$

$$= \frac{\partial f}{\partial p_i}(\mathbf{x}^*(\mathbf{p}); \mathbf{p}) + \sum_{j=1}^{m} \lambda_j^*(\mathbf{p}) \frac{\partial g^j}{\partial p_i}(\mathbf{x}^*(\mathbf{p}); \mathbf{p})$$

since all terms in brackets are zero

$$= \frac{\partial L}{\partial p_i}(\mathbf{x}^*(\mathbf{p}), \boldsymbol{\lambda}^*(\mathbf{p}); \mathbf{p})$$

It is important to note the order of events. To find the effect of a parameter change on the optimized value of the objective function, first take the regular partial derivative of the Lagrangian with respect to the parameter and then evaluate the result at the original parameter values and the original optimizers. When taking the regular partial derivative, it is important to recognize all places where the parameter appears in the Lagrangian.

EXAMPLE: For the problem of maximizing $f(x, p) = x + p$ subject to $g(x, p) = 2x - p \leq 0$ with Lagrangian $L(x, \lambda; p) = x + p - \lambda(2x - p)$

the solution is $x^*(p) = p/2$, $\lambda^*(p) = 1/2$. Then $f^*(p) = 3p/2$, $\partial f/\partial p = 1$, $\partial g/\partial p = -1$ and

$$\frac{\partial L^*(x^*(p), \lambda^*(p); p)}{\partial p} = \frac{\partial f(x^*(p), p)}{\partial p} - \lambda^*(p) \frac{\partial g(x^*(p), p)}{\partial p}$$

$$= 1 - (1/2)(-1) = 3/2 = df^*(p)/dp.$$

EXAMPLE: Maximize utility $u(x, y) = x^2 y$ subject to the budget constraints $I = p_x x + p_y y$. Form the Lagrangian $L(x, y, \lambda; I, p_x, p_y) = x^2 y + \lambda(I - p_x x - p_y y)$. First-order conditions and the second-order condition matrix are

$$L_\lambda = I - p_x x - p_y y,$$

$$L_x = 2xy - \lambda p_x,$$

$$L_y = x^2 - \lambda p_y,$$

$$\begin{bmatrix} L_{\lambda\lambda} & L_{\lambda x} & L_{\lambda y} \\ L_{x\lambda} & L_{xx} & L_{xy} \\ L_{y\lambda} & L_{yx} & L_{yy} \end{bmatrix} = \begin{bmatrix} 0 & -p_x & -p_y \\ -p_x & 2y & 2x \\ -p_y & 2x & 0 \end{bmatrix}.$$

Setting $\nabla L = 0$ and solving for x, y, and λ, given that $(I, p_x, p_y) = (3, 2, 1)$, we get $x^* = y^* = \lambda^* = 1$ and $|D_1| = 6 > 0$, so the solution is a local (and global) maximizer. The conditions of the IFT are satisfied, and thus the conditions of the envelope theorem are satisfied and we can use the envelope theorem to determine how optimized utility changes when a parameter changes. Define the indirect utility function: $v(I, p_x, p_y) = $ maximum $\{u(x, y) | I = p_x x + p_y y\}$. Recall the Lagrangian is $L(x, y, \lambda; I, p_x, p_y) = x^2 y + \lambda(I - p_x x - p_y y)$. By the envelope theorem

$$\frac{\partial v}{\partial I}(3, 2, 1) = \frac{\partial L}{\partial I}(1, 1, 1; 3, 2, 1) = \lambda^*(3, 2, 1) = 1,$$

$$\frac{\partial v}{\partial p_x}(3, 2, 1) = \frac{\partial L}{\partial p_x}(1, 1, 1; 3, 2, 1) = -\lambda^*(3, 2, 1) x^*(3, 2, 1) = -1,$$

$$\frac{\partial v}{\partial p_y}(3, 2, 1) = \frac{\partial L}{\partial p_y}(1, 1, 1; 3, 2, 1) = -\lambda^*(3, 2, 1) y^*(3, 2, 1) = -1.$$

EXAMPLE: Minimize the cost of producing $Y^0 > 0$ according to the production function $Y = 1 + (KL - 1)^{1/3}$ when factor prices are $r^0 > 0$ and $w^0 > 0$. Since we are using L for labor, write the Lagrangian as $M(K, L, \lambda; Y, r, w) = rK + wL + \lambda(Y - 1 - (KL - 1)^{1/3})$. The first-order conditions and the second-order condition matrix are

$$M_\lambda = Y - 1 - (KL - 1)^{1/3} = 0,$$

$$M_K = r - \frac{\lambda}{3}L(KL - 1)^{-2/3} = 0,$$

$$M_L = w - \frac{\lambda}{3}K(KL - 1)^{-2/3} = 0,$$

$$\begin{bmatrix} M_{\lambda\lambda} & M_{\lambda K} & M_{\lambda L} \\ M_{K\lambda} & M_{KK} & M_{KL} \\ M_{L\lambda} & M_{LK} & M_{LL} \end{bmatrix}$$

$$= \begin{bmatrix} 0 & -(L/3)(KL-1)^{-2/3} & -(K/3)(KL-1)^{-2/3} \\ -(L/3)(KL-1)^{-2/3} & \frac{2\lambda}{9}L^2(KL-1)^{-5/3} & \frac{\lambda}{3}(KL-1)^{-5/3}\left(1 - \frac{KL}{3}\right) \\ -(K/3)(KL-1)^{-2/3} & \frac{\lambda}{3}(KL-1)^{-5/3}\left(1 - \frac{KL}{3}\right) & \frac{2\lambda}{9}K^2(KL-1)^{-5/3} \end{bmatrix}.$$

At $Y^0 = 3$ and $r^0 = w^0 = 1$, the optimal solution is $K^* = L^* = 3$ and $\lambda^* = 4$. To see this, note that $M_K = 0$ implies $r^0 = (\lambda/3)L(KL - 1)^{-2/3}$ and $M_L = 0$ implies $w^0 = (\lambda/3)K(KL - 1)^{-2/3}$, so $r^0/w^0 = L/K$. With $r^0 = w^0 = 1$, $L = K$, and using $Y^0 = 3$ in $M_\lambda = 0$, we get $(K^2 - 1)^{1/3} = 2$ or $K^2 = 9$. Clearly K and L must be positive to make economic sense, so $K^* = L^* = 3$. Substituting back into $M_K = 0$, we find $\lambda^* = 4$. Substituting $K = L = 3$ and $\lambda = 4$ into the matrix of second partials, we find $|D_1| = -1/24$, so the solution is a local (and global) minimizer. Letting

$$F^1(K, L, \lambda; Y, r, w) = Y - 1 - (KL - 1)^{1/3}(= M_\lambda),$$

$$F^2(K, L, \lambda; Y, r, w) = r - \frac{\lambda}{3}L(KL - 1)^{-2/3}(= M_K),$$

$$F^3(K, L, \lambda; Y, r, w) = w - \frac{\lambda}{3}K(KL - 1)^{-2/3}(= M_L),$$

we see that each F^i is continuously differentiable near

$(K^*, L^*, \lambda^*; Y^0, r^0, w^0) = (3, 3, 4; 3, 1, 1)$, and $F^i(3, 3, 4; 3, 1, 1) = 0$ for $i = 1, 2, 3$.

Evaluated at $(3, 3, 4; 3, 1, 1)$, the determinant is

$$\begin{vmatrix} F^1_\lambda & F^1_K & F^1_L \\ F^2_\lambda & F^2_K & F^2_L \\ F^3_\lambda & F^3_K & F^3_L \end{vmatrix} = |D_1| = -\frac{1}{24} \neq 0,$$

so the conditions of the IFT are satisfied, and there are continuously differentiable functions $K^*(Y, r, w)$, $L^*(Y, r, w)$, and $\lambda^*(Y, r, w)$ such that $K^*(3, 1, 1) = 3$, $L^*(3, 1, 1) = 3$, and $\lambda^*(3, 1, 1) = 4$; $K^*(Y, r, w)$ and $L^*(Y, r, w)$ are the optimal input levels as functions of (Y, r, w) for (Y, r, w) near $(3, 1, 1)$. $K^*(Y, r, w)$ and $L^*(Y, r, w)$ satisfy the sufficient conditions for a strict local minimizer with Lagrange multiplier $\lambda^*(Y, r, w)$.

For the cost function $C(Y, r, w) = \text{minimum } \{rK + wL | Y = 1 + (KL - 1)^{1/3}\}$, we know by the envelope theorem that

$$\frac{\partial C}{\partial Y}(3, 1, 1) = \frac{\partial M}{\partial Y}(3, 3, 4; 3, 1, 1) = \lambda^*(3, 1, 1) = 4,$$

$$\frac{\partial C}{\partial r}(3, 1, 1) = \frac{\partial M}{\partial r}(3, 3, 4; 3, 1, 1) = K^*(3, 1, 1) = 3,$$

$$\frac{\partial C}{\partial w}(3, 1, 1) = \frac{\partial M}{\partial w}(3, 3, 4; 3, 1, 1) = L^*(3, 1, 1) = 3.$$

Notice how useful the envelope theorem is. We are able to find the partial derivatives of the cost function without having to compute the partial derivatives of K^* and L^*. We could have computed the result from

$$\frac{\partial C}{\partial Y}(3, 1, 1) = r\frac{\partial K^*}{\partial Y}(3, 1, 1) + w\frac{\partial L^*}{\partial Y}(3, 1, 1).$$

Suppose we also want to find out how the conditional factor demand functions, $K^*(Y, r, w)$, and $L^*(Y, r, w)$, change as the parameters change. By Eq. (3) of Section 7.3, for the functions $F^i(K, L, \lambda; Y, r, w)$, $i = 1, 2, 3$, as previously defined,

$$
\begin{bmatrix}
\dfrac{\partial \lambda^*}{\partial Y} & \dfrac{\partial \lambda^*}{\partial r} & \dfrac{\partial \lambda^*}{\partial w} \\[2ex]
\dfrac{\partial K^*}{\partial Y} & \dfrac{\partial K^*}{\partial r} & \dfrac{\partial K^*}{\partial w} \\[2ex]
\dfrac{\partial L^*}{\partial Y} & \dfrac{\partial L^*}{\partial r} & \dfrac{\partial L^*}{\partial w}
\end{bmatrix}
$$

$$
= -
\begin{bmatrix}
\dfrac{\partial F^1}{\partial \lambda} & \dfrac{\partial F^1}{\partial K} & \dfrac{\partial F^1}{\partial L} \\[2ex]
\dfrac{\partial F^2}{\partial \lambda} & \dfrac{\partial F^2}{\partial K} & \dfrac{\partial F^2}{\partial L} \\[2ex]
\dfrac{\partial F^3}{\partial \lambda} & \dfrac{\partial F^3}{\partial K} & \dfrac{\partial F^3}{\partial L}
\end{bmatrix}^{-1}
\begin{bmatrix}
\dfrac{\partial F^1}{\partial Y} & \dfrac{\partial F^1}{\partial r} & \dfrac{\partial F^1}{\partial w} \\[2ex]
\dfrac{\partial F^2}{\partial Y} & \dfrac{\partial F^2}{\partial r} & \dfrac{\partial F^2}{\partial w} \\[2ex]
\dfrac{\partial F^3}{\partial Y} & \dfrac{\partial F^3}{\partial r} & \dfrac{\partial F^3}{\partial w}
\end{bmatrix}
$$

where all entries in the left-hand matrix are evaluated at $(Y, r, w) = (3, 1, 1)$ and all entries in the two right-hand matrices are evaluated at $(K, L, \lambda; Y, r, w) = (3, 3, 4; 3, 1, 1)$. Notice that the matrix being inverted is just the matrix of second partials of M, D_1. Thus the right-hand side is

$$
-\begin{bmatrix} 0 & -\dfrac{1}{4} & -\dfrac{1}{4} \\ -\dfrac{1}{4} & \dfrac{1}{4} & -12 \\ -\dfrac{1}{4} & -12 & \dfrac{1}{4} \end{bmatrix}^{-1} \begin{bmatrix} 1 & 0 & 0 \\ 0 & 1 & 0 \\ 0 & 0 & 1 \end{bmatrix} = \begin{bmatrix} 4/3 & 2 & 2 \\ 2 & -3/2 & 3/2 \\ 2 & 3/2 & -3/2 \end{bmatrix}.
$$

We can use these results to check our previous computations which used the envelope theorem: $C(Y, r, w) = rK^*(Y, r, w) + wL^*(Y, r, w)$ so

$$
\frac{\partial C}{\partial Y}(3, 1, 1) = r\frac{\partial K^*}{\partial Y}(3, 1, 1) + w\frac{\partial L^*}{\partial Y}(3, 1, 1)
$$

$$
= (1) \cdot (2) + (1) \cdot (2) = 4,
$$

$$
\frac{\partial C}{\partial r}(3, 1, 1) = K^*(3, 1, 1) + r\frac{\partial K^*}{\partial r}(3, 1, 1) + w\frac{\partial L^*}{\partial r}(3, 1, 1)
$$

$$
= 3 + (1)\left(-\frac{3}{2}\right) + (1)\left(\frac{3}{2}\right) = 3,
$$

$$
\frac{\partial C}{\partial w}(3, 1, 1) = r\frac{\partial K^*}{\partial w}(3, 1, 1) + L^*(3, 1, 1) + w\frac{\partial L^*}{\partial w}(3, 1, 1)
$$

$$
= (1)\left(\frac{3}{2}\right) + 3 + (1)\left(-\frac{3}{2}\right) = 3.
$$

As a further check on all the results we can check that the optimal solutions are

$$
K^*(Y, r, w) = \left(\left[1 + (Y - 1)^3\right]\frac{w}{r}\right)^{1/2},
$$

$$
L^*(Y, r, w) = \left(\left[1 + (Y - 1)^3\right]\frac{r}{w}\right)^{1/2},
$$

$$
\lambda^*(Y, r, w) = \frac{3(Y - 1)^2}{\left(\left[1 + (Y - 1)^3\right]/rw\right)^{1/2}}
$$

and compute all derivatives directly.

7.6 INEQUALITY CONSTRAINTS

Inequality constraints can be treated with the same methods. Nonbinding inequality constraints should be ignored. With strict complementary slackness, the active inequality constraints may be treated as equality constraints for small changes in the parameters. (It is important to have the unique global optimizer at the starting parameter values.) The only potential new difficulty involves a failure of strict complementary slackness, where some active constraint has corresponding multiplier zero. In this case, the constraint may be just at the borderline between active and inactive as the exogenous parameters change.

EXAMPLE: Consider the problem of minimizing $px + y$ subject to $x \geq 0$, $y \geq 0$, and $(x + 1)(y + 1) \geq 2$. When $p = 2$, the optimizer is $x^*, y^*, \lambda_1^*, \lambda_2^*, \lambda_3^*) = (0, 1, 0, 0, 1)$. The $x \geq 0$ constraint is active but the corresponding multiplier is zero. For $1/2 \leq p \leq 2$ the optimizer is $(\sqrt{2/p} - 1, \sqrt{2p} - 1, 0, 0, \sqrt{p/2})$, while for $p > 2$ the optimizer is $(0, 1, p - 2, 0, 1)$. At $p = 2$ the $x \geq 0$ constraint is just at the borderline of being active. Note that $x^*(p)$ is not differentiable at $p = 2$: for $p > 2$, $x^*(p) = 0$, while for $1/2 \leq p \leq 2$, $x^*(p) = \sqrt{2/p} - 1$. Note however that

$$f^*(p) = px^*(p) + y^*(p) = \begin{cases} 2\sqrt{2p} - p - 1 & \text{if } p \leq 2, \\ 1 & \text{if } p > 2 \end{cases}$$

is differentiable even at $p = 2$, with $df^*(p)/dp = x^*(p)$.

EXAMPLE: Minimize $(x + 1)^2 + (y + 1)^2$ subject to $x + y \geq 0$ and $(x + 1)(y + 1) \geq p^2$. For $0 < p \leq 1$ the solution is $x^*(p) = y^*(p) = 0$ with $f^*(p) = 2$. For $1 < p$ the solution is $x^*(p) = y^*(p) = p - 1$ with $f^*(p) = 2p^2$. Here none of $x^*(p)$, $y^*(p)$, and $f^*(p)$ are differentiable at $p = 1$. Note the active constraint switches from $x + y \geq 0$ to $(x + 1)(y + 1) \geq p^2$ and the constraint qualification condition fails at $p = 1$.

EXAMPLE: Let

$$b(p) = \begin{cases} \sqrt{p} & \text{if } p \geq 0, \\ -\sqrt{-p} & \text{if } p < 0. \end{cases}$$

Minimize $(x + 1)^2 + (y + 1)^2$ subject to $x + y \geq 0$ and $x - y \geq b(p)$. For $p \leq 0$ the solution is $x^*(p) = y^*(p) = 0$ with $f^*(p) = 2$. For $p > 0$ the solution is $x^*(p) = -y^*(p) = \sqrt{p}/2$ with $f^*(p) = 2 + p/2$. Here none of $x^*(p)$, $y^*(p)$, and $f^*(p)$ are differentiable at $p = 0$. Note that the constraint $x + y \geq 0$ is always active, the constraint $x - y \geq b(p)$ becomes active at $p = 0$, and $b(p)$ is not differentiable at $p = 0$.

The previous examples examined the properties of optimal choices and the optimized objective function at parameter values where the active constraints change. Now we will compare the responses to parameter changes of the optimal choices and the optimized objective function under two different sets of constraints, an original set and an expanded set. A typical example would be a comparison of a firm's short-run and long-run responses to a parameter change. The application of the *Le Châtelier principle* explains why, for example, long-run demands are more elastic than short-run demands.

Example: Consider a competitive firm facing fixed input and output prices with a technology specified by the function g. Divide the goods into two groups: let $\mathbf{x}$ be the vector of inputs and outputs that are variable in both long and short run, with prices given by the vector $\mathbf{p}$, and let $\mathbf{z}$ be the vector of inputs that are variable in the long run but fixed in the short run, with prices given by the vector $\mathbf{q}$. The production plan $(\mathbf{x}, \mathbf{z})$ is feasible if and only if $g(\mathbf{x}, \mathbf{z}) \leq 0$. A positive coordinate of $(\mathbf{x}, \mathbf{z})$ corresponds to an output and a negative coordinate corresponds to an input. Then the profit corresponding to production plan $(\mathbf{x}, \mathbf{z})$ is $\mathbf{p} \cdot \mathbf{x} + \mathbf{q} \cdot \mathbf{z}$. Throughout this example we assume the appropriate IFT conditions hold, so all comparative statics derivatives are well defined. The firm's long-run problem is to choose $\mathbf{x}$ and $\mathbf{z}$ to maximize $\mathbf{p} \cdot \mathbf{x} + \mathbf{q} \cdot \mathbf{z}$ subject to $g(\mathbf{x}, \mathbf{z}) \leq 0$. Denote the optimizers by $\mathbf{x}^*(\mathbf{p}, \mathbf{q})$ and $\mathbf{z}^*(\mathbf{p}, \mathbf{q})$, with corresponding optimized profit $\pi(\mathbf{p}, \mathbf{q})$. By the envelope theorem, $\partial \pi(\mathbf{p}, \mathbf{q})/\partial p_i = x_i^*(\mathbf{p}, \mathbf{q})$. The firm's short-run problem given fixed $\mathbf{z}$ is to choose $\mathbf{x}$ to maximize $\mathbf{p} \cdot \mathbf{x} + \mathbf{q} \cdot \mathbf{z}$ subject to $g(\mathbf{x}, \mathbf{z}) \leq 0$. Denote the optimizers by $\mathbf{x}^s(\mathbf{p}, \mathbf{q}, \mathbf{z})$, with corresponding optimized profit $\pi^s(\mathbf{p}, \mathbf{q}, \mathbf{z})$. By the envelope theorem,

$$\frac{\partial \pi^s(\mathbf{p}, \mathbf{q}, \mathbf{z})}{\partial p_i} = x_i^s(\mathbf{p}, \mathbf{q}, \mathbf{z}).$$

Let $\mathbf{z}^0 = \mathbf{z}^*(\mathbf{p}^0, \mathbf{q}^0)$. Then $x^s(\mathbf{p}^0, \mathbf{q}^0, \mathbf{z}^0) = \mathbf{x}^*(\mathbf{p}^0, \mathbf{q}^0)$. Let $f(\mathbf{p}, \mathbf{q}) = \pi(\mathbf{p}, \mathbf{q}) - \pi^s(\mathbf{p}, \mathbf{q}, \mathbf{z}^0)$. Then $f(\mathbf{p}, \mathbf{q}) \geq 0$ for all $\mathbf{p}, \mathbf{q}$ and $f(\mathbf{p}^0, \mathbf{q}^0) = 0$, so f is minimized at $\mathbf{p}^0, \mathbf{q}^0$. By the first-order necessary conditions for unconstrained minimization, $\nabla f(\mathbf{p}^0, \mathbf{q}^0) = \mathbf{0}$ or

$$\frac{\partial \pi(\mathbf{p}^0, \mathbf{q}^0)}{\partial p_i} = \frac{\partial \pi^s(\mathbf{p}^0, \mathbf{q}^0, \mathbf{z}^0)}{\partial p_i} \quad \text{for all } i,$$

$$\frac{\partial \pi(\mathbf{p}^0, \mathbf{q}^0)}{\partial q_j} = \frac{\partial \pi^s(\mathbf{p}^0, \mathbf{q}^0, \mathbf{z}^0)}{\partial q_j} \quad \text{for all } j.$$

Thus the long-run and short-run effects of price changes on profit are equal if the short-run fixed factors are optimal. (This is similar to the result that long-run and short-run marginal costs are equal when the short-run plant is optimal for producing the given output.) By the second-order necessary conditions for minimization, $[f_{ij}(\mathbf{p}^0, \mathbf{q}^0)]$ must be positive semidefinite, so the diagonal entries must be nonnegative. Thus

$$\frac{\partial x_i(\mathbf{p}^0, \mathbf{q}^0)}{\partial p_i} = \frac{\partial^2 \pi(\mathbf{p}^0, \mathbf{q}^0)}{\partial p_i^2} \geq \frac{\partial^2 \pi^s(\mathbf{p}^0, \mathbf{q}^0, \mathbf{z}^0)}{\partial p_i^2} = \frac{\partial x^s(\mathbf{p}^0, \mathbf{q}^0, \mathbf{z}^0)}{\partial p_i}$$

and the long-run responses to own price changes must be at least as elastic as the short-run responses.

The general result is similar and is proved in a similar manner. For a maximization problem, the long-run optimized value of the objective function is the upper envelope of the corresponding short-run optimized functions and thus must be "more convex" (or "less concave") than the short-run function with the optimal values for the fixed variables. For minimization problems (such as cost minimization for the firm), the long-run function is the lower envelope of the short-run functions and thus must be less convex (or more convcave) than the short-run function with the optimal values for the fixed variables. As in the example above, this often leads to important economic implications for the optimizing choices. The second order results are sometimes referred to as generalized envelope theorem or Le Châtelier principle results.

7.7 APPLICATION TO CONSUMER THEORY

In this section we examine some of the economic applications of duality and the envelope theorem in the context of a consumer problem with two goods and strictly increasing utility. For brevity, we ignore all second-order conditions and assume nonnegativity constraints are never binding.

7.7.1 Generalized Demand Functions

The usual consumer problem is to maximize utility subject to a budget constraint. The variables are the amounts of the commodities, x and y, and the Lagrange multiplier λ, while the parameters are prices p_x and p_y for commodities x and y, respectively, and income M. The solution to this problem will yield the optimal variable values as functions of the parameters: $x^*(p_x, p_y, M)$, $y^*(p_x, p_y, M)$, and $\lambda^*(p_x, p_y, M)$. The x^* and y^* are the generalized (ordinary or regular) demand functions.

1. Set up the Lagrangian:

$$L(x, y, \lambda; p_x, p_y, M) = u(x, y) - \lambda(-M + p_x x + p_y y).$$

2. Differentiate with respect to variables to get the first-order conditions:

$$L_x = u_x - \lambda p_x = 0,$$

$$L_y = u_y - \lambda p_y = 0,$$

$$L_\lambda = M - p_x x - p_y y = 0.$$

3. Solve for x, y and λ as functions of p_x, p_y, and M.

EXAMPLE: $u(x, y) = xy$

1. $L(x, y, \lambda; p_x, p_y, M) = xy - \lambda(-M + p_x x + p_y y).$
2.
$$L_x = y - \lambda p_x = 0,$$

$$L_y = x - \lambda p_y = 0,$$

$$L_\lambda = M - p_x x - p_y y = 0.$$

3.
$$x^*(p_x, p_y, M) = M/2p_x,$$

$$y^*(p_x, p_y, M) = M/2p_y,$$

$$\lambda^*(p_x, p_y, M) = M/2p_x p_y.$$

7.7.2 Indirect Utility Function

The indirect utility function specifies the utility attained at the solution to the generalized demand problem. Since generalized demands are functions of the parameters p_x, p_y, M, so is the indirect utility.

$$u^*(p_x, p_y, M) = u\big(x^*(p_x, p_y, M), y^*(p_x, p_y, M)\big).$$

For the example in Section 7.7.1, $u^*(p_x, p_y, M) = x^* y^* = M^2/4p_x p_y$.

If we start with the indirect utility function, we can recover the generalized demand functions by using the envelope theorem.

1. Write the Lagrangian corresponding to the original generalized demand problem: $L(x, y, \lambda; p_x, p_y, M) = u(x, y) - \lambda(-M + p_x x + p_y y)$.
2. Differentiate with respect to the parameters.

$$L_{p_x} = -\lambda x,$$

$$L_{p_y} = -\lambda y,$$

$$L_M = \lambda.$$

3. Evaluate the answers in step 2 at x^*, y^*, λ^*.

$$L_{p_x} = -\lambda^*(p_x, p_y, M)x^*(p_x, p_y, M),$$

$$L_{p_y} = -\lambda^*(p_x, p_y, M)y^*(p_x, p_y, M)$$

$$L_M = \lambda^*(p_x, p_y, M).$$

4. By the envelope theorem, the partials of u^* are equal to the corresponding partials in step 3.

$$\frac{\partial u^*}{\partial p_x} = -\lambda^*(p_x, p_y, M)x^*(p_x, p_y, M) \text{ etc.}$$

To recover the generalized demands, note that $-L_{p_x}/L_M = x^*$ so

$$x^*(p_x, p_y, M) = -\frac{\partial u^*/\partial p_x}{\partial u^*/\partial M}$$

can be used to find x^* given $u^*(p_x, p_y, M)$.

EXAMPLE: Given $u^*(p_x, p_y, M) = M^2/4p_x p_y$, find the demand for y at $p_x = 11$, $p_y = 7$, $M = 28$.

$$y^*(p_x, p_y, M) = -\frac{\partial u^*/\partial p_y}{\partial u^*/\partial M} = -\frac{-M^2/4p_x p_y^2}{2M/4p_x p_y} = \frac{M}{2p_y}$$

Thus $y^*(11, 7, 28) = 28/(2)(7) = 2$.

7.7.3 Generalized Compensated Demand Functions

This problem is useful in evaluating consumer's surplus. The problem is to minimize the expenditure necessary to attain a target utility level. The variables are x, y, and the Lagrange multiplier μ, while the parameters are p_x, p_y, and the target utility level U. The solutions include the generalized compensated demand functions, $x_c^*(p_x, p_y, U)$ and $y_c^*(p_x, p_y, U)$.

1. Set up the Lagrangian:

$$L(x, y, \mu; p_x, p_y, U) = p_x x + p_y y - \mu(-U + u(x, y)).$$

2. Differentiate with respect to variables to get the first order conditions:

$$L_x = p_x - \mu u_x = 0,$$

$$L_y = p_y - \mu u_y = 0,$$

$$L_\mu = U - u(x, y) = 0.$$

3. Solve for x, y, and μ as functions of p_x, p_y, U.

EXAMPLE: $u(x, y) = xy$

1. $L(x, y, \mu; p_x, p_y, U) = p_x x + p_y y - \mu(-U + xy)$.

2.
$$L_x = p_x - \mu y = 0,$$

$$L_y = p_y - \mu x = 0,$$

$$L_\mu = U - xy = 0.$$

3.
$$x_c^*(p_x, p_y, U) = \sqrt{\frac{p_y U}{p_x}},$$

$$y_c^*(p_x, p_y, U) = \sqrt{\frac{p_x U}{p_y}},$$

$$\mu^*(p_x, p_y, U) = \sqrt{\frac{p_x p_y}{U}}.$$

7.7.4 Expenditure Function

The expenditure function specifies the expenditure necessary at the solution to the generalized compensated demand problem. It is a function of p_x, p_y, and U:

$$M^*(p_x, p_y, U) = p_x x_c^*(p_x, p_y, U) + p_y y_c^*(p_x, p_y, U).$$

For the example in Section 7.7.3,

$$M^*(p_x, p_y, U) = p_x x_c^* + p_y y_c^* = 2\sqrt{p_x p_y U}.$$

If we start with the expenditure function, we can recover the generalized compensated demand functions by using the envelope theorem.

1. Write the Lagrangian corresponding to the original generalized compensated demand problem:

$$L(x, y, \mu; p_x, p_y, U) = p_x x + p_y y - \mu(-U + u(x, y)).$$

2. Differentiate with respect to the parameters:

$$L_{p_x} = x,$$

$$L_{p_y} = y,$$

$$L_U = \mu.$$

3. Evaluate the answers in step 2 at x_c^*, y_c^*, μ^*:

$$L_{p_x} = x_c^*(p_x, p_y, U),$$

$$L_{p_y} = y_c^*(p_x, p_y, U),$$

$$L_U = \mu^*(p_x, p_y, U).$$

4. By the envelope theorem, the partials of M^* are equal to the corresponding partials in (3). In particular, $\partial M^*/\partial p_x = x_c^*(p_x, p_y, U)$ and $\partial M^*/\partial p_y = y_c^*(p_x, p_y, U)$.

EXAMPLE: Given $M^*(p_x, p_y, U) = 2\sqrt{p_x p_y U}$, find the compensated demand for x at $p_x = 4$, $p_y = 8$, $U = 2$. $x_c^*(p_x, p_y, U) = \partial M^*/\partial p_x = \sqrt{p_y U/p_x}$. Thus $x_c^*(4, 8, 2) = \sqrt{(8)(2)/4} = 2$.

7.7.5 Relationship between Regular and Compensated Demands

Recall that if a problem of maximizing (minimizing) $f(x, y)$ subject to $g(x, y) = c$ has solution x^*, y^* and $f^* = f(x^*, y^*)$, then the dual problem of minimizing (maximizing) $g(x, y)$ subject to $f(x, y) = f^*$ has solution x^*, y^* and $g^* = g(x^*, y^*) = c$.

Regular and compensated demands can be put into this framework in two ways:

1. If we start with regular demand and income M, then the dual problem for compensated demand should have utility level $U = u^*(p_x, p_y, M)$. Thus $x^*(p_x, p_y, M) \equiv x_c^*(p_x, p_y, u^*(p_x, p_y, M))$.

2. If we start with compensated demand and utility U, then the dual problem for regular demand should have income level $M = M^*(p_x, p_y, U)$. Thus $x^*(p_x, p_y, M^*(p_x, p_y, U)) \equiv x_c^*(p_x, p_y, U)$.

These relationships tell us how to tie together regular and compensated demand at a single point. Often we start from a point on the regular demand curve and use the relationship in method 1 to find the appropriate level for the corresponding compensated demand.

EXAMPLE: Verify the Slutsky equation holds for x, when $u(x, y) = xy$.

$$x^*(p_x, p_y, M) = \frac{M}{2p_x}, \quad \text{so} \quad \frac{\partial x^*}{\partial p_x} = -\frac{M}{2p_x^2} \quad \text{and} \quad \frac{\partial x^*}{\partial M} = \frac{1}{2p_x}.$$

$$x_c^*(p_x, p_y, U) = \sqrt{\frac{p_y U}{p_x}} \quad \text{so} \quad \frac{\partial x_c^*}{\partial p_x} = -\frac{1}{2}\sqrt{\frac{p_y U}{p_x^3}}.$$

To combine x^* and x_c^* in the same equation, we need to evaluate x_c^* at $U = u^*(p_x, p_y, M) = M^2/4p_x p_y$. Thus,

$$\frac{\partial x_c^*}{\partial p_x}\left(p_x, p_y, \frac{M^2}{4p_x p_y}\right) = -\frac{1}{2}\sqrt{\frac{p_y\left[\dfrac{M^2}{4p_x p_y}\right]}{p_x^3}} = -\frac{M}{4p_x^2} \quad \text{and}$$

$$\frac{\partial x_c^*}{\partial p_x} - x^*\frac{\partial x^*}{\partial M} = -\frac{M}{4p_x^2} - \frac{M}{2p_x}\frac{1}{2p_x} = -\frac{M}{2p_x^2} = \frac{\partial x^*}{\partial p_x},$$

which verifies the Slutsky equation for this example.

EXAMPLE: For $u(x, y) = xy$, $p_y = 1$, and $M = 4$, the demand function for x is $x^*(p_x, 1, 4) = 2/p_x$. If $p_x = 2$, what utility level is needed so that the regular and compensated demand functions agree? If we set

$$U = u^*(2, 1, 4) = 2, \text{ then } x_c^*(2, 1, 2) = 1 = x^*(2, 1, 4).$$

EXAMPLE: For $u(x, y) = xy$,

$$x_c^*\big(p_x, p_y, u^*(p_x, p_y, M)\big) \equiv \sqrt{\frac{p_y\left[\dfrac{M^2}{4p_x p_y}\right]}{p_x}} \equiv \frac{M}{2p_x} \equiv x^*(p_x, p_y, M),$$

$$x^*\big(p_x, p_y, M^*(p_x, p_y, U)\big) \equiv \frac{2\sqrt{p_x p_y U}}{2p_x} \equiv \sqrt{\frac{p_y U}{p_x}} \equiv x_c^*(p_x, p_y, U).$$

EXAMPLE: Differentiating the identity in method 2 with respect to p_x, using the result that

$$\frac{\partial M^*(p_x, p_y, U)}{\partial p_x} = x_c^*(p_x, p_y, U) = x^*\big(p_x, p_y, M^*(p_x, p_y, U)\big),$$

and setting $M = M^{B^*}(p_x, p_y, U)$ and $U = u^*(p_x, p_y, M)$ gives a simple proof of the Slutsky equation:

$$\frac{\partial x^*(p_x, p_y, M)}{\partial p_x} + \frac{\partial x^*(p_x, p_y, M)}{\partial M}x^*(p_x, p_y, M)$$

$$= \frac{\partial x_c^*\big(p_x, p_y, u^*(p_x, p_y, M)\big)}{\partial p_x}.$$

PROBLEMS

7.1 (a) Maximize xy subject to $-1 \leq x + y \leq 2$.

   (b) Suppose the "price" of y in (a) changes to p so the constraint becomes $-1 \leq x + py \leq 2$. Use the IFT to find out how the optimized values of x and y change as p changes, evaluated at $p = 1$.

   (c) Let $M(q)$ be the maximized value of xy subject to $-1 \leq qx + y \leq 2$. What is $dM(1)/dq$?

   (d) Let $V(t)$ be the maximized value of xy subject to $t \leq x + y \leq 2$. What is $dV(-1)/dt$?

7.2 Can the intersection of the surfaces $x^2 + y^2 + z^2 = 5$ and $(x - 1)^2 + (y - 1)^2 + (z - 1)^2 = 2$ be written in the form of differentiable functions $x^*(z)$ and $y^*(z)$ near $(x, y, z) = (1, 2, 0)$?

7.3 True-False/Explain: If we solve the optimization problem maximize (with respect to $\mathbf{x}$) $f(\mathbf{x}, t)$ subject to $g(\mathbf{x}, t) \leq 0$ and obtain the solution at $t = 0$, then for $f^*(t)$ defined to equal $f(\mathbf{x}^*(t), t)$, $f^*(0)/dt = \partial f(\mathbf{x}^*(0), 0)/\partial t$.

7.4 The Zealand Sheep Shop has a national monopoly in the production of both wool and mutton. The company buys sheep from farmers at a fixed price of \$10 per head. Each sheep is then sheared to produce 1 kilo of wool and butchered to produce 25 kilos of mutton. The wool is sold in a market where average revenue (price) per kilo is $p_w = 100 - 6\sqrt{q_w}$ where q_w is the number of kilos of wool sold per day. The mutton is sold in a market where average revenue (price) per kilo is $p_m = 200 - (q_m/25)$ where q_m is the number of kilos of mutton sold per day.

   (a) What is the firm's profit per day if it buys x sheep per day and sells the resulting wool and mutton in the appropriate markets?

   (b) Show that $x = 100$ is the unique global profit maximizing input of sheep per day.

   (c) Suppose the government is considering imposing a tax t per kilo on the sale of mutton. How does the monopolist's optimal input of sheep change as the tax rate changes infinitesimally from zero?

   (d) How does the market price for wool change as the tax on mutton changes infinitesimally from zero?

7.5 The amount of savings available for investment purposes is given by $S(Y, r)$ where Y is national income and r is the interest rate. The demand for funds for investment is given by $I(r, E)$ where E is an index measuring how firms feel about the outlook for the economy (i.e., whether future conditions will be better than current ones). The index depends on current conditions and is given by $E = f(Y, r)$. The demand for money (in real terms) is given by $L(Y, r)$. Given that

$\partial I/\partial E$, $\partial S/\partial Y$, $\partial S/\partial r$, and $\partial L/\partial Y$ are strictly positive while $\partial I/\partial r$, $\partial L/\partial r$, $\partial f/\partial Y$, and $\partial f/\partial r$ are strictly negative and that all markets are initially in equilibrium, what happens to national income when the real money stock, M is increased?

7.6 EG is a monopolist in the market for a particular durable good. For simplicity assume that there are only two periods. In the first period EG can produce q_1 units at cost $C_1(q_1) = q_1$ and can sell q_1 units at a price given by the average revenue function $P_1(q_1) = 3 - 2q_1$. In the second period EG can produce q_2 units at cost $C_2(q_2) = q_2$ and can sell q_2 units in the second period at a price given by the average revenue function $P_2(q_2, q_1) = 3 - 2q_2 - 2bq_1$ where q_1 is the amount sold in the first period and b is a fixed durability parameter. (If $b = 0$ then all units sold in period one completely "disintegrate" before the second period, while if $b = 1$ then all units sold in period one do not deteriorate at all between periods.) The monopolist is interested in picking a production plan (q_1, q_2) so as to maximize the present value of profit. Thus all second period revenues and costs must be discounted by multiplying by a factor t which is less than one.

(a) What is the present value of producing and selling the bundle (q_1, q_2) (i.e., producing and selling q_1 units in the first period and q_2 units in the second period)?

(b) Given that $(b, t) = (1, 1/2)$, show that $(q_1^*, q_2^*) = (3/7, 2/7)$ is the unique global (present value of) profit-maximizing production plan.

(c) Show that optimal production plans $(q_1^*(b, t), q_2^*(b, t))$ exist for (b, t) near $(1, 1/2)$ and use implicit differentiation to find

$$\frac{\partial q_1^*}{\partial b}(1, 1/2), \quad \frac{\partial q_1^*}{\partial t}(1, 1/2), \quad \frac{\partial q_2^*}{\partial b}(1, 1/2), \quad \frac{\partial q_2^*}{\partial t}(1, 1/2).$$

(d) How does the maximized present value of profit change as b changes (t changes) infinitesimally starting from $(b, t) = (1, 1/2)$?

7.7 Given the production function $Y = f(K, L) = K^{1/2}L^{1/2}$, the firm's cost function is $C(Y; r, w) = \text{minimum} \{rK + wL | K^{1/2}L^{1/2} = Y\}$. The minimum cost depends on output level Y and factor prices r and w.

(a) For $Y = r = w = 1$ use the Lagrange multiplier method to find the inputs K^* and L^* that minimize cost.

(b) Find $\partial C(1, 1, 1)/\partial Y$.

(c) Show that (with $Y \equiv 1$) $K^*(r, w)$ and $L^*(r, w)$, the input demand functions, exist for (r, w) near $(1, 1)$.

(d) Use the envelope theorem to find

$$\frac{\partial C}{\partial r}(1, 1, 1) \quad \text{and} \quad \frac{\partial C}{\partial w}(1, 1, 1).$$

7.8 The demand for coffee is a function of the price paid by consumers for coffee, p_c^c, and the price paid by consumers for tea, p_T^c, given by $D_c(p_c^c, p_T^c)$ where $0 < \partial D_c/\partial p_T^c < -\partial D_c/\partial p_c^c$. Similarly, the demand for tea is given by $D_T(p_c^c, p_T^c)$ where $0 < \partial D_T/\partial p_c^c < -\partial D_T/\partial p_T^c$. The supply of coffee is a function of the price received by firms for coffee, p_c^f, given by $S_c(p_c^f)$ where $dS_c/dp_c^f > 0$. Similarly, the supply of tea is $S_T(p_T^f)$ where $dS_c/dp_T^f > 0$. Starting from an equilibrium with no taxes (so $p_c^c = p_c^f$, $p_T^c = p_T^f$), suppose a tax of t per unit is introduced for coffee only (so $p_c^c = p_c^f + t$). What happens to the equilibrium price of tea when t increases infinitesimally from zero; i.e., does it increase or decrease?

7.9 For the problem of maximizing xy subject to $0 \le x + y \le 2e$, with Lagrangian $L(x, y, \lambda_1, \lambda_2) = xy - \lambda_1(x + y - 2e) - \lambda_2(-x - y)$ the potential solution $(x, y, \lambda_1, \lambda_2) = (e, e, e, 0)$ has SOC matrix

$$\begin{bmatrix} 0 & 1 & -1 \\ 1 & 0 & -1 \\ -1 & -1 & 0 \end{bmatrix}$$

and is the unique global maximizer. Now consider the problem of maximizing $x'y$ subject to $0 \le x + y \le 2te$. Define $x^*(t)$ and $y^*(t)$ as the optimal choices for x and y given t and let $\pi(t)$ be the corresponding optimized value of $x'y$.
(a) Find $dx^*(1)/dt$ and $dy^*(1)/dt$.
(b) Find $d\pi(1)/dt$.

7.10 (a) For the problem of maximizing $x^2 + 2y^2$ subject to $x \ge 0$, $y \ge 0$, and $3x + 2y \le 10$, setting up the problem in standard form and solving, the unique global solution is $(x^*, y^*, \lambda_1^*, \lambda_2^*, \lambda_3^*) = 0, 5, 30, 0, 10)$. Now consider a new objective function $f(x, y, t) = x^2 + 2(y/t)^2$. What is the appropriate system of equations for performing comparative statics to find the effect of a change in t, evaluated at $t = 1$?
(b) If we define $f^*(t) = f(x^*(t), y^*(t), t)$, what is df^*/dt evaluated at $t = 1$?

7.11 For the problem of maximizing $x^2 + y^2$ subject to $x \ge 0$, $y \ge 0$, and $2x + y \le 4$, setting up the problem in standard form and solving, the unique global solution is $(x^*, y^*, \lambda_1^*, \lambda_2^*, \lambda_3^*) = (0, 4, 16, 0, 8)$. Now consider a new objective function $f(x, y, t) = x^2 + ty^2$. What is the appropriate system of equations for performing comparative statics to find the effect of a change in t, evaluated at $t = 1$?

7.12 For the problem of maximizing $(x + 1)y^2z$ subject to $x \ge 0$, $y \ge 0$, $z \ge 0$, and $3x + 2y + z \le 6$, setting up the problem in standard form and solving, the unique global solution is

$$(x^*, y^*, z^*, \lambda_1^*, \lambda_2^*, \lambda_3^*, \lambda_4^*) = (0, 2, 2, 4, 0, 0, 4).$$

(a) Now consider a new problem of maximizing $(x + t)y^2 z$ subject to $x \geq 0$, $y \geq 0$, $z \geq 0$, and $(2 + t)x + 2y + z \leq 6$. What is the appropriate system of equations for performing comparative statics to find the effect on the optimal choices of x, y, and z of a change in t, evaluated at $t = 1$?

(b) For the problem in part (a), let $f^*(t)$ be the maximized value of the objective function given the constraints corresponding to t. What is $df^*(1)/dt$?

8

COMPARATIVE
STATICS
SUMMARY

8.1 INTRODUCTION

This chapter summarizes our results concerning comparative statics problems by setting out a step-by-step solution procedure. The chapter can also be read as a "cookbook" introduction to comparative statics before reading the background material contained in previous chapters (especially Chapter 7).

How does a competitive consumer's demand for a commodity change when a price changes? How does a market equilibrium price change when a tax rate changes? In order to answer these questions we need to understand how to perform comparative statics. The second section of this chapter contains a step-by-step procedure for solving these problems. The third section contains solved examples to illustrate the procedure. The fourth section contains an alternative representation of the results, in terms of partial derivatives rather than differentials. An additional type of question to be addressed is: How much better off (in utility terms) is a consumer when she is allowed to adjust her demand optimally in response to a decrease in one of the prices? This could be solved using the procedure laid out in Section 8.2, but the use of the envelope theorem makes the solution much easier. This is discussed in the final section. A reader who has not read the previous chapters will probably find it useful to read through one or more of the solved examples in Section 8.3 along with the solution procedure of Section 8.2.

8.2 SOLUTION PROCEDURE

We treat two types of comparative statics problems: (1) single-agent optimization problems (e.g., how does a competitive consumer's demand change when a price changes? and (2) equilibrium problems (e.g., how does a market equilibrium price change when a tax rate changes?). The procedure is the same in the two types of problems but as we shall see, several of the steps are trivial or already completed as part of the original optimization for optimization problems.

For an optimization problem it is important that there be a unique optimizer initially. Otherwise we could not be sure which optimizer to use at the start of our procedure. For an equilibrium problem it is important that the initial equilibrium we use be (at least locally) stable for an appropriate dynamic adjustment process. Otherwise, when the market is perturbed by the comparative statics change, there is no reason to believe the market would converge to the new equilibrium indicated by our procedure. This stability requirement is very important, though it is often ignored or glossed over in practice.

Step A: Distinguish exogenous and endogenous variables.

Endogenous variables are those being determined in the model or problem, while exogenous variables are determined outside the model. For a single competitive consumer, prices are exogenous while quantities demanded are endogenous in the standard utility maximization problem. In an equilibrium model for a single competitive market, the market price is endogenously determined by supply-equals-demand conditions, while tax rates are exogenous (determined by some government body). A variable that is exogenous in one problem (the price for the consumer maximization) may be endogenous for another (the market equilibrium).

Comparative statics question ask how some endogenous variables change when an endogenous variable is changed. This is the first clue to the nature of the variables: what comparative statics changes are needed? The second clue is "commonsense" understanding of the model: what variables are likely to be determined within the model? For example, in a model of a competitive market, it is reasonable to think of market price as being determined in the model, but not tax rates.

In a well-specified optimization problem this step is trivial: the endogenous variables are those treated as variables in the Lagrangian.

Step B: Set up the system of equations.

For an optimization problem these are just the relevant first-order conditions, from the Lagrangian L^*, with inactive constraints ignored. As in the nonlinear programming summary in Chapter 6, we assume strict complementary slackness, so all the active inequality constraints have strictly positive multipliers. Given this information, the first-order condition "$\partial L^*/\partial \lambda_i \geq 0$, $\lambda_i \geq 0$, $\lambda_i(\partial L^*/\partial \lambda_i) = 0$" can be written as the equality $\partial L^*/\partial \lambda_i = 0$. This system of $n + s$ first-order condition equalities has $n + s$ endogenous variables (the x_t and the λ_i from active constraints).

For an equilibrium model this system includes all known relationships defining functions and/or the equilibrium. In particular, the "supply equals demand" type of equations must be included for all relevant markets. The number of equations must equal the number of endogenous variables.

Step C: Check conditions for legitimacy of the procedure.

The conditions of a mathematical result known as the implicit function theorem must be satisfied for our procedure to work. Given the systems of equations from step B, the relevant conditions are (1) the functions are differentiable, (2) we have a starting point satisfying the equations, and (3) a certain determinant (to be specified below) is nonzero.

The starting point condition means we are starting from an initial equilibrium (in equilibrium problems) or an initial unique global optimizer (in optimization problems). The starting point might be abstract, "starting from the equilibrium $y^* \ldots$," or concrete, "starting from the initial maximizer $(1, 1) \ldots$."

If the system of equations is

$$F_1(\mathbf{x}, \mathbf{y}) = 0,$$

$$\vdots$$

$$F_n(\mathbf{x}, \mathbf{y}) = 0,$$

where x_i, $i = 1, \ldots, n$, are the endogenous variables and the y_j are the exogenous variables, then the last condition is that the determinant of $[\partial F_i/\partial x_j]$ is nonzero where the $n \times n$ matrix $[\partial F_i/\partial x_j]$ has as its entry in row i, column j the term $\partial F_i(\mathbf{x}^0, \mathbf{y}^0)/\partial x_j$ where $(\mathbf{x}^0, \mathbf{y}^0)$ is the starting point. This is the Jacobian matrix of $\mathbf{F} = (F_1, F_2, \ldots, F_n)$ and its determinant is the Jacobian of $\mathbf{F}$.

This step is trivial for optimization problems. The system of equations is given by $n + s$ first-order condition equations with $n + s$ endogenous variables. The starting point is the initial unique global optimizer, so the system of equations is satisfied. The matrix $[\partial F_i/\partial x_j]$ evaluated at $(\mathbf{x}^0, \mathbf{y}^0)$ is exactly the $(n + s) \times (n + s)$ second-order condition matrix corresponding to the Lagrangian L^*. If the original optimizer satisfied all the conditions for our optimization procedure (and $s < n$), then by the check of second-order conditions we already know the determinant is nonzero.

Step D: Write out the comparative static results using differentials.

By step C, the matrix inverse $[\partial F_i(\mathbf{x}^0, \mathbf{y}^0)/\partial x_j]^{-1}$ is well defined. Taking total differentials and rearranging,

$$
\begin{pmatrix} dx_1 \\ \vdots \\ dx_n \end{pmatrix} = -\left[\frac{\partial F_i(\mathbf{x}^0, \mathbf{y}^0)}{\partial x_j}\right]^{-1} \begin{pmatrix} \sum_j \dfrac{\partial F_1(\mathbf{x}^0, \mathbf{y}^0)}{\partial y_j} \, dy_j \\ \vdots \\ \sum_j \dfrac{\partial F_n(\mathbf{x}^0, \mathbf{y}^0)}{\partial y_j} \, dy_j \end{pmatrix}.
$$

Step E: Solve.

If only some exogenous variables have changed, then the other dy_j can be set equal to zero. If we are interested in all or many of the dx_i, then it is easiest to compute the inverse matrix $[\partial F_i(\mathbf{x}^0, \mathbf{y}^0)/\partial x_j]^{-1}$. If only one or two of the dx_i are of interest, Cramer's rule may be used. Let B_t be the matrix obtained by replacing the entry in the kth row and tth column of $[\partial F_i(\mathbf{x}^0, \mathbf{y}^0)/\partial x_j]$ with the entry $\sum_j (\partial F_k(\mathbf{x}^0, \mathbf{y}^0)/\partial y_j)\, dy_j$ for $k = 1, \ldots, n$. Then by Cramer's rule,

$$
dx_t = -\frac{\text{determinant of } B_t}{\text{determinant of} \left[F_i(\mathbf{x}^0, \mathbf{y}^0)/\partial x_j \right]}.
$$

The minus sign arises because we start with a system of the form $A\mathbf{x} + \mathbf{b} = \mathbf{0}$ rather than $A\mathbf{x} = \mathbf{b}$.

8.3 EXAMPLES

(A) (Continuation of Example A of Chapter 6, Section 6.3.) For the problem of minimizing $x + 2y + 4z$ subject to $x^2 + y^2 + z^2 = 21 + w$, how does the optimal choice of x change as w changes from $w = 0$? [In Chapter 6 we found that $(-1, -2, -4)$ solved the problem for $w = 0$.]

Switching to maximization of $-x - 2y - 4z$, the Lagrangian is $L = -x - 2y - 4z - \mu(21 + w - x^2 - y^2 - z^2)$. The endogenous variables are x, y, z, and μ. The exogenous variable is w. The system of equations (first-order conditions) is

$$\frac{\partial L}{\partial x} = -1 + 2\mu x = 0,$$

$$\frac{\partial L}{\partial y} = -2 + 2\mu y = 0,$$

$$\frac{\partial L}{\partial z} = -4 + 2\mu z = 0,$$

$$\frac{\partial L}{\partial \mu} = -21 - w + x^2 + y^2 + z^2 = 0.$$

When $w = 0$ we already know $(-1, -2, -4, -\frac{1}{2})$ is the global maximizer (minimizer for the original problem) and satisfies the first-order conditions. The Jacobian, determinant of "$[\partial F_i(\mathbf{x}^0, \mathbf{y}^0)/\partial x_j]$" is exactly the determinant we already checked as part of the second-order conditions. It was $D_2 = -84 \neq 0$. The second-order condition matrix was

$$M = \begin{bmatrix} -1 & 0 & 0 & -2 \\ 0 & -1 & 0 & -4 \\ 0 & 0 & -1 & -8 \\ -2 & -4 & -8 & 0 \end{bmatrix}$$

so

$$\begin{pmatrix} dx \\ dy \\ dz \\ d\mu \end{pmatrix} = -M^{-1} \begin{pmatrix} \dfrac{\partial^2 L}{\partial w \, \partial x} dw \\ \dfrac{\partial^2 L}{\partial w \, \partial y} dw \\ \dfrac{\partial^2 L}{\partial w \, \partial z} dw \\ \dfrac{\partial^2 L}{\partial w \, \partial \mu} dw \end{pmatrix} = -M^{-1} \begin{pmatrix} 0 \\ 0 \\ 0 \\ -dw \end{pmatrix}.$$

Even though we are not interested in $d\mu$, μ was one of the endogenous variables in the first-order conditions so it must be included in this stage, making M a 4×4 matrix. Also, note that almost all terms can be just read off from our previous problem (with $w = 0$). The only new terms are in the final vector above.

Using Cramer's rule,

$$dx = -\frac{\begin{vmatrix} 0 & 0 & 0 & -2 \\ 0 & -1 & 0 & -4 \\ 0 & 0 & -1 & -8 \\ -dw & -4 & -8 & 0 \end{vmatrix}}{\begin{vmatrix} -1 & 0 & 0 & -2 \\ 0 & -1 & 0 & -4 \\ 0 & 0 & -1 & -8 \\ -2 & -4 & -8 & 0 \end{vmatrix}} = -\frac{-2\,dw}{-84} = -\frac{dw}{42}.$$

(B) (Continuation of Example C of Chapter 6, Section 6.3.) For the problem of minimizing $x^2 + y^2 + z^2$ subject to $x + y + z \geq 3 + w$, how does the optimal choice of z change as w changes from $w = 0$? [In Chapter 6 we found that $(1, 1, 1)$ solved the problem for $w = 0$.]

Switching to maximization of $-x^2 - y^2 - z^2$ and writing the constraint as $-x - y - z + 3 + w \leq 0$, the Lagrangian is $L = -x^2 - y^2 - z^2 - \lambda(-x - y - z + 3 + w)$.

The endogenous variables are x, y, z, and λ. The exogenous variable is w. The system of equations (first-order conditions) is

$$-2x + \lambda = 0,$$
$$-2y + \lambda = 0,$$
$$-2z - \lambda = 0,$$
$$x + y + z - 3 - w = 0.$$

The last condition is written as an equation (rather than the usual inequality conditions) because we already know for $w = 0$, $\lambda = 2 \neq 0$.

We know $(1, 1, 1, 2)$ is the global maximizer (minimizer for the original problem) and satisfies the first-order conditions when $w = 0$. The Jacobian, determinant of "$[\partial F_i / \partial x_j]$," is exactly the determinant we already checked as part of the second-order conditions, and it is nonzero. The second-order condition matrix was

$$M = \begin{bmatrix} -2 & 0 & 0 & 1 \\ 0 & -2 & 0 & 1 \\ 0 & 0 & -2 & 1 \\ 1 & 1 & 1 & 0 \end{bmatrix}$$

so

$$\begin{pmatrix} dx \\ dy \\ dz \\ d\lambda \end{pmatrix} = -M^{-1} \begin{pmatrix} 0 \\ 0 \\ 0 \\ -dw \end{pmatrix}.$$

Using Cramer's rule,

$$
dz = - \frac{\begin{vmatrix} -2 & 0 & 0 & 1 \\ 0 & -2 & 0 & 1 \\ 0 & 0 & 0 & 1 \\ 1 & 1 & -dw & 0 \end{vmatrix}}{\begin{vmatrix} -2 & 0 & 0 & 1 \\ 0 & -2 & 0 & 1 \\ 0 & 0 & -2 & 1 \\ 1 & 1 & 1 & 0 \end{vmatrix}} = - \frac{4\,dw}{-12} = \frac{dw}{3}.
$$

(C) (Continuation of Example D of Chapter 6, Section 6.3.) For the problem of maximizing $y - x^2$ subject to $x \geq 0$, $y \geq 0$, and $y \leq 2x - 1$, what happens to the optimal value of x as one of the constraints becomes more restrictive? From Chapter 6 we know that $(1, 1)$ is the unique global maximizer. Since the $x \geq 0$ and $y \geq 0$ constraints are not binding, making them slightly more restrictive has no effect. The last constraint is binding, so we need to go through our procedure. If the constraint becomes $y \leq 2x - 1 - w$, we can ask what happens to the optimal x as w changes from $w = 0$.

The unique global maximizer for $w = 0$ is $x = y = 1$, so the nonnegativity constraints are not binding and are ignored in the Lagrangian $L^* = y - x^2 - \lambda(-2x + 1 + w + y)$. The endogenous variables are x, y, and λ. The exogenous variable is w. The system of equations (first-order conditions) is

$$-2x + 2\lambda = 0,$$

$$1 - \lambda = 0,$$

$$2x - 1 - w - y = 0.$$

Again the third condition is written as an equation rather than the set of inequalities because we know $\lambda > 0$ at the starting point.

We know $(1, 1, 1)$ is the global maximizer and satisfies the first-order conditions. The Jacobian is the determinant of the second-order condition matrix

$$
M = \begin{bmatrix} -2 & 0 & 2 \\ 0 & 0 & -1 \\ 2 & -1 & 0 \end{bmatrix},
$$

already known to be nonzero. Thus

$$
\begin{pmatrix} dx \\ dy \\ d\lambda \end{pmatrix} = -M^{-1} \begin{pmatrix} 0 \\ 0 \\ -dw \end{pmatrix}
$$

and, by Cramer's rule,

$$dx = -\frac{\begin{vmatrix} 0 & 0 & 2 \\ 0 & 0 & -1 \\ -dw & -1 & 0 \end{vmatrix}}{\begin{vmatrix} -2 & 0 & 2 \\ 0 & 0 & -1 \\ 2 & -1 & 0 \end{vmatrix}} = 0.$$

Even though the constraint is binding, as it changes, it does not affect the optimal x. (It does affect the optimal y.)

(D) How does x change as y changes when moving along the intersection of the surfaces $x^2 + y^2 + z^2 = 5$ and $(x - 1)^2 + (y - 1)^2 + (z - 1)^2 = 2$ near $(1, 2, 0)$? This is an "equilibrium" problem, so we must actually do some work to go through the steps of the procedure. The endogenous variables are x and z, and the exogenous variable is y. The system of equations consists of the two equations defining the surfaces

$$x^2 + y^2 + z^2 - 5 = 0,$$

$$(x - 1)^2 + (y - 1)^2 + (z - 1)^2 - 2 = 0.$$

The point $(1, 2, 0)$ does satisfy both equations. The Jacobian matrix has entries corresponding to partial derivatives of the two functions on the left-hand side of the equations above with respect to the endogenous variables,

$$\begin{bmatrix} 2x & 2z \\ 2(x - 1) & 2(z - 1) \end{bmatrix}.$$

The determinant of this matrix evaluated at $(x, z) = (1, 0)$ is nonzero so the conditions are satisfied.

$$\begin{pmatrix} dx \\ dz \end{pmatrix} = -\begin{bmatrix} 2x & 2z \\ 2(x - 1) & 2(z - 1) \end{bmatrix}^{-1} \begin{pmatrix} 2y\,dy \\ 2(y - 1)\,dy \end{pmatrix}$$

or, evaluated at $(1, 2, 0)$,

$$\begin{pmatrix} dx \\ dz \end{pmatrix} = -\begin{bmatrix} 2 & 0 \\ 0 & -2 \end{bmatrix}^{-1} \begin{pmatrix} 4\,dy \\ 2\,dy \end{pmatrix} = \begin{pmatrix} -2\,dy \\ dy \end{pmatrix}.$$

(E) A client of an economic consulting group believes that the nominal money supply, M, will increase in the near future and, in order to decide whether or not it is advisable to purchase bonds now, asks the consulting group to determine whether the rate of interest on bonds, r, will increase or decrease in response. The model builders in the group believe that: aggregate consumption is a function of aggregate income, Y, given by $C(Y)$; aggregate investment is a function of the rate of interest on bonds given by $I(r)$; the demand for real money balances is a function of aggregate income and the Treasury bill rate, b, given by $L(Y, b)$, and the demand for real Treasury bills is given by $G(Y, r, b)$. The price level, P, the quantity of Treasury bills, B, and the money supply, M, are assumed to be exogenous. The system is in equilibrium when all three markets are simultaneously in equilibrium, i.e., when

(aggregate income) $\qquad\qquad\qquad Y = C(Y) + I(r),$

(real money balances) $\qquad\qquad M/P = L(Y, b),$

(real Treasury bills) $\qquad\qquad \dfrac{B}{(1 + b)P} = G(Y, r, b).$

The econometricians in the group have estimated the derivatives of all the relevant functions and have found that $0 < dC/dY < 1$, $dI/dr < 0$, $0 < \partial L/\partial Y < 1$, $\partial L/\partial b < 0$, and $0 < \partial G/\partial Y < 1$, $\partial G/\partial r < 0$, $\partial G/\partial b > 0$.

Using this information and assuming that the system is initially in equilibrium, how should the client's question be answered? In implicit form, the equilibrium conditions are

$$F_1 \equiv Y - C(Y) - I(r) = 0, \tag{1}$$

$$F_2 \equiv M/P - L(Y, b) = 0, \tag{2}$$

$$F_3 \equiv \frac{B}{(1 + b)P} - G(Y, r, b) = 0 \tag{3}$$

with endogenous variables Y, r, b and exogenous variables M, P, B. By definition, at the initial equilibrium (1), (2), and (3) are satisfied. By assumption the functions are continuously differentiable. The Jacobian matrix of partials of F_i, $i = 1, 2, 3$ with respect to the endogenous variables is given by

$$J = \begin{bmatrix} \left(1 - \dfrac{dC}{dY}\right) & -\dfrac{dI}{dr} & 0 \\[2ex] -\dfrac{\partial L}{\partial Y} & 0 & -\dfrac{\partial L}{\partial b} \\[2ex] -\dfrac{\partial G}{\partial Y} & -\dfrac{\partial G}{\partial r} & -\left(\dfrac{B}{(1 + b)^2 P} + \dfrac{\partial G}{\partial b}\right) \end{bmatrix}.$$

So,

$$|J| = \frac{\partial L}{\partial b}\left[-\frac{\partial G}{\partial r}\left(1 - \frac{dC}{dy}\right) - \frac{\partial G}{\partial Y}\frac{\partial I}{\partial r}\right]$$

$$-\left(\frac{B}{(1+b^2)P} + \frac{\partial G}{\partial b}\right)\left(-\frac{\partial L}{\partial Y}\frac{\partial I}{\partial r}\right) < 0$$

by the econometricians' information. Hence the conditions of the IFT hold. Totally differentiating (1), (2), and (3),

$$\begin{bmatrix} \left(1 - \dfrac{dC}{dY}\right) & -\dfrac{dI}{dr} & 0 \\[2ex] -\dfrac{\partial L}{\partial Y} & 0 & -\dfrac{\partial L}{\partial b} \\[2ex] -\dfrac{\partial G}{\partial Y} & -\dfrac{\partial G}{\partial r} & -\left(\dfrac{B}{(1+b)^2 P} + \dfrac{\partial G}{\partial b}\right) \end{bmatrix} \begin{bmatrix} dy \\[2ex] dr \\[2ex] db \end{bmatrix} = \begin{bmatrix} 0 \\[2ex] -\dfrac{dM}{P} \\[2ex] 0 \end{bmatrix}.$$

By Cramer's rule and the econometricians' information,

$$\frac{dr}{dM} = \frac{1}{|J|P}\left[\left(1 - \frac{dC}{dY}\right)\left(\frac{B}{(1+b)^2 P} + \frac{\partial G}{\partial b}\right)\right] < 0.$$

(F) What difficulties arise if we attempt our procedure for an optimization problem at which strict complementary slackness fails? As we will see in the following example, at such a point the active constraint with the zero multiplier may be just switching between being active and being inactive. At such a point the endogenous solution variables (e.g., x^*) may not be differentiable functions of the exogenous parameters, and the correct results may depend on whether the parameter increases or decreases. Typically, these cases require extra work to be solved correctly. In particular, one must determine whether the active constraint with zero multiplier should or should not be included in the Lagrangian L^* and the subsequent first-order conditions.

Consider the problem of maximizing $(x + 1)y$ subject to $x \geq 0$, $y \geq 0$, and $px + qy \leq m$ where p, q, and m are (strictly positive) exogenous parameters of the problem. (This is a utility maximization problem subject to a budget constraint.) The Lagrangian is $L(x, y, \lambda_1, \lambda_2, \lambda_3) = (x + 1)y - \lambda_1(-x) - \lambda_2(-y) - \lambda_3(px + qy - m)$.

If $m > p$ the solution is

$$(x, y, \lambda_1, \lambda_2, \lambda_3) = \left(\frac{m-p}{2p}, \frac{m+p}{2q}, 0, 0, \frac{m+p}{2pq}\right),$$

while if $m \leq p$ the solution is

$$(x, y, \lambda_1, \lambda_2, \lambda_3) = \left(0, \frac{m}{q}, \frac{p - m}{q}, 0, \frac{1}{q}\right).$$

If we had first solved the problem for the case $m = p = q = 1$, we would have found the solution $(0, 1, 0, 0, 1)$. The $x \geq 0$ constraint is active but $\lambda_1 = 0$, so strict complementary slackness fails. To see how the optimal y changes as p changes starting from $m = p = q = 1$, we can use the general solution from the previous paragraph: if $y^*(m, p, q)$ is the optimal y given the parameters,

$$y^*(1, p, 1) = \begin{cases} \dfrac{1 + p}{2} & \text{if } p < 1, \\ 1 & \text{if } p \geq 1. \end{cases}$$

Note that y^* is not differentiable at $(1, 1, 1)$. If p increases from 1, there is no effect on y^*, while if p decreases from 1, then y^* also decreases half as fast. Given $m = q = 1$, at $p = 1$ the constraint $x \geq 0$ is just at the borderline between being active and inactive.

Using our procedure with the $x \geq 0$ constraint included (as $x = 0$) gives the correct comparative statics results for increases in p but the wrong results for decreases.

The system of equations is

$$y + \lambda_1 - p\lambda_3 = 0,$$

$$x + 1 - \lambda_3 = 0,$$

$$x = 0,$$

$$1 - px - y = 0,$$

and

$$dy = -\frac{\begin{vmatrix} 0 & -dp & 1 & -1 \\ 1 & 0 & 0 & -1 \\ 1 & 0 & 0 & 0 \\ -1 & 0 & 0 & 0 \end{vmatrix}}{\begin{vmatrix} 0 & 1 & 1 & -1 \\ 1 & 0 & 0 & -1 \\ 1 & 0 & 0 & 0 \\ -1 & -1 & 0 & 0 \end{vmatrix}} = 0,$$

which is correct for $dp > 0$ but not for $dp < 0$.

On the other hand, using our procedure without the $x \geq 0$ constraint included gives the correct comparative statics results for decreases in p but the wrong results for increases. The system of equations is

$$y - p\lambda_3 = 0,$$

$$x + 1 - \lambda_3 = 0,$$

$$1 - px - y = 0,$$

and

$$dy = -\frac{\begin{vmatrix} 0 & -dp & -1 \\ 1 & 0 & -1 \\ -1 & 0 & 0 \end{vmatrix}}{\begin{vmatrix} 0 & 1 & -1 \\ 1 & 0 & -1 \\ -1 & -1 & 0 \end{vmatrix}} = -\frac{-dp}{2} = \frac{dp}{2},$$

which is correct for $dp < 0$ but not for $dp > 0$.

When strict complementary slackness fails we must do additional work beyond our basic comparative statics procedure in order to determine the effect of a change in the parameters. The effect might depend on the direction of change as in this example.

(G) The procedure uses a linear approximation to the true functions to obtain the comparative statics results. If the exogenous changes dy are infinitesimal, the endogenous changes dx are exactly correct. If the changes dy are not infinitesimal, the solutions for dx are only approximations to the true changes. Since the functions are differentiable (and the determinant is nonzero), the percentage relative error is small for small dy. Unfortunately, it is not possible to determine how small dy must be in order to guarantee no more than (say) 5% relative error without examining the specific problem.

For example, suppose the endogenous variable r and the exogenous variable t are related by $r - kt^2 \equiv 0$ where k is a positive constant. At the starting point $(r^0, t^0) = (0, 0)$ the procedure yields $dr = 0 \, dt = 0$. Given $dt > 0$, the percentage relative error is the absolute value of 100% times the difference between the estimated value of dr, $0 \, dt = 0$, and the true change in r, $k(dt)^2$, all divided by the change in t, dt. This equals $(k \, dt)$ 100%. To get less than 5% relative error requires $dt < 1/(20k)$, which depends on the constant k. The absolute error is $|0 \, dt - k(dt)^2| = k(dt)^2$. For any fixed $dt > 0$, no matter how small, the relative and absolute errors could still be very large if k was sufficiently large. We only know that for any fixed k, the errors go to zero as dt does.

8.4 ALTERNATIVE PROCEDURE

Comparative statics are sometimes done in terms of partial derivatives instead of differentials. If $\mathbf{x}$ are the endogenous variables and $\mathbf{y}$ are the exogenous variables, after step C of our procedure, by the implicit function theorem we know $\mathbf{x}$ can be written as a function of $\mathbf{y}$, $\mathbf{x}^*(\mathbf{y})$, for $\mathbf{y}$ near the starting point $\mathbf{y}^0$; i.e., the endogenous variables can be written as functions of the exogenous variables. Asking how the equilibrium (or optimizing) value of x_i changes when y_j changes is asking for $\partial x_i^*/\partial y_j$. Step D can be written in terms of partial derivatives as

$$
\begin{pmatrix} \dfrac{\partial x_1^*(\mathbf{y}^0)}{\partial y_k} \\ \vdots \\ \dfrac{\partial x_n^*(\mathbf{y}^0)}{\partial y_k} \end{pmatrix} = - \left[\dfrac{\partial F_i(\mathbf{x}^0, \mathbf{y}^0)}{\partial x_j} \right]^{-1} \begin{pmatrix} \dfrac{\partial F_1(\mathbf{x}^0, \mathbf{y}^0)}{\partial y_k} \\ \vdots \\ \dfrac{\partial F_n(\mathbf{x}^0, \mathbf{y}^0)}{\partial y_k} \end{pmatrix}.
$$

Thus $dx_i = \partial x_i^*(\mathbf{y}^0)/\partial y_k \, dy_k$ relates the differential and partial derivative versions of step D when only y_k changes.

8.5 ENVELOPE THEOREM

In previous sections we considered both optimization and equilibrium problems and examined the effect on the endogenous variables of a change in the exogenous parameters. For the optimization problems this involves changes in the optimal choices as parameters changed. The envelope theorem applies only to optimization problems, and it gives a simplified procedure for finding the effect on the optimized value of the objective function (not the optimal choice variables) of changes in the parameters.

For the original optimization problem, assume we are following the procedure used in Chapter 6 and strict complementary slackness holds. Suppose the original problem was to maximize $f(\mathbf{x}; \mathbf{p})$ subject to constraints where $\mathbf{x}$ are the choice variables and $\mathbf{p}$ are the exogenous parameters. (Note the parameters may appear in either the objective function or the constraints or both.) Suppose $\mathbf{x}^0$ is the unique global maximizer when the parameters are $\mathbf{p}^0$ with corresponding Lagrangian $L^*(\mathbf{x}, \boldsymbol{\lambda}; \mathbf{p})$ (writing only active constraints in the Lagrangian) and Lagrange multipliers $\boldsymbol{\lambda}^0$ at the solution. Also assume the second-order condition matrix $[L^*_{ij}(\mathbf{x}^0, \boldsymbol{\lambda}^0; \mathbf{p}^0)]$ is nonsingular.

By the implicit function theorem we know the functions $\mathbf{x}^*(\mathbf{p})$ and $\boldsymbol{\lambda}^*(\mathbf{p})$ corresponding to the unique global maximizers exist for $\mathbf{p}$ near $\mathbf{p}^0$, are differentiable at $\mathbf{p}^0$, and satisfy $\mathbf{x}^*(\mathbf{p}^0) = \mathbf{x}^0$, $\boldsymbol{\lambda}^*(\mathbf{p}^0) = \boldsymbol{\lambda}^0$.

If we define $f^*(\mathbf{p})$ as the optimized value of the objective function given $\mathbf{p}$ [i.e., $f^*(\mathbf{p}) := f(\mathbf{x}^*(\mathbf{p}); \mathbf{p})$], we are interested in the derivative of f^* with respect to, say, p_j, evaluated at $\mathbf{p}^0$. Note $f^*(\mathbf{p}) \equiv f(\mathbf{x}^*(\mathbf{p}); \mathbf{p}) \equiv L^*(\mathbf{x}^*(\mathbf{p}), \boldsymbol{\lambda}^*(\mathbf{p}); \mathbf{p})$, since at $(\mathbf{x}^*(\mathbf{p}), \boldsymbol{\lambda}^*(\mathbf{p}); \mathbf{p})$ all active constraints hold as equalities. By the chain rule

$$\frac{\partial f^*(\mathbf{p})}{\partial p_j} = \sum_i \frac{\partial L^*}{\partial x_i} \frac{\partial x_i^*}{\partial p_j} + \sum_k \frac{\partial L^*}{\partial \lambda_k} \frac{\partial \lambda_k^*}{\partial p_j} + \frac{\partial L^*}{\partial p_j}$$

where the partial derivatives of L^* are evaluated at $(\mathbf{x}^*(\mathbf{p}), \boldsymbol{\lambda}^*(\mathbf{p}); \mathbf{p})$ and the partial derivatives of the x_i^* and λ_k^* are evaluated at $\mathbf{p}$. Setting $\mathbf{p} = \mathbf{p}^0$, we get the desired derivative, $\partial f^*(\mathbf{p}^0)/\partial p_j$. Thus the desired change in the optimized value of f^* could be determined using the derivatives of L^* evaluated at $(\mathbf{x}^0, \boldsymbol{\lambda}^0; \mathbf{p}^0)$ along with the comparative statics terms (e.g., $\partial x_i^*(\mathbf{p}^0)/\partial p_j$) discussed in the previous sections.

The envelope theorem offers a shortcut by observing that $\partial L^*(\mathbf{x}^0, \boldsymbol{\lambda}^0; \mathbf{p}^0)/\partial x_i = 0$ for all i and $\partial L^*(\mathbf{x}^0, \boldsymbol{\lambda}^0; \mathbf{p}^0)/\partial \lambda_k = 0$ for all k by the first-order conditions for optimization in the original problem. Thus $\partial f^*(\mathbf{p}^0)/\partial p_j = \partial L^*(\mathbf{x}^0, \boldsymbol{\lambda}^0; \mathbf{p}^0)/\partial p_j$. When the conditions of the implicit function theorem hold (and we have a unique global maximizer), we can find the effect of a change in parameter p_j on the optimized value of the objective function by just differentiating the Lagrangian L^* with respect to p_j and evaluating the result at the original solution. This procedure works with and without constraints.

EXAMPLE: From Example D of Chapter 6, Section 6.3, we know $(1, 1)$ is the unique global maximizer of $y - x^2$ subject to $x \geq 0$, $y \geq 0$, and $y \leq 2x - 1$, with corresponding Lagrangian $L^* = y - x^2 - \lambda(-2x + 1 + y)$ and $\lambda^* = 1$ at the solution.

Suppose this is just the special case corresponding to $p^0 = 1$ of the problem maximize $y^p - x^2$ subject to $x \geq 0$, $y \geq 0$, and $y \leq 2x - 1$. Then $f^*(p)$ is the optimized value of $y^p - x^2$, and $L^*(x, y, \lambda; p) = y^p - x^2 - \lambda(-2x + 1 + y)$ so $\partial L^*/\partial p = \partial y^p/\partial p = y^p(\ln y)$. Thus $df^*(1)/dp = \partial L^*(1, 1, 1; 1)/\partial p = \ln 1 = 0$.

Suppose the original problem is just the special case corresponding to $p^0 = 1$ of the problem maximize $y - x^2$ subject to $x \geq 0$, $y \geq 0$, and $y \leq 2x - p$. Then $f^*(p)$ is the optimized value of $y - x^2$ subject to the constraints, and $L^*(x, y, \lambda; p) = y - x^2 - \lambda(-2x + p + y)$ so $\partial L^*/\partial p = -\lambda$. Thus $df^*(1)/dp = \partial L^*(1, 1, 1; 1)/\partial p = -1$.

Use of the envelope theorem makes this comparative statics problem easy. Assuming we have a unique global optimizer with nonsingular $[L^*_{ij}]$, we need only:

1. Write out the Lagrangian, L^*, including the relevant parameters (a parameter may appear in several places in L^*, either as part of the objective function or as part of one or more of the constraints or in both the objective function and constraints).
2. Differentiate L^* with respect to the relevant parameter.
3. Evaluate $\partial L^*/\partial p_j$ at the original parameter value $\mathbf{p}^0$ and the solution corresponding to the original parameter value, $(\mathbf{x}^0, \boldsymbol{\lambda}^0)$.

Then $\partial f^*(\mathbf{p}^0)/\partial p_j = \partial L^*(\mathbf{x}^0, \boldsymbol{\lambda}^0; \mathbf{p}^0)/\partial p_j$.

PROBLEMS

8.1 (a) Minimize $(x - 1)^2 + (y - 1)^2 + (z - 1)^2$ subject to $x + y + z = 2$.

 (b) Suppose the constraint in part (a) contained a parameter t with $x + y + z = 2 + t$. Without explicitly solving the minimization problem for nonzero t, find out how the optimal values of x, y, and z change when t changes from $t = 0$.

8.2 In a neighborhood of $(1, 0, 1)$ can the intersection of the surfaces $x^2 + 2y^2 + (z - 1)^2 = 1$ and $x - y + z^2 = 2$ be written as $x = g(z)$ and $y = h(z)$? If so, find $dg(1)/dz$ and $dh(1)/dz$.

8.3 Find the slope of the tangent to the curve defined by $x^2y + x \ln y = 0$ at the point $(x, y) = (e, 1/e)$.

8.4 A profit-maximizing monopolist produces a single output to be sold in a single market. The cost to produce q units is $C(q) = q + \frac{1}{2}q^2$, and the market demand is such that the average revenue for selling q units is $D^{-1}(q) = 4 - q^5/6$. The monopolist must also pay a tax of \$1 per unit.

 (a) Show that the monopolist's unique optimal output is $q^* = 1$.

 (b) How does the monopolist's optimal output change when the tax rate changes?

8.5 Show that the intersection of the surface $x^2 + y + z^2 = 4$ with the surface $y - xz = 1$ near $(x, y, z) = (1, 2, 1)$ can be written in the form $x = g(z)$ and $y = h(z)$. Find $dg(1)/dz$ and $dh(1)/dz$.

8.6 (a) Minimize $x^2 + y^2 + z^2$ subject to $x \geq 0$, $y \geq 0$, and $x + y + 2z = 6$.

(b) How does the minimized value of $x^2 + y^2 + z^2$ change if the equality constraint in part (a) is changed to $x + y + 2z = 6 + dt$.

8.7 For the problem of maximizing $(x + 3)(y + 1)$ subject to $y \geq 0$, $x - y \geq -2$, and $0 \geq x$, setting up the problem in standing form and solving, the unique global solution is $(x^*, y^*, \lambda_1^*, \lambda_2^*, \lambda_3^*) = (0, 2.0, 3, 6)$.

(a) Now consider a new problem of maximizing $(x + 3)(y + t)$ subject to the same constraints. What is the appropriate system of equations for performing comparative statics to find the effect on the optimal choices of x and y of a change in t, evaluated at $t = 1$?

(b) Consider the problem of maximizing $(x + 3)(y + 1)$ subject to $y \geq t$, $x - y \geq -2(1 + t)$, and $t \geq x$. Let $f^*(t)$ be the maximized value of the objective function given the constraints corresponding to t. What is $df^*(0)/dt$?

8.8 Consider the intersection of the surfaces $xyz = 3$ and $x^2 + y^2 + (z - 1)^2 = 10$.

(a) Can the intersection be written in the form of differentiable functions $x^*(z)$ and $y^*(z)$ near $(x, y, z) = (3, 1, 1)$?

(b) Show the intersection can be written in the form of differentiable functions $x^*(y)$ and $z^*(y)$ near $(1, 3, 1)$ and find $dx^*(3)/dy$ and $dz^*(3)/dy$.

8.9 For the problem of maximizing $2x + y$ subject to $0 \geq x$, $y \geq 0$, and $(x - 1)^2 + (y + 1)^2 \leq 10$, setting up the problem in standard form and solving, the unique global solution is $(x^*, y^*, \lambda_1^*, \lambda_2^*, \lambda_3^*) = (0, 2, 7/3, 0, 1/6)$.

(a) Now consider a new problem of maximizing $(2x + y)^t$ subject to the same constraints. What is the appropriate system of equations for performing comparative statics to find the effect on the optimal choices of x and y of a change in t, evaluated at $t = 1$?

(b) Consider the problem of maximizing $2x + yt + y$ subject to $t \geq x$, $y \geq t$, and $(x - 1)^2 + (y + 1)^2 \leq 10 + t$. Let $f^*(t)$ be the maximized value of the objective function given the constraints corresponding to t. What is $df^*(0)/dt$?

8.10 Show the intersection of the surfaces $xy + xz + yz = 11$ and $z^2 + y \ln x = 4$ can be written in the form of differentiable functions $x^*(y)$ and $z^*(y)$ near $(1, 3, 2)$ and find $dx^*(3)/dy$ and $dz^*(3)/dy$.

8.11 For the problem of maximizing $(x - 2)(y + 1)$ subject to $x + y \geq -1$ and $2x + y \leq 4$ with Lagrangian $L(x, y, \lambda_1, \lambda_2) = (x - 2)(y + 1) - \lambda_1(-1 - x - y) - \lambda_2(2x + y - 4)$, the potential solution $(1, -2, 1, 0)$

satisfies the second-order conditions and is the unique global maximizer. Now consider the problem of maximizing $(x - 2)(y + p)$ subject to $x + py \geq -p$ and $2x + py \leq 4$. Define $x^*(p)$ and $y^*(p)$ as the optimal choices for x and y given p and let $f^*(p)$ be the corresponding optimized value of $(x - 2)(y + p)$.

(a) Find $dx^*(1)/dp$ and $dy^*(1)/dp$.

(b) Find $df^*(1)/dp$.

8.12 For the problem of maximizing $(3 - x)(5 - y)$ subject to $x \geq 0$, $y \geq 0$, and $2x + y \leq 4$ setting up the problem in standard form and solving, the unique global solution is $(x^*, y^*, \lambda_1^*, \lambda_2^*, \lambda_3^*) = (0, 0, 5, 3, 0)$.

(a) Now consider a new problem of maximizing $(3 - tx)(5 - y)$ subject to $x \geq 0$, $y \geq 0$, and $2x + y \leq 4t$. What is the appropriate system of equations for performing comparative statics to find the effect on the optimal x and y of a change in t, evaluated at $t = 1$?

(b) For the problem in part (a), let $f^*(t)$ be the maximized value of the objective function given the constraints corresponding to t. What is $df^*(1)/dt$?

8.13 Consider the intersection of the surfaces $x^2 + zy = 7$ and $xy - z = 5$. Show the intersection can be written in the form of differentiable functions $y^*(x)$ and $z^*(x)$ near $(2, 3, 1)$ and find $dy^*(2)/dx$ and $dz^*(2)/dx$.

8.14 For the problem of maximizing x^4y subject to $x \geq 0$, $y \geq 0$, and $x^2 + y^2 \leq 5$ with Lagrangian $L(x, y, \lambda_1, \lambda_2, \lambda_3) = x^4y - \lambda_1(-x) - \lambda_2(-y) - \lambda_3(x^2 + y^2 - 5)$, the potential solution $(2, 1, 0, 0, 8)$ satisfies the second-order conditions and is the unique global maximizer. Now consider the problem of maximizing px^4y subject to $x \geq 0$, $y \geq p - 1$, and $px^2 + y^2 \leq 5p$. Define $x^*(p)$ and $y^*(p)$ as the optimal choices for x and y given p and let $f^*(p)$ be the corresponding optimized value of px^4y.

(a) Find $dx^*(1)/dp$ and $dy^*(1)/dp$.

(b) Find $df^*(1)/dp$.

9

LINE
INTEGRALS

9.1 INTRODUCTION

The area under a demand curve is sometimes used as a measure of value
to consumers. Such areas are often used to evaluate the effect on consumers of price changes. (We will not discuss the appropriateness of this
use here.) For example, if the utility function is $u(x, y) = xy$, the price of
the second good is fixed at 1, and income is $4, then at $p_x = 1$ the optimal
consumption is $x^* = y^* = 2$, with corresponding utility $u^* = 4$. If p_x
increases to 4, we can use the area under the compensated demand
function $x_c^*(p_x, p_y, u) = \sqrt{up_y/p_x}$ to evaluate the effect of the price
increase on the consumer's welfare. Setting $p_y = 1$ and $u = 4$ and integrating over the range of the price change, $\int_1^4 x_c^*(p_x, 1, 4)\, dp_x =$
$\int_1^4 (2/\sqrt{p_x})\, dp_x = 4$. This means that at the new higher price, $p_x = 4$, the
consumer would need an additional $4 in income to be as well off as at the
initial prices and income.

　　If several prices change, we might consider the changes one at a time,
adding up the individual effects to find the overall effect. Unfortunately,
the result can depend on the order in which we consider the changes. For
example, with utility function $u(x, y) = (x + 1)y$, income m, and prices
p_x and p_y, the (regular) demand functions are $x^*(p_x, p_y, m) = (m -
p_x)/2p_x$ and $y^*(p_x, p_y, m) = (m + p_x)/2p_y$ as long as $m \geq p_x$. Using the
area under the (regular) demands to evaluate the effect of a change from
$(p_x, p_y, m) = (1, 1, 5)$ to $(4, 9/16, 5)$ leads to path-specific answers. If p_x is

changed first, then p_y, the change is

$$\int_1^4 \left[(5 - p_x)/2p_x\right] dp_x + \int_1^{9/16} \left[(5 + 4)/2p_y\right] dp_y$$

$$= (5/2)(\ln 4) - (3/2) + (9/2)(\ln(9/16))$$

$$\approx -0.6 < 0,$$

while if p_y is changed first, then p_x, the change is

$$\int_1^{9/16} \left[(5 + 1)/2p_y\right] dp_y + \int_1^4 \left[(5 - p_x)/2p_x\right] dp_x$$

$$= 3(\ln(9/16)) + (5/2)(\ln 4) - (3/2)$$

$$\approx 0.2 > 0.$$

For this procedure to make sense when several prices change, the result should be independent of the order in which prices are changed. This leads us to examine line integrals and the conditions under which the value is independent of the path. This is a specialized topic and we are only interested in certain results, so only a brief treatment of line integrals is provided.

9.2 LINE INTEGRALS AND PATH INDEPENDENCE

We now investigate conditions under which the answer will be independent of the path. Let $\mathbf{a}, \mathbf{b}, \in \mathbb{R}^n$ with $a_i < b_i$, $i = 1, \ldots, n$, and let $\Omega = \{\mathbf{x} \in \mathbb{R}^n | a_i < x_i < b_i \ i = 1, \ldots, n\}$.

DEFINITION: A *path* from $\mathbf{x}^0 \in \Omega$ to $\mathbf{x}^1 \in \Omega$ is a continuous, piecewise continuously differentiable function $\mathbf{w}: [0, 1] \to \Omega$ such that $\mathbf{w}(0) = \mathbf{x}^0$ and $\mathbf{w}(1) = \mathbf{x}^1$.

Thus a path is just a piecewise smooth curve in Ω connecting $\mathbf{x}^0$ and $\mathbf{x}^1$. The curve is *oriented* since it starts at $\mathbf{x}^0$ and ends at $\mathbf{x}^1$.

DEFINITION: A *vector field* on Ω is a function $F: \Omega \to \mathbb{R}^n$.

The function F is represented by coordinate functions, $F = (f_1, \ldots, f_n)$, where for each i, $f_i: \Omega \to \mathbb{R}$. We say F is continuous if each coordinate function is continuous, we say F is differentiable if each coordinate function is differentiable, etc.

DEFINITION: A *potential function* for a vector field F is a differentiable function $V: \Omega \to \mathbb{R}$ such that $\nabla V(\mathbf{x}) = F(\mathbf{x})$ for all $\mathbf{x} \in \Omega$.

Note that if $V(\mathbf{x})$ is a potential function for F, then so is $V(\mathbf{x}) + c$ for any $c \in \mathbb{R}$. Also, if $V(\mathbf{x})$ and $W(\mathbf{x})$ are potential functions for F, then $V(\mathbf{x}) - W(\mathbf{x})$ is constant.

THEOREM: *Let $F = (f_1, \ldots, f_n)$ be a continuously differentiable vector field on Ω. Then F has a potential function if and only if $\partial f_i(\mathbf{x})/\partial x_j = \partial f_j(\mathbf{x})/\partial x_i$ for all $\mathbf{x} \in \Omega$, for all $i, j \in \{1, 2, \ldots, n\}$.*

EXAMPLE: $F(x, y) = ((1 - x)/x, (1 + x)/y)$ does not have a potential function on $\Omega = (0, 1)^2$ because $\partial f_1/\partial y = 0 \neq \partial f_2/\partial x = 1/y$.

EXAMPLE: $F(x, y) = (2xy, x^2)$ has a potential function on $\mathbb{R}^2$ since $\partial f_1/\partial y = 2x = \partial f_2/\partial x$ for all x, y. To find the potential function, V, note $f_2(x, y) = x^2 = \partial V/\partial y$, so integrating with respect to y, $V(x, y) = x^2 y + g(x)$. Similarly, $f_1(x, y) = 2xy = \partial V/\partial x$ so integrating with respect to x, $V(x, y) = x^2 y + h(y)$. Since $h(y) \equiv g(x)$, both functions must be constant and $V(x, y)$ must be $x^2 y + c$ for some constant c.

Let $\mathbf{w}$ be a path from $\mathbf{x}^0$ to $\mathbf{x}^1$, and let F be a continuous vector field on Ω. To define the integral of F along the path $\mathbf{w}$ note for $t \in [0, 1], \mathbf{w}(t)$ is a point in Ω, so $F(\mathbf{w}(t))$ is a vector in $\mathbb{R}^n$. By the piecewise continuous differentiability of $\mathbf{w}$, for all but a finite number of t values, $\mathbf{w}'(t) = (dw_1(t)/dt, dw_2(t)/dt, \ldots, dw_n(t)/dt)$ is a well-defined vector in $\mathbb{R}^n$. Thus $F(\mathbf{w}(t)) \cdot \mathbf{w}'(t)$ is a scalar, and it is used to define the line (or curve) integral of F along $\mathbf{w}$ as $\int_w F = \int_0^1 F(\mathbf{w}(t)) \cdot w'(t) \, dt$.

DEFINITION: The continuous vector field F on Ω satisfies *path independence* if for any $\mathbf{x}^0 \in \Omega$ and $\mathbf{x}^1 \in \Omega$ and any two paths $\mathbf{w}^0$ and $\mathbf{w}^1$ from $\mathbf{x}^0$ to $\mathbf{x}^1$, $\int_{w^0} F = \int_{w^1} F$.

THEOREM: *Let F be a continuous vector field on Ω. Then F satisfies path independence if and only if F has a potential function.*

By the previous theorem, if F is a continuously differentiable vector field on Ω and $\partial f_i(\mathbf{x})/\partial x_j = \partial f_j(\mathbf{x})/\partial x_i$ for all $\mathbf{x}$, for all i and j, then F has a potential function and thus satisfies path independence. This gives us a way to check for path independence. If F satisfies path independence, then the path can be chosen to make the integration as simple as possible (e.g., changing only one price at a time in the consumer examples at the start of this chapter). If the potential function V is known, then $\int_w F = V(\mathbf{w}(1)) - V(\mathbf{w}(0))$.

EXAMPLE: For $F(x, y) = (2xy, x^2)$, find the line integral of F over the path $\mathbf{w}(t) = (t, t^2)$, $t \in [0, 1]$.

1. This can be done directly via the definition: $F(\mathbf{w}(t)) = (2tt^2, t^2) = (2t^3, t^2)$ and $\mathbf{w}'(t) = (1, 2t)$, so

$$\int_w F = \int_0^1 (2t^3, t^2) \cdot (1, 2t) \, dt = \int_0^1 4t^3 \, dt = 1.$$

2. Noting F satisfies path independence, this can be done via the path

$$\mathbf{w}^0(t) = \begin{cases} (2t, 0) & 0 \le t \le 1/2, \\ (1, 2t - 1) & 1/2 < t \le 1. \end{cases}$$

Then

$$F(\mathbf{w}^0(t)) = \begin{cases} (0, 4t^2) & 0 \le t \le 1/2, \\ (4t - 2, 1) & 1/2 < t \le 1 \end{cases}$$

and

$$\mathbf{w}^{0\prime}(t) = \begin{cases} (2, 0) & 0 < t < 1/2, \\ (0, 2) & 1/2 < t < 1 \end{cases}$$

so

$$\int_w F = \int_{w^0} F = \int_0^{1/2} (0, 4t^2) \cdot (2, 0) \, dt + \int_{1/2}^1 (4t - 2, 1) \cdot (0, 2) \, dt$$

$$= \int_0^{1/2} 0 \, dt + \int_{1/2}^1 2 \, dt = 1.$$

This can also be done using the path $\mathbf{w}^1(t) = (t, t)$. Then $F(\mathbf{w}^1(t)) = (2t^2, t^2)$ and $\mathbf{w}^{1\prime}(t) = (1, 1)$ so

$$\int_w F = \int_{w^1} F = \int_0^1 (2t^2, t^2) \cdot (1, 1) \, dt = \int_0^1 3t^2 \, dt = 1.$$

3. Noting F has potential function $V(x, y) = x^2 y$, this can be done as $\int_w F = V(\mathbf{w}(1)) - V(\mathbf{w}(0)) = V(1, 1) - V(0, 0) = 1$.

EXAMPLE: For $F(x, y) = (x/\sqrt{x^2 + y^2}, y/\sqrt{x^2 + y^2})$ find the line integral of F over the path $\mathbf{w}(t) = (1 - t, t)$, $t \in [0, 1]$. This could be done directly from the definition, but noting F satisfies path independence allows us to choose a more convenient path from $(1, 0)$ to $(0, 1)$. In particular, for the path $\mathbf{w}^0(t) = (1 - t, \sqrt{2t - t^2})$ $t \in [0, 1]$, $F(\mathbf{w}^0(t)) = (1 - t, \sqrt{2t - t^2}) = \mathbf{w}^0(t)$ and $\mathbf{w}^{0\prime}(t) = (-1, (1 - t)/\sqrt{2t - t^2})$ so

$$\int_0^1 F(\mathbf{w}^0(t)) \cdot \mathbf{w}^{0\prime}(t) \, dt = \int_0^1 [(-1 + t) + (1 - t)] \, dt = \int_0^1 0 \, dt = 0.$$

A potential function for F is $V(x, y) = \sqrt{x^2 + y^2}$ so $\int_w F = V(1, 0) - V(0, 1) = 1 - 1 = 0$ is the solution via the third method.

9.3 SURPLUS MEASURES USING LINE INTEGRALS

For economic problems involving consumer's surplus, path independence for the use of compensated demand follows from the symmetry of the Slutsky matrix. For initial prices and income $(\mathbf{p}^0, y^0)$ and final prices and income $(\mathbf{p}^1, y^1)$, $V(\mathbf{p}, y) = y - m^*(\mathbf{p}, u^*(\mathbf{p}^1, y^1))$ is a potential function for $F(\mathbf{p}, y) = (-h_1(\mathbf{p}, u^*(\mathbf{p}^1, y^1)), \ldots, -h_l(\mathbf{p}, u^*(\mathbf{p}^1, y^1)), 1)$ where u^* is the indirect utility function, m^* is the expenditure function, and h_i is the compensated demand function for good i. Then

$$\int_{y^0}^{y^1} dy + \sum_{i=1}^{l} \int_{p_i^0}^{p_i^1} - h_i\left((p_1^1, \ldots, p_{i-1}^1, p_i, p_{i+1}^0, \ldots, p_l^0), u^*(\mathbf{p}^1, y^1)\right) dp_i$$

$$= V(\mathbf{p}^1, y^1) - V(\mathbf{p}^0, y^0)$$

is the amount of money that would have to be given to the consumer at $(\mathbf{p}^0, y^0)$ to make her as well off as at $(\mathbf{p}^1, y^1)$. This is the *equivalent variation* measure. As written, it is evaluated by taking price changes one at a time, which is legitimate since path independence is satisfied. If we replace $u^*(\mathbf{p}^1, y^1)$, the final utility level, with $u^*(\mathbf{p}^0, y^0)$, the initial utility level, we get the *compensating variation* measure, and the corresponding $V(\mathbf{p}^1, y^1) - V(\mathbf{p}^0, y^0)$ is the amount of income that would have to be taken away at $(\mathbf{p}^1, y^1)$ in order to make her as well off as at $(\mathbf{p}^0, y^0)$. Once again path independence is satisfied, so this measure may be evaluated by integrating compensated demands with one price changing at a time.

As exhibited at the start of this chapter, path independence does not generally hold for the use of regular demand functions. For this case, path independence requires the extra condition of homothetic preferences.

For the example near the start of this chapter, with utility function $u(x, y) = (x + 1)y$, preferences are not homothetic. The corresponding compensated demand functions are $h_1(p_x, p_y, u) = \sqrt{p_y u / p_x} - 1$ and $h_2(p_x, p_y, u) = \sqrt{p_x u / p_y}$ with expenditure function $m^*(p_x, p_y, u) = 2\sqrt{p_x p_y u} - p_x$ and indirect utility function

$$u^*(p_x, p_y, m) = (m + p_x)^2 / 4 p_x p_y.$$

Using the potential function, the equivalent variation measure for the change from $(1, 1, 5)$ to $(4, 9/16, 5)$ is $\{5 - m^*(4, 9/16, u^*(4, 9/16, 5))\} - \{5 - m^*(1, 1, u^*(4, 9/16, 5))\} = 3 - \sqrt{u^*(4, 9/16, 5)} = 0$. Thus the consumer is indifferent between the two budgets. They both lead to $u^* = 9$.

10

STABILITY

10.1 INTRODUCTION

For many economic models the dynamic behavior of the system is modeled
by the solution curves of a differential equation or system of differential
equations. For example, in the general equilibrium price adjustment
tatonnement, the rate of change of prices depends on the differences
between demand and supply for each good, $\mathbf{p}' = \mathbf{f}(\mathbf{p})$. Given some initial
state, $\mathbf{p}^0$, at time t^0, we are interested in the price path over time, $\mathbf{p}(t)$.
Two issues are of particular interest. First, which states are *equilibrium
states* in the sense that they do not change over time? Obviously $\mathbf{p}^*$ is an
equilibrium if and only if $\mathbf{f}(\mathbf{p}^*) = \mathbf{0}$. Second, are the equilibrium states
"stable"? If not, they are unlikely to be observed, since after any distur-
bance the system will not return to the original equilibrium. Alternatively,
if we start from an initial equilibrium and change some policy instrument
(e.g., a tax rate), our comparative statics procedure determines the effect
on the equilibrium. Unless that new equilibrium is stable, the comparative
statics are meaningless since the economy will not move to the new
equilibrium tracked by the comparative statics.

Consider the usual price adjustment story for a single competitive
market: price rises if demand exceeds supply and falls if supply exceeds
demand. For the typical partial equilibrium example, the equilibrium price
is the unique price p^* at which supply equals demand. The equilibrium is
stable since demand exceeds supply for $p < p^*$ while supply exceeds
demand for $p > p^*$. In a general equilibrium context in which the feed-

back effects of ownership of resources and firms are accounted for, there may be multiple equilibria. Some equilibria may be stable for small perturbations, while others may not be stable.

In this chapter we will examine some ways to determine whether a particular equilibrium is stable under a given adjustment process. The adjustment process itself is not explained here. The economic aspects of the situation suggest appropriate adjustment processes.

10.2 LOCAL AND GLOBAL STABILITY

The following definitions of stability will be useful for our purposes. However, it is important to note that terminology in this area is not standardized so one must be very careful to check the sense in which "stable" is being used. Let $\mathbf{f}: W \to \mathbb{R}^m$ and let $\mathbf{p}(t; \mathbf{p}^0)$ be the state of the dynamical system (e.g., the price vector) at time t following a solution curve for the adjustment process $\mathbf{p}' = \mathbf{f}(\mathbf{p})$ starting at $\mathbf{p}^0$ at time t^0. (Sometimes we will use a dot over a variable to indicate the derivative of the variable with respect to time, as in $\dot{V}$.)

DEFINITION: $\mathbf{p}^*$ is *globally asymptotically stable* if $\mathbf{p}(t; \mathbf{p}^0) \to \mathbf{p}^*$ as $t \to \infty$ for all $\mathbf{p}^0 \in W$.

DEFINITION: $\mathbf{p}^*$ is *locally asymptotically stable* if there exists a $\delta > 0$ such that $\mathbf{p}(t; \mathbf{p}^0) \to \mathbf{p}^*$ as $t \to \infty$ for all $\mathbf{p}^0 \in W$ satisfying $\|\mathbf{p}^0 - \mathbf{p}^*\| < \delta$.

Local stability requires that after "small" disturbances the system returns to the original equilibrium, while global stability requires convergence to $\mathbf{p}^*$ from any starting point. Global stability implies local stability, but local stability does not imply global stability. Clearly there cannot be more than one equilibrium if some equilibrium is globally stable.

10.3 LINEAR SYSTEMS

Consider a linear system, $\mathbf{f}: \mathbb{R}^m \to \mathbb{R}^m$ given by $\mathbf{f}(\mathbf{p}) = A\mathbf{p}$ or $\mathbf{f}(\mathbf{p}) = A(\mathbf{p} - \mathbf{p}^*)$ where A is an $m \times m$ matrix. We proceed by examining first the case $m = 1$, then the case $m > 1$ with A a diagonal matrix, and finally the general linear case.

For $m = 1$ let $f(p) = ap$ with initial state p^0 at time t^0. Solving the differential equation $dp(t)/dt = ap(t)$ (see Chapter 1, Section 1.25), the solution is $p(t) = ce^{at}$ where the constant c is determined by the initial condition $p(t^0) = p^0$. Thus $c = p^0/e^{at^0}$, and the solution path is $p(t) = p^0 e^{at}/e^{at^0} = p^0 e^{a(t-t^0)}$. There are three possible cases. If $a > 0$, $p^* = 0$ is the unique equilibrium, but it is not stable [$e^{a(t-t^0)} \to \infty$ as $t \to \infty$, so

$p(t) \to \infty$ if $p^0 > 0$ and $p(t) \to -\infty$ if $p^0 < 0$]. If $a = 0$, every $p \in \mathbb{R}$ is an equilibrium, but no equilibrium is locally stable [$p(t) \equiv p^0$ for every p^0]. Finally, if $a < 0$, then $p^* = 0$ is the unique equilibrium, and it is globally stable [$e^{a(t-t^0)} \to 0$ as $t \to \infty$, so $p(t) \to 0$ as $t \to \infty$ for any p^0].

For $m = 1$ and $f(p) = a(p - p^*)$, the solution is $p(t) = p^* + (p^0 - p^*))e^{a(t-t^0)}$, and p^* plays the role of zero (i.e., p^* is the unique equilibrium unless $a = 0$, and it is stable if and only if $a < 0$).

Similar results hold for $m > 1$. First consider the case in which A is a diagonal matrix. Then each variable is independent of all other variables, and we obtain an m-tuple of single-variable solutions as above. However, the overall system is stable if and only if all m components are stable, i.e., if and only if all diagonal entries of A are strictly negative. For a general matrix A, solving the system of differential equations $\mathbf{p}'(t) = A(\mathbf{p}(t) - \mathbf{p}^*)$ with initial condition $\mathbf{p}(t^0) = \mathbf{p}^0$, the solution path is $\mathbf{p}(t) = \mathbf{p}^* + e^{A(t-t^0)}(\mathbf{p}^0 - \mathbf{p}^*)$ where $e^{At} = I + At/1! + A^2t^2/2! + \cdots + A^n t^n/n! + \cdots$. The properties for the general system are similar to those for the diagonal system but use the eigenvalues of A rather than the diagonal entries.

THEOREM: *For the system* $\mathbf{p}' = A(\mathbf{p} - \mathbf{p}^*)$, $\mathbf{p}^*$ *is globally asymptotically stable if and only if every eigenvalue of A has a strictly negative real part.*

We know two conditions under which a matrix has eigenvalues with negative real parts: negative dominant diagonal and negative definite (defined for symmetric matrices).

10.4 LINEAR APPROXIMATION SYSTEMS

Most dynamical systems are not linear, but a linear approximation system can be used to check local stability of a general system. Given the system $\mathbf{p}' = \mathbf{f}(\mathbf{p})$ with equilibrium $\mathbf{p}^*$, let A be the $m \times m$ matrix with entries $a_{ij} = \partial f_i(\mathbf{p}^*)/\partial p_j$; i.e., A is the Jacobian matrix of f evaluated at the equilibrium. The *linear approximation system* at the equilibrium $\mathbf{p}^*$ is $\mathbf{p}' = A(\mathbf{p} - \mathbf{p}^*)$. At equilibrium $\mathbf{p}^*$, the linear approximation system uses the fact that for $\mathbf{p}$ near $\mathbf{p}^*$,

$$f(\mathbf{p}) \approx f(\mathbf{p}^*) + \left[\frac{\partial f_i(\mathbf{p}^*)}{\partial p_j}\right](\mathbf{p} - \mathbf{p}^*) = \left[\frac{\partial f_i(\mathbf{p}^*)}{\partial p_j}\right](\mathbf{p} - \mathbf{p}^*).$$

THEOREM: *Let* $\mathbf{f}$ *be continuously differentiable and* $\mathbf{p}' = A(\mathbf{p} - \mathbf{p}^*)$ *be the linear approximation system corresponding to $\mathbf{f}$ at equilibrium $\mathbf{p}^*$.*

1. *If every eigenvalue of A has a strictly negative real part, then $\mathbf{p}^*$ is locally asymptotically stable under the dynamical system* $\mathbf{p}' = \mathbf{f}(\mathbf{p})$.

2. *If $\mathbf{p}^*$ is locally asymptotically stable under* $\mathbf{p}' = \mathbf{f}(\mathbf{p})$, *then no eigenvalue of A has a strictly positive real part.*

Notice that there are three cases. If all eigenvalues have strictly negative real parts, then $\mathbf{p}^*$ is locally stable. If any eigenvalue has a strictly positive real part, then $\mathbf{p}^*$ is not locally stable. If no eigenvalue has a strictly positive real part but some eigenvalue has real part 0, then $\mathbf{p}^*$ might or might not be locally stable. The linear approximation system cannot answer the question in this third case.

EXAMPLE: For

$$\mathbf{p}' = \begin{bmatrix} -2 & 0 \\ 1 & -1 \end{bmatrix}\mathbf{p},$$

$\mathbf{0}$ is globally stable since A has a dominant negative diagonal.

EXAMPLE: For

$$p'_1 = -2p_1 + p_2^2,$$

$$p'_2 = p_1 + p_1^2 - p_2 + p_2^2$$

$\mathbf{p} = \mathbf{0}$ is an equilibrium and the linear approximation system is

$$\mathbf{p}' = \begin{bmatrix} -2 & 0 \\ 1 & -1 \end{bmatrix}\mathbf{p},$$

so by the previous example, the original system is locally stable.

EXAMPLE: The linear approximation system may fail to be stable while the true system is stable. By the theorem, this can occur only if some eigenvalue for the linear approximation system has real part zero. For example, if $p' = [1 - p]^3$, then the equilibrium is $p^* = 1$. The linear approximation system is $p' = 0(p - 1)$, which is not stable. However, as we will see below, the original system is locally asymptotically stable.

10.5 LIAPUNOV FUNCTIONS

An additional method for determining stability uses Liapunov's second method. The idea for this method follows from the proof for the linear case, where it is shown that for an appropriate notion of distance, the distance from $\mathbf{p}(t)$ to $\mathbf{p}^*$ decreases over time if and only if all eigenvalues have negative real parts (the notion of distance depends on the actual eigenvalues and eigenvectors). Liapunov showed that other functions satisfying certain properties could be used to play the role of the distance (i.e., would decrease with time until the equilibrium was reached). Such a function is called a *Liapunov function*. The difficult part of this procedure is to find an appropriate Liapunov function (if one exists) for a particular problem. Sometimes functions such as utility, profit, or social welfare can be modified to be so used. In the following theorem, V is the Liapunov function and $\dot{V}$ is the time derivative of V.

THEOREM: *Let* $\mathbf{p}' = \mathbf{f}(\mathbf{p})$ *where* $\mathbf{f}: W \to \mathbb{R}^m$ *is a continuously differentiable function on the open set* $W \subset \mathbb{R}^m$ *with* $\mathbf{f}(\mathbf{p}^*) = \mathbf{0}$. *Let* $V: S \to \mathbb{R}$ *be a continuous function defined on a neighborhood* $S \subset W$ *of* $\mathbf{p}^*$ *and differentiable* (*except possibly at* $\mathbf{p}^*$) *satisfying*
1. $V(\mathbf{p}) > 0$ *for all* $\mathbf{p} \neq \mathbf{p}^*$, $V(\mathbf{p}^*) = 0$,
2. $\dot{V} = \nabla V(\mathbf{p}) \cdot \mathbf{f}(\mathbf{p}) < 0$ *for all* $\mathbf{p} \neq \mathbf{p}^*$.
Then $\mathbf{p}^*$ *is locally asymptotically stable.*

A Liapunov function can also be used to show global stability if appropriate properties hold everywhere, not just on neighborhood S.

EXAMPLE: For $p' = (1 - p)^3$ let $V(p) = (1 - p)^2$. Then $\dot{V} = -2(1 - p)(1 - p^3) = -2(1 - p)^4 < 0$ for $p \neq 1$. All the conditions of the theorem are satisfied, so $p^* = 1$ is locally asymptotically stable. (Recall that the linear approximation system was not stable for this example.) Since the properties hold globally for V, $p^* = 1$ is globally asymptotically stable.

If the adjustment process is defined by $\mathbf{f}(\mathbf{x}) = -\nabla H(\mathbf{x})$ for some function H, the system is called a *gradient system*. Note that $\dot{H} = \nabla H \cdot f = -\|\nabla H\|^2$, so the function H decreases over time except where $\nabla H(\mathbf{x}^*) = \mathbf{0}$ (i.e., except at an equilibrium). Thus if $\mathbf{x}^*$ is an equilibrium, a candidate Liapunov function is $H(\mathbf{x}) - H(\mathbf{x}^*)$. However, not all conditions of the theorem are necessarily satisfied. In particular, condition 1 of the theorem requires that $\mathbf{x}^*$ be a strict local minimizer. (The minimum is sometimes called an *isolated* minimum because there is no other minimum "nearby.") When H has an isolated minimum at $\mathbf{x}^*$, all the conditions of the theorem hold and $\mathbf{x}^*$ is asymptotically stable.

EXAMPLE: Let $H: \mathbb{R}^2 \to \mathbb{R}^1$ be defined by $H(x, y) = x^2(x - 1)^2 + y^2$ and let

$$\mathbf{f}(x, y) = -\nabla H(x, y) = -\begin{pmatrix} 2x(x - 1)(2x - 1) \\ 2y \end{pmatrix}.$$

To find all equilibria set $\nabla H = \mathbf{0}$ and solve for (x, y) to get the three equilibria $(0, 0)$, $(1/2, 0)$, and $(1, 0)$. The second-order condition matrix for minimizing H (to check for isolated minima) is

$$B(x, y) = \begin{bmatrix} 2(6x^2 - 6x + 1) & 0 \\ 0 & 2 \end{bmatrix}.$$

Evaluated at $(0, 0)$ or at $(1, 0)$,

$$B = \begin{bmatrix} 2 & 0 \\ 0 & 2 \end{bmatrix},$$

which is positive definite, so these are isolated minima of H and therefore locally asymptotically stable equilibria of the system. Evaluated at $(1/2, 0)$,

$$B = \begin{bmatrix} -1 & 0 \\ 0 & 2 \end{bmatrix},$$

so $(1/2, 0)$ is not a local minimizer of H, and this equilibrium is unstable.

PROBLEMS

10.1 Consider an equilibrium $x^* = 0$ and a corresponding adjustment process $\dot{x} = -x^3$.
   (a) Can the linear approximation system be used to show the equilibrium is locally stable?
   (b) Can the function $V(x) = x^2$ be used as a Liapunov function to show the equilibrium is stable?

10.2 Which of the following systems are stable?
   (a) $\dot{x} = -2x + y, \ \dot{y} = 2x - 3y$
   (b) $\dot{x} = x - 5y, \ \dot{y} = x - 3y$
   (c) $\dot{x} = x - 4y, \ \dot{y} = 4x - 7y$

10.3 Consider the set of price vectors $P = \{\mathbf{p} \in \mathbb{R}^l | p_i \geq 0 \forall i \text{ and } \|\mathbf{p}\| = 1\}$. Suppose the excess demand vector, $\mathbf{z}(\mathbf{p})$, for a competitive economy with price vector $\mathbf{p}$ satisfies:
   (i) $\mathbf{p} \cdot \mathbf{z}(p) = 0$ for all $\mathbf{p} \in P$ (Walras' law), and
   (ii) $\mathbf{p} \cdot \mathbf{z}(\mathbf{q}) \leq 0$ implies $\mathbf{q} \cdot \mathbf{z}(\mathbf{p}) > 0$ for all $\mathbf{p}, \mathbf{q} \in P$ (the weak axiom of revealed preference).
   Suppose $\mathbf{p}^* \in P$ is an equilibrium price vector [i.e. $\mathbf{z}(\mathbf{p}^*) = \mathbf{0}$]. Starting from any $\mathbf{p} \in P$ prices adjust in proportion to excess demand; i.e., $d\mathbf{p}/dt = \mathbf{z}(\mathbf{p})$. Show:
   (a) $d(\mathbf{p} \cdot \mathbf{p})/dt = 0$ (so the adjustment process stays in P) and
   (b) $(\mathbf{p} - \mathbf{p}^*) \cdot (\mathbf{p} - \mathbf{p}^*)$ can be used as a Liapunov function to prove the equilibrium is stable.

10.4 Is the following dynamical system locally stable?

$$\dot{x} = -3x + 2y,$$

$$\dot{y} = -4y + 2x,$$

$$\dot{z} = -3z + 3.$$

10.5 Given $H(x, y) = (x^2 - 1)^2 + (y - 2)^2$ define the dynamical system

$$\begin{pmatrix} \dot{x} \\ \dot{y} \end{pmatrix} = -\nabla H(x, y).$$

Find all equilibria and determine which equilibria are locally or globally stable.

10.6 Is the following system stable?

$$\dot{x} = -3x + 4y,$$
$$\dot{y} = -2y - 6z,$$
$$\dot{z} = -4z + 4.$$

10.7 True/False. The function $g(x, y) = x^4 - 2x^2 + y^2$ can be used as a Liapunov function to show $(0, 0)$ is a locally stable equilibrium of the dynamical system

$$\dot{x} = -4x^3 + 4x,$$
$$\dot{y} = -2y.$$

10.8 True/False. Suppose the dynamical system $\dot{x} = f(x)$ has equilibrium 0 and a linear approximation system $\dot{x} = Ax$ at 0. If the linear approximation system is not stable, then the original system is not stable.

10.9 True/False. Suppose the dynamical system $\dot{x} = f(x)$ has equilibrium 0. Suppose the function g has $g(0) = 10$ and $g(x) < 10$ for all $x \neq 0$. If $\nabla g(x) \cdot f(x)$ is strictly positive at all $x \neq 0$, then 0 is a stable equilibrium of the system.

10.10 What is the equilibrium for the following system and is it stable?

$$\dot{x} = -2x + y - 8z,$$
$$\dot{y} = 2x - 3y + 4z,$$
$$\dot{z} = -5z - 10.$$

10.11 Can the function $h(x, y) = x^4 - 4x^3 + 8x^2 - 8x + y^2 + 3$ be used as a Liapunov function to show $(1, 0)$ is a locally stable equilibrium for the following system?

$$\dot{x} = -4x^3 + 12x^2 - 16x + 8,$$
$$\dot{y} = -2y.$$

10.12 What are the equilibria for the following system and are they stable?

$$\dot{x} = -3x + 6,$$
$$\dot{y} = x - y^2 + 7z,$$
$$\dot{z} = 2x - 4z.$$

11

DYNAMIC
PROGRAMMING

11.1 INTRODUCTION

Dynamic programming is an approach used to solve sequential decision problems. The sequential nature of the problem may be natural (a sequence of choices made at different dates) or artificial (simultaneous allocation of production among n machines thought of as sequential allocation to machine 1, then 2,..., then n). The key idea of this approach is Bellman's principle of optimality: whatever has been done in previous steps, the remaining decisions must be optimal given the current situation. The mathematical form of this principle is the functional equation known as Bellman's equation. This approach allows very general formulations and yields sufficient conditions for optimization. Its disadvantage is the "curse of dimensionality": computational requirements for a solution expand exponentially as the dimension of the state space expands.

For concreteness, in what follows "time" is used as the sequential parameter of the problem. We will first consider finite horizon discrete time problems, then infinite horizon problems, and finally stochastic problems.

11.2 FINITE HORIZON DISCRETE TIME PROBLEMS

The standard dynamic programming (DP) problem assumes time separability of the overall objective function. Thus the overall payoff is the sum of returns in each of the periods. The "state" of the system (e.g., the consumer's wealth) at time t is $x(t)$. An initial condition for the problem is the state in the initial period: $x(0) = x_0$. The agent chooses a "control" (e.g., a vector of consumption and investment decisions) at time t, $u(t)$. The set of feasible controls at time t is Ω_t. When a control is chosen, the state is updated according to the dynamics

$$x(t + 1) = f(t, x(t), u(t))$$

for $t = 0, 1, \ldots, N - 1$. Note that the updating rule could depend on the period. The "return" in period t is $g(t, x(t), u(t))$ for $t = 0, 1, \ldots, N - 1$ and $h(x(N))$ for the final period N when no control choice is made. Note that the return function could depend on the period. The basic problem is to choose the controls $u(t)$ to maximize

$$\left\{ \sum_{t=0}^{N-1} g(t, x(t), u(t)) \right\} + h(x(N))$$

subject to the constraints on the controls, the updating rule, and the initial condition that the state is x_0 at date 0.

The idea of the DP approach is to consider a family of related problems. For each integer k with $0 \le k \le N - 1$ and each possible state x consider the problem of choosing controls for periods $k, k + 1, k + 2, \ldots, N - 1$ in order to maximize

$$\left\{ \sum_{t=k}^{N-1} g(t, x(t), u(t)) \right\} + h(x(N))$$

subject to the constraints on the controls, the updating rule, and the initial condition that the state is x at date k. When $k > 0$ this is in some sense a subproblem of the original problem.

Assume an optimal solution to the subproblem exists for all $0 \le k \le N - 1$ and all possible x. Let $V(k, x)$ be the maximized value for the subproblem and define $V(N, x) := h(x)$. V is called the *value function*.

For $0 \le k \le N - 1$, the value function satisfies Bellman's equation (or "the optimality equation")

$$V(k, x) = \max_{u \in \Omega_k} \left\{ g(k, x, u) + V(k + 1, f(k, x, u)) \right\}.$$

This equation means that the value function can be solved recursively backward, using $V(k + 1, \cdot)$ to solve for $V(k, \cdot)$. When choosing the control $u \in \Omega_k$, we must optimally trade off return "today" in $g(k, x, u)$ versus future return from a modified state in $V(k + 1, f(k, x, u))$. The economic intuition generated by this approach to problems comes from this trade-off. The optimal choice for the control given k and x, $\varphi(k, x)$, is called an *optimal control*. While solving the problem we will determine the optimal control function, i.e., $\varphi(k, x)$ for each k and x.

Before proceeding to some examples, a word on notation is in order. Our procedure started at $t = 0$ and counted time periods forward. It is also common to work without a period zero and/or to count time periods backwards so t refers to the number of periods remaining. These choices are usually dictated by the nature of the problem at hand. It is important to note the notation used in any particular problem. In many economic problems, the overall objective is the present discounted value of a stream of payoffs (e.g., profits in each period). When defining the value function and setting up Bellman's equation there are two commonly used alternatives. The first alternative discounts all values back to period zero. The second alternative discounts all values to the current period being examined. In the first method all values are measured in common units (value discounted to date zero), while in the second method, the value in period $t + 1$ must be discounted in order to make it comparable to the value in period t. The choice of method will affect the algebra involved but not the overall solution. We will use both alternatives.

The following facts will be useful in solving problems. For any z,

$$1 + z^1 + z^2 + \cdots + z^k = (1 - z^{k+1})/(1 - z),$$

$$z^1 + z^2 + \cdots + z^k = z(1 - z^k)/(1 - z),$$

$$z^0 = 1, \quad \text{and} \quad z^{bi} = \left(z^b\right)^i.$$

EXAMPLE: A consumer has initial wealth w_0. In each period $t = 0, 1, 2, \ldots, N - 1$ she chooses how much of her wealth to consume, c_t, and invests the rest at interest rate r. Thus for $t = 0, 1, \ldots, N - 1$, wealth in period $t + 1$ is $w_{t+1} = (w_t - c_t)(1 + r)$. She will die at the end of period $N - 1$, with any remaining wealth in period N, w_N, bequeathed to her offspring. Her utility function is time separable, with utility for consumption and bequest plan $(c_0, c_1, \ldots, c_{N-1}, b)$ equal to

$$\sum_{t=0}^{N-1} \delta^t \sqrt{c_t} + \delta^N \sqrt{b}, \quad \text{where } \delta \in (0, 1).$$

To find her optimal consumption plan and utility using dynamic programming, first translate into the DP notation. In this problem we will discount all values to period zero. Let $u(t) = c_t$, $x(t) = w_t$, $h(x) = \delta^N \sqrt{x}$, $g(t, x(t), u(t)) = \delta^t \sqrt{u(t)}$, $f(t, x(t), u(t)) = (1 + r)[x(t) - u(t)]$, $x_0 = w_0$, and $\Omega_t = \mathbb{R}_+$ for all t. The value function satisfies $V(N, x) = \delta^N \sqrt{x}$

and the optimality equation is

$$V(k, x) = \max_u \{\delta^k \sqrt{u} + V(k + 1, (1 + r)(x - u))\}.$$

Consider the case $r = 0$ (for $r > 0$ see the Problems). $V(N, x) = \delta^N \sqrt{x}$.

Using backward recursion, $V(N - 1, x) = \max_u \{\delta^{N-1} \sqrt{u} + \delta^N \sqrt{x - u}\}$. The optimization problem on the right-hand side is solved with optimal control $u^* = \varphi(N - 1, x) = x/(1 + \delta^2)$ and optimized value $V(N - 1, x) = \delta^{N-1} \sqrt{x(1 + \delta^2)}$.

Then

$$V(N - 2, x) = \max_u \left\{\delta^{N-2} \sqrt{u} + \delta^{N-1} \sqrt{(x - u)(1 + \delta^2)}\right\}.$$

The optimization problem on the right-hand side is solved with optimal control $u^* = \varphi(N - 2, x) = x/(1 + \delta^2 + \delta^4)$, and optimized value $V(N - 2, x) = \delta^{N-2} \sqrt{x(1 + \delta^2 + \delta^4)}$.

The pattern in these solutions suggests that $V(k, x)$ might be equal to $\delta^k \sqrt{x \sum_{i=0}^{N-k} \delta^{2i}}$, which can be checked by induction. The formula is correct for $V(N, x)$. For $0 \leq k < N$, assume the formula is correct for $k + 1$, $k + 2, \ldots, N$. Then

$$V(k, x) = \max_u \left\{\delta^k \sqrt{u} + \delta^{k+1} \sqrt{(x - u) \sum_{i=0}^{N-k-1} \delta^{2i}}\right\}.$$

The optimization problem on the right-hand side is solved with optimal control $\varphi(k, x) = x/\sum_{i=0}^{N-k} \delta^{2i}$ and value $\delta^k \sqrt{x \sum_{i=0}^{N-k} \delta^{2i}}$ as desired. By induction, the value function is $V(k, x) = \delta^k \sqrt{x \sum_{i=0}^{N-k} \delta^{2i}}$ and the optimal control is $\varphi(k, x) = x/\sum_{i=0}^{N-k} \delta^{2i}$. The optimal consumption plan is found as follows. Consumption in period 0 is $c_0 = \varphi(0, w_0)$. Then the state is updated to $f(0, w_0, \varphi(0, w_0))$. Consumption in period 1 is $c_1 = \varphi(1, f(0, w_0, \varphi(0, w_0)))$, etc. The optimal consumption plan is $c_t = \delta^{2t} w_0/\sum_{i=0}^{N} \delta^{2i}$, $t = 0, 1, \ldots, N - 1$, with bequest $b = \delta^{2N} w_0/\sum_{i=0}^{N} \delta^{2i}$. The corresponding maximized utility is $V(0, w_0) = \sqrt{w_0 \sum_{i=0}^{N} \delta^{2i}}$.

EXAMPLE: Minimize the sum of squares of n numbers subject to the constraint that they total to c. For $t = 0, 1, \ldots, n - 2$, let $u(t)$ be the $(t + 1)$st number. Let the state, $x(t)$, be the amount (out of total length c) that remains to be used up at period t. The state is updated according to $x(t + 1) = x(t) - u(t)$, and the initial condition is $x(0) = c$. To make this a maximization problem, the return in period t is $g(t, x(t), u(t)) = -[u(t)]^2$ for $t = 0, 1, \ldots, n - 2$ and $h(x(n - 1)) = -[x(n - 1)]^2$. The control constraint is $u(t) \in \mathbb{R}$. In the final period, we define the value function as $V(n - 1, x) = -x^2$. For the next-to-last period, by Bellman's equation

$$V(n - 2, x) = \max_u \left\{ -u^2 - (x - u)^2 \right\}$$

Solving the optimization problem on the right-hand side of this equation, we get the optimal control $\varphi(n - 2, x) = x/2$ and $V(n - 2, x) = 2(x/2)^2$. For the previous period, by Bellman's equation $V(n - 3, x) = \max_u \{ -u^2 - (x - u)^2/2 \}$. Solving the optimization problem, we get the optimal control $\varphi(n - 3, x) = x/3$ and $V(n - 3, x) = -3(x/3)^2$. By induction, $\varphi(n - k, x) = x/k$ and $V(n - k, x) = -k(x/k)^2$. For the original problem, $V(0, c) = -n(c/n)^2$ and $u^*(0) = u^*(1) = \cdots = u^*(n - 2) = c/n$.

Note the interpretation of the first-order condition used in solving the maximization problem,

$$\max_u \left\{ g(k, x, u) + V(k + 1, f(k, x, u)) \right\} : \frac{\partial g}{\partial u} + \frac{\partial V}{\partial x} \frac{\partial f}{\partial u} = 0.$$

The agent must trade off the effect on the current period return against the effect on the value function for the future position

$$\left(\frac{\partial V}{\partial x} \frac{\partial f}{\partial u} \right).$$

In the second example, increasing u reduced the current return ($\partial g/\partial u = -2u$) but improved the value of the future position by reducing the amount of length remaining to be used up ($\partial V(n - k, x)/\partial x = -2x/1$ and $\partial f/\partial u = -1$). In the first example, increasing u increased the current return but reduced the value of the future position by decreasing the wealth available for future consumption.

11.3 INFINITE TIME HORIZON

In many economic optimization problems with infinite horizon, except for discounting, there is no difference between the problem at $t = 0$ with state x and the problem at $t = k$ with state x, because, except for discounting, the return (and updating) functions are identical in each period. This is not true in the finite horizon case because we are closer to the end of time at later periods. In infinite horizon problems it is often useful to introduce a period-free value function $V(x)$ by discounting to the current period rather than to period zero. In the optimality equation, the future value must then be discounted:

$$V(x) = \max_u \left\{ g(x, u) + \delta V(f(x, u)) \right\}.$$

The undiscounted return in any period is $g(x, u)$, independent of t, and the updating function is $f(x, u)$, independent of t. The point of view here is that, because of the separability and time independence, whatever period we are in should be thought of as "today" for discounting purposes, with all previous returns sunk costs or benefits. For current and future decisions, the past matters only through its determination of the current state, x. The time period is irrelevant as long as all values are discounted to current values. The optimality equation exhibits the trade-off between current return, $g(x, u)$, and the discounted value of next periods problem, faced with the new, updated state, $f(x, u)$.

With no final period for an infinite horizon problem, we cannot use the simple backward recursion method of the finite horizon case. However, in some problems the infinite horizon solutions will be the limit of finite horizon solutions, with the limit taken as the horizon grows without bound. In other problems, even though there is no final period, the optimal decisions will lead to a finite date after which no further action occurs. We will consider both cases via simple examples.

EXAMPLE: Consider an infinite horizon version of the investment problem in the previous section, again with $r = 0$ (for $r > 0$ see the Problems). The investor is infinitely lived (or considers the string of consumptions of an infinite sequence of her offspring) with consumption plan $(c_0, c_1, c_2, \ldots)$ yielding utility $\sum_{t=0}^{\infty} \delta^t \sqrt{c_t}$, which is to be maximized subject to $\sum_{t=0}^{\infty} c_t = w_0$. The optimality equation is $V(x) = \max_u \{\sqrt{u} + \delta V(x - u)\}$, and we are seeking a function $V(x)$ satisfying it. There is no final period, so we cannot work backward as in the finite horizon problem. A natural candidate to consider for $V(x)$ is the limit of the maximized utilities $V(0, x)$ for the finite horizon problem as N gets large. This limit is

$$V(x) = \sqrt{x \sum_{i=0}^{\infty} \delta^{2i}} = \sqrt{x/(1 - \delta^2)} \ .$$

To check this as the value function note that $\sqrt{u} + \delta\sqrt{(x - u)/(1 - \delta^2)}$ is maximized at $u = (1 - \delta^2)x$ with maximized value $\sqrt{x/(1 - \delta^2)}$. Thus the value function is $V(x) = \sqrt{x/(1 - \delta^2)}$, and the optimal control is $\varphi(x) = (1 - \delta^2)x$.

EXAMPLE: A monopolist owns a mine containing A tons of ore. In each time period $t = 0, 1, 2, \ldots$ the monopolist decides how many tons to extract and sell. Extraction has constant average cost of \$100 per ton and, in each time period, the market price is given by the inverse demand function $p = 102 - q$ where q is the number of tons sold. The present value of the profit stream corresponding to an extraction plan $q_0, q_1, q_2, \ldots$, with discount factor $\delta \in (0, 1)$ is $\sum_{t=0}^{\infty} \delta^t [(102 - q_t)q_t - 100q_t]$, and this must be maximized subject to $q_t \geq 0$ and $\Sigma_{t=0}^{\infty} q_t = A$. The optimality equation is $V(x) = \max_{q \geq 0} \{(2 - q)q + \delta V(x - q)\}$.

Despite having an infinite horizon, in the optimal solution to this problem, all the ore will be extracted in a finite number of periods. Part of the problem is to determine the date at which the last ore should be extracted. Rather than working backward from the (unknown) final period, we can work forward, asking when it would be profitable for the monopolist to leave ore in the ground today (and thus forgo current profit) and extract it k periods in the future. The marginal profit today is

$$\frac{d}{dq}[(2 - q)q] = 2 - 2q.$$

In the future, the ore can never be sold for a price (net of extraction cost) above \$2, so the discounted marginal profit from extracting k periods in the future is never more than $2\delta^k$. Thus it does not pay for the monopolist to retain any ore for extraction k periods in the future unless $2 - 2q < 2\delta^k$ or $q > 1 - \delta^k$ where q is current extraction. This analysis applies to any period as the current period and to any k. For any two periods s and t with positive extraction, the (appropriately discounted) marginal profits must be equal, or, for $t < s$, $2 - 2q_t = \delta^{s-t}(2 - 2q_s)$ or $q_t = 1 - \delta^{s-t}(1 - q_s)$. Combining these facts, the last ore is extracted in period s if the following conditions hold: (1) $0 < q_s \leq 1 - \delta$ (if $q_s > 1 - \delta$ it pays to reduce q_s and set $q_{s+1} > 0$); (2) for $0 \leq t < s$, $q_t = 1 - \delta^{s-t}(1 - q_s)$; and (3) total production of $\Sigma_{j=0}^{s} q_j = \Sigma_{j=0}^{s}(1 - \delta)^j(1 - q_s)) = s + 1 - (1 - q_s)(1 - \delta^{s+1})/(1 - \delta)$ is equal to the total ore available, A.

Thus the last extraction period is s such that $s + 1 - (1 - \delta^{s+1})/(1 - \delta) < A \leq s + 2 - (1 - \delta^{s+2})/(1 - \delta)$ and $q_t = 1 - \delta^{s-t}(s + 1 - A)(1 - \delta)/(1 - \delta^{s+1})$ for $t = 0, 1, \ldots, s$. The corresponding present value of profit is

$$V(A) = \sum_{t=0}^{s} (2 - q_t)q_t$$

$$= \sum_{t=0}^{s} \left[1 - \delta^{2(s-t)}(s + 1 - A)^2(1 - \delta)^2/(1 - \delta^{s+1})^2\right].$$

EXAMPLE: Consider another infinite horizon investment problem with interest rate $r > 0$, discount $\delta \in (0, 1)$, and per period felicity ("utility") ln c for consumption of c. We approach the infinite horizon problem by first solving a corresponding finite horizon problem.

Let $V(N, x) = \delta^N \ln x$ and

$$V(N - 1, x) = \max_{u} \{\delta^{N-1} \ln u + V(N, (x - u)(1 + r))\}.$$

Solving the optimization problem, $u^* = \varphi(N - 1, x) = x/(1 + \delta)$, and the optimized value is $V(N - 1, x) = (\delta^{N-1} + \delta^N)\ln(x/(1 + \delta)) + \delta^N \ln(\delta(1 + r))$.

Then

$$V(N - 2, x) = \max_u \left\{ \delta^{N-2} \ln u + V(N - 1, (x - u)(1 + r)) \right\}.$$

Solving the optimization problem, $u^* = \varphi(N - 2, x) = x/(1 + \delta + \delta^2)$, and the optimized value is

$$V(N - 2, x) = (\delta^{N-2} + \delta^{N-1} + \delta^N)\ln\big(x/(1 + \delta + \delta^2)\big)$$

$$+ (\delta^{N-1} + 2\delta^N)\ln(\delta(1 + r)).$$

If we guess that

$$V(N - j, x) = (\delta^{N-j} + \delta^{N-j+1} + \cdots + \delta^N)\ln\big(x/(1 + \delta + \cdots + \delta^j)\big)$$

$$+ (\delta^{N-j} + 2\delta^{N-j+1} + 3\delta^{N-j+2} + \cdots + j\delta^N)$$

$$\times \ln(\delta(1 + r)),$$

we can check by using this formula for $V(N - j + 1, x)$ and using the optimality equation (we already know the formula works for $j = 1, 2$).

$$V(N - j, x) = \max_u \big\{ \ln u + (\delta^{N-j+1} + \cdots + \delta^N)$$

$$\times \ln((x - u)(1 + r)/(1 + \delta + \cdots + \delta^{j-1}))$$

$$+ (\delta^{N-j+1} + \cdots + (j - 1)\delta^N)\ln(\delta(1 + r)) \big\}.$$

Solving the optimization problem, $u^* = x/(1 + \delta + \cdots + \delta^j)$ and the optimized value is

$$V(N - j, x) = (\delta^{N-j} + \cdots + \delta^N)\ln\big(x/(1 + \delta + \cdots + \delta^j)\big)$$

$$+ (\delta^{N-j} + \cdots + j\delta^N)\ln(\delta(1 + r)),$$

confirming our guess.

Thus the value for the finite horizon problem is

$$V(0, x) = (1 + \delta + \cdots + \delta^N)\ln\big(x/(1 + \delta + \cdots + \delta^N)\big)$$

$$+ (\delta + 2\delta^2 + \cdots + N\delta^N)\ln(\delta(1 + r))$$

with optimal control $\varphi(N - j, x) = x/(1 + \delta + \cdots + \delta^j)$. For a potential solution to the infinite horizon problem consider the limit of the finite horizon solution as $N \to \infty$. This suggests $V(x) = (1/(1 - \delta))\ln(x(1 - \delta)) + (\delta/(1 - \delta^2)\ln(\delta(1 + r))$ and $\varphi(x) = x(1 - \delta)$ as solutions to the infinite horizon problem. The infinite horizon optimality equation to check is whether

$$V(x) = \max_u \Big\{ \ln u + (\delta/(1 - \delta))\ln((x - u)(1 + r)(1 - \delta))$$

$$+ \big(\delta^2/(1 - \delta)^2 \ln(\delta(1 + r))\big) \Big\}.$$

Solving the optimization problem, $u^* = x(1 - \delta)$, and the optimized value is $V(x) = (1/(1 - \delta))\ln(x(1 - \delta)) + (\delta/(1 - \delta^2)\ln(\delta(1 + r))$, so our guess is correct. Starting with wealth w_0, the optimal infinite horizon path of consumption $c_0, c_1, c_2, \ldots$ has $c_t = (1 - \delta)\delta^t(1 + r)^t w_0$, which increases with t if $\delta > 1/(1 + r)$ and decreases with t if $\delta < 1/(1 + r)$.

11.4 STOCHASTIC DYNAMIC PROGRAMMING

The dynamic programming problem could include random variables. The return given state x and control u could be a random variable, or the transition function for updating states could be random. In this case the value function must be thought of as the maximized expected value, and the optimality equation must reflect the randomness appropriately.

EXAMPLE: At the beginning of each of N time periods, an individual must decide how much of her fortune to save and how much to consume. Borrowing is allowed (at interest rate 0) so consumption is unrestricted in periods $0, 1, \ldots, N - 1$. If her fortune is x and she consumes y in period t, her felicity ("utility") is $-e^{-y}$ and the amount saved is $x - y$. The interest rate on savings is zero, and she does not discount future periods. In the final period, N, she consumes her wealth $x_N \in \mathbb{R}$ and has felicity $-e^{-x_N}$. In addition to her initial wealth, at the end of each period (except period N), after the consumption decision is made, she receives a random nonnegative wage w_t. The wage in different periods is independent and identically distributed and has an exponential distribution with mean λ [i.e., the density is $f(w) = (1/\lambda)e^{-w/\lambda}$ for $w \geq 0$, and the cumulative distribution is $F(w) = 1 - e^{-w/\lambda}$ for $w \geq 0$]. If we let x_t represent the wealth in period t before consuming, then the updating rule is $x_{t+1} = x_t - y_t + w_t$. Let $V(j, x)$ represent the value at the start of period j with wealth x. Then $V(N, x) = -e^{-x}$ and the optimality equation yields

$$V(N - 1, x) = \max_y \left\{ -e^{-y} + \int_0^\infty V(N, x - y + w)f(w)\,dw \right\}$$

$$= \max_y \left\{ -e^{-y} - \int_0^\infty e^{-(x-y+w)}(1/\lambda)e^{-w/\lambda}\,dw \right\}$$

$$= \max_y \left\{ -e^{-y} - (1/(1 + \lambda))e^{-x+y} \right\}$$

Solving the optimization problem, $y^* = (x + \ln(1 + \lambda))/2$ with optimized value $V(N - 1, x) = -2e^{-(x+\ln(1+\lambda))/2}$.

Then

$$V(N - 2, x) = \max_y \left\{ -e^{-y} + \int_0^\infty V(N - 1, x - y + w)f(w)\,dw \right\}$$

$$= \max_y \left\{ -e^{-y} - \int_0^\infty 2e^{-(x-y+w+\ln(1+\lambda))/2}(1/\lambda)e^{-w/\lambda}\,dw \right\}$$

$$= \max_y \left\{ -e^{-y} - (4/(\lambda + 2))e^{-(x-y+\ln(1+\lambda))/2} \right\}$$

Solving the optimization problem,

$$y^* = (x + \ln(1 + \lambda) + 2\ln((1 + \lambda)/2))/3$$

with optimized value $V(N - 2, x) = -3e^{-(x+\ln(1+\lambda)+2\ln((2+\lambda)/2))/3}$.

By induction, we can show the form of the value function is

$$V(N - j, x) = -(j + 1)\exp\left[-\left(x + \sum_{i=1}^j i\ln((i + \lambda)/i)\right)\Big/(j + 1)\right]$$

with corresponding optimal control $\varphi(N - j, x) = (x + \sum_{i=1}^j i\ln((i + \lambda)/i))/(j + 1)$.

PROBLEMS

11.1 Solve the finite horizon investment example of Section 11.2 for the case $r > 0$. Find the value function $V(k, x)$, the optimal control $\varphi(k, x)$, and the optimal consumption stream, bequest, and maximized utility with initial wealth W_0.

11.2 Consider a dynamic programming problem with return in period k equal to $g(k, x, u) = \sqrt{u}$ where x is the state and $u \geq 0$ is the control. For the final period, N, the return is $h(x) = \sqrt{x}$. The state is updated by $x(t + 1) = x(t) - u(t)$. Find the value function $V(k, x)$ and the optimal control $\varphi(k, x)$.

11.3 (a) Consider the problem of choosing $(y_0, y_1, \ldots, y_N)$ to maximize $\sum_{t=0}^{N}(\alpha)^t \ln y_t$ subject to $\sum_{t=0}^{N} y_t = 100$. If this problem is set up in the dynamic programming framework (with x_t as the part of the 100 remaining at t) what is the optimality equation for $V(j, x)$?

(b) True/False. For $\alpha = 1$ and $N = 99$ in (a),

$$V(j, x) = (100 - j)\ln\left(\frac{x}{100 - j}\right)$$

is the value function.

11.4 A consumer must decide how to allocate her wealth, W, over consumption in N periods. If she has remaining wealth x_t at the start of period t and consumes wealth y_t in period t, her felicity ("utility") for that period is $y_t - e^{-y_t}$. Any wealth unused in period t is carried over to period $t + 1$. The time periods are short so the effective interest rate is zero and future periods are not discounted. With final period N, find the value function $V(N - j, x)$ and the optimal control $\varphi(N - j, x)$ for a general period $N - j$ with remaining wealth x.

11.5 A firm with initial capital level K_0 is interested in maximizing the present discounted value (with discount β) of its dividends over the period $t = 0, 1, 2, \ldots, T$. In each period t, $t = 0, 1, \ldots, T - 1$, the current capital level K_t produces net revenues $\sqrt{K_t} - K_t$ (after replenishing the capital stock to counterbalance depreciation), and the firm must decide how much of the revenues to pay out as dividends and how much to invest in increasing the capital stock. If the firm invests i_t, the current dividend is $\sqrt{K_t} - K_t - i_t$ and the capital stock in the next period is $K_{t+1} = K_t + i_t$. (Note that i_t need not be positive since $i_t < 0$ just means the capital stock is allowed to depreciate partially. The only constraint is $i_t \geq -K_t$.) In period T the capital stock is allowed to depreciate completely, there is no investment, and the dividend is $\sqrt{K_T}$.

(a) Find the value function $V(T - j, K)$ and the optimal (investment) control $\varphi(T - j, K)$ for a general period $T - j$ with capital K.

(b) With initial capital stock K_0 in period 0 find the optimal sequence of capital stocks $K_0, K_1, K_2, \ldots, K_T$ and investments $i_0, i_1, i_2, \ldots, i_{T-1}$.

11.6 A consumer must decide how to allocate her wealth over consumption in N periods. If she consumes c_t in period t, her felicity ("utility") for that period is $(c_t)^2$. Any wealth not consumed in period t is invested at interest rate $r > 0$ and carried over to period $t + 1$.

She is now allowed to borrow in any period. She discounts the future, with $\delta \in (0, 1)$. In final period, N, she consumes her remaining wealth. Find the value function $V(N - j, x)$ and the optimal control $\varphi(N - j, x)$ for a general period $N - j$ with remaining wealth x.

11.7 Solve the first infinite horizon investment problem of Section 11.3 for the case $0 < r < (1 - \delta^2)/\delta^2$. Find the value function $V(x)$, the optimal control $\varphi(x)$, and the optimal consumption stream and maximized utility with initial wealth W_0.

11.8 Suppose the firm in the ore extraction example of Section 11.3 had been competitive, facing a sequence of markets with (fixed) price P_t in period t, $t = 0, 1, 2 \ldots$. Given $\delta \in (0, 1)$, what must be true about the sequence of prices so that the firm is willing to extract a strictly positive amount in every period? (This result is known as Hotelling's rule.)

11.9 Solve a problem similar to the random wage problem of Section 11.4 in which the wage is nonrandom: $w_t = \lambda$ with probability one.

SAMPLE
SOLUTIONS

A.1 INTRODUCTION

This appendix contains sample solutions to almost all parts of all problems. Most solutions contain at least a sketch of the procedure followed to obtain the final answer. For many problems, the solution is very complete, laying out the procedure in detail. This is especially true for the initial problems in Chapters 6 and 8. The problems and detailed solutions can be used as additional examples to help the reader understand how to approach problems and why particular techniques work. Although the procedure is presented in detail, the explanations have often been abbreviated by the use of phrases rather than complete sentences and by the use of symbols such as $\exists$, $\nexists$, $\forall$, and s.t. to represent there exists, there does not exist, for all, and such that, respectively. The symbol $\Rightarrow$ is used not only to mean "implies" but also as a general indicator of the next step in the solution procedure. The terms FOC and SOC mean first-order conditions and second-order conditions, respectively.

A.2 SOLUTIONS FOR CHAPTER 1

1.1
$$\frac{d}{dx}\int_{-1}^{2x}e^{xt^2}\,dt = \left(\frac{d}{dx}(2x)\right)e^{x(2x)^2} + \int_{-1}^{2x}\left(\frac{d}{dx}(e^{xt^2})\right)dt$$

$$= 2e^{4x^3} + \int_{-1}^{2x}t^2e^{xt^2}\,dt.$$

At $x = 0$ this is

$$2e^0 + \int_{-1}^{0} t^2 e^0 \, dt = 2 + \int_{-1}^{0} t^2 \, dt = 2 + [t^3/3]_{-1}^{0} = 7/3.$$

1.2
$$\frac{d}{dx} \int_{3-x}^{4} \ln(t - x) \, dt = -\frac{d(3 - x)}{dx} \ln((3 - x) - x)$$

$$+ \int_{3-x}^{4} \frac{d \ln(t - x)}{dx} \, dt$$

$$= \ln(3 - 2x) + \int_{3-x}^{4} (-1/(t - x)) \, dt.$$

At $x = 1$ this is

$$\ln 1 + \int_{2}^{4} (-1/(t - 1)) \, dt = -\ln(t - 1)]_{2}^{4} = -\ln 3 + \ln 1 = -\ln 3.$$

1.3
$$\frac{d}{dx} \int_{2x}^{ex} \ln(xt) \, dt = \left(\frac{dex}{dx}\right) \ln(ex^2) - \left(\frac{d2x}{dx}\right) \ln(2x^2)$$

$$+ \int_{2x}^{ex} \left(\frac{d \ln(xt)}{dx}\right) dt$$

$$= e \ln(ex^2) - 2 \ln(2x^2) + \int_{2x}^{ex} \left(\frac{1}{x}\right) dt.$$

At $x = 1$ this is

$$e \ln e - 2 \ln 2 + \int_{2}^{e} dt = e - 2 \ln 2 + e - 2 = 2e - 2 - 2 \ln 2.$$

A.3 SOLUTIONS FOR CHAPTER 2

2.1 Writing system as $A\mathbf{x} = \mathbf{b}$, where

$$A = \begin{bmatrix} -3 & 3 & -1 \\ 3 & -4 & 1 \\ -1 & 1 & -1 \end{bmatrix}, \qquad \mathbf{x} = \begin{bmatrix} x_1 \\ x_2 \\ x_3 \end{bmatrix}, \qquad \mathbf{b} = \begin{bmatrix} 1 \\ 3 \\ 1 \end{bmatrix},$$

$|A| = -2 \neq 0 \Rightarrow$ there is a unique solution.

$$\mathbf{x} = A^{-1}\mathbf{b} = \begin{bmatrix} -3/2 & -1 & 1/2 \\ -1 & -1 & 0 \\ 1/2 & 0 & -3/2 \end{bmatrix} \begin{bmatrix} 1 \\ 3 \\ 1 \end{bmatrix} \quad \text{or} \quad \begin{bmatrix} x_1 \\ x_2 \\ x_3 \end{bmatrix} = \begin{bmatrix} -4 \\ -4 \\ -1 \end{bmatrix}$$

2.2

$$y = \frac{\begin{vmatrix} 1 & 2 & -1 \\ 3 & -2 & -3 \\ -1 & 2 & 2 \end{vmatrix}}{\begin{vmatrix} 1 & 0 & -1 \\ 3 & 2 & -3 \\ -1 & 4 & 2 \end{vmatrix}} = -\frac{8}{2} = -4.$$

2.3 (a) Denote $\mathbf{a} = (1, -3, 0, -5)$, $\mathbf{b} = (-2, 6, 0, 10)$, $\mathbf{c} = (1, 2, 1, -1)$, and $\mathbf{d} = (3, 1, 2, -7)$. Show $\mathbf{a} \cdot \mathbf{c} = 0 = \mathbf{b} \cdot \mathbf{c}$; this implies $\{\mathbf{a}, \mathbf{c}\}$ and $\{\mathbf{b}, \mathbf{c}\}$ are orthogonal.

  (b) Note that $\mathbf{b} = -2\mathbf{a}$. Also $\mathbf{a} + 2\mathbf{c} - \mathbf{d} = 0$. Hence, the set of vectors are not independent. One can also show the determinant is zero.

  (c) Using (b) to eliminate $\mathbf{b}$ and $\mathbf{d}$ from the set, we are left with $\{\mathbf{a}, \mathbf{c}\}$ as a basis.

  (d) $(1, 0, 0, 0)$ is not in the subspace spanned by $\mathbf{a}$, $\mathbf{b}$, $\mathbf{c}$, and $\mathbf{d}$. Otherwise, since $\{\mathbf{a}, \mathbf{c}\}$ is basis, the following must hold:

$$(1, 0, 0, 0) = \lambda_1(1, -3, 0, 5) + \lambda_2(1, 2, 1, -1).$$

  But no λ_1, λ_2 can satisfy this, which implies $(1, 0, 0, 0)$ cannot be expressed as linear combination of $\mathbf{a}$ and $\mathbf{c}$. Hence $(1, 0, 0, 0)$ must be outside subspace.

2.4 (a) Let $\mathbf{a} = (1/\sqrt{2}, 0, -1/\sqrt{2})$ and $\mathbf{b} = (0, 1, 0)$. Orthonormality requires $\mathbf{a} \cdot \mathbf{b} = 0$, $\mathbf{a} \cdot \mathbf{a} = 1$, and $\mathbf{b} \cdot \mathbf{b} = 1$. Since these hold, $\{\mathbf{a}, \mathbf{b}\}$ do form orthonormal set.

  (b) Check the determinant of matrix formed by the three vectors:

$$\begin{vmatrix} 1 & 1/\sqrt{2} & 0 \\ 2 & 0 & 1 \\ 3 & -1/\sqrt{2} & 0 \end{vmatrix} = \frac{4}{\sqrt{2}} \neq 0$$

  $\Rightarrow (1, 2, 3)$ is not in subspace spanned.

  (c) Let $\mathbf{x} = (x_1, x_2, x_3)$ be required vector. From orthonormality,

$$\mathbf{x} \cdot \mathbf{a} = 0 \Rightarrow (x_1, x_2, x_3) \cdot (1/\sqrt{2}, 0, -1/\sqrt{2}) = 0 \Rightarrow x_1 = x_3.$$

  Also,

$$\mathbf{x} \cdot \mathbf{b} = 0 \Rightarrow x_2 = 0.$$

  Furthermore,

$$\mathbf{x} \cdot \mathbf{x} = 1 \Rightarrow x_1^2 + x_2^2 + x_3^2 = 1$$

or

$$2x_1^2 = 1 \Rightarrow x_1 = \pm 1/\sqrt{2}.$$

So, the required vector is

$$\left(\frac{1}{\sqrt{2}}, 0, \frac{1}{\sqrt{2}}\right) \quad \text{or} \quad \left(-\frac{1}{\sqrt{2}}, 0 - \frac{1}{\sqrt{2}}\right),$$

and the basis is formed by

$$\left\{\left(\frac{1}{\sqrt{2}}, 0, -\frac{1}{\sqrt{2}}\right), (0, 1, 0), \left(\frac{1}{\sqrt{2}}, 0, \frac{1}{\sqrt{2}}\right)\right\}$$

or

$$\left\{\left(\frac{1}{\sqrt{2}}, 0, -\frac{1}{\sqrt{2}}\right), (0, 1, 0), \left(-\frac{1}{\sqrt{2}}, 0, -\frac{1}{\sqrt{2}}\right)\right\}.$$

(d) Let $\{(1/\sqrt{2}, 0, -1/\sqrt{2}), (0, 1, 0), (1/\sqrt{2}, 0, 1/\sqrt{2})\}$ be the basis. Then $(1, 1, 1)$ must be expressible as a linear combination of these vectors, or

$$\lambda_1\left(\frac{1}{\sqrt{2}}, 0, -\frac{1}{\sqrt{2}}\right) + \lambda_2(0, 1, 0) + \lambda_3\left(\frac{1}{\sqrt{2}}, 0, \frac{1}{\sqrt{2}}\right) = (1, 1, 1).$$

And thus:

$$\frac{\lambda_1}{\sqrt{2}} + \frac{\lambda_3}{\sqrt{2}} = 1 \Rightarrow \lambda_1 + \lambda_3 = \sqrt{2}, \tag{1}$$

$$\lambda_2 = 1, \tag{2}$$

$$-\frac{\lambda_1}{\sqrt{2}} + \frac{\lambda_3}{\sqrt{2}} = 1 \Rightarrow -\lambda_1 + \lambda_3 = \sqrt{2}. \tag{3}$$

From (1) and (3), $\lambda_3 = \sqrt{2} \Rightarrow$ from (1), $\lambda_1 = 0$. So,

$$\sqrt{2}\left(\frac{1}{\sqrt{2}}, 0, +\frac{1}{\sqrt{2}}\right) + 1(0, 1, 0) = (1, 1, 1)$$

is unique representation.

2.5 Check the determinant:

$$D = \begin{vmatrix} -1 & 2 & 0 & 1 \\ 3 & 6 & 1 & 0 \\ 0 & -2 & 3 & 4 \\ 1 & 4 & 0 & 3 \end{vmatrix} = -122 \neq 0$$

$\Rightarrow$ full row rank $\Rightarrow$ linearly independent set of vectors.

2.6 (a)

$$(3, -1)\begin{pmatrix} v_1 \\ v_2 \end{pmatrix} = 3 \quad \text{or} \quad 3v_1 - v_2 = 3.$$

So, the required set is $\{v \in \mathbb{R}^2: 3v_1 - v_2 = 3\}$

(b) Max$(3, -1)(v_1, v_2)$ s.t. $\|v\| = 1$.

Let $v = (v_1, v_2)$. Then $\|v\| = \sqrt{v_1^2 + v_2^2} = 1$. So the problem can be written as: Max $3v_1 - v_2$ s.t. $\sqrt{v_1^2 + v_2^2} = 1$. Solve, to get $v_1 = 3/\sqrt{10}$, $v_2 = -1/\sqrt{10}$. So $v = (3/\sqrt{10}, -1/\sqrt{10})$ maximizes $(3, -1) \cdot v$ subject to $\|v\| = 1$.

(c) $H_{(-1,2)}(0) = \{x \in \mathbb{R}^2: x(-1, 2) = 0\} \Rightarrow -x_1 + 2x_2 = 0.$

This is the equation of a straight line with slope $1/2$ through the origin and perpendicular to $(-1, 2)$.

$$H_{(-1,2)}(1) = \{x \in \mathbb{R}^2: x \cdot (-1, 2) = 1\} \Rightarrow -x_1 + 2x_2 = 1.$$

This is the equation of a straight line with intercept $1/2$ and parallel to $H_{(-1/2)}(0)$.

(d) The subspace spanned by $\{(-1, -2)\}$ is the line containing $(0, 0)$ and $(-1, -2)$. The subspace $\{v \in \mathbb{R}^2 | (-1, -2) \cdot v = 0\}$ is the line through $(0, 0)$, perpendicular to the first subspace.

2.7 (a)

$$A = \begin{bmatrix} 1 & 2 \\ 2 & 1 \end{bmatrix}, \quad A_1 = 1 > 0, \quad A_2 = \begin{vmatrix} 1 & 2 \\ 2 & 1 \end{vmatrix} = -3 < 0,$$

so neither positive (semi) definite nor negative (semi) definite.

(b)

$$A = \begin{bmatrix} -1 & 1 \\ 1 & -1 \end{bmatrix}, \quad A_1 = -1 < 0, \quad A_2 = 0 \Rightarrow \text{NSD.}$$

(c)
$$A = \begin{bmatrix} 1 & 0 & -1 \\ 0 & 3 & 0 \\ -1 & 0 & 4 \end{bmatrix}, \quad A_1 = 1 > 0, \quad A_2 = 3 > 0,$$

$$A_3 = 9 > 0 \Rightarrow A \text{ is PD.}$$

(d)
$$A = \begin{bmatrix} 1 & 7 & 0 \\ 7 & 4 & -1 \\ 0 & -1 & 1 \end{bmatrix}, \qquad A_1 = 1 > 0, \; A_2 < 0 \Rightarrow \text{indefinite}$$

(e) $A_1 = 1 > 0, \; A_2 = -4 < 0 \Rightarrow$ indefinite

2.8 (a) Can show rank = 3.

(b) A basis is
$$\left\{ \begin{pmatrix} 1 \\ 3 \\ 5 \\ -2 \end{pmatrix} \begin{pmatrix} 3 \\ -2 \\ -7 \\ 5 \end{pmatrix} \begin{pmatrix} 3 \\ 4 \\ 5 \\ 1 \end{pmatrix} \right\}.$$

2.9 (a) (i)
$$\text{Rank} \begin{bmatrix} 3 & -9 & 2 \\ 1 & -3 & 1 \end{bmatrix} = 2 > \text{Rank} \begin{bmatrix} 3 & -9 \\ 1 & -3 \end{bmatrix} = 1$$

$\Rightarrow$ no solution.

(ii) det $A = 0$, where
$$A = \begin{bmatrix} 3 & -9 \\ 1 & -3 \end{bmatrix}.$$

(iii) An inverse does not exist.

(iv) No solution.

(b)
$$\overset{A}{\begin{bmatrix} 3 & -1 \\ -9 & 3 \end{bmatrix}} \overset{\mathbf{x}}{\begin{bmatrix} x \\ y \end{bmatrix}} = \overset{\mathbf{b}}{\begin{bmatrix} 2 \\ -6 \end{bmatrix}}$$

(i)
$$\text{Rank} \begin{pmatrix} 3 & -1 & 2 \\ -9 & 3 & -6 \end{pmatrix} = 1 = \text{Rank} \begin{pmatrix} 3 & -1 \\ -9 & 3 \end{pmatrix} < 2 = r.$$

Therefore there exists an infinite number of solutions: $3x - y = 2$.

(ii) det $A = 9 - 9 = 0$.

(iii) No inverse since the determinant is zero.

(iv) No unique solution.

(c)

$$\overset{A}{\begin{bmatrix} 3 & 3 \\ -1 & -9 \end{bmatrix}} \overset{\mathbf{x}}{\begin{bmatrix} x \\ y \end{bmatrix}} = \overset{\mathbf{b}}{\begin{bmatrix} 1 \\ -1 \end{bmatrix}}.$$

(i)

$$\text{Rank} \begin{bmatrix} 3 & 3 & 1 \\ -1 & -9 & -1 \end{bmatrix} = 2 = \text{Rank } A = n.$$

Therefore a unique solution exists.

(ii) det $A = -24 = |A|$.

(iii)

$$A^{-1} = \frac{1}{|A|} \text{ adj. } A = \frac{-1}{24} \begin{bmatrix} -9 & -3 \\ -1 & 3 \end{bmatrix} = \begin{bmatrix} 3/8 & 1/8 \\ 1/24 & -1/8 \end{bmatrix}.$$

(iv)

$$\begin{pmatrix} x \\ y \end{pmatrix} = A^{-1} \begin{pmatrix} 1 \\ -1 \end{pmatrix} = -\frac{1}{24} \begin{bmatrix} -9 & -3 \\ -1 & 3 \end{bmatrix} \begin{bmatrix} 1 \\ -1 \end{bmatrix} = \begin{bmatrix} 1/4 \\ 1/12 \end{bmatrix}.$$

(d)

$$\overset{A}{\begin{bmatrix} 1 & 0 & -1 \\ 3 & 2 & -3 \\ -1 & 4 & 1 \end{bmatrix}} \overset{\mathbf{x}}{\begin{bmatrix} x \\ y \\ z \end{bmatrix}} = \overset{\mathbf{b}}{\begin{bmatrix} 0 \\ -1 \\ -2 \end{bmatrix}}.$$

(i) Rank$(A) = 2 = \text{Rank}(A, \mathbf{b}) < 3 = n$. Hence, there exists an infinite number of solutions: $x = z$ and $y = -\frac{1}{2}$.

(ii) det $A = 0$.

(iii) No inverse exists.

(iv) No unique solution.

A.4   SOLUTIONS FOR CHAPTER 3

3.1 (a) $A = [-10, 1]$.

(i) Closed: any convergent sequence in A converges to a point in A.

(ii) Not open: $\mathbb{R} \setminus A$ is not closed.

(iii) Compact: A is closed and bounded (a ball with radius, say 11, contains A).

      (iv) Convex: $\forall \ x, x' \in [-10, 1]$, $\lambda x + (1 - \lambda)x' \in [-10, 1]$ for all $\lambda \in [0, 1]$.

(b) $A = (-\infty, 0]$

      (i) Closed: every contingent sequence in A converges to a point in A.

     (ii) Not open: complement $\mathbb{R} \setminus A$ is not closed.

    (iii) Not compact: A is closed but not bounded.

    (iv) Convex: $\lambda x + (1 - \lambda)x' \in A \ \forall \ x, x' \in A$ and $\lambda \in [0, 1]$.

(c) $A = (-\infty, 0)$

      (i) Not closed: we can find a limit point not belonging to A. Consider the sequence $x_n = -1/n$, $n = 1, 2, \ldots$. Then $\lim_{n \to \infty} x_n = 0 \notin A \Rightarrow A$ not closed.

     (ii) Open: $\mathbb{R} \setminus A = [0, \infty)$ is closed.

    (iii) Not compact because not bounded.

    (iv) Convex: as above.

(d) $A = [-10, 0)$

      (i) Not closed: Let $\{x_n\} = -1/n$, $n = 1, 2, \ldots$. Then $x_n \in A \ \forall$ n and $\lim_{n \to \infty} x_n = 0$, but $0 \notin A$.

     (ii) Not open: $\nexists$ open ball around -10 that is contained in A.

    (iii) Not compact because not closed.

    (iv) Convex: all convex combinations belong to A.

(e) $A = \{\mathbf{x} \in \mathbb{R}^2 : x_i \geq 0, i = 1, 2 \text{ and } x_1^2 + x_2^2 \geq 1\}$.

      (i) Closed: $\forall \ \{x_i\}$ converging to $\bar{x}, \bar{x} \in A$. (A contains its boundary.)

     (ii) Not open: For any point on $x_1^2 + x_2^2 = 1$, $\nexists$ open ball which is entirely contained in A.

    (iii) Not compact: not bounded.

    (iv) Not convex: Let $\mathbf{x} = (1, 0)$ and $\mathbf{x}' = (0, 1)$. For $\lambda = \frac{1}{2}$,

$$\lambda \mathbf{x} + (1 - \lambda)\mathbf{x}' = \left(\tfrac{1}{2}, \tfrac{1}{2}\right) \notin A.$$

(f) $A = \{\mathbf{x} \in \mathbb{R}^2 : x_i \geq 0, i = 1, 2 \text{ and } x_1^2 + x_2^2 < 1\}$.

      (i) Not closed: Take sequence $\{x_n\} = \{1/n, 1 - 1/n\}$, $n = 1, 2, \ldots$ Then

$$\lim_{n \to \infty} x_n = (0, 1) = \bar{\mathbf{x}} \quad \text{but} \quad \bar{x}_1^2 + \bar{x}_2^2 = 0^2 + 1^2 = 1 \Rightarrow \bar{x} \notin A.$$

     (ii) Not open: $\nexists$ open ball around say, $(0, 0)$ entirely contained in A.

    (iii) Not compact: not closed.

    (iv) Convex.

(g) $A = \{\mathbf{x} \in \mathbb{R}^2 : -10 \leq x_1 \leq 1\}$.

      (i) Closed: All convergent sequences in A converge to points in A.

     (ii) Not open: $\nexists$ open balls around points along $x_1 = 1$ or $x_1 = -10$ that are entirely contained in A.

(iii) Not compact: A is not bounded.

(iv) Convex.

(h) $A = \{\mathbf{x} \in \mathbb{R}^2: x_i \geq 1, \ i = 1, 2 \text{ and } x_1 x_2 \leq 2\}$.

   (i) Closed: A contains its own boundary.

   (ii) Not open: $\not\exists$ open ball around $(1, 1)$ that lies entirely in A.

   (iii) Compact: closed and bounded.

   (iv) Not convex: convex combination of $(1, 2)$ and $(2, 1)$ for $\lambda = \frac{1}{2}$ is $(3/2, 3/2) \notin A$.

3.2 $A = \{\mathbf{x} \in \mathbb{R}^2: 0 \leq x_1 \leq 1 \text{ and } 2 \leq x_2 \leq 3\}$,

   $B = \{\mathbf{x} \in \mathbb{R}^2: 0 \leq x_1 \leq 1 \text{ and } x_2 = x_1\}$.

   (a) $A + B = \{\mathbf{x} \in \mathbb{R}^2: 0 \leq x_1 \leq 2, \ 2 \leq x_2 \leq 4, \ 1 \leq x_2 - x_1 \leq 3\}$.

   (b) Any straight line $x_2 = a$, $1 < a < 2$, can separate A and B.

3.3 For any c with $1 < c < 2$, any vertical line through $(c, 0)$, or any horizontal line through $(0, c)$, or any line $x + y = 2c$ will work.

3.4 (a) $A = \{(x, y) \in \mathbb{R}^2: x^2 + y^2 = 1\}$.

   (i) Closed: contains its boundary.

   (ii) Not open: $\mathbb{R}^2 / A$ is not closed.

   (iii) Compact: closed and bounded.

   (iv) Not convex: e.g., $\frac{1}{2}(1, 0) + \frac{1}{2}(0, 1) = (\frac{1}{2}, \frac{1}{2}) \notin A$.

(b) $A = \{(x, y) \in \mathbb{R}^2: x \geq 0, \ y \geq 0 \text{ and } xy \geq 1\}$.

   (i) Closed: all convergent sequences converge to points in A.

   (ii) Not open: $\not\exists$ open ball around, say, $(1, 1)$ that is entirely contained in A.

   (iii) Not compact: not bounded.

   (iv) Convex.

(c) $A = \{(x, y) \in \mathbb{R}^2: -1 < x < 1 \text{ and } y = x\}$.

   (i) Not closed: Consider $\{x_n, y_n\} = \{1 - 1/n, 1 - 1/n\}$,

$$n = 1, 2, \ldots \ \lim_{n \to \infty} \left\{1 - \frac{1}{n}, 1 - \frac{1}{n}\right\} = (1, 1) \notin A.$$

   (ii) Not open: Cannot find open ball around $(0, 0) \in A$ that is contained entirely in A.

   (iii) Not compact: not closed.

   (iv) Convex.

3.5 False. A counterexample is sufficient to demonstrate this. The key lies in the fact that if a set is not closed then it is not compact. Define $S = \{(x, y) \in \mathbb{R}_+^2: x + y = 1, \ x \neq 1\}$. Note that due to the hole at $(x, y) = (1, 0)$, S is not compact. Yet the function $x^2 + y^2$ attains a unique global maximum at $(0, 1) \in S$.

3.6 Here

$$X = \{(x, y) \in \mathbb{R}^2: x^2 + y^2 < 1\},$$

$$A = \{(x, y) | 0 \leq x < 1 \quad \text{and} \quad y = 0\}.$$

A is not open because no open ball around, say, $(\frac{1}{2}, 0)$ can ever be contained in A. However, A is closed relative to X because for any convergent sequence in A converging to a point $\bar{x}$ in X, $\bar{x} \in A$. Observe that the definition of X rules out the point $(1, 0)$ where A has a "hole" if $\mathbb{R}^2$ is considered rather than X.

3.7 $A = \{(x, y)|0 < x \le 10 \text{ and } 0 \le y \le \ln x\}$.

Noting that $\ln x$ is an increasing, strictly concave function with $\ln 1 = 0$, the set A is clearly compact, convex, and closed. It is closed because it contains its boundary, convex because all convex combinations also belong to it, and compact because it is also bounded.

3.8 $S = \{(x, y) \in \mathbb{R}^2: xy < 1\}$.

  (i) S is open because $S^c = \{(x, y) \in \mathbb{R}^2: xy \ge 1\}$ is closed.

  (ii) Not closed. Consider convergent sequence $(x_n, y_n) = (1 - 1/2n, 1 - 1/2n)$, $n = 1, 2, \ldots$. Then, $x_n \cdot x_y < 1 \; \forall \, n = 1, 2, \ldots$ and $(x_n, y_n) \to (1, 1)$. But $(1, 1) \notin S \Rightarrow$ not closed.

  (iii) Not compact because not closed.

  (iv) Not convex. For example, $(4, 0)$ and $(0, 4) \in S$, but $\frac{1}{2}(4, 0) + \frac{1}{2}(0, 4) = (2, 2) \notin S$.

3.9 $S = \{x \in \mathbb{R}: x^2 \ge 1\} = (-\infty, -1] \cup [1, \infty)$.

  (i) No ball around 1 is contained in S so S is not open.

  (ii) S is closed because all convergent sequences in S have limit points in S.

  (iii) Not compact because not bounded.

  (iv) Not convex; e.g., $\frac{1}{2}(-1) + \frac{1}{2}(1) = 0 \notin S$.

3.10 (a) Open: yes. If $x^2 > 1$ then $(x \pm \varepsilon)^2 > 1$ for small ε.

        Closed: no. $1 + 1/n$ is in the set for all n but $1 + 1/n \to 1$, which is not in the set.

        Compact: no. Not closed, not bounded $(2, 3, 4, \ldots$ in set).

        Convex: no. 2 and -2 are in the set but $0 = \frac{1}{2}(2) + \frac{1}{2}(-2)$ is not.

   (b) Open: no. $(1, 1)$ is in the set but any ball around it contains points with $x < 1$ so not in set.

        Closed: yes. It is the intersection of closed sets

$$\{(x, y \in \mathbb{R}^2 | x \ge 1\}, \quad \{(x, y) \in \mathbb{R}^2 | y \ge 1\},$$

$$\text{and} \quad \{(x, y) \in \mathbb{R}^2 | xy \le 9\}.$$

        Compact: yes. Closed and bounded (the set is contained in a ball of radius 20 around the origin).

        Convex: no. $(1, 9)$ and $(9, 1)$ are in the set but $\frac{1}{2}(1, 9) + \frac{1}{2}(9, 1) = (5, 5)$ is not.

3.11 (a) Not open: $(1/\sqrt{2}, -1\sqrt{2})$ is in the set but no ball around it is contained in the set.

   (b) Not closed: $(1/n, -1/n)$ is in the set for all $n > 1$ but $\lim_{n \to \infty}(1/n, -1/n) = (0, 0)$ is not in the set.

(c) Not compact: bounded but not closed.

(d) Not convex: $(1/\sqrt{2}, -1/\sqrt{2})$ and $(-1/\sqrt{2}, 1/\sqrt{2})$ are both in the set but $(0,0) = \frac{1}{2}(1/\sqrt{2}, -1/\sqrt{2}) + \frac{1}{2}(-1/\sqrt{2}, 1/\sqrt{2})$ is not.

3.12 Not open: $(4,0)$ is in the set, but every open ball around it contains points of the form $(4 + 2\varepsilon, -\varepsilon)$, which do not satisfy $y \geq 0$ or $x + y \leq 4$.

Closed: If $(x_n, y_n) \to (x^0, y^0)$ and (x_n, y_n) is in the set for all n then

(i) $x_n \geq 0$ for all n and $x_n \to x^0$, so $x^0 \geq 0$

(ii) $y_n \geq 0$ for all n and $y_n \to y^0$, so $y^0 \geq 0$

(iii) $x_n^2 + y_n^2 \geq 1$ for all n and $x_n^2 + y_n^2 \to (x^0)^2 + (y^0)^2$, so $(x^0)^2 + (y^0)^2 \geq 1$

(iv) $x_n + y_n \leq 4$ for all n and $x_n + y_n \to x^0 + y^0$, so $x^0 + y^0 \leq 4$.

Thus (x^0, y^0) is in the set.

Compact: The set is contained in the ball $\{(x, y) | x^2 + y^2 \leq 25\}$ so it is bounded. Closed by previous part.

Not convex: $(1,0)$ and $(0,1)$ are in the set, but $(1/2)(1,0) + (1/2)(0,1) = (1/2, 1/2)$ which is not in the set $[(1/2)^2 + (1/2)^2 = 1/2 < 1]$.

3.13 Not open: $(1,1)$ is in the set, but every ball around $(1,1)$ contains points of the form $(1, 1 - \varepsilon)$, which are not in the set.

Closed: If (x_n, y_n) is in the set for all n and $(x_n, y_n) \to (x^0, y^0)$, then $y_n \geq x_n$ for all n, so $y^0 \geq x^0$ and $x_n y_n \geq 1$ for all n, so $x^0 y^0 \geq 1$. Thus (x^0, y^0) is in the set.

Not compact: The set is not bounded since (n, n) is in the set for $n = 1, 2, 3, \ldots$.

Not convex: $(1,1)$ and $(-1,-1)$ are in the set, but $(1/2)(1,1) + (1/2)(-1, -1) = (0,0)$ is not.

A.5 SOLUTIONS FOR CHAPTER 4

4.1 $\varphi(0) = \{0\}$. For any open V with $\varphi(0) \subset V$, there is an $\varepsilon > 0$ such that $(-\varepsilon, \varepsilon) \subset V$. For $x \in (-\sqrt{\varepsilon}, \sqrt{\varepsilon})$, $\varphi(x) \subset (-\varepsilon, \varepsilon) \subset V$ so φ is uhc at 0. For any open V with $\varphi(0) \cap V \neq \varnothing$, $0 \in V$. But $0 \in \varphi(x)$ for all x, so φ lhc at 0.

$\varphi(1) = (-1, 1)$. For any open V with $\varphi(1) \subset V$, for all x, $\varphi(x) \subset (-1, 1) \subset V$ so φ is uhc at 1. For any open V with $\varphi(1) \cap V \neq \varnothing$, let $z \in \varphi(1) \cap V$. Let z^* be the absolute value of z. Then $\sqrt{z^*} < 1$ and for all $x > \sqrt{z^*}$, $z \in \varphi(x) \cap V$. Thus φ is lhc at 1.

4.2 (a) $\{0\} \cup \{x | 1/2 < x \leq 1\}$.

(i) At $0 < x < 1/2$, $V = (x, 1)$ contains $\varphi(x)$ but does not contain $\varphi(x')$ for any $x' < x$. Thus not uhc.

(ii) At $x = 0$, if V contains $\varphi(0)$, then it contains $(0, 1/2 + \varepsilon)$ for some $\varepsilon > 0$. Thus $\varphi(x') \subset V$ for all x' near 0, and uhc at 0.

(iii) At $x = 1/2$, $V = (1/4, 3/4)$ contains $\varphi(1/2)$ but does not contain $\varphi(x')$ for any $x' < 1/2$, so not uhc.

(iv) At $1/2 < x \leq 1$ uhc since "continuous function."

(b) $\{x \mid 0 \leq x \leq 1\}$.

(i) At $0 \leq x < 1/2$, if $V \cap \varphi(x) \neq \emptyset$ then $V \cap \varphi(x') \neq \emptyset$ for x' near x, so lhc.

(ii) At $x = 1/2$ if $V \cap \varphi(x) \neq \emptyset$, then V contains $(1/2 - \varepsilon, 1/2 + \varepsilon)$ for some $\varepsilon > 0$ and $V \cap \varphi(x') \neq \emptyset$ for all x' near $1/2$, so lhc.

(iii) At $1/2 < x \leq 1$ lhc since "continuous function."

4.3 (a) $\varphi(x) = (x, 2]$.

(i) Not uhc: Let $V = (1, 2]$. Note V is open relative to $[0, 2]$. Then $\varphi(1) = (1, 2] \subset V$. But for any $\varepsilon > 0$,

$$\varphi(1 - \varepsilon) = (1 - \varepsilon, 2] \not\subset (1, 2] = V.$$

So for all $x < 1$, $\varphi(x)$ is not contained in $V \Rightarrow$ not uhc at $x = 1$.

(ii) lhc: For any $x \in [0, 1]$, for any open set V with $V \cap \varphi(x) \neq \emptyset$, V must contain some point $y > x$. Let $\varepsilon = (y - x)/2$, and $N = (x - \varepsilon, x + \varepsilon) \cap [0, 2]$. For any $x' \in N$, $y \in \varphi(x')$.

(iii) Convex valued: Image set $(x, 2]$ is convex for all x.

(iv) Not compact valued: Image set $(x, 2]$ is not closed.

(b) $\varphi(x) = \{2 - 2x, 2x\}$.

(i) uhc: For any open V containing $\varphi(x)$, for t near x $\varphi(t) \subset V$ since φ is made up of two continuous strands, $2x$ and $2 - 2x$.

(ii) lhc: For any open set V having a nonempty intersection with $\varphi(x)$, the appropriate strand ($2t$ or $2 - 2t$) will stay in V for small changes in t.

(iii) Not convex valued: $\varphi(0) = \{2, 0\}$, which is not a convex set.

(iv) Compact valued: $\varphi(x)$ is closed and bounded for all x.

(c) $\varphi(x) = \{2 - 2x, 3x\}$ for $x \leq 2/3$ and $\varphi(x) = \{2 - 2x\}$ for $x > 2/3$.

(i) uhc: Similar to part (b).

(ii) Not lhc: $2 \in \varphi(\frac{2}{3})$. Taking small arbitrary open set $(2 - \varepsilon, 2 + \varepsilon) = V$, notice that for any neighborhood N, however small, $\varphi(x) = \{2 - 2x\}$ for all $x > \frac{2}{3}$. Clearly then $\varphi(x) \cap V = \emptyset$.

(iii) Not convex valued: $\varphi(0) = \{2, 0\}$, which is not a convex set.

(iv) Compact valued: $\varphi(x)$ is closed and bounded for all x.

(d) (i) uhc: For $0 < p \leq 1$, $\varphi(p)$ is a usual budget set [with prices p and $1 - p$ and income p so the bundle $(1, 0)$ is always just affordable]. The budget set varies smoothly with p. For any open set V, the complement of V is closed and the distance from $\varphi(p)$ to the complement of V (i.e., the minimum distance between two points, one from each set) is a continuous function of p. If V contains $\varphi(p)$, then the distance is strictly positive and stays strictly positive for small changes in p. For $p = 0$, $\varphi(0) = \{(x, 0)|x \geq 0\}$. If V contains $\varphi(0)$, then the idea above can be applied using $\varphi^*(0) = \{(x, 0)|1 \geq x \geq 0\}$ instead of $\varphi(0)$.

(ii) Not lhc: $(2, 0) \in \varphi(0)$. Let V be a ball around $(2, 0)$ with radius 0.1. For $p > 0$, get $px + (1 - p)y \leq p$ or

$$x \leq 1 - ((1 - p)/p)y \leq 1 \quad \text{for all } y \geq 0 \Rightarrow \varphi(p) \cap V = \varnothing.$$

(iii) Convex valued.

(iv) Not compact valued: $\varphi(0)$ is unbounded.

4.4 (a) (i) Not uhc: Let $V = (1, 2) = \varphi(1)$. For $x < 1$, $\varphi(x) \not\subset V$.

(ii) lhc: If V has a nonempty intersection with $\varphi(x)$, let z be in the intersection. Then $z - 1 < x < z < x + 1$ and $z \in \varphi(t)$ for all $t \in (z - 1, z) \cap [0, 2]$.

(b) Graph is rectangular hyperbola with shifted origin $(1, 0)$.

(i) Not uhc: At $x = 1$, $\varphi(x) = 0$. Choose $V = (-\varepsilon, \varepsilon) \supset \varphi(1)$. But $\varphi(x) \not\subset V$ for x near 1 but $x \neq 1$.

(ii) Not lhc: Using the same V, $\varphi(1) = 0 \in V$, but $\varphi(x) \cap V = \varnothing$ for x near 1 but $x \neq 1$.

(c) (i) uhc: $\varphi(x) = \{0\}$ for $x > 0$ and $\varphi(0) = [0, 2]$. If V contains $\varphi(0)$, then it contains $\varphi(x)$ for all x. If $x > 0$ and V contains $\varphi(x)$, then V contains $\varphi(z)$ for all $z \lessdot 0$.

(ii) Not lhc: Let $V = (1, 2)$. Then $V \cap \varphi(0) \neq \varnothing$. But $V \cap \varphi(x) = \varnothing$ for all $x \in (0, 1]$.

4.5 (a) $\varphi: [0, 1] \mapsto [0, 1]$ defined by

$$\varphi(x) = \begin{cases} & 0 \leq y \leq 1, & x = 0, \\ y: & 0 \leq y \leq x, & 0 < x \leq \dfrac{1}{2}, \\ & 0 \leq y < 1 - x \text{ or } y = x, & \dfrac{1}{2} < x \leq 1. \end{cases}$$

(b) $\varphi(x)$ is uhc for all $x \in [0, \frac{1}{2}]$. For $x \geq \frac{1}{2}$ note that $\varphi(x) = \{x\} \cup [0, 1 - x]$. Let $V = A \cup (0, 1 - x)$, where A is an open ball containing x but not $1 - x$. Then $V \supset \varphi(x)$. For $\frac{1}{2} < z < x$, $1 - x$ is in $\varphi(z)$ but not in V, so not uhc for $x > \frac{1}{2}$.

(c) lhc for all $x \in (0, 1]$. At $x = 0$, $\frac{3}{4} \in V = (\frac{1}{2}, 1)$ but $\varphi(x) \cap V = \varnothing$ for $0 < x < \frac{1}{2}$.

A.6 SOLUTIONS FOR CHAPTER 5

5.1 $Y = f(K, L) = 1 + (KL - 1)^{1/3}$.
(a) The equation of tangent plane to production surface at (K^0, L^0) is

$$Y = f(K^0, L^0) + \nabla f(K^0, L^0) \cdot (K - K^0, L - L^0)$$
$$= 2 + \tfrac{2}{3}(K - 1) + \tfrac{1}{3}(L - 2) \quad \text{at } (K^0, L^0) = (1, 2),$$

or $Y = \tfrac{2}{3}K + \tfrac{1}{3}L + \tfrac{2}{3}$ is required equation.
(b) Equation of tangent plane to level curve at $(1, 9)$ given by

$$0 = (K - 1, L - 9)\nabla f(1, 9) = \tfrac{3}{4}(K - 1) + \tfrac{1}{12}(L - 9)$$

or $9(K - 1) + L - 9 = 0$ or $9K + L - 18 = 0$ is equation.
(c) Equation of tangent plane to level curve at $(K, L) = (2, 1)$ is

$$0 = (\Delta K, \Delta L) \cdot (f_K(2, 1), f_L(2, 1)) = (\Delta K, \Delta L) \cdot (\tfrac{1}{3}, \tfrac{2}{3})$$

$$\Rightarrow \text{MRS} = \frac{\Delta K}{\Delta L} = -2.$$

(d) Equation of tangent plane to production surface at $(2, 1)$ is

$$y = f(2, 1) + (\Delta K, \Delta L) \cdot (\tfrac{1}{3}, \tfrac{2}{3})$$
$$\text{or} \quad y - f(2, 1) = (\Delta K, \Delta L) \cdot (\tfrac{1}{3}, \tfrac{2}{3})$$

$\Rightarrow$ Increase in output is maximized when scalar product of $(\Delta K, \Delta L)$ and $\nabla f(2, 1)$ is maximized

$$\Rightarrow (\Delta K, \Delta L) = \frac{\varepsilon}{\|\tfrac{1}{3}, \tfrac{2}{3}\|}(\tfrac{1}{3}, \tfrac{2}{3}) = \left(\frac{\varepsilon}{\sqrt{5}}, \frac{2\varepsilon}{\sqrt{5}}\right) \Rightarrow \frac{\Delta L}{\Delta K} = 2.$$

Note that direction of fastest increase is always along gradient vector.
5.2 $z = ye^x + t^2$, $x = \ln(y + t)$, and $y = t^3 - 9$.

$$dz = \frac{\partial z}{\partial x}\, dx + \frac{\partial z}{\partial y}\, dy + \frac{\partial z}{\partial t}\, dt.$$

$$dx = \frac{1}{y + t}(dy + dt)$$

$$dy = 3t^2\, dt$$

$$\Rightarrow dx = \frac{1}{y + t}(3t^2 + 1)\, dt.$$

So,

$$dz = \frac{ye^x}{y+t}(dy + dt) + e^x 3t^2\, dt + 2t\, dt$$

or

$$\frac{dz}{dt} = \frac{ye^x}{y+t}(3t^2 + 1) + e^x 3t^2 + 2t.$$

When $t = 2$, $y = -1$, $x = 0$, so

$$\frac{dz}{dt} = \frac{(-1)}{2-1}(12 + 1) + 12 + 4 \quad \text{or} \quad \left.\frac{dz}{dt}\right|_{t=2} = 3.$$

5.3 Given $y = f(K, L) = K^{1/4} \cdot L^{1/2}$.

(a) Equation of tangent plane to production surface at $(K, L) = (16, 9)$ is given by $y = f(16, 9) + (K - 16, L - 9) \cdot \nabla f(16, 9)$. Get

$$y = 6 + \tfrac{3}{32}(K - 16) + \tfrac{1}{3}(L - 9) \quad \text{or} \quad y = \tfrac{3}{32}K + \tfrac{1}{3}L + \tfrac{3}{2}.$$

(b) Equation of tangent plane to level curve at $(1, 4)$ given by $0 = (K - 1, L - 4) \cdot \nabla f(1, 4)$. Since $f_K(1, 4) = \tfrac{1}{2}$ and $f_L(1, 4) = \tfrac{1}{4}$, get

$$(K - 1)\tfrac{1}{2} + (L - 4)\tfrac{1}{4} = 0 \quad \text{or} \quad 2K + L - 6 = 0.$$

(c) Tangent plane to isoquant at $(1, 9)$ is $0 = (\Delta K, \Delta L) \cdot (3/4, 1/6) \Rightarrow \text{MRS} = \Delta L/\Delta K = -9/2$.

5.4 (a) Setting $Y = 1$ get level curve $K^\alpha L^\beta = 1$.

(b) Equation of tangent plane to production surface at $K = L = Y = 1$ given by

$$Y = 1 + (K - 1)\frac{\partial f}{\partial K}(1, 1) + (L - 1)\frac{\partial f}{\partial L}(1, 1)$$

$$= 1 + \alpha(K - 1) + \beta(L - 1) \quad \text{as} \quad \nabla f(1, 1) = \begin{bmatrix} \alpha \\ \beta \end{bmatrix}$$

$$= \alpha K + \beta L - (\alpha + \beta) + 1.$$

(c) Required equation given by

$$0 = \alpha(K - 1) + \beta(L - 1) \quad \text{or} \quad \alpha K + \beta L = \alpha + \beta.$$

(d) Use $0 = (\Delta K, \Delta L) \cdot (\alpha, \beta) \Rightarrow \alpha \Delta K + \beta \Delta L = 0 \Rightarrow \Delta L/\Delta K = -\alpha/\beta = \text{MRS}$.

(e) We know that for small changes near $K = L = Y = 1$, $Y = 1 + (\Delta K, \Delta L) \cdot (\alpha, \beta)$. So Y will be maximized by maximizing the scalar product of $(\Delta K, \Delta L)$ and (α, β). This will occur when

$$(\Delta K, \Delta L) = \frac{c}{\sqrt{\alpha^2 + \beta^2}} (\alpha, \beta)$$

5.5 $z = x^2 + y(x + 1)$.

$$\frac{\partial z}{\partial s} = \frac{\partial z}{\partial x} \cdot \frac{\partial x}{\partial s} + \frac{\partial z}{\partial y} \cdot \frac{\partial y}{\partial s} = (2x + y)\frac{\partial x}{\partial s} + (x + 1)\frac{\partial y}{\partial s}.$$

Now,

$$x = rs + s^2 \Rightarrow \text{"}\frac{\partial x}{\partial s}\text{"} = \frac{\partial x}{\partial r} \cdot \frac{\partial r}{\partial s} + \frac{\partial x}{\partial s} = s\frac{\partial r}{\partial s} + r + 2s.$$

Given $r = st$, $\partial r/\partial s = t$. Thus $\partial x/\partial s = st + r + 2s$. Also $y = t + s(t - 1)$, so $\partial y/\partial s = t - 1$. Therefore,

$$\partial z/\partial s = (2x + y)(st + r + 2s) + (x + 1)(t - 1).$$

When $s = 0 = t$, then $r = 0$, $x = 0$, and $y = 0$ so $\Rightarrow \partial z/\partial s|_{s=t=0} = -1$.

5.6

$$z = (s - 1)(t + 1) \quad \text{and} \quad \frac{\partial z}{\partial x} = (t + 1)\frac{\partial s}{\partial x} + (s - 1)\frac{\partial t}{\partial x},$$

$$s = x - 1 \Rightarrow \frac{\partial s}{\partial x} = 1,$$

$$t = 2x + r^2 \Rightarrow \text{"}\frac{\partial t}{\partial x}\text{"} = 2 + 2r\frac{\partial r}{\partial x},$$

$$r = x^2 + y^2 \Rightarrow \frac{\partial r}{\partial x} = 2x.$$

So, $\partial z/\partial x = (t + 1) + (s - 1)(2 + 4rx)$. When $x = 1 = y$, get $r = 2$, $s = 0$, and $t = 6$. $\Rightarrow$ at $x = y = 1$, $\partial z/\partial x = -3$.

5.7 Given $z = f(x, y)$;

$$dz = \frac{\partial f}{\partial x}\left(\frac{\partial g}{\partial s}\,ds + \frac{\partial g}{\partial t}\,dt\right) + \frac{\partial f}{\partial y}\left(\frac{\partial h}{\partial s}\,ds + \frac{\partial h}{\partial r}\,dr\right).$$

Now

$$dt = \frac{\partial m}{\partial r} dr = \frac{\partial m}{\partial r} \left(\frac{\partial n}{\partial s} ds + \frac{\partial n}{\partial q} dq \right) \quad \text{or} \quad dt = \frac{\partial m}{\partial r} \cdot \frac{\partial n}{\partial s} ds,$$

when $dq = 0$, and

$$dr = \frac{\partial n}{\partial s} ds + \frac{\partial n}{\partial q} dq = \frac{\partial n}{\partial s} ds,$$

when $dq = 0$. So,

$$dz = \frac{\partial f}{\partial x} \left[\frac{\partial g}{\partial s} ds + \frac{\partial g}{\partial t} \frac{\partial m}{\partial r} \frac{\partial n}{\partial s} ds \right] + \frac{\partial f}{\partial y} \left(\frac{\partial h}{\partial s} ds + \frac{\partial h}{\partial r} \frac{\partial n}{\partial s} ds \right)$$

$$= y \left[2s - 1r\frac{1}{q} \right] ds + x \left[r^3 + 3sr^2\frac{1}{q} \right] ds.$$

When $s = 2$, $q = 1$ we have $r = 2$, $t = 2$, $y = 16$, and $x = 2$. So,

$$\partial z/\partial s = 16(4 - 2) + 2(8 + 3 \cdot 2 \cdot 4) = 32 + 64 = 96.$$

5.8 Given $f(x, y) = x^2 - y^2$,
  (a) $f_x = 2x$, $f_{yx} = 0$, $f_{xx} = 2$, $f_y = -2y$, $f_{xy} = 0$, $f_{yy} = -2$. Then Hessian is

$$H = \begin{bmatrix} 2 & 0 \\ 0 & -2 \end{bmatrix}.$$

Since

$$|2| = 2 > 0 \quad \text{and} \quad \begin{vmatrix} 2 & 0 \\ 0 & -2 \end{vmatrix} = -4 < 0,$$

H is not NSD so f is not concave.
  (b) Bordering Hessian with first partials, get

$$B(x, y) = \begin{bmatrix} 0 & 2x & -2y \\ 2x & 2 & 0 \\ -2y & 0 & -2 \end{bmatrix},$$

$$(-1)^{2+1}|B_2| = (-1)^3(-4x^2) > 0 \quad \forall \, x \neq 0,$$

$$(-1)^{3+1}|B_3| = (-1)^4 8(x^2 - y^2) > 0 \quad \text{as } |y| < x.$$

So since $(-1)^{r+1}|B_r| > 0$, $r = 2, 3$, we conclude that f is quasi-concave.

5.9 Given $U(x_1, x_2) = \sqrt{x_1} + \sqrt{x_2}$, the Hessian is

$$H = \begin{bmatrix} U_{11} & U_{12} \\ U_{21} & U_{22} \end{bmatrix} = \begin{bmatrix} -1/4(x_1)^{3/2} & 0 \\ 0 & -1/4(x_2)^{3/2} \end{bmatrix}.$$

$$|U_{11}| < 0 \quad \forall \, (x_1, x_2) \in \mathbb{R}^2_{++},$$

$$|H| = \frac{1}{16} x_1^{-3/2} \cdot x_2^{-3/2} > 0 \quad \forall \, (x_1, x_2) \in \mathbb{R}^2_{++}.$$

Hence H is ND $\Rightarrow U(x_1, x_2)$ is strictly concave on $\mathbb{R}^2_{++}$. Since concavity $\Rightarrow$ quasiconcavity, $U(x_1, x_2)$ is also quasiconcave on $\mathbb{R}^2_{++}$.

5.10 $f(x, y) = \sqrt{xy}$. For $(x, y) \in \mathbb{R}^2_{++}$, $f_x = \frac{1}{2} x^{-1/2} \cdot y^{1/2}$, $f_{xy} = \frac{1}{4} x^{-1/2} \cdot y^{-1/2}$, $f_y = \frac{1}{2} x^{1/2} \cdot y^{-1/2}$, $f_{xx} = -\frac{1}{4} x^{-3/2} \cdot y^{1/2}$, and $f_{yy} = -\frac{1}{4} x^{1/2} \cdot y^{-3/2}$.

$$H = \begin{bmatrix} -\dfrac{1}{4} x^{-3/2} y^{1/2} & \dfrac{1}{4} x^{-1/2} y^{-1/2} \\ \dfrac{1}{4} x^{-1/2} y^{-1/2} & -\dfrac{1}{4} x^{1/2} y^{-3/2} \end{bmatrix} = \frac{1}{4} x^{-1/2} y^{-1/2} \begin{bmatrix} -\dfrac{y}{x} & 1 \\ 1 & -\dfrac{x}{y} \end{bmatrix}.$$

So $H_1 < 0$, and $|H| = \frac{1}{4} x^{-1/2} y^{-1/2}(1 - 1) = 0$. $\Rightarrow H$ is NSD and therefore concave on $\mathbb{R}^2_{++}$. This result can be extended to $\mathbb{R}^2_+$.

5.11 Given $f(x, y) = x^2 y^2$,

$$f_x = 2xy^2, \qquad f_{xy} = 4xy, \qquad f_{xx} = 2y^2,$$

$$f_y = 2x^2 y, \qquad f_{xy} = 4xy, \qquad f_{yy} = 2x^2,$$

$$H = \begin{bmatrix} 2y^2 & 4xy \\ 4xy & 2x^2 \end{bmatrix}.$$

$|H_1| = 2y^2 \geq 0 \quad \forall \; x, y \geq 0$ and $|H| = 4x^2 y^2 - 16x^2 y^2 \leq 0 \quad \forall \; x, y \geq 0$. So H is not NSD $\Rightarrow f$ is not concave on $\mathbb{R}^2_+$ (and also not concave on $\mathbb{R}^2$). Checking quasiconcavity:

$$B(x, y) = \begin{bmatrix} 0 & 2xy^2 & 2x^2 y \\ 2xy^2 & 2y^2 & 4xy \\ 2x^2 y & 4xy & 2x^2 \end{bmatrix}.$$

So $(-1)^{2+1} B_2 = +4x^2 y^4 > 0 \quad \forall \; x, y > 0$, and $(-1)^{3+1} B_3 = 16x^4 y^4 > 0 \; \forall \; x, y > 0$. For $(x, y) \in \mathbb{R}^2_{++}$, the sufficient conditions for quasiconcavity hold (the inequalities are both strict). It remains to check $\mathbb{R}^2_+ \setminus \mathbb{R}^2_{++}$, i.e., points where x and/or y is 0. On $\mathbb{R}^2_{++}$, $f > 0$, while $f = 0$ if either x or y is 0. But $\{(x, y) \in \mathbb{R}^2_+ \,|\, f(x, y) \geq 0\} = \mathbb{R}^2_+$, so all upper contour sets are convex, and f is quasiconcave on $\mathbb{R}^2_+$.

f is not quasiconcave on $\mathbb{R}^2$ since $f(1, 1) = f(-1, -1) = 1$, but $f((1/2)(1, 1) + (1/2)(-1, -1)) = f(0, 0) = 0$.

5.12 (a) $\lambda_i < 0$, so minimization problem. $n = s = 2$, so no SOC to check. $(1, -1)$ is strict local minimizer.

(b) $\lambda_2 < 0$, so minimization problem. $n = 3$, $s = 1$, so need to check 3×3 and 4×4 determinants for minimum:

$$(-1)^1 D_1 = 17 > 0 \quad \text{and} \quad (-1)^1 D_2 = 51 > 0.$$

Thus, $(-4, 0, 1)$ is strict local minimizer.

(c) No binding constraints, so could be maximization or minimization. $n = 2$, $s = 0$, so need to check 1×1 and 2×2. Note the matrix is PSD everywhere [the upper left 1×1 is 2 and $\det(2 \times 2) = (1 + x_1)^2 \geq 0$], so $(4, -7)$ is a global minimizer.

5.13 Given $f(x, y) = e^{x+y} = e^x \cdot e^y$,

$$f_x = e^x \cdot e^y, \qquad f_{xy} = e^x \cdot e^y, \qquad f_{xx} = e^{x+y},$$

$$f_y = e^{x+y} = f_{yx} = f_{yy}.$$

So,

$$H = \begin{bmatrix} e^{x+y} & e^{x+y} \\ e^{x+y} & e^{x+y} \end{bmatrix}.$$

Since $e^{x+y} > 0 \;\forall\; x, y \in \mathbb{R}^2$, H is not NSD $\Rightarrow f$ not concave.

5.14 $f(x, y) = \ln(xy)$, $(x, y) \in \mathbb{R}^2_{++}$,

$$f_x = \frac{1}{x}, \qquad f_{xy} = 0, \qquad f_{xx} = -\frac{1}{x^2},$$

$$f_y = \frac{1}{y}, \qquad f_{xy} = 0, \qquad f_{yy} = -\frac{1}{y^2}.$$

So Hessian is

$$H = \begin{bmatrix} -\dfrac{1}{x^2} & 0 \\ 0 & -\dfrac{1}{y^2} \end{bmatrix}.$$

Since $H_1 = -1/x^2 < 0 \;\forall\; x > 0$ and $|H| = 1/x^2 y^2 > 0 \;\forall\; x, y > 0$, H is ND everywhere on $\mathbb{R}^2_{++} \Rightarrow$ strictly concave $\Rightarrow$ quasiconcave.

5.15 Let us first check the Hessian.

$$f(x) = e^{-x^2},$$

$$f'(x) = e^{-x^2}(-2x),$$

$$f''(x) = (-2)\big[x(-2x)e^{-x^2} + e^{-x^2}\big] = (-2)e^{-x^2}[1 - 2x^2].$$

Now e^{-x^2} is always > 0. So $f(x)$ is concave ($f'' \leq 0$) if and only if $1 - 2x^2 \geq 0$; i.e., $\frac{1}{2} \geq x^2 \Rightarrow -1/\sqrt{2} \leq x \leq 1/\sqrt{2}$. So largest interval on which f is concave is $[-1/\sqrt{2}, 1/\sqrt{2}]$. To examine quasiconcavity we need to check convexity of the upper contour sets. Note:

$$\{x \in \mathbb{R} | f(x) \geq \alpha\} = \begin{cases} \mathbb{R} & \text{if } \alpha \leq 0, \\ \big[-\sqrt{-\ln\alpha}, \ \sqrt{-\ln\alpha}\big] & \text{if } 0 < \alpha \leq 1, \\ \varnothing & \text{if } \alpha > 1. \end{cases}$$

Since this set is convex for all α, e^{-x^2} is quasiconcave.

5.16 False. The function

$$f(x, y) = \begin{cases} |xy| & \text{if } y \geq 0, \\ y & \text{if } y < 0 \end{cases}$$

is quasiconcave in each of the desired regions, but $\{(x, y) \in \mathbb{R}^2 | f(x, y) \geq 1\}$ contains $(1, 1)$ and $(-1, 1)$ but not $(0, 1)$.

5.17 False. For $f(x) = 1/x$ defined on $\mathbb{R}_{++}$, upper contour set $\{x: f(x) \geq c\}$ is convex for all c; e.g., for $c = 1$, the upper contour set is the interval $(0, 1]$. Here the function is strictly convex ($f''(x) = 2/x^3 > 0$ for all $x > 0$), and upper contour sets are convex, so f is quasiconcave.

5.18 True. Suppose (x^*, y^*) is a global maximizer of $x + y$ s.t. $(x, y) \in S$. Since S is open, we can always find ε small enough so that an open ε ball around (x^*, y^*) is entirely contained in S. But then a point such as $(x^* + \varepsilon/2, y^* + \varepsilon/2)$ would lie in S with a value of the objective function $(x^* + \varepsilon/2) + (y^* + \varepsilon/2)$; i.e.,

$$f\left(x^* + \frac{\varepsilon}{2}, y^* + \frac{\varepsilon}{2}\right) = x^* + y^* + \varepsilon > x^* + y^* = f(x^*, y^*).$$

$\Rightarrow (x^*, y^*)$ cannot be a global maximizer. $\Rightarrow$ Original assumption must be false. $\Rightarrow \nexists (x, y) \in S$, which is a global maximizer of $f(x, y) = x + y$.

5.19 False. Consider the constant function $f(x, y) = c$, $c > 0$. The graph of this function is a plane in three dimensions, parallel to the x–y plane. If S is defined as $\{(x, y) \in \mathbb{R}^2: x > 0, y > 0\}$, then S^c is closed. $\Rightarrow S$ is open. Furthermore, f is continuous, and clearly all $(x, y) \in S$ are global maximizers (and minimizers) since f has the same value everywhere.

5.20 (a) $L = - \sqrt{x + y} - \lambda_1(-x) - \lambda_2(108 - x^2 y)$.
FOC:

$$L_x = -1/2\sqrt{x + y} + \lambda_1 + 2\lambda_2 xy = 0,$$

$$L_y = -1/2\sqrt{x + y} + \lambda_2 x^2 = 0,$$

$$L_{\lambda_1} = x \geq 0, \qquad\qquad \lambda_1 \geq 0, \lambda_1 x = 0,$$

$$L_{\lambda_2} = x^2 y - 108 \geq 0, \qquad \lambda_2 \geq 0, \lambda_2(x^2 y - 108) = 0.$$

Both $\lambda_2 = 0$ and $\lambda_1 > 0$ ($x = 0$) are inconsistent with $L_y = 0$. Thus $\lambda_2 > 0$ and $\lambda_1 = 0$ is the only possible case, and the unique potential solution is $(6, 3, 0, 1/216)$.
SOC: $L^* = - \sqrt{x + y} - \lambda_2(108 - x^2 y)$.

$$[L_{ij}^*] = \begin{bmatrix} 2\lambda_2 y + (x + y)^{-3/2}/4 & 2\lambda_2 x + (x + y)^{-3/2}/4 & 2xy \\ 2\lambda_2 x + (x + y)^{-3/2}/4 & (x + y)^{-3/2}/4 & x^2 \\ 2xy & x^2 & 0 \end{bmatrix}$$

$$= \begin{bmatrix} 1/27 & 7/108 & 36 \\ 7/108 & 1/108 & 36 \\ 36 & 36 & 0 \end{bmatrix}.$$

$n - s = 1$, so one determinant to check: $(-1)^{1+1} \det[L_{ij}^*] = 108 > 0$. Thus $(x^*, y^*) = (6, 3)$ is a strict local maximizer and is the only local maximizer.

(b) First note that both x and y must be strictly positive to be feasible, so the feasible set turns out to be the subset of $\mathbb{R}^2_{++}$, where $g(x, y) = x^2 y \geq 108$. Checking the bordered Hessian for g, we find g is strictly quasiconcave on $\mathbb{R}^2_{++}$. Thus the feasible set, an upper contour set for g, is convex. The objective function is quasiconcave: for any $c \leq 0$, the set of (x, y) such that $- \sqrt{x + y} \geq c$ is $\{(x, y) \in \mathbb{R}^2 | 0 \leq x + y \leq c^2\}$, which is convex (for $c > 0$ the set is empty). With quasiconcave objective and convex feasible set, the unique local maximizer is the unique global maximizer.

5.21 The Hessian

$$\begin{bmatrix} -1/4x^{3/2} & 0 & 0 \\ 0 & -1/4y^{3/2} & 0 \\ 0 & 0 & 2 \end{bmatrix}$$

is not negative semidefinite, so the function is not concave. The bordered Hessian

$$\begin{bmatrix} 0 & 1/2\sqrt{x} & 1/2\sqrt{y} & 2z \\ 1/2\sqrt{x} & -1/4x^{3/2} & 0 & 0 \\ 1/2\sqrt{y} & 0 & -1/4y^{3/2} & 0 \\ 2z & 0 & 0 & 2 \end{bmatrix}$$

has determinant $(\sqrt{x} + \sqrt{y} - 2z^2)/8x^{3/2}y^{3/2}$, which is positive for some $(x, y, z) \in \mathbb{R}^3_{++}$ and negative for others. Thus the function is not quasiconcave on $\mathbb{R}^3_{++}$.

5.22 (a) $(\mathbf{x}^*, \lambda^*_1, \lambda^*_2) = (2, 4, -1, 1, 0)$. FOC for maximizer, so not a minimizer. $n = 3$, $s = 1 \Rightarrow n - s = 2$, and two determinants to check.

$$(-1)^{1+1}D_1 = \begin{vmatrix} 2 & 0 & -1 \\ 0 & 1 & 0 \\ -1 & 0 & 0 \end{vmatrix} = (-1)(1) = -1 < 0.$$

SOC for maximum fails $\Rightarrow (2, 4, -1)$ is not a maximizer (note: $D_2 = 2D_1 = -2$). Conclusion: neither maximizer nor minimizer.

(b) $(\mathbf{x}^*, \lambda^*_1, \lambda^*_2) = (-2, 1, -3, -2, -2)$. FOC for minimizer, so not a maximizer. $n = 3$, $s = 2 \Rightarrow$ one determinant to check.

$$(-1)^2 D_1 = |L^*_{ij}| = (-x_1)\begin{vmatrix} 2 & 0 & 0 & 1 \\ 0 & -1 & -1 & 0 \\ 0 & -1 & 0 & 0 \\ 1 & 0 & 0 & 0 \end{vmatrix}$$

$$= (-x_1)(-1)\begin{vmatrix} 0 & -1 & -1 \\ 0 & -1 & 0 \\ 1 & 0 & 0 \end{vmatrix}$$

or $D_1 = x_1(1)(0 - 1) = -x_1 = -(-2) = 2$ at potential solution. SOC hold, so strict local minimizer. Conclusion: strict local minimizer.

(c) $(\mathbf{x}^*, \lambda^*_1, \lambda^*_2) = (1, 1, 2, 0, 1)$. FOC for maximizer so not a minimizer. $n = 3$, $s = 1 \Rightarrow$ two determinants to check. $(-1)^2 \cdot D_1 = (1)(-1) = -1 < 0 \Rightarrow$ SOC fails $\Rightarrow$ not a maximizer. Conclusion: neither a maximizer nor a minimizer.

(d) $(\mathbf{x}^*, \lambda^*_1, \lambda^*_2) = (1, 1, 2, 0, 0)$. FOC for either maximizer or minimizer. $n = 3$, $s = 0 \Rightarrow$ three determinants to check. $(-1)^{0+1}D_1 = (-1)(1 + x_1)^2 < 0$ at $x_1 = 1 \Rightarrow$ not maximizer. Note that since no constraints are binding, the SOC matrix is also the Hessian. Here the Hessian is always positive definite $\Rightarrow$ strictly convex objective function $\Rightarrow$ global minimizer. Conclusion: unique global minimizer.

(e) $(x^*, \lambda_1^*, \lambda_2^*) = (1, 1, 2, 1, 0)$. FOC for maximizer, so not a minimizer. $n = 3$, $s = 1 \Rightarrow$ two determinants to check.

$$(-1)^{1+1} D_1 = 1 > 0,$$

$$(-1)^{1+2} D_2 = (-1)(-1) D_1 = 1 > 0.$$

SOC hold, so $(1, 1, 2)$ is strict local maximizer. Conclusion: strict local maximizer.

(f) $(x^*, \lambda_1^*, \lambda_2^*) = (1, 1, 2, -1, -2)$. FOC for minimizer, so not a maximizer. $n = 3$, $s = 2 \Rightarrow$ one determinant to check

$$(-1)^2 D_1 = (1)(-1) \begin{vmatrix} 2 & 0 & 0 & 1 \\ 0 & -1 & 1 & 0 \\ 0 & 1 & 0 & 0 \\ 1 & 0 & 0 & 0 \end{vmatrix}$$

$$= (-1)(-1) \begin{vmatrix} 0 & -1 & 1 \\ 0 & 1 & 0 \\ 1 & 0 & 0 \end{vmatrix}$$

$$= (1)(-1) = -1.$$

Thus, SOC for minimizer fail. Conclusion: neither a maximizer nor a minimizer.

(g) FOC for maximizer, so not a minimizer. $n = 2 = s \Rightarrow$ no SOC to check, and $(1, 1)$ is a strict local maximizer.

5.23 (a) False. $f(x) = 2x^3 - 3x^2$ on feasible set $[-1, 2]$ and has local maximizers at 0 and 2, but $f(2) > f(0)$ so only 2 is a global maximizer.

(b) False. $f(x) = 2x^3 - 3x^2$ is not quasiconcave on the nonconvex feasible set $[-5, -4] \cup [-1, 2]$ but has local maximizers at -4, 0, and 2.

(c) True. The objective function is both concave and convex. Each constraint defines a convex feasible region, so the intersection (i.e., the feasible set) is convex.

5.24

$$\nabla f = \begin{pmatrix} 2xy \\ x^2 \end{pmatrix}. \qquad H = [f_{ij}] = \begin{bmatrix} 2y & 2x \\ 2x & 0 \end{bmatrix}$$

is not NSD since $2y > 0$.
Thus not concave. The bordered Hessian is

$$B = \begin{bmatrix} 0 & 2xy & x^2 \\ 2xy & 2y & 2x \\ x^2 & 2x & 0 \end{bmatrix}.$$

$(-1)^3 \det[\text{upper left } 2 \times 2] = 4x^2y^2 > 0$ for all $(x, y) \in \mathbb{R}^2_{++}$. $(-1)^4 \det B = 6x^4y > 0$ for all $(x, y) \in \mathbb{R}^2_{++}$. Thus quasiconcave.

5.25 (a) False, since S need not be convex. Example: $f(x) = \sqrt{x}$ on $S = \{x \in \mathbb{R} \mid 0 \leq x \leq 1 \text{ or } 2 \leq x \leq 3\}$. Then $x^* = 1$ satisfies all FOC, but 3 is the global maximizer of the concave function f.

(b) False, since S need not be closed. Example: $f(x) = x^3 - 3x$ on $S = [-2, 3)$. The unique local maximizer is -1 with value 2, but $f(x) \to 18$ as $x \to 3$. The problem is $3 \notin S$.

(c) False. Example: $f: [-1, 2] \to \mathbb{R}$ is not quasiconcave for $f(x) = x^2$ $(\{x \mid f(x) \geq 1\} = \{-1\} \cup \{x \mid 1 \leq x \leq 2\})$, but the solutions to FOC (with constraints $-1 \leq x \leq 2$) are -1 and 2, with 2 the global maximizer.

(d) False. Since the feasible set is convex, if the objective function f is quasiconcave, then any point satisfying the FOC (with $\nabla f \neq \mathbf{0}$) is a global maximizer. Example: $f(x, y) = -\sqrt{x} + 1$ is not concave but is quasiconcave $(\{(x, y) \mid f \geq c\} = \{(x, y) \in \mathbb{R}^2_+ \mid x \leq c^2 - 1\}$ for any $c \leq -1$; the set is empty for $c > -1)$. All local maximizers $((x^*, y^*) \in \{(x, y) \mid x = 0, \ y \geq 0\})$ are global maximizers without "direction check."

5.26 $x^2 + y^2 + z^2$ is strictly convex (the matrix of second partials is

$$\begin{bmatrix} 2 & 0 & 0 \\ 0 & 2 & 0 \\ 0 & 0 & 2 \end{bmatrix},$$

which is positive definite everywhere), and the feasible set $\{(x, y, z) \mid y \geq x + 4\} \cap \{(x, y, z) \mid z \leq 2x + 5\}$ is convex so the unique solution to the FOC is the global minimizer.

$$L(x, y, z, \lambda_1, \lambda_2) = x^2 + y^2 + z^2 - \lambda_1(x + 4 - y)$$

$$- \lambda_2(z - 2x - 5)$$

FOC: $L_x = 2x - \lambda_1 + 2\lambda_2 = 0,$

$L_y = 2y + \lambda_1 = 0,$

$L_z = 2z - \lambda_2 = 0,$

$L_{\lambda_1} = -x - 4 + y \geq 0, \quad \lambda_1 \leq 0, \lambda_1(-x - 4 + y) = 0,$

$L_{\lambda_2} = -z + 2x + 5 \geq 0, \quad \lambda_2 \leq 0, \lambda_2(-z + 2x + 5) = 0.$

Case 1. $\lambda_1 = \lambda_2 = 0$. Then $x = y = z = 0$. But this violates $L_{\lambda_1} \geq 0$.
Case 2. $\lambda_1 = 0$, $\lambda_2 < 0$. Solving $2x + 2\lambda_2 = 0$, $2z - \lambda_2 = 0$ and $-z + 2x + 5 = 0$, we obtain $z = 1$, $x = -2$, $\lambda_2 = 2$, which violates $\lambda_2 \leq 0$.

Case 3. $\lambda_1 < 0$, $\lambda_2 < 0$. Solving $2x - \lambda_1 + 2\lambda_2 = 0$, $2y + \lambda_1 = 0$, $2z - \lambda_2 = 0$, $-x - 4 + y = 0$, and $-z + 2x + 5 = 0$, we obtain $(x, y, z, \lambda_1, \lambda_2) = (-7/3, 5/3, 1/3, -10/3, 2/3)$, which violates $\lambda_2 \leq 0$.

Case 4. $\lambda_1 < 0$, $\lambda_2 = 0$. Solving $2x - \lambda_1 = 0$, $2y + \lambda_1 = 0$ and $-x - 4 + y = 0$, we obtain $(x, y, z, \lambda_1, \lambda_2) = (-2, 2, 0, -4, 0)$, which satisfies all FOC and is the unique global minimizer.

5.27

$$\nabla f = \begin{pmatrix} 2x \\ 1/y \\ 1/z \end{pmatrix}, \qquad [f_{ij}] = \begin{bmatrix} 2 & 0 & 0 \\ 0 & -1/y^2 & 0 \\ 0 & 0 & -1/z^2 \end{bmatrix}$$

is not NSD, so f is not concave. To check for quasiconcavity form the bordered Hessian:

$$\begin{bmatrix} 0 & 2x & 1/y & 1/z \\ 2x & 2 & 0 & 0 \\ 1/y & 0 & -1/y^2 & 0 \\ 1/z & 0 & 0 & -1/z^2 \end{bmatrix},$$

$$\det \begin{bmatrix} 0 & 2x \\ 2x & 2 \end{bmatrix} = -4x^2 < 0 \quad \text{for } x > 0,$$

$$\det \begin{bmatrix} 0 & 2x & 1/y \\ 2x & 2 & 0 \\ 1/y & 0 & -1/y^2 \end{bmatrix} = (4x^2 - 2)/y^2,$$

which does not have the same sign on all of $\mathbb{R}^3_{++}$ so f is not quasiconcave.

A.7 SOLUTIONS FOR CHAPTER 6

6.1 $f(x, y, z) = x^2 + x(z - 2) + 3(y - 1)^2 + z^2$.

FOC for extrema: $\qquad \dfrac{\partial f}{\partial x} = 2x + z - 2 = 0,$

$$\dfrac{\partial f}{\partial y} = 6(y - 1) = 0,$$

$$\dfrac{\partial f}{\partial z} = x + 2z = 0.$$

Solve to get $(x, y, z) = (\frac{4}{3}, 1, -\frac{2}{3})$. SOC matrix (Hessian) is

$$H = \begin{bmatrix} 2 & 0 & 1 \\ 0 & 6 & 0 \\ 1 & 0 & 2 \end{bmatrix}.$$

The corresponding determinants are

$$|2| > 0,$$

$$\begin{bmatrix} 2 & 0 \\ 0 & 6 \end{bmatrix} = 12 > 0,$$

$$|H| = 18 > 0.$$

H is PD $\Rightarrow f$ is strictly convex $\Rightarrow$ the solution is the unique global minimizer (and obviously also a local minimizer).

6.2 Rewriting the constraint as $-1 - x \le 0$, the Lagrangian is

$$L = \mu[x^3 - 6x^2 + 9x + 1] - \lambda(-1 - x),$$

where

$$\mu = \begin{cases} 1 & \text{for the maximization problem,} \\ -1 & \text{for the minimization problem.} \end{cases}$$

(a) Maximization problem, $\mu = 1$

FOC: $\dfrac{\partial L}{\partial x} = 3x^2 - 12x + 9 + \lambda = 0,$ \hfill (1)

$$\frac{\partial L}{\partial \lambda} = x + 1 \ge 0, \ \lambda \ge 0, \ \lambda(x + 1) = 0. \tag{2}$$

Case 1. $\lambda = 0$. (1) $\Rightarrow 3x^2 - 12x + 9 = 0$, or $(x - 3)(x - 1) = 0$, $\Rightarrow x = 1$ or $x = 3$. Checking SOC, and noting that constraint is not binding for either value of x:

$$\frac{\partial^2 L}{\partial x^2} = 6x - 12$$

When $x = 1$, $\partial^2 L / \partial x^2 = -6 < 0$; when $x = 3$, $\partial^2 L / \partial x^2 = 6 > 0$. Note $n = 1$, $s = 0$ and $D_1 = \partial^2 L / \partial x^2$. Since $(-1)^1 D_1 > 0$ for a maximum to exist, $x = 1$ satisfies SOC, while $x = 3$ violates the SOC. Hence $x = 1$ is local maximizer.

Case 2. $\lambda > 0$. From (2), $x = -1$ since the constraint is binding. By substituting $x = -1$ in (1) we get $\lambda = -24 < 0 \Rightarrow$ contradiction, since we started by assuming λ positive. So $x = -1$ is not a maximizer.

(b) Minimization problem, $\mu = -1$. The transformed problem is Max $-x^3 + 6x^2 - 9x - 1$ s.t. $x \geq -1$.

$$L = -x^3 + 6x^2 - 9x - 1 - \lambda(-x - 1).$$

FOC: $\dfrac{\partial L}{\partial x} = -3x^2 + 12x - 9 + \lambda = 0,$ (3)

$\dfrac{\partial L}{\partial x} = x + 1 \geq 0,\ \lambda \geq 0,\ \lambda(x + 1) = 0.$ (4)

Case 1. $\lambda = 0$. (3) $\Rightarrow (x - 3)(x - 1) = 0 \Rightarrow x = 3$ or $x = 1$. The constraint is inactive for either value. Checking SOC (for max of transformed problem):

$$\frac{\partial^2 L}{\partial x^2} = -6x + 12 = D_1.$$

When $x = 1$, $(-1)^1 D_1 = -6 < 0$, and SOC violated. When $x = 3$, $(-1)^1 D_1 = 6 > 0$, and SOC satisfied. Hence $x = 3$ is local maximizer for the transformed problem and local minimizer for the original problem.

Case 2. $\lambda > 0$. From (4), $x = -1$. Plugging into (3), we get $\lambda = 24$, which is consistent. Furthermore, since $n = 1 = s$ there are no SOC to be checked $\Rightarrow x = -1$ is local minimizer.

Global Solutions

Maximization problem: $x = 1$ is local maximizer but not global because $\lim_{x \to \infty} f(x) = \infty > f(1) = 5$. In fact, there is no global maximizer.

Minimization problem: Since the constraint requires $x \geq -1$, $x \to -\infty$ is not feasible. Also $\lim_{x \to \infty} f(x) = \infty$. Compare the values of objective function for the two local minimizers, $x = 3$ and $x = -1$: $f(3) = 1$, $f(-1) = -15$. Since $f(-1) < f(3)$, $x = -1$ is the unique global minimizer.

6.3 Max xy s.t. $x + y = 1$.

$$L = xy - \mu(1 - x - y).$$

FOC: $\dfrac{\partial L}{\partial x} = y + \mu = 0,$

$\dfrac{\partial L}{\partial y} = x + \mu = 0,$

$\dfrac{\partial L}{\partial \mu} = -1 + x + y = 0.$

Solve to get $(x, y, \mu) = (1/2, 1/2, -1/2)$ as a potential solution.
Checking sufficiency, SOC matrix is

$$D = \begin{bmatrix} 0 & 1 & 1 \\ 1 & 0 & 1 \\ 1 & 1 & 0 \end{bmatrix}.$$

Here $n = 2$, $s = 1$ so $n - s = 1 \Rightarrow$ only one determinant to check of order $(2s + i) \times (2s + i) = 3 \times 3$. The determinant is 2, so $(-1)^{s+1}D_1 = (-1)^2 D_1 > 0 \Rightarrow$ SOC holds, and $(x, y) = (1/2, 1/2)$ is a strict local maximizer.

Global: By the constraint, if either of $|x|$ or $|y|$ is greater than 1, then x and y have opposite signs and xy is negative. Thus $(x, y) = (1/2, 1/2)$ is the unique global maximizer.

6.4 Min $x^2 + y^2$ s.t. $x + 2y = 3$.

$$L = -x^2 - y^2 - \mu(3 - x - 2y)$$

FOC:
$$\frac{\partial L}{\partial x} = -2x + \mu = 0,$$

$$\frac{\partial L}{\partial y} = -2y + 2\mu = 0,$$

$$\frac{\partial L}{\partial \mu} = x + 2y - 3 = 0.$$

Solve to get $(x, y, \mu) = (\frac{3}{5}, \frac{6}{5}, \frac{6}{5})$ as a potential solution.
Checking sufficiency, SOC matrix is

$$D = \begin{bmatrix} \dfrac{\partial^2 L}{\partial x^2} & \dfrac{\partial^2 L}{\partial x\, \partial y} & \dfrac{\partial^2 L}{\partial x\, \partial \mu} \\[2mm] \dfrac{\partial^2 L}{\partial y\, \partial x} & \dfrac{\partial^2 L}{\partial y^2} & \dfrac{\partial^2 L}{\partial y\, \partial \mu} \\[2mm] \dfrac{\partial^2 L}{\partial \mu\, \partial x} & \dfrac{\partial^2 L}{\partial \mu\, \partial y} & \dfrac{\partial^2 L}{\partial \mu^2} \end{bmatrix} = \begin{bmatrix} -2 & 0 & 1 \\ 0 & -2 & 2 \\ 1 & 2 & 0 \end{bmatrix}.$$

Here $n = 2$, $s = 1 \Rightarrow n - s = 1 \Rightarrow$ only one determinant to check of order $(2s + i) \times (2s + i) = 3 \times 3$. Then

$$D_1 = \begin{vmatrix} -2 & 0 & 1 \\ 0 & -2 & 2 \\ 1 & 2 & 0 \end{vmatrix} = 10.$$

So, $(-1)^{s+1}D_1 = (-1)^2 D_1 > 0 \Rightarrow$ SOC holds, and $(x, y) = (\frac{3}{5}, \frac{6}{5})$ is a local minimizer for original problem.

Global: Checking the Hessian, we find it is PD:

$$H = \begin{bmatrix} f_{11} & f_{12} \\ f_{21} & f_{22} \end{bmatrix} = \begin{bmatrix} 2 & 0 \\ 0 & 2 \end{bmatrix}, \qquad |2| > 0 \quad \text{and} \quad |H| = 4 > 0.$$

Thus the objective function is strictly convex. Since the feasible set is a line, and hence both concave and convex, $(x, y) = (\frac{3}{5}, \frac{6}{5})$ is also the unique global minimizer.

6.5 Min $x^2 + y^2 + z^2$ s.t. $2x + 2y + 2z = 1$.

$$L = -x^2 - y^2 - z^2 - \mu(1 - 2x - 2y - 2z).$$

FOC:
$$\frac{\partial L}{\partial x} = -2x + 2\mu = 0,$$

$$\frac{\partial L}{\partial y} = -2y + 2\mu = 0,$$

$$\frac{\partial L}{\partial z} = -2z + 2\mu = 0,$$

$$\frac{\partial L}{\partial \mu} = 2x + 2y + 2z - 1 = 0.$$

Solve to get $(x, y, z, \mu) = (\frac{1}{6}, \frac{1}{6}, \frac{1}{6}, \frac{1}{6})$ as a potential solution. Checking sufficiency, the required SOC matrix is

$$D = \begin{bmatrix} -2 & 0 & 0 & 2 \\ 0 & -2 & 0 & 2 \\ 0 & 0 & -2 & 2 \\ 2 & 2 & 2 & 0 \end{bmatrix}.$$

Here, $n = 3$, $s = 1 \Rightarrow n - s = 2 \Rightarrow$ need to check D_1 and D_2:

$$D_1 = \begin{vmatrix} -2 & 0 & 2 \\ 0 & -2 & 2 \\ 2 & 2 & 0 \end{vmatrix} = 16 > 0,$$

$$D_2 = -2D_1 - 2 \begin{vmatrix} 0 & 0 & 2 \\ -2 & 0 & 2 \\ 0 & -2 & 2 \end{vmatrix} = -32 - 16 = -48 < 0.$$

So $(-1)^{1+1}D_1 = (-1)^2 16 > 0$ and $(-1)^{1+2}D_2 = (-1)^3(-48) > 0 \Rightarrow$ SOC holds, and $(x, y, z) = (\frac{1}{6}, \frac{1}{6}, \frac{1}{6})$ is a local minimizer.

Global: Checking the Hessian, it can be shown to be PD:

$$H = \begin{bmatrix} 2 & 0 & 0 \\ 0 & 2 & 0 \\ 0 & 0 & 2 \end{bmatrix}.$$

Therefore, the objective function is strictly convex. A strictly convex objective function, along with the convex feasible set, implies $(\frac{1}{6}, \frac{1}{6}, \frac{1}{6})$ is the unique global minimizer.

6.6 Max $x + y$ s.t. $2x^2 + y^2 \leq 54$.

$$L = x + y - \lambda(2x^2 + y^2 - 54).$$

FOC:
$$\frac{\partial L}{\partial x} = 1 - 4\lambda x = 0, \tag{1}$$

$$\frac{\partial L}{\partial y} = 1 - 2\lambda y = 0, \tag{2}$$

$$\frac{\partial L}{\partial \lambda} = 54 - 2x^2 - y^2 \geq 0, \lambda \geq 0,$$

$$\lambda(54 - 2x^2 - y^2) = 0. \tag{3}$$

Case 1. $\lambda = 0$. When $\lambda = 0$ FOC (1) and (2) are violated $\Rightarrow$ no solution.

Case 2. $\lambda > 0$. (3) $\Rightarrow 2x^2 + y^2 = 54$; (1) $\Rightarrow x = 1/4\lambda$, and (2) $\Rightarrow$ $y = 1/2\lambda$. Plugging (1) and (2) into (3), we get

$$2\left(\frac{1}{4\lambda}\right)^2 + \left(\frac{1}{2\lambda}\right)^2 = 54,$$

which yields $\lambda = \pm \frac{1}{12}$. $\lambda = -\frac{1}{12}$ is ruled out by (3). So we get $x = 1/4\lambda = 1/4(\frac{1}{12}) = 3$ and $y = 1/2\lambda = 1/2(\frac{1}{12}) = 6$, and (x, y) $= (3, 6)$ is a potential local maximizer.

Checking sufficiency, the SOC matrix is

$$D = \begin{bmatrix} -4\lambda & 0 & -4x \\ 0 & -2\lambda & -2y \\ -4x & -2y & 0 \end{bmatrix}.$$

Note the constraint is active at $(x, y) = (3, 6)$. Here $n = 2$, $s = 1 \Rightarrow$ only D_1 to check. $D_1 = -4\lambda(-4y^2) - 4x(-8\lambda x) = 16\lambda(y^2 + 2x^2)$ $= 72 > 0$ at $(x, y, \lambda) = (3, 6, \frac{1}{12})$. So, $(-1)^2 D_1 = 72 > 0 \Rightarrow$ SOC holds, and $(x, y) = (3, 6)$ is a local maximizer.

Global: Since the upper contour sets are convex, the objective function is quasiconcave while the feasible set is bounded and convex. Hence $(x, y) = (3, 6)$ is also a global maximizer.

6.7 Max $x - y$ s.t. $3x^2 + 2y^2 \leq 30$.

$$L = x - y - \lambda(3x^2 + 2y^2 - 30).$$

FOC:
$$\frac{\partial L}{\partial x} = 1 - 6\lambda x = 0,$$

$$\frac{\partial L}{\partial y} = -1 - 4\lambda y = 0,$$

$$\frac{\partial L}{\partial \lambda} = 30 - 3x^2 - 2y^2 \geq 0,$$

$$\lambda \geq 0, \ \lambda(30 - 3x^2 - 2y^2) = 0.$$

Case 1. $\lambda = 0 \Rightarrow$ no solution.

Case 2. $\lambda > 0 \Rightarrow (x, y, \lambda) = (2, -3, \frac{1}{12})$ is a potential solution.

SOC: $n = 2$, $s = 1 \Rightarrow n - s = 1$, and we need only check D_1:

$$D_1 = \begin{vmatrix} -6\lambda & 0 & -6x \\ 0 & -4\lambda & -4y \\ -6x & -4y & 0 \end{vmatrix} = 120 > 0.$$

So, $(-1)^2 D_1 = 120 > 0 \Rightarrow$ SOC holds, and $(x, y) = (2, -3)$ is a local maximizer. Furthermore, since the objective function is quasiconcave and the feasible set is convex, $(2, -3)$ is also a global maximizer.

6.8 Max $2x + y$ s.t. $x \geq 0$, $y \geq 0$ and $(x + 1)(y + 1) = 9/2$.

$$L = 2x + y + \lambda_1 x + \lambda_2 y - \mu[(x + 1)(y + 1) - 9/2].$$

FOC:
$$\frac{\partial L}{\partial x} = 2 + \lambda_1 - \mu(y + 1) = 0,$$

$$\frac{\partial L}{\partial y} = 1 + \lambda_2 - \mu(x + 1) = 0,$$

$$\frac{\partial L}{\partial \lambda_1} = x \geq 0, \qquad \lambda_1 \geq 0 \quad \text{and} \quad \lambda_1 x = 0,$$

$$\frac{\partial L}{\partial \lambda_2} = y \geq 0, \qquad \lambda_2 \geq 0 \quad \text{and} \quad \lambda_2 y = 0,$$

$$\frac{\partial L}{\partial \mu} = \frac{9}{2} - (x + 1)(y + 1) = 0.$$

Case 1. $\lambda_1 = 0 = \lambda_2$. Potential solution: $(x, y, \lambda_1, \lambda_2, \mu) = (\frac{1}{2}, 2, 0, 0, \frac{2}{3})$.

Case 2. $\lambda_1 > 0$, $\lambda_2 = 0$. Potential solution: $(x, y, \lambda_1, \lambda_2, \mu) = (0, \frac{7}{2}, \frac{5}{2}, 0, 1)$.

Case 3. $\lambda_1 = 0$, $\lambda_2 > 0$. Potential solution: $(x, y, \lambda_1, \lambda_2, \mu) = (\frac{7}{2}, 0, 0, 8, 2)$.

Case 4. $\lambda_1 > 0$, $\lambda_2 > 0$. No solution.

Check SOC for each potential solution:

(i) $(\frac{1}{2}, 2, 0, 0, \frac{2}{3})$.

Here, $n = 2$, $s = 1 \Rightarrow n - s = 1 \Rightarrow$ check only D_1:

$$D_1 = \begin{vmatrix} 0 & -\mu & -(y+1) \\ -\mu & 0 & -(x+1) \\ -(y+1) & -(x+1) & 0 \end{vmatrix} = -6 \quad \text{at } (\tfrac{1}{2}, 2, 0, 0, \tfrac{2}{3}).$$

So, $(-1)^2 D_1 = -6 < 0 \Rightarrow$ SOC fails, and $(\frac{1}{2}, 2, 0, 0, \frac{2}{3})$ is not a local maximizer.

(ii) $(0, \frac{7}{2}, \frac{5}{2}, 0, 1)$.

Here, $n = 2 = s \Rightarrow$ no SOC to check. So $(x, y) = (0, \frac{7}{2})$ is a local maximizer, and $f(0, \frac{7}{2}) = \frac{7}{2}$.

(iii) $(\frac{7}{2}, 0, 0, 8, 2)$.

Again, no SOC to check. So $(x, y) = (\frac{7}{2}, 0)$ is a local maximizer; $f(\frac{7}{2}, 0) = 7$.

The feasible set is compact so best local maximizer is the global maximizer. Comparing $(x, y) = (\frac{7}{2}, 0)$ is global max.

6.9 Max $x - y$ s.t. $3x^2 + 2y^2 = 1$.

$$L = x - y - \mu(3x^2 + 2y^2 - 1).$$

FOC:
$$\frac{\partial L}{\partial x} = 1 - 6\mu x = 0,$$

$$\frac{\partial L}{\partial y} = -1 - 4\mu y = 0,$$

$$\frac{\partial L}{\partial \mu} = 1 - 3x^2 - 2y^2 = 0.$$

Potential solutions are

$$(x, y, \mu) = \begin{cases} \left(\dfrac{1}{6}\sqrt{\dfrac{24}{5}}, \ -\dfrac{1}{4}\sqrt{\dfrac{24}{5}}, \ \sqrt{\dfrac{5}{24}} \right), \\[3mm] \left(-\dfrac{1}{6}\sqrt{\dfrac{24}{5}}, \ \dfrac{1}{4}\sqrt{\dfrac{24}{5}}, \ -\sqrt{\dfrac{5}{24}} \right). \end{cases}$$

Checking sufficiency, the SOC matrix is

$$D = \begin{bmatrix} -6\mu & 0 & -6x \\ 0 & -4\mu & -4y \\ -6x & -4y & 0 \end{bmatrix}.$$

Here, $n = 2$, $s = 1 \Rightarrow n - s = 1 \Rightarrow$ check D_1. $D_1 = -6\mu(-16y^2)$
$- 6x(-24\mu x) = 48\mu(2y^2 + 3x^2) \Rightarrow (-1)^2 D_1 > 0$ for

$$(x, y, \mu) = \left(\frac{1}{6}\sqrt{\frac{24}{5}}, -\frac{1}{4}\sqrt{\frac{24}{5}}, \sqrt{\frac{5}{24}} \right)$$

and < 0 for other potential solution $\Rightarrow$

$$\left(\frac{1}{6}\sqrt{\frac{24}{5}}, -\frac{1}{4}\sqrt{\frac{24}{5}}, \sqrt{\frac{5}{24}} \right)$$

is a local maximizer; it is also a global maximizer because the feasible set is bounded.

6.10 Max$(x + 1)^2 + (y - 1)^2$ s.t. $x \geq 0$, $y \geq 0$ and $2x + y \leq 4$.

$$L = (x + 1)^2 - (y - 1)^2 + \lambda_1 x + \lambda_2 y - \lambda_3(2x + y - 4).$$

FOC: $\dfrac{\partial L}{\partial x} = 2(x + 1) + \lambda_1 - 2\lambda_3 = 0,$ \hfill (1)

$$\frac{\partial L}{\partial y} = 2(y - 1) + \lambda_2 - \lambda_3 = 0, \tag{2}$$

$$\frac{\partial L}{\partial \lambda_1} = x \geq 0, \qquad\qquad \lambda_1 \geq 0, \lambda_1 x = 0, \tag{3}$$

$$\frac{\partial L}{\partial \lambda_2} = y \geq 0, \qquad\qquad \lambda_2 \geq 0, \lambda_2 y = 0, \tag{4}$$

$$\frac{\partial L}{\partial \lambda_3} = 4 - 2x - y \geq 0, \quad \lambda_3 \geq 0, \lambda_3(4 - 2x - y) = 0. \tag{5}$$

There are $2^3 = 8$ cases to consider; we find three potential solutions:
(i) $(x, y, \lambda_1, \lambda_2, \lambda_3) = (2, 0, 0, 5, 3)$.
   SOC: $n = 2 = s \Rightarrow$ no SOC to check $\Rightarrow$ this is local maximizer.
(ii) $(x, y, \lambda_1, \lambda_2, \lambda_3) = (0, 4, 10, 0, 6)$.
   SOC: Again no SOC to check and $(x, y) = (0, 4)$ is local maximizer.
(iii) $(x, y, \lambda_1, \lambda_2, \lambda_3) = (1, 2, 0, 0, 2)$.
   SOC: $n = 2$, $s = 1 \Rightarrow$ check D_1:

$$D_1 = \begin{vmatrix} 2 & 0 & -2 \\ 0 & 2 & -1 \\ -2 & -1 & 0 \end{vmatrix} = -10 < 0.$$

So, $(-1)^2 D_1 = -10 < 0 \Rightarrow$ SOC fails $\Rightarrow$ not local maximizer.
Here the feasible set is bounded and "∞" cannot dominate; thus,

there are two global maxima; i.e., $(2,0)$ and $(0,4)$ are both global maximizers, and $f(2,0) = f(0,4) = 10$.

6.11 Min $x + y$ s.t. $x \geq 0$, $y \geq 0$ and $(x + 1)(y + 1) \geq 2$.

$$L = -x - y + \lambda_1 x + \lambda_2 y - \lambda_3 [2 - (x + 1)(y + 1)].$$

FOC:

$$\frac{\partial L}{\partial x} = -1 + \lambda_1 + \lambda_3(y + 1) = 0,$$

$$\frac{\partial L}{\partial y} = -1 + \lambda_2 + \lambda_3(x + 1) = 0,$$

$$\frac{\partial L}{\partial \lambda_1} = x \geq 0, \qquad \lambda_1 \geq 0, \lambda_1 x = 0,$$

$$\frac{\partial L}{\partial \lambda_2} = y \geq 0, \qquad \lambda_2 \geq 0, \lambda_2 y = 0,$$

$$\frac{\partial L}{\partial \lambda_3} = (x + 1)(y + 1) - 2 \geq 0,$$

$$\lambda_3 \geq 0, \lambda_3[(x + 1)(y + 1) - 2] = 0.$$

There are $2^3 = 8$ cases to consider; we find only one potential solution:

$$(x, y, \lambda_1, \lambda_2, \lambda_3) = (\sqrt{2} - 1, \sqrt{2} - 1, 0, 0, 1/\sqrt{2}).$$

SOC: $n = 2$, $s = 1 \Rightarrow 1$ determinant to check. The appropriate Lagrangian is

$$L^* = -x - y - \lambda_3[2 - (x + 1)(y + 1)].$$

So SOC matrix is

$$D = \begin{bmatrix} 0 & \lambda_3 & y + 1 \\ \lambda_3 & 0 & x + 1 \\ y + 1 & x + 1 & 0 \end{bmatrix}.$$

$D_1 = 2\lambda_3(x + 1)(y + 1) = 2\sqrt{2}$ at the potential solution $\Rightarrow (-1)^2 D_1 > 0 \Rightarrow$ SOC holds, and $(\sqrt{2} - 1, \sqrt{2} - 1, 0, 0, 1/\sqrt{2})$ is a local minimizer. $(x, y) = (\sqrt{2} - 1, \sqrt{2} - 1)$ is also the global minimizer because the objective function is convex and the feasible set is convex.

6.12 Min $4K + 2L$ s.t. $KL = 1$, $K \geq 0$.

$$M = -4K - 2L + \lambda_1 K - \mu(1 - KL).$$

FOC: $$\frac{\partial M}{\partial K} = -4 + \lambda_1 + \mu L = 0, \tag{1}$$

$$\frac{\partial M}{\partial L} = -2 + \mu K = 0, \tag{2}$$

$$\frac{\partial M}{\partial \lambda_1} = K \geq 0, \qquad \lambda_1 \geq 0, \lambda_1 K = 0, \tag{3}$$

$$\frac{\partial M}{\partial \mu} = KL - 1 = 0. \tag{4}$$

Case 1. $\lambda_1 > 0$. $K = 0 \Rightarrow$ (4) fails $\Rightarrow$ no solution.
Case 2. $\lambda_1 = 0$. Get $(K, L, \lambda_1, \mu) = (1/\sqrt{2}, \sqrt{2}, 0, 2\sqrt{2})$ as a potential solution.

SOC: $n = 2$, $s = 1 \Rightarrow 1$ determinate to check. The matrix of second partials is

$$D = \begin{bmatrix} 0 & \mu & L \\ \mu & 0 & K \\ L & K & 0 \end{bmatrix}.$$

$D_1 = 2\mu KL = 4\sqrt{2}$ at the potential solution $\Rightarrow (-1)^2 D_1 > 0 \Rightarrow$ SOC holds. Since the objective function is quasiconvex and the feasible set is the boundary of the convex set $\{(K, L)|KL \geq 1, K \geq 0\}$, $(K, L) = (1/\sqrt{2}, \sqrt{2})$ is also global minimizer.

6.13 $\text{Min}(x + 1)^2 + (y - 1)^2$ s.t. $x \geq 0$ $y \geq 0$ and $2x + y \leq 4$.

$$L = -(x + 1)^2 - (y - 1)^2 + \lambda_1 x + \lambda_2 y - \lambda_3[2x + y - 4].$$

FOC: $$\frac{\partial L}{\partial x} = -2(x + 1) + \lambda_1 - 2\lambda_3 = 0,$$

$$\frac{\partial L}{\partial y} = -2(y - 1) + \lambda_2 - \lambda_3 = 0,$$

$$\frac{\partial L}{\partial \lambda_1} = x \geq 0, \qquad\qquad \lambda_1 \geq 0, \lambda_1 x = 0,$$

$$\frac{\partial L}{\partial \lambda_2} = y \geq 0, \qquad\qquad \lambda_2 \geq 0, \lambda_2 y = 0,$$

$$\frac{\partial L}{\partial \lambda_3} = 4 - 2x - y \geq 0, \qquad \lambda_3 \geq 0, \lambda_3(4 - 2x - y) = 0.$$

Only one potential solution: $(x, y, \lambda_1, \lambda_2, \lambda_3) = (0, 1, 2, 0, 0)$.
SOC: $n = 2$, $s = 1 \Rightarrow 1$ determinant to check

$$D = \begin{bmatrix} -2 & 0 & 1 \\ 0 & -2 & 0 \\ 1 & 0 & 0 \end{bmatrix}.$$

$D_1 = 2$ at the potential solution $\Rightarrow (-1)^2 D_1 = 2 > 0 \Rightarrow$ SOC holds, and $(x, y) = (0, 1)$ is local minimizer. Since objective function is strictly convex (Hessian is positive definite) and the feasible set is convex, $(0, 1)$ is unique global minimizer.

6.14 Min $2x + y$ s.t. $x \geq 0$, $y \geq 0$, and $(x + 1)(y + 1) \geq 2$.

$$L = -2x - y + \lambda_1 x + \lambda_2 y - \lambda_3 [2 - (x + 1)(y + 1)]$$

FOC:
$$\frac{\partial L}{\partial x} = -2 + \lambda_1 + \lambda_3 (y + 1) = 0,$$

$$\frac{\partial L}{\partial y} = -1 + \lambda_2 + \lambda_3 (x + 1) = 0,$$

$$\frac{\partial L}{\partial \lambda_1} = x \geq 0, \qquad \lambda_1 \geq 0, \lambda_1 x = 0,$$

$$\frac{\partial L}{\partial \lambda_2} = y \geq 0, \qquad \lambda_2 \geq 0, \lambda_2 y = 0,$$

$$\frac{\partial L}{\partial \lambda_3} = (x + 1)(y + 1) - 2 \geq 0,$$

$$\lambda_3 \geq 0, \lambda_3 [(x + 1)(y + 1) - 2] = 0.$$

There are $2^3 = 8$ cases to check; there is only one potential solution: $(x, y, \lambda_1, \lambda_2, \lambda_3) = (0, 1, 0, 0, 1)$.
SOC: There are two active constraints, $x = 0$ and $(x + 1)(y + 1) = 2$, at $(x, y) = (0, 1)$, so $n = 2 = s$. However, note that strict complementary slackness does not hold because $\lambda_1 = 0$ and $\partial L / \partial \lambda_1 = 0$. So $n = s$ does not guarantee $(x, y) = (0, 1)$ is a minimizer. Checking SOC using only the third constraint, $L^* = -2x - y - \lambda_3 [2 - (x + 1)(y + 1)]$ and $n = 2$, $s = 1$, so there is one determinant to check:

$$D_1 = \begin{vmatrix} 0 & 1 & 2 \\ 1 & 0 & 1 \\ 2 & 1 & 0 \end{vmatrix}$$

and $(-1)^{1+1} D_1 = 4 > 0$. Since SOC holds both ways, $(0, 1)$ is a minimizer. The objective function is convex, and the feasible set is convex, so $(0, 1)$ is a global minimizer.

6.15 Min $x^2 + y^2$ s.t. $x + 2y = 3$.

$$L = -x^2 - y^2 - \mu(3 - x - 2y).$$

FOC:
$$\frac{\partial L}{\partial x} = -2x + \mu = 0,$$

$$\frac{\partial L}{\partial y} = -2y + 2\mu = 0,$$

$$\frac{\partial L}{\partial \mu} = x + 2y - 3 = 0.$$

Solve to get $(x, y, \mu) = (\frac{3}{5}, \frac{6}{5}, \frac{6}{5})$.

SOC: $n = 2$, $s = 1$, $n - s = 1 \Rightarrow 1$ determinant to check

$$D_1 = \begin{vmatrix} -2 & 0 & 1 \\ 0 & -2 & 2 \\ 1 & 2 & 0 \end{vmatrix}.$$

$D_1 = 8 + 2 = 10$ and $(-1)^{1+1}D_1 = 10 > 0 \Rightarrow$ SOC holds, and $(x, y) = (\frac{3}{5}, \frac{6}{5})$ is a local minimizer.

Global: The Hessian of the original function is

$$H = \begin{bmatrix} 2 & 0 \\ 0 & 2 \end{bmatrix} = \begin{bmatrix} f_{11} & f_{12} \\ f_{21} & f_{22} \end{bmatrix}.$$

$|f_{11}| = 2 > 0$, $|H| = 4 > 0 \Rightarrow H$ is positive definite $\Rightarrow f(x, y) = x^2 + y^2$ is strictly convex. Furthermore, the feasible set is convex, so $(\frac{3}{5}, \frac{6}{5})$ is also unique global minimizer.

6.16 Max xy s.t. $x \geq 0$, $y \geq 0$ and $2x + y \leq 4$.

$$L = xy + \lambda_1 x + \lambda_2 y - \lambda_3(2x + y - 4).$$

FOC: $\dfrac{\partial L}{\partial x} = y + \lambda_1 - 2\lambda_3 = 0,$

$\dfrac{\partial L}{\partial y} = x + \lambda_2 - \lambda_3 = 0,$

$\dfrac{\partial L}{\partial \lambda_1} = x \geq 0,$ $\qquad \lambda_1 \geq 0, \lambda_1 x = 0,$

$\dfrac{\partial L}{\partial \lambda_2} = y \geq 0,$ $\qquad \lambda_2 \geq 0, \lambda_2 y = 0,$

$\dfrac{\partial L}{\partial \lambda_3} = 4 - 2x - y \geq 0,$ $\qquad \lambda_3 \geq 0, \lambda_3(4 - 2x - y) = 0.$

There are eight possible cases. There are two potential solutions: $(0, 0, 0, 0, 0)$ fails strict complementary slackness but it is obviously not a maximizer; $(1, 2, 0, 0, 1)$ satisfies strict complementary slackness. SOC: The matrix of second partials at the potential solution is

$$\begin{bmatrix} 0 & 1 & -2 \\ 1 & 0 & -1 \\ -2 & -1 & 0 \end{bmatrix}.$$

At $(1, 2, 0, 0, 1)$ $n = 2$ and $s = 1$ so there is one determinant to check. $(-1)^{1+1} D_1 = 4 > 0$ so $(x, y) = (1, 2)$ is a strict local maximizer. The feasible set is compact so it is also a global maximizer.

6.17 Min $3x + y$ s.t. $x \geq 0$, $y \geq 0$ and $(x + 1)(y + 1) = 2$.

$$L = -(3x + y) - \lambda_1(-x) - \lambda_2(-y) + \lambda_3['(x + 1)(y + 1) - 2].$$

FOC:
$$\frac{\partial L}{\partial x} = -3 + \lambda_1 + \lambda_3(1 + y) = 0, \tag{1}$$

$$\frac{\partial L}{\partial y} = -1 + \lambda_2 + \lambda_3(1 + x) = 0, \tag{2}$$

$$\frac{\partial L}{\partial \lambda_1} = x \geq 0, \qquad \lambda_1 \geq 0, \lambda_1 x = 0, \tag{3}$$

$$\frac{\partial L}{\partial \lambda_2} = y \geq 0, \qquad \lambda_2 \geq 0, \lambda_2 y = 0, \tag{4}$$

$$\frac{\partial L}{\partial \lambda_3} = [(x + 1)(y + 1) - 2] = 0. \tag{5}$$

There are four cases in this problem.

Case 1. $\lambda_1 = \lambda_2 = 0$. From (1) and (2), $(x + 1) = 1/\lambda_3$, and $(y + 1) = 3/\lambda_3$. Plug into (5) to get $3/\lambda_3^2 = 2 \Rightarrow \lambda_3 = \sqrt{\frac{3}{2}} \Rightarrow x = \sqrt{\frac{2}{3}} - 1 < 0$, which violates (3). No solution in this case.

Case 2. $\lambda_1 > 0$, $\lambda_2 > 0$. $x = y = 0$ violates (5). No solution.

Case 3. $\lambda_1 = 0$, $\lambda_2 > 0$. Immediate that $y = 0$. From (5), $x = 1$; from (1), $\lambda_3 = 3$; from (2), $\lambda_2 = -5$, which is a contradiction. No solution.

Case 4. $\lambda_1 > 0$, $\lambda_2 = 0$. Immediate that $x = 0$. From (5), $y = 1$; from (2), $\lambda_3 = 1$; from (1), $\lambda_1 = 1$, so the potential solution is $(x, y, \lambda_1, \lambda_2, \lambda_3) = (0, 1, 1, 0, 1)$.

SOC: Since $n = s = 2$, it is local maximizer $\Rightarrow$ local minimizer for the original problem. Since the feasible set is bounded (not convex), $(0, 1)$ is a global minimizer for the original problem.

6.18 $\text{Min}(x - 1)^2 + (y - 1)^2 + (z - 2)^2$ s.t. $x + y + z = 2$.

$$L = -(x - 1)^2 - (y - 1)^2 - (z - 2)^2 - \mu(2 - x - y - z)$$

FOC:
$$\frac{\partial L}{\partial x} = -2(x - 1) + \mu = 0, \tag{1}$$

$$\frac{\partial L}{\partial y} = -2(y - 1) + \mu = 0, \tag{2}$$

$$\frac{\partial L}{\partial z} = -2(z - 2) + \mu = 0, \tag{3}$$

$$\frac{\partial L}{\partial \mu} = -(2 - x - y - z) = 0. \tag{4}$$

From (1)–(3), we get $x = 1 + \mu/2$, $y = 1 + \mu/2$, $z = 2 + \mu/2$. Plug them into (4) and solve for $\mu = -\frac{4}{3}$. The potential solution is $(x, y, z, \mu) = (\frac{1}{3}, \frac{1}{3}, \frac{4}{3}, -\frac{4}{3})$.

SOC: The matrix of second partials is

$$\begin{bmatrix} -2 & 0 & 0 & 1 \\ 0 & -2 & 0 & 1 \\ 0 & 0 & -2 & 1 \\ 1 & 1 & 1 & 0 \end{bmatrix}.$$

Here, $n = 3$, $s = 1$, $n - s = 2$, so we need to check D_1 and D_2:

$$D_1 = \begin{vmatrix} -2 & 0 & 1 \\ 0 & -2 & 1 \\ 1 & 1 & 0 \end{vmatrix} = 4,$$

$$D_2 = (-2)\begin{vmatrix} -2 & 0 & 1 \\ 0 & -2 & 1 \\ 1 & 1 & 0 \end{vmatrix} + (-1)\begin{vmatrix} 0 & -2 & 0 \\ 0 & 0 & -2 \\ 1 & 1 & 1 \end{vmatrix}$$

$$= -8 - 4 = -12.$$

$(-1)^{1+1}D_1 = 4 > 0$ and $(-1)^{2+1}D_2 = 12 > 0 \Rightarrow$ SOC holds, and $(\frac{1}{3}, \frac{1}{3}, \frac{4}{3})$ is a local maximizer (a local minimizer for original problem). The solution is global since the objective function is concave (convex for the original function) and the feasible set is convex.

6.19 Max$(3 - x)(5 - y)$ s.t. $x \geq 0$, $y \geq 0$ and $2x + y \leq 4$.

$$L = (3 - x)(5 - y) - \lambda_1(-x) - \lambda_2(-y) - \lambda_3(2x + y - 4)$$

FOC: $\dfrac{\partial L}{\partial x} = -5 + y + \lambda_1 - 2\lambda_3 = 0,$

$\dfrac{\partial L}{\partial y} = x - 3 + \lambda_2 - \lambda_3 = 0,$

$\dfrac{\partial L}{\partial \lambda_1} = x \geq 0, \qquad \lambda_1 \geq 0, \lambda_1 x = 0,$

$\dfrac{\partial L}{\partial \lambda_2} = y \geq 0, \qquad \lambda_2 \geq 0, \lambda_2 y = 0,$

$\dfrac{\partial L}{\partial \lambda_3} = -(2x + y - 4) \geq 0, \quad \lambda_3 \geq 0, -\lambda_3(2x + y - 4) = 0.$

The only potential solution is $(x, y, \lambda_1, \lambda_2, \lambda_3) = (0, 0, 5, 3, 0)$. Here, $n = 2$, $s = 2$ so no SOC to check; the potential solution is a local maximizer. To check for global solution, note the objective function is quasiconcave over the feasible set:

$$B = \begin{bmatrix} 0 & -(5 - y) & -(3 - x) \\ -(5 - y) & 0 & 1 \\ -(3 - x) & 1 & 0 \end{bmatrix}.$$

$(-1)^{2+1}\{-(5 - y)^2\} = (5 - y)^2 > 0$ because $y \leq 4$.

$(-1)^{3+1}\{(5 - y)(3 - x) + (3 - x)(5 - y)\} > 0$

since $y \leq 4$ and $x \leq 2$.

The feasible set is convex, so $(0, 0)$ is a global maximizer.

6.20 $\text{Min}(x - 2)^2 + (y - 2)^2 + (z - 2)^2$ s.t. $x + y + z = 2$, $x \geq 0$, $y \geq 0$ and $z \geq 0$.

$$L = -(x - 2)^2 - (y - 2)^2 - (z - 2)^2$$
$$+ \lambda_1 x + \lambda_2 y + \lambda_3 z + \mu[x + y + z - 2].$$

FOC:
$$\frac{\partial L}{\partial x} = -2(x - 2) + \lambda_1 + \mu = 0, \tag{1}$$

$$\frac{\partial L}{\partial y} = -2(y - 2) + \lambda_2 + \mu = 0, \tag{2}$$

$$\frac{\partial L}{\partial z} = -2(z - 2) + \lambda_3 + \mu = 0, \tag{3}$$

$$\frac{\partial L}{\partial \lambda_1} = x \geq 0, \qquad \lambda_1 \geq 0, \lambda_1 x = 0, \tag{4}$$

$$\frac{\partial L}{\partial \lambda_2} = y \geq 0, \qquad \lambda_2 \geq 0, \lambda_2 y = 0, \tag{5}$$

$$\frac{\partial L}{\partial \lambda_3} = z \geq 0, \qquad \lambda_3 \geq 0, \lambda_3 z = 0, \tag{6}$$

$$\frac{\partial L}{\partial \mu} = x + y + z - 2 = 0. \tag{7}$$

There are eight cases:

Case 1. $\lambda_1 = \lambda_2 = 0$, $\lambda_3 > 0$. Then $z = 0$, (1)(2) $\Rightarrow x = y$, (7) $\Rightarrow x = y = 1 \Rightarrow \mu = -2$, (3) $\Rightarrow \lambda_3 = -2$, which contradicts (6).
By symmetry of x, y, z, we can eliminate the corresponding two cases:

$$\lambda_1 = \lambda_3 = 0, \lambda_2 > 0 \quad \text{and} \quad \lambda_2 = \lambda_3 = 0, \lambda_1 > 0.$$

Case 2. $\lambda_1 = 0$, $\lambda_2 > 0$, $\lambda_3 > 0$. (5)(6) $\Rightarrow y = z = 0$, $\Rightarrow x = 2$ from (7), $\Rightarrow \mu = 0$ from (1), $\Rightarrow \lambda_2 = -4$ from (2), which violates (5).
By symmetry of x, y, z, we can eliminate the corresponding two cases:

$$\lambda_1 > 0, \lambda_2 > 0, \lambda_3 = 0 \quad \text{and} \quad \lambda_1 > 0, \lambda_2 = 0, \lambda_3 > 0$$

Case 3. $\lambda_1 > 0$, $\lambda_2 > 0$, $\lambda_3 > 0$. $x = y = z = 0$, which violates (7).
Case 4. $\lambda_1 = \lambda_2 = \lambda_3 = 0$. (1)(2)(3) $\Rightarrow x = y = z$. Combined with (7) $\Rightarrow x = y = z = \frac{2}{3}$, (1) $\Rightarrow \mu = -\frac{8}{3}$. Thus the only potential solu-

tion is $(x, y, z, \lambda_1, \lambda_2, \lambda_3, \mu) = (\frac{2}{3}, \frac{2}{3}, \frac{2}{3}, 0, 0, 0, -\frac{8}{3})$.

Checking sufficiency, the SOC matrix is

$$\begin{bmatrix} -2 & 0 & 0 & 1 \\ 0 & -2 & 0 & 1 \\ 0 & 0 & -2 & 1 \\ 1 & 1 & 1 & 0 \end{bmatrix}.$$

Here, $n = 3$, $s = 1$ so there are two determinants to check:

$$(-1)^{1+1} \begin{vmatrix} -2 & 0 & 1 \\ 0 & -2 & 1 \\ 1 & 1 & 0 \end{vmatrix} = 4 > 0,$$

$$(-1)^{1+2} \left\{ -2 \begin{vmatrix} -2 & 0 & 1 \\ 0 & -2 & 1 \\ 1 & 1 & 0 \end{vmatrix} - \begin{vmatrix} 0 & -2 & 0 \\ 0 & 0 & -2 \\ 1 & 1 & 1 \end{vmatrix} \right\}$$

$$= (-1)(-8 - 4) = 12 > 0.$$

Thus, the potential solution is a local maximizer. The original objective function is strictly convex, and the feasible set is convex, so $(\frac{2}{3}, \frac{2}{3}, \frac{2}{3})$ is the unique global minimizer.

6.21 Min $x^2 + (y - 5)^2$ s.t. $x \geq 0$, $y \geq 0$ and $2x + y \leq 4$.

$$L = -x^2 - (y - 5)^2 + \lambda_1 x + \lambda_2 y + \lambda_3 (4 - 2x - y).$$

FOC: $\dfrac{\partial L}{\partial x} = -2x + \lambda_1 - 2\lambda_3 = 0,$ (1)

$\dfrac{\partial L}{\partial y} = -2(y - 5) + \lambda_2 - \lambda_3 = 0,$ (2)

$\dfrac{\partial L}{\partial \lambda_1} = x \geq 0,$ $\lambda_1 \geq 0, \lambda_1 x = 0,$ (3)

$\dfrac{\partial L}{\partial \lambda_2} = y \geq 0,$ $\lambda_2 \geq 0, \lambda_2 y = 0,$ (4)

$\dfrac{\partial L}{\partial \lambda_3} = 4 - 2x - y \geq 0,$ $\lambda_3 \geq 0, \lambda_3(4 - 2x - y) = 0.$ (5)

There are eight cases to consider. The only potential solution is

$$(x, y, \lambda_1, \lambda_2, \lambda_3) = (0, 4, 4, 0, 2).$$

Since $n = s = 2$, there is no determinant to check. It is local minimizer for the original problem. Note the original objective function is strictly convex:

$$H = \begin{bmatrix} \dfrac{\partial^2 f}{\partial x^2} & \dfrac{\partial^2 f}{\partial x \partial y} \\[2mm] \dfrac{\partial^2 f}{\partial y 2x} & \dfrac{\partial^2 f}{\partial y^2} \end{bmatrix} = \begin{bmatrix} 2 & 0 \\ 0 & 2 \end{bmatrix}.$$

H is positive definite, so the original function is strictly convex. The feasible set is convex so $(0, 4)$ is the unique global minimizer.

6.22 Max $x - y + z$ s.t. $x \geq 0$, $y \geq 0$, $z \geq 0$, and $x^2 + y^2 + z^2 = 2$.

$$L = x - y + z + \lambda_1 x + \lambda_2 y + \lambda_3 z + \mu(x^2 + y^2 + z^2 - 2).$$

FOC:
$$\frac{\partial L}{\partial x} = 1 + \lambda_1 + 2\mu x = 0, \tag{1}$$

$$\frac{\partial L}{\partial y} = -1 + \lambda_2 + 2\mu y = 0, \tag{2}$$

$$\frac{\partial L}{\partial z} = 1 + \lambda_3 + 2\mu z = 0, \tag{3}$$

$$\frac{\partial L}{\partial \lambda_1} = x \geq 0, \qquad \lambda_1 \geq 0, \lambda_1 x = 0, \tag{4}$$

$$\frac{\partial L}{\partial \lambda_2} = y \geq 0, \qquad \lambda_2 \geq 0, \lambda_2 y = 0, \tag{5}$$

$$\frac{\partial L}{\partial \lambda_3} = z \geq 0, \qquad \lambda_3 \geq 0, \lambda_3 z = 0, \tag{6}$$

$$\frac{\partial L}{\partial \mu} = x^2 + y^2 + z^2 - 2 = 0. \tag{7}$$

There are eight cases to consider. The only potential solution is

$$(x, y, z, \lambda_1, \lambda_2, \lambda_3, \mu) = (1, 0, 1, 0, 1, 0, -\tfrac{1}{2}).$$

SOC: The matrix of second partials is

$$
\begin{bmatrix}
2\mu & 0 & 0 & 0 & 2x \\
0 & 2\mu & 0 & 1 & 2y \\
0 & 0 & 2\mu & 0 & 2z \\
0 & 1 & 0 & 0 & 0 \\
2x & 2y & 2z & 0 & 0
\end{bmatrix}
=
\begin{bmatrix}
-1 & 0 & 0 & 0 & 2 \\
0 & -1 & 0 & 1 & 0 \\
0 & 0 & -1 & 0 & 2 \\
0 & 1 & 0 & 0 & 0 \\
2 & 0 & 2 & 0 & 0
\end{bmatrix}
$$

at $(x, y, z, \lambda_2, \mu) = (1, 0, 1, 1, -\frac{1}{2})$. Here $n = 3$, $s = 2$, $n - s = 1$ so there is one determinant to check:

$$
D_1 =
\begin{vmatrix}
-1 & 0 & 0 & 0 & 2 \\
0 & -1 & 0 & 1 & 0 \\
0 & 0 & -1 & 0 & 2 \\
0 & 1 & 0 & 0 & 0 \\
2 & 0 & 2 & 0 & 0
\end{vmatrix}
= (-1)
\begin{vmatrix}
-1 & 0 & 1 & 0 \\
0 & -1 & 0 & 2 \\
1 & 0 & 0 & 0 \\
0 & 2 & 0 & 0
\end{vmatrix}
$$

$$
+ (2)
\begin{vmatrix}
0 & -1 & 0 & 1 \\
0 & 0 & -1 & 0 \\
0 & 1 & 0 & 0 \\
2 & 0 & 2 & 0
\end{vmatrix}
= 8.
$$

So $(-1)^{2+1}D_1 = 8 > 0$, and $(x, y, z) = (1, 0, 1)$ is a local maximizer. The feasible set is compact so it is also a global maximizer.

6.23 Max $x^2 + (y - 5)^2$ s.t. $x \geq 0$, $y \geq 0$, and $2x + y \leq 4$.

$$
L = x^2 + (y - 5)^2 + \lambda_1(x) + \lambda_2(y) + \lambda_3(4 - 2x - y).
$$

FOC: $\dfrac{\partial L}{\partial x} = 2x + \lambda_1 - 2\lambda_3 = 0$,

$$
\dfrac{\partial L}{\partial y} = 2(y - 5) + \lambda_2 - \lambda_3 = 0,
$$

$$
\dfrac{\partial L}{\partial \lambda_1} = x \geq 0, \qquad\qquad \lambda_1 \geq 0, \lambda_1 x = 0,
$$

$$
\dfrac{\partial L}{\partial \lambda_2} = y \geq 0, \qquad\qquad \lambda_2 \geq 0, \lambda_2 y = 0,
$$

$$
\dfrac{\partial L}{\partial \lambda_3} = -(2x + y - 4) \geq 0, \quad \lambda_3 \geq 0, -\lambda_3(2x + y - 4) = 0
$$

Potential solutions are $(x, y, \lambda_1, \lambda_2, \lambda_3) = (2, 0, 0, 12, 2)$ and $(0, 0, 0, 10, 0)$. The second potential solution violates strict complementary slackness. For $(2, 0, 0, 12, 2)$, $n = 2$, $s = 2 \Rightarrow n = s$, so there is no determinant to check. $(2,0)$ is local maximizer for $f(x, y) = x^2 + (y - 5)^2$; $f(2,0) = 4 + (-5)^2 = 29 > f(0,0) = 25$. The feasible set is compact so $(2,0)$ is also global maximizer.

6.24 Min y s.t. $x \geq 2$, $x^3/3 - x = y$. Note this is equivalent to Min $x^3/3 - x$ s.t. $x \geq 2$.

$$L = -\left(\frac{x^3}{3} - x\right) + \lambda(x - 2).$$

FOC:
$$\frac{\partial L}{\partial x} = 1 - x^2 + \lambda = 0, \tag{1}$$

$$\frac{\partial L}{\partial \lambda} = x - 2 \geq 0, \qquad \lambda \geq 0, \lambda(x - 2) = 0. \tag{2}$$

Case 1. $\lambda = 0$. From (1) $x^2 = 1$ so $x = \pm 1$, which violates (2).
Case 2. $\lambda > 0$. From (2), $x = 2$. From (1), $\lambda = 3$. Thus $(x, \lambda) = (2, 3)$ is a potential solution.

SOC: $n = s = 1$ so $(2, 3)$ is a local maximizer. The feasible set $(x \geq 2)$ is convex and the objective function $(x^3/3 - x)$ is strictly convex on the feasible set, so $x = 2$ is the unique global minimizer for the equivalent problem. For the original problem, $(x, y) = (2, 2/3)$ is the unique global minimizer.

6.25 Min $x^2 + 2y^2 + 3z^2$ s.t. $3x + 2y + z \geq 17$.

$$L = -(x^2 + 2y^2 + 3z^2) + \lambda(3x + 2y + z - 17).$$

FOC:
$$\frac{\partial L}{\partial x} = -2x + 3\lambda = 0, \tag{1}$$

$$\frac{\partial L}{\partial y} = -4y + 2\lambda = 0, \tag{2}$$

$$\frac{\partial L}{\partial z} = -6z + \lambda = 0, \tag{3}$$

$$\frac{\partial L}{\partial \lambda} = 3x + 2y + z - 17 \geq 0,$$

$$\lambda \geq 0, \lambda(3x + 2y + z - 17) = 0. \tag{4}$$

Case 1. $\lambda = 0$. From (1)–(3), $x = 0$, $y = 0$, $z = 0$, which violates (4).
Case 2. $\lambda > 0$. From (4), $3x + 2y + z - 17 = 0$. Solving (1), (2), (3), and this equation, $(x, y, z, \lambda) = (\frac{9}{2}, \frac{3}{2}, \frac{1}{2}, 3)$.

SOC: The matrix of second partials is

$$\begin{bmatrix} -2 & 0 & 0 & 3 \\ 0 & -4 & 0 & 2 \\ 0 & 0 & -6 & 1 \\ 3 & 2 & 1 & 0 \end{bmatrix}.$$

Here, $n = 3$, $s = 1$, so we need to check two determinants:

$$(-1)^2 D_1 = \begin{vmatrix} -4 & 0 & 2 \\ 0 & -6 & 1 \\ 2 & 1 & 0 \end{vmatrix} = 4 + 24 = 28 > 0,$$

$$(-1)^3 D_2 = - \begin{vmatrix} -2 & 0 & 0 & 3 \\ 0 & -4 & 0 & 2 \\ 0 & 0 & -6 & 1 \\ 3 & 2 & 1 & 0 \end{vmatrix} = 272 > 0,$$

so $(\frac{9}{2}, \frac{3}{2}, \frac{1}{2})$ is a strict local maximizer. The original objective function is strictly convex, and the feasible set is convex, so $(\frac{9}{2}, \frac{3}{2}, \frac{1}{2})$ is the unique global minimizer.

6.26 Min $x^2 + y^2$ s.t. $x + y \leq -2$ and $x \geq -3$.

$$L = -x^2 - y^2 - \lambda_1(x + y + 2) - \lambda_2(-3 - x).$$

FOC: $\dfrac{\partial L}{\partial x} = -2x - \lambda_1 + \lambda_2 = 0,$

$\dfrac{\partial L}{\partial y} = -2y - \lambda_1 = 0,$

$\dfrac{\partial L}{\partial \lambda_1} = -x - y - 2 \geq 0, \qquad \lambda_1 \geq 0, \lambda_1(-x - y - 2) = 0,$

$\dfrac{\partial L}{\partial \lambda_2} = 3 + x \geq 0, \qquad \lambda_2 \geq 0, \lambda_2(3 + x) = 0.$

There are four possible cases. There is one potential solution: $(-1, -1, 2, 0)$.

SOC: $n = 2$, $s = 1$ so there is one determinant to check. The matrix of second partials is

$$\begin{bmatrix} -2 & 0 & -1 \\ 0 & -2 & -1 \\ -1 & -1 & 0 \end{bmatrix}.$$

$(-1)^{1+1}D_1 = 4 > 0$ so strict local maximizer. The original objective function is strictly convex and the feasible set is convex, so $(-1, -1)$ is the unique global minimizer.

6.27 There is no SOC matrix to check here. Note that we have three active constraints $x = 0$, $z = 0$, and $2x + y + z = 1$ at $(x, y, z) = (0, 1, 0)$. Furthermore, strict complementary slackness holds (the multipliers λ_1, λ_3, and λ_4 associated with active constraints are nonzero). Hence the potential solution is a local maximizer.

6.28 $L = -x^2y + 2yz - \lambda_1(-x) - \lambda_2 y - \lambda_3(x + 2y - z + 2) - \mu(xyz - 6x - 2z)$.

FOC:

$$\frac{\partial L}{\partial x} = -2xy + \lambda_1 - \lambda_3 - \mu(yz - 6) = 0,$$

$$\frac{\partial L}{\partial y} = -x^2 + 2z - \lambda_2 - 2\lambda_3 - \mu xz = 0,$$

$$\frac{\partial L}{\partial z} = 2y + \lambda_3 - \mu(xy - 2) = 0,$$

$$\frac{\partial L}{\partial \lambda_1} = x \geq 0, \qquad \lambda_1 \geq 0, \lambda_1 x = 0,$$

$$\frac{\partial L}{\partial \lambda_2} = -y \geq 0, \quad \lambda_2 \geq 0, \lambda_2(-y) = 0,$$

$$\frac{\partial L}{\partial \lambda_3} = -x - 2y + z - 2 \geq 0, \qquad \lambda_3 \geq 0, \lambda_3(-x - 2y + z - 2) = 0,$$

$$\frac{\partial L}{\partial \mu} = -xyz + 6x + 2z = 0.$$

6.29 Here $n = 2$, $s = 1$, $n - s = 1 \Rightarrow$ one determinant to check. Note that at $(x, y) = (\frac{1}{2}, \frac{1}{2})$, $2y \leq 4x - 1$ holds as strict equality while the other constraints do not.

$$L = 2y - 4x^2 - \lambda_3(1 + 2y - 4x),$$

$$\frac{\partial L}{\partial x} = -8x + 4\lambda_3,$$

$$\frac{\partial L}{\partial y} = 2 - 2\lambda_3,$$

$$\frac{\partial L}{\partial \lambda_3} = 4x - 1 - 2y.$$

The SOC matrix is then the matrix of second partials of the Lagrangian with respect to x, y and λ_3.

$$
D = \begin{bmatrix}
\dfrac{\partial^2 L}{\partial x^2} & \dfrac{\partial^2 L}{\partial y\, \partial x} & \dfrac{\partial^2 L}{\partial \lambda_3\, \partial x} \\[2ex]
\dfrac{\partial^2 L}{\partial x\, \partial y} & \dfrac{\partial^2 L}{\partial y^2} & \dfrac{\partial^2 L}{\partial \lambda_3\, \partial y} \\[2ex]
\dfrac{\partial^2 L}{\partial x\, \partial \lambda_3} & \dfrac{\partial^2 L}{\partial y\, \partial \lambda_3} & \dfrac{\partial^2 L}{\partial \lambda_3^2}
\end{bmatrix}
= \begin{bmatrix}
-8 & 0 & 4 \\
0 & 0 & -2 \\
4 & -2 & 0
\end{bmatrix}
$$

is the required SOC matrix.

6.30 $L(x, y, \lambda_1, \lambda_2, \mu) = -x^2 - (y - 5)^2 - \lambda_1(-x) - \lambda_2(2x + y - 4) - \mu(y - 3.5 + x^2)$

FOC: $L_x = -2x + \lambda_1 - 2\lambda_2 - 2\mu x = 0$

$L_y = -2(y - 5) - \lambda_2 - \mu = 0$

$L_{\lambda_1} = x \geq 0, \qquad\qquad\qquad \lambda_1 \geq 0, \lambda_1 x = 0$

$L_{\lambda_2} = -2x - y + 4 \geq 0, \qquad \lambda_2 \geq 0, \lambda_2(-2x - y + 4) = 0$

$L_\mu = -y + 3.5 - x^2 = 0$

6.31 **Case 1.** $\lambda_1 = \lambda_2 = 0$. Then $y = 0$ by second equation, contrary to $-2 + y \geq 0$. No potential solution.

Case 2. $\lambda_1 > 0$, $\lambda_2 = 0$ (same as case 1) so no potential solution.

Case 3. $\lambda_1 = 0$, $\lambda_2 > 0$. Then $x = 1$ by first equation, contrary to $-3 + x \geq 0$. No potential solution.

Case 4. $\lambda_1 > 0$, $\lambda_2 > 0$ By third line $\lambda_1(-3 + x) = 0$, so $x = 3$. By fourth line $\lambda_2(-2 + y) = 0$, so $y = 2$. By first line $-2(3) + 2 + \lambda_1 = 0$, so $\lambda_1 = 4$. By second line $-2(2) + \lambda_2 = 0$, so $\lambda_2 = 4$. All equations and inequalities hold. The unique potential solution is $(x^*, y^*, \lambda_1^*, \lambda_2^*) = (3, 2, 4, 4)$.

6.32 The binding constraints are $y \geq 0$ and $x^2 + y^2 + z^2 - 2 = 0$.

$$L^*(x, y, z, \lambda_2, \mu) = x - y + z - \lambda_2(-y) - \mu(x^2 + y^2 + z^2 - 2).$$

$$L_x = 1 - 2\mu x,$$

$$L_y = -1 + \lambda_2 - 2\mu y,$$

$$L_z = 1 - 2\mu z,$$

$$L_{\lambda_2} = y,$$

$$L_\mu = -x^2 - y^2 - z^2 + 2,$$

$$[L_{ij}] = \begin{bmatrix} -2\mu & 0 & 0 & 0 & -2x \\ 0 & -2\mu & 0 & 1 & -2y \\ 0 & 0 & -2\mu & 0 & -2z \\ 0 & 1 & 0 & 0 & 0 \\ -2x & -2y & -2z & 0 & 0 \end{bmatrix}.$$

At the potential solution the matrix is

$$\begin{bmatrix} -1 & 0 & 0 & 0 & -2 \\ 0 & -1 & 0 & 1 & 0 \\ 0 & 0 & -1 & 0 & -2 \\ 0 & 1 & 0 & 0 & 0 \\ -2 & 0 & -2 & 0 & 0 \end{bmatrix}$$

6.33 In the answers below, the word "maximizer*" means the maximizer of the objective f^* (which may be $f^* = -f$).
   (a) $n = 1$, $s = 0$. No constraint is binding, $f'(-2) = 0$, and $f''(x) = -6 < 0$ for all x. Thus -2 is the unique global maximizer*.
   (b) $n = 2$, $s = 2$. $(1, -1)$ is a strict local maximizer* subject to the constraints since $n - s = 0$.
   (c) $n = 2$, $s = 1$.

$$(-1)^{1+1} \text{Det} \begin{bmatrix} 0 & 0 & 1 \\ 0 & 2 & 0 \\ 1 & 0 & 0 \end{bmatrix} = -2 < 0.$$

Thus the second-order condition fails, and $(0, 1)$ is not a local maximizer* of f^* subject to the constraints.
   (d) $n = 3$, $s = 1$. We must check the 3×3 and 4×4 determinants at $x_1 = -4$:

$$(-1)^{1+1} \text{Det} \begin{bmatrix} -1 & 0 & 1 \\ 0 & -4 & 0 \\ 1 & 0 & 0 \end{bmatrix} = 4 > 0 \quad \text{so } 3 \times 3 \text{ is OK.}$$

$$(-1)^{1+2} \text{Det} \begin{bmatrix} 1 & 0 & 0 & -1 \\ 0 & -1 & 0 & 1 \\ 0 & 0 & -4 & 0 \\ -1 & 1 & 0 & 0 \end{bmatrix} = 0.$$

So, we cannot tell; it might be an optimizer, but it might not.
   (e) $n = 2$, $s = 0$. Must check the 1×1 and 2×2 at $x_1 = 4$ and $x_2 = -7$.

$$(-1)^{0+1} \text{Det}[-7] = 7 > 0 \quad \text{so } 1 \times 1 \text{ is OK.}$$

$$(-1)^{0+2} \text{Det} \begin{bmatrix} -3 & 4 \\ 4 & -7 \end{bmatrix} = 5 > 0 \quad \text{so } 2 \times 2 \text{ is OK.}$$

Thus $(4, -7)$ is a strict local maximizer*.

6.34 $L(x, y, z, \lambda_1, \lambda_2, \mu) = -xy + zy^2 - \lambda_1(-x) - \lambda_2(y + z) - \mu(x^2 + y^2 + z^2 - 1)$.

FOC: $L_x = -y + \lambda_1 - 2\mu x = 0$,

$$L_y = -x + 2zy - \lambda_2 - 2\mu y = 0,$$

$$L_z = y^2 - \lambda_2 - 2\mu z = 0,$$

$$L_{\lambda_1} = x \geq 0, \qquad\qquad \lambda_1 \geq 0, \lambda_1 x = 0,$$

$$L_{\lambda_2} = -y - z \geq 0, \qquad \lambda_2 \geq 0, \lambda_2(-y - z) = 0,$$

$$L_\mu = -x^2 - y^2 - z^2 + 1 = 0.$$

6.35 The only binding constraint is $x + y + z - 2 = 0$.

$$L^* = -(x - 2)^2 - (y - 2)^2 - (z - 2)^2 - \mu(x + y + z - 2).$$

$$L_x = -2(x - 2) - \mu,$$

$$L_y = -2(y - 2) - \mu,$$

$$L_z = -2(z - 2) - \mu,$$

$$L_\mu = -x - y - z + 2,$$

$$[L_{ij}] = \begin{bmatrix} -2 & 0 & 0 & -1 \\ 0 & -2 & 0 & -1 \\ 0 & 0 & -2 & -1 \\ -1 & -1 & -1 & 0 \end{bmatrix}.$$

6.36 (a) $n = 3$, $s = 1$, $n - s = 2$.

$$(-1)^{1+1} \det \begin{bmatrix} 2 & 0 & 1 \\ 0 & 0 & 0 \\ 1 & 0 & 0 \end{bmatrix} = 0$$

$(-1)^{1+2} \det[4 \times 4] = -1 < 0$, so not a maximizer.

(b) $n = 2$, $s = 1$, $n - s = 1$.

$$(-1)^{1+1} \det \begin{bmatrix} 0 & 0 & 1 \\ 0 & -3 & 0 \\ 1 & 0 & 0 \end{bmatrix} = 3 > 0.$$

Strict local maximizer.

(c) $n = 2$, $s = 2$, $n - s = 0$. Strict local maximizer.

A.8 SOLUTIONS FOR CHAPTER 7

7.1 Max xy s.t. $-(x + y + 1) \leq 0$ and $x + y - 2 \leq 0$.
(a) $L = xy + \lambda_1(x + y + 1) - \lambda_2(x + y - 2)$

FOC: $L_x = y + \lambda_1 - \lambda_2 = 0,$ (1)

        $L_y = x + \lambda_1 - \lambda_2 = 0,$ (2)

        $L_{\lambda_1} = x + y + 1 \geq 0,$ $\lambda_1 \geq 0, \lambda_1(x + y + 1) = 0,$ (3)

        $L_{\lambda_2} = 2 - x - y \geq 0,$ $\lambda_2 \geq 0, \lambda_2(2 - x - y) = 0.$ (4)

Case 1. $\lambda_1 = 0 = \lambda_2$. From (1) and (2), $x = 0 = y$. But $(0, 0, 0, 0)$ violates SOC because

$$D_2 = \begin{vmatrix} 0 & 1 \\ 1 & 0 \end{vmatrix} = -1 \Rightarrow (-1)^2 D_2 < 0.$$

Case 2. $\lambda_1 = 0, \lambda_2 > 0$. From (4), $x + y = 2$ while (1) and (2) $\Rightarrow$ $x = \lambda_2 = y = 1$. Thus $(x, y, \lambda_1, \lambda_2) = (1, 1, 0, 1)$ is a potential solution.

SOC: $n = 2$, $x = 1 \Rightarrow$ one determinant to check

$$D_1 = \begin{bmatrix} 0 & 1 & -1 \\ 1 & 0 & -1 \\ -1 & -1 & 0 \end{bmatrix} \Rightarrow (-1)^{1+1} D_1 = 2 > 0 \Rightarrow \text{SOC holds.}$$

So $(1, 1, 0, 1)$ is local maximizer.

Case 3. $\lambda_1 > 0, \lambda_2 = 0$. From (3), $x + y = -1$. From (1) and (2) $x = -\lambda_1 = y$. Hence $\lambda_1 = \frac{1}{2}$, $x = -\frac{1}{2} = y$. So $(-\frac{1}{2}, -\frac{1}{2}, \frac{1}{2}, 0)$ is a potential solution.

SOC: $n = 2$, $s = 1 \Rightarrow$ one determinant to check.

$$D_1 = \begin{bmatrix} 0 & 1 & 1 \\ 1 & 0 & 1 \\ 1 & 1 & 0 \end{bmatrix} \Rightarrow (-1)^2 D_1 = 2 > 0 \Rightarrow \text{SOC holds.}$$

Thus, $(-\frac{1}{2}, -\frac{1}{2})$ is a local maximizer.
Case 4. $\lambda_1, \lambda_2 > 0$. (3) and (4) $\Rightarrow x + y = 2$ and $x + y = -1$. Rewriting the first equation as $y = 2 - x$ and substituting into the second, we get $x + (2 - x) = -1$ or $2 = -1$, which is not consistent. Hence no solution for this case.
Global: Draw the graph of the feasible set. Note that the points in the feasible set in second and fourth quadrants are ruled out because they give $xy \leq 0$. Comparing $f(-\frac{1}{2}, -\frac{1}{2}) = \frac{1}{4}$ with

$f(1, 1) = 1$, one concludes that $(1, 1)$ is the unique, global maximizer.

(b) Noting that $-1 \leq x + y$ is inactive when $p = 1$, formulate the Lagrangian as

$$L^*(x, y, \lambda_2; p) = xy - \lambda_2(x + py - 2).$$

FOC:
$$F^1(x, y, \lambda_2; p) = y - \lambda_2 = 0, \quad (5)$$

$$F^2(x, y, \lambda_2; p) = x - \lambda_2 p = 0, \quad (6)$$

$$F^3(x, y, \lambda_2; p) = 2 - x - py = 0. \quad (7)$$

Check IFT:

(i) $F^1(1, 1, 1, 1) = F^2(1, 1, 1, 1) = F^3(1, 1, 1, 1) = 0$.

(ii) F^i are continuously differentiable $\forall i = 1, 2, 3$.

(iii)
$$|J| = \begin{vmatrix} 0 & 1 & -1 \\ 1 & 0 & -1 \\ -1 & -1 & 0 \end{vmatrix} = 2 \neq 0.$$

Hence IFT holds, and comparative statics valid. Totally differentiate (5)–(7) to get

$$dy^* - d\lambda_2^* = 0,$$

$$dx^* - pd\lambda_2^* - \lambda_2^* dp = 0,$$

$$- dx^* - pdy^* - y^* dp = 0 \quad \text{or}$$

$$\begin{bmatrix} 0 & 1 & -1 \\ 1 & 0 & -1 \\ -1 & -1 & 0 \end{bmatrix} \begin{bmatrix} dx^* \\ dy^* \\ d\lambda_2^* \end{bmatrix} = \begin{bmatrix} 0 \\ dp \\ dp \end{bmatrix} \quad \text{at } (1, 1, 1, 1).$$

By Cramer's rule,

$$\frac{dx^*}{dp} = \frac{1}{|J|} \begin{vmatrix} 0 & 1 & -1 \\ 1 & 0 & -1 \\ 1 & -1 & 0 \end{vmatrix} = 0 \quad \text{at } p = 1,$$

$$\frac{dy^*}{dp} = \frac{1}{|J|} \begin{vmatrix} 0 & 0 & -1 \\ 1 & 1 & -1 \\ -1 & 1 & 0 \end{vmatrix} = -1 \quad \text{at } p = 1.$$

(c) Write Lagrangian as

$$L^*(x, y, \lambda_2, q) = xy - \lambda_2(-2 + qx + y)$$

By the envelope theorem,

$$\frac{dM(1)}{dq} = \frac{\partial L}{\partial q}(1, 1, 1, 1) = -\lambda_2^* x^* = -1.$$

(d) At $t = -1$ $(x, y) = (1, 1)$ is the unique global maximizer with $-1 \leq x + y$ an inactive constraint. Hence, a change in t around $t = -1$ will not alter optimized value; i.e., $dV(-1)/dt = 0$.

7.2 Checking the conditions of the IFT:
   (i) Both equations hold at $(1, 2, 0)$.
   (ii) The functions $F^1 = x^2 + y^2 + z^2 - 5$ and $F^2 = (x - 1)^2 + (y - 1)^2 + (z - 1)^2 - 2$ are differentiable.

   (iii)
   $$\begin{bmatrix} \dfrac{\partial F^1}{\partial x} & \dfrac{\partial F^1}{\partial y} \\[2mm] \dfrac{\partial F^2}{\partial x} & \dfrac{\partial F^2}{\partial y} \end{bmatrix} = \begin{bmatrix} 2x & 2y \\ 2(x - 1) & 2(y - 1) \end{bmatrix} \quad \text{so at } (1, 2, 0),$$

   $$\det\left[\frac{\partial F^i}{``\partial x_j"}\right] = \det\begin{bmatrix} 2 & 4 \\ 0 & 2 \end{bmatrix} \neq 0.$$

   Thus all conditions are satisfied, and the intersection can be written in the form of differentiable functions $x^*(z)$ and $y^*(z)$ near $(1, 2, 0)$.

7.3 False. Given Max $f(\mathbf{x}, t)$ s.t. $g(\mathbf{x}, t) \leq 0$, set up the Lagrangian $L(\mathbf{x}, t) = f(\mathbf{x}, t) - \lambda g(\mathbf{x}, t)$. Then by the envelope theorem

   $$\frac{df^*(t)}{dt} = \frac{\partial L}{\partial t}(\mathbf{x}^*(t), t) = \frac{\partial f}{\partial t}(\mathbf{x}^*(t), t) - \lambda^*(t)\frac{\partial g}{\partial t}(\mathbf{x}^*(t), t),$$

   so

   $$\frac{df^*(0)}{dt} = \frac{\partial f}{\partial t}(\mathbf{x}^*(0), 0) - \lambda^*(0)\frac{\partial g}{\partial t}(\mathbf{x}^*(0), 0) \neq \frac{\partial f}{\partial t}(\mathbf{x}^*(0), 0)$$

   in general.

7.4 In general, $\Pi = p_w q_w + p_m q_m - c$.
   (a) Since x sheep give x wool and $25x$ mutton

   $$\Pi(x) = (100 - 6x^{1/2})x + (200 - x)25x - 10x$$

   $$= 5090x - 6x^{3/2} - 25x^2.$$

   (b) FOC: $d\Pi/dx = 5090 - 9x^{1/2} - 50x = 0$.
   Putting $x^{1/2} = z$ get $z = 10$ or -10.18. Since $x \geq 0$ and $x^{1/2} \geq 0$, $z = -10.18$ is ruled out. Hence $z = 10 \Rightarrow x = 100$.
   SOC: $\partial^2\Pi/dx^2 = -9x^{-1/2} - 50 < 0$ for $x = 100$. Furthermore, $\partial^2\Pi/\partial x^2 < 0 \ \forall x \geq 0 \Rightarrow$ profit is strictly concave in x. Hence $x = 100$ is unique, global profit maximizer.

(c) Show IFT conditions satisfied:

$$\Pi(x;t) = 5090x - 6x^{3/2} - 25x^2 - 25tx.$$

FOC: $\partial\Pi/\partial x = 5090 - 9x^{1/2} - 50x - 25t = 0$.
At $t = 0$,

$$F(100,0) \equiv \frac{\partial\Pi}{\partial x}(100,0) = 0$$

holds, and $\partial F/\partial x = \partial^2\Pi/\partial x^2 \neq 0$.
Differentiating with respect to t,

$$-\left(\frac{9}{2}x^{-1/2} + 50\right)\frac{dx}{dt} - 25 = 0$$

and at $t = 0$,

$$\frac{dx}{dt} = -\frac{500}{1009}.$$

(i) Given $p_w = 100 - 6x^{1/2}$, at $t = 0$,

$$\frac{dp_w}{dt} = -\frac{6}{2}x^{-1/2}\frac{dx}{dt} = -\frac{6}{2}\left(\frac{-500}{1009}\right)\frac{1}{10} = \frac{150}{1009}.$$

7.5 System of equations:

$$F^1(Y,r;M) \equiv S(Y,r) - I(r,f(Y,r)) = 0,$$

$$F^2(Y,r;M) \equiv L(Y,r) - M = 0,$$

$$J = \begin{bmatrix} \left(\dfrac{\partial S}{\partial Y} - \dfrac{\partial I}{\partial E}\dfrac{\partial f}{\partial Y}\right) & \left(\dfrac{\partial S}{\partial r} - \dfrac{\partial I}{\partial r} - \dfrac{\partial I}{\partial E}\dfrac{\partial f}{\partial r}\right) \\[2ex] \dfrac{\partial L}{\partial y} & \dfrac{\partial L}{\partial r} \end{bmatrix},$$

$$|J| = \left(\frac{\partial S}{\partial Y} - \frac{\partial I}{\partial E}\frac{\partial f}{\partial Y}\right)\left(\frac{\partial L}{\partial r}\right) - \frac{\partial L}{\partial Y}\left(\frac{\partial S}{\partial r} - \frac{\partial I}{\partial r} - \frac{\partial I}{\partial E}\frac{\partial f}{\partial r}\right) < 0.$$
$$((+) \ - (+)(-)) \ \ (-) \ \ - (+)((+) \ - (-) \ - (+)(-))$$

Using IFT,

$$J\begin{bmatrix} dY \\ dr \end{bmatrix} = \begin{bmatrix} 0 \\ dM \end{bmatrix}, \quad \text{or}$$

$$\frac{dY}{dM} = -\frac{1}{|J|}\left[\frac{\partial S}{\partial r} - \frac{\partial I}{\partial r} - \frac{\partial I}{\partial E}\frac{\partial f}{\partial r}\right] > 0.$$
$$[(+) \ - (-) \ - (+)(-)]$$

An increase in real money stock increases Y.

7.6 (a) $\quad \Pi = R_1 - C_1 + t(R_2 - C_2)$

$$= (3 - 2q_1)q_1 - q_1 + t[(3 - 2q_2 - 2bq_1)q_2 - q_2]$$

$$= 2q_1 - 2q_1^2 + t(2q_2 - 2q_2^2 - 2bq_1q_2).$$

(b) $(b, t) = (1, 1/2).$

FOC yield $\partial \Pi / \partial q_1 = 0 \Rightarrow 2 - 4q_1 - q_2 = 0$ and $\partial \Pi / \partial q_2 = 0 \Rightarrow 1 - 2q_2 - q_1 = 0.$

Solution: $(q_1^*, q_2^*) = (3/7, 2/7).$

SOC: $\qquad\qquad H = \begin{bmatrix} -4 & -1 \\ -1 & -2 \end{bmatrix}.$

$|-4| < 0$ and $|H| = 7 > 0 \Rightarrow H$ is $ND \Rightarrow$ strictly concave profit function. So $(3/7, 2/7)$ is unique, global maximizer.

(c) $\partial \Pi / \partial q_1$ and $\partial \Pi / \partial q_2$ are differentiable; $(q_1, q_2, b, t) = (3/7, 2/7, 1, 1/2)$ satisfies FOC, and $|J| \neq 0$. Hence, IFT holds. Optimal $(q_1^*(b, t), q_2^*(b, t))$ exists for (b, t) near $(1, 1/2)$. So (evaluated at $(3/7, 2/7, 1, 1/2)$)

$$\begin{bmatrix} \dfrac{\partial q_1^*}{\partial b} & \dfrac{\partial q_1^*}{\partial t} \\[2mm] \dfrac{\partial q_2^*}{\partial b} & \dfrac{\partial q_2^*}{\partial t} \end{bmatrix} = \begin{bmatrix} -4 & -1 \\ -1 & -2 \end{bmatrix}^{-1} \begin{bmatrix} \dfrac{-2}{7} & \dfrac{-4}{7} \\[2mm] \dfrac{-3}{7} & 0 \end{bmatrix}$$

$$= \frac{1}{7} \begin{bmatrix} 2 & -1 \\ -1 & 4 \end{bmatrix} \begin{bmatrix} -2/7 & -4/7 \\ -3/7 & 0 \end{bmatrix}$$

$$= \begin{bmatrix} \dfrac{-1}{49} & \dfrac{-8}{49} \\[2mm] \dfrac{-10}{49} & \dfrac{4}{49} \end{bmatrix}.$$

(d) By the envelope theorem,

$$\frac{\partial \Pi^*}{\partial b}(b, t) = \frac{\partial \Pi}{\partial b}(q_1^*(b, t), q_2^*(b, t); b, t),$$

$$\frac{\partial \Pi^*}{\partial b}(1, 1/2) = \frac{\partial \Pi}{\partial b}(3/7, 2/7; 1, 1/2) = -2tq_1^*q_2^*$$

$$= -2(1/2)(3/7)(2/7) = \frac{-6}{49},$$

$$\frac{\partial \Pi^*}{\partial t}(1, 1/2) = 2q_2^* - 2q_2^{*2} - 2bq_1^*q_2^* = \frac{8}{49}.$$

7.7 Min $C = rK + wL$ s.t. $Y = K^{1/2}L^{1/2}$.

$$M = -rK - wL - \lambda(Y - K^{1/2}L^{1/2})$$

FOC:

$$\frac{\partial M}{\partial K} = -r + \frac{1}{2}\lambda K^{-1/2}L^{1/2} = 0, \qquad (1)$$

$$\frac{\partial M}{\partial L} = -w + \frac{1}{2}\lambda K^{1/2}L^{-1/2} = 0, \qquad (2)$$

$$\frac{\partial M}{\partial \lambda} = K^{1/2}L^{1/2} - Y = 0. \qquad (3)$$

(a) Given $r, w > 0$, $\lambda = 0$ is not possible as (1) and (2) would not hold. Hence $\lambda \neq 0$. Dividing (1) by (2), we get

$$\frac{r}{w} = \frac{L}{K} \quad \text{or} \quad L = \frac{r}{w}K. \qquad (4)$$

Using (4) in (3), we get

$$K^{1/2}\left(\frac{r}{w}K\right)^{1/2} = Y \quad \text{or} \quad K\left(\frac{r}{w}\right)^{1/2} = Y \quad \text{or}$$

$$\left.\begin{array}{l} K^* = Yr^{-1/2}w^{1/2} = 1 \\ L^* = Yr^{1/2}w^{-1/2} = 1 \\ \lambda^* = 2r^{1/2}w^{1/2} = 2 \end{array}\right\} \quad \text{when } Y = r = w = 1.$$

SOC:

$$\begin{bmatrix} -\frac{1}{4}\lambda K^{-3/2}L^{1/2} & \frac{1}{4}\lambda K^{-1/2}L^{-1/2} & \frac{1}{2}K^{-1/2}L^{1/2} \\ \frac{1}{4}\lambda K^{-1/2}L^{1/2} & -\frac{1}{4}\lambda K^{1/2}L^{-3/2} & \frac{1}{2}K^{1/2}L^{-1/2} \\ \frac{1}{2}K^{-1/2}L^{1/2} & \frac{1}{2}K^{1/2}L^{-1/2} & 0 \end{bmatrix}.$$

$n = 2, s = 1 \Rightarrow$ one determinant to check. At $(K, L, \lambda) = (1, 1, 2)$ the SOC matrix is

$$\begin{bmatrix} -\dfrac{1}{2} & \dfrac{1}{2} & \dfrac{1}{2} \\ \dfrac{1}{2} & -\dfrac{1}{2} & \dfrac{1}{2} \\ \dfrac{1}{2} & \dfrac{1}{2} & 0 \end{bmatrix}.$$

$D_1 = \frac{1}{8} + \frac{1}{8} - (-\frac{1}{8} - \frac{1}{8}) = \frac{1}{2} > 0 \Rightarrow$ SOC holds. So $K^* = 1 = L^*$ minimizes cost.

(b)
$$C(Y, r, w) = rK^* + wL^*$$
$$= Yr^{1/2}w^{1/2} + Yr^{1/2}w^{1/2}$$
$$= 2(rw)^{1/2}Y.$$

Therefore, $\partial C / \partial Y = 2(rw)^{1/2} = 2$ at $(1, 1, 1)$.

(c) Let
$$F^1(K, L, \lambda; Y, r, w) = -r + \tfrac{1}{2}\lambda K^{-1/2}L^{1/2},$$
$$F^2(K, L, \lambda; Y, r, w) = -w + \tfrac{1}{2}\lambda K^{1/2}L^{-1/2},$$
$$F^3(K, L, \lambda; Y, r, w) = K^{1/2}L^{1/2} - Y.$$

From FOC we know that
$$F^1(1,1,2;1,1,1) = F^2(1,1,2;1,1,1) = F^3(1,1,2;1,1,1) = 0.$$

Furthermore, F^1, F^2, and F^3 are continuously differentiable while the Jacobian is nonzero ($|J| = \tfrac{1}{2}$). Hence, IFT applies, and input demand functions exist for (r, w) near $(1, 1)$.

(d) Since $C^* = rK + wL = -M$, by the envelope theorem,
$$\frac{\partial C^*}{\partial r}(1,1,1) = \frac{-\partial M}{\partial r}(1,1,2,1,1,1) = K^*(1,1,1) = 1,$$
$$\frac{\partial C^*}{\partial w}(1,1,1) = \frac{-\partial M}{\partial w}(1,1,2,1,1,1) = L^*(1,1,1) = 1.$$

7.8 When both markets are in equilibrium, we get
$$D_C(p_c^c, p_T^c) - S_C(p_c^f) = 0, \tag{1}$$
$$D_T(p_c^c, p_T^c) - S_T(p_T^f) = 0. \tag{2}$$

Totally differentiating (1) and (2) with respect to $p_c^c, p_T^c, p_c^f, p_T^f$,
$$\frac{\partial D_c}{\partial p_c^c} \cdot dp_c^c + \frac{\partial D_c}{\partial p_T^c} dp_T^c - \frac{\partial S_c}{\partial p_c^f} \cdot dp_c^f = 0, \tag{3}$$
$$\frac{\partial D_T}{\partial p_c^c} dp_c^c + \frac{\partial D_T}{\partial p_T^c} dp_T^c - \frac{\partial S_T}{\partial p_T^f} dp_T^f = 0. \tag{4}$$

$p_c^c = p_c^f + t \Rightarrow dp_c^c = dp_c^f + dt$; while $p_T^c = p_T^f \Rightarrow dp_T^c = dp_T^f$. Using these in (3) and (4), one gets
$$\frac{\partial D_c}{\partial p_c^c} dp_c^c + \frac{\partial D_c}{\partial p_T^c} dp_T^c - \frac{\partial S_c}{\partial p_c^f}(dp_c^c - dt) = 0,$$
$$\frac{\partial D_T}{\partial p_c^c} dp_c^c + \frac{\partial D_T}{\partial p_T^c} dp_T^c - \frac{\partial S_T}{\partial p_T^f} dp_T^c = 0.$$

Rearranging,

$$
\begin{bmatrix}
\left(\dfrac{\partial D_c}{\partial p_c^c} - \dfrac{\partial S_c}{\partial p_c^f} \right) & \dfrac{\partial D_c}{\partial p_T^c} \\[2ex]
\dfrac{\partial D_T}{\partial p_c^c} & \left(\dfrac{\partial D_T}{\partial p_T^c} - \dfrac{\partial S_T}{\partial p_T^f} \right)
\end{bmatrix}
\begin{bmatrix}
dp_c^c \\[1ex]
dp_T^c
\end{bmatrix}
=
\begin{bmatrix}
- \dfrac{\partial S_c}{\partial p_c^f}\, dt \\[2ex]
0
\end{bmatrix}.
$$

Letting A be the 2×2 matrix in the above equation:

$$
|A| = \left(\frac{\partial D_c}{\partial p_c^c} - \frac{\partial S_c}{\partial p_c^f} \right)\left(\frac{\partial D_T}{\partial p_T^c} - \frac{\partial S_T}{\partial p_T^f} \right) - \frac{\partial D_T}{\partial p_c^c}\frac{\partial D_c}{\partial p_T^c}
$$

$$
= \underset{(-)}{\frac{\partial D_c}{\partial p_c^c}} \cdot \underset{(-)}{\frac{\partial D_T}{\partial p_T^c}} - \underset{(-)}{\frac{\partial D_c}{\partial p_c^c}} \cdot \underset{(+)}{\frac{\partial S_T}{\partial p_T^f}} - \underset{(+)}{\frac{\partial S_c}{\partial p_c^f}} \cdot \underset{(-)}{\frac{\partial D_T}{\partial p_T^c}} + \underset{(+)}{\frac{\partial S_c}{\partial p_c^f}} \cdot \underset{(+)}{\frac{\partial S_T}{\partial p_T^f}} - \underset{(+)}{\frac{\partial D_T}{\partial p_c^c}} \cdot \underset{(+)}{\frac{\partial D_c}{\partial p_T^c}}.
$$

Comparing the first and last terms, note that since $|\partial D_c/\partial p_c^c| > |\partial D_c/\partial p_T^c|$ and $|\partial D_t/\partial p_T^c| > |\partial D_T/\partial p_c^c|$ we have

$$
\left(\frac{\partial D_c}{\partial p_c^c} \cdot \frac{\partial D_T}{\partial p_T^c} - \frac{\partial D_c}{\partial p_T^c} \cdot \frac{\partial D_T}{\partial p_c^c} \right) > 0,
$$

which implies $|A| > 0$.
Applying Cramer's rule,

$$
dp_T^c = \frac{1}{|A|}
\begin{vmatrix}
\left(\dfrac{\partial D_c}{\partial p_c^c} - \dfrac{\partial S_c}{\partial p_c^f} \right) & -\dfrac{\partial S_c}{\partial p_c^f}\, dt \\[2ex]
\dfrac{\partial D_T}{\partial p_c^c} & 0
\end{vmatrix}
= \underset{(+)}{\frac{1}{|A|}} \cdot \underset{(+)}{\frac{\partial D_T}{\partial p_c^c}} \cdot \underset{(+)}{\frac{\partial S_c}{\partial p_c^f}}\, dt,
$$

or $dp_T^c/dt > 0$. Hence an increase in tax in the coffee market leads to a rise in equilibrium price in the tea market.

7.9 Noting that constraint $x + y \geq 0$ is not binding, formulate the Lagrangian:

$$
L^* = x^t y - \lambda_1 (x + y - 2te).
$$

FOC:
$$
\frac{\partial L^*}{\partial x} = t x^{t-1} y - \lambda_1 = 0,
$$

$$
\frac{\partial L^*}{\partial y} = x^t - \lambda_1 = 0,
$$

$$
\frac{\partial L^*}{\partial \lambda_1} = 2te - x - y = 0 \quad (\text{noting } \lambda_1 \text{ is strictly positive}).
$$

Totally differentiating FOC, we get (noting $d(a^x)/dx = a^x \ln a$):

$$t(t-1)x^{t-2}y\,dx + tx^{t-1}\,dy - d\lambda_1 = -x^{t-1}y[1 + t\ln x]\,dt,$$

$$tx^{t-1}\,dx - d\lambda_1 = -x^t \ln_e x\,dt,$$

$$-dx - dy = -2e\,dt.$$

At $t = 1$, $x = e = y$ satisfy FOC, and we get

$$\begin{bmatrix} 0 & 1 & -1 \\ 1 & 0 & -1 \\ -1 & -1 & 0 \end{bmatrix}\begin{bmatrix} dx^* \\ dy^* \\ d\lambda_1^* \end{bmatrix} = \begin{bmatrix} -2e\,dt \\ -e\,dt \\ -2e\,dt \end{bmatrix},$$

$$\frac{dx^*}{dt}(1) = \frac{1}{|D|}\begin{vmatrix} -2e & 1 & -1 \\ -e & 0 & -1 \\ -2e & -1 & 0 \end{vmatrix}$$

$$= \frac{1}{2}[-2e(-1) + e(-1) - 2e(-1)] = \frac{3e}{2}.$$

Similarly, $dy^*(1)/dt = e/2$ using Cramer's rule. By the envelope theorem,

$$\frac{d\pi}{dt}(1) = \frac{dL^*}{dt} = y \cdot x^t \ln x + 2e\lambda_1 = 3e^2 \quad \text{at } t = 1.$$

7.10 (a) Noting that the second constraint is inactive, rewrite the Lagrangian:

$$L^*(x, y, \lambda_1, \lambda_3; t) = x^2 + 2\left(\frac{y}{t}\right)^2 + \lambda_1 x - \lambda_3(3x + 2y - 10)$$

Considering all constraints as equalities, the FOC for this problem give us the appropriate system of equations for comparative statics:

FOC: $\dfrac{\partial L^*}{\partial x} = 2x + \lambda_1 - 3\lambda_3 \equiv F^1(x, y, \lambda_1, \lambda_3; t) = 0,$

$\dfrac{\partial L^*}{\partial y} = \dfrac{4y}{t^2} - 2\lambda_3 \equiv F^2(x, y, \lambda_1, \lambda_3; t) = 0,$

$\dfrac{\partial L^*}{\partial \lambda_1} = x \equiv F^3(x, y, \lambda_1, \lambda_3; t) = 0,$

$\dfrac{\partial L^*}{\partial \lambda_3} = 10 - 3x - 2y \equiv F^4(x, y, \lambda_1, \lambda_3; t) = 0.$

(b) By the envelope theorem,

$$\frac{\partial f^*}{\partial t} = \frac{\partial L^*}{\partial t}(x(1), y(1), \lambda_1(1), \lambda_3(1); 1) = 2[y(1)]^2(-2)(1)^{-3}.$$

At $t = 1$, $y^* = 5 = y(1)$. So, we get $\partial f^*/dt = (-4)25 = -100$.

7.11 Noting that $y \geq 0$ is not binding, rewrite the Lagrangian as

$$L^*(x, y, \lambda_1, \lambda_3; t) = x^2 + ty^2 + \lambda_1 x - \lambda_3(2x + y - 4)$$

FOC:
$$L_x^* = F^1(x, y, \lambda_1, \lambda_3; t) = 2x + \lambda_1 - 2\lambda_3 = 0,$$

$$L_y^* = F^2(x, y, \lambda_1, \lambda_3; t) = 2ty \quad - \lambda_3 \quad = 0,$$

$$L_{\lambda_1}^* = F^3(x, y, \lambda_1, \lambda_3; t) = x \qquad\qquad = 0,$$

$$L_{\lambda_3}^* = F^4(x, y, \lambda_1, \lambda_3; t) = 4 - 2x - y \quad = 0.$$

This is the appropriate system of equations. Note that at $t = 1$, $(x^*, y^*) = (0, 4)$ is the unique global maximizer. Furthermore, all IFT conditions are satisfied.

7.12 (a) When $t = 1$ this is the original problem. Binding constraints are $x \geq 0$ and $(2 + t)x + 2y + z \leq 6$.

$$L^*(x, y, z, \lambda_1, \lambda_4; t) = (x + t)y^2z - \lambda_1(-x)$$
$$- \lambda_4((2 + t)x + 2y + z - 6)$$

The system of equations in endogenous variables x, y, z, λ_1, λ_4 and exogenous parameter t is found by setting the partial derivatives of L^* with respect to the endogenous variables equal to zero.

$$y^2z + \lambda_1 - (2 + t)\lambda_4 = 0,$$

$$2(x + t)yz - 2\lambda_4 = 0,$$

$$(x + t)y^2 - \lambda_4 = 0,$$

$$x = 0,$$

$$-(2 + t)x - 2y - z + 6 = 0.$$

(b) By the envelope theorem,

$$\frac{df^*(1)}{dt} = \frac{\partial L^*(x^*(1), y^*(1), z^*(1), \lambda_1^*(1), \lambda_4^*(1); 1)}{\partial t}$$

$$= [y^*(1)]^2 z^*(1) - \lambda_4^*(1)x^*(1)$$

$$= [2]^2(2) - (4)(0)$$

$$= 8.$$

A.9 SOLUTIONS FOR CHAPTER 8

8.1 (a) $L = -(x - 1)^2 - (y - 1)^2 - (z - 1)^2 - \mu(2 - x - y - z)$.

FOC:
$$\frac{\partial L}{\partial x} = -2(x - 1) + \mu = 0, \tag{1}$$

$$\frac{\partial L}{\partial y} = -2(y - 1) + \mu = 0, \tag{2}$$

$$\frac{\partial L}{\partial z} = -2(z - 1) + \mu = 0, \tag{3}$$

$$\frac{\partial L}{\partial \mu} = x + y + z - 2 = 0. \tag{4}$$

From (1)–(3), we get $x = y = z = \mu/2 + 1$. Using (4), $\mu = -\frac{2}{3} \Rightarrow x = y = z = \frac{2}{3}$. So $(x, y, z, \mu) = (\frac{2}{3}, \frac{2}{3}, \frac{2}{3}, -\frac{2}{3})$ is a potential solution.

SOC:

$$D = \begin{bmatrix} -2 & 0 & 0 & 1 \\ 0 & -2 & 0 & 1 \\ 0 & 0 & -2 & 1 \\ 1 & 1 & 1 & 0 \end{bmatrix}.$$

$n = 3$, $s = 1 \Rightarrow n - s = 2$, and two determinants to check

$$D_1 = \begin{vmatrix} -2 & 0 & 1 \\ 0 & -2 & 1 \\ 1 & 1 & 0 \end{vmatrix} = 4 > 0,$$

$$D_2 = -2D_1 - 1 \begin{vmatrix} 0 & 0 & 1 \\ -2 & 0 & 1 \\ 0 & -2 & 1 \end{vmatrix} = -8 - 4 = -12 < 0.$$

$(-1)^2 D_1 = 4 > 0$ and $(-1)^3 D_2 = 12 > 0 \Rightarrow$ SOC holds, and $(x, y, z) = (\frac{2}{3}, \frac{2}{3}, \frac{2}{3})$ is local minimizer. Furthermore, Hessian is PD:

$$H = \begin{bmatrix} 2 & 0 & 0 \\ 0 & 2 & 0 \\ 0 & 0 & 2 \end{bmatrix}.$$

Thus, $f(x, y, z)$ is strictly convex $\Rightarrow (x, y, z) = (\frac{2}{3}, \frac{2}{3}, \frac{2}{3})$ is unique global minimizer since the feasible set is convex.

(b) The Lagrangian now becomes

$$L = -(x - 1)^2 - (y - 1)^2 - (z - 1)^2 - \mu(2 + t - x - y - z).$$

FOC: $F_1 \equiv \dfrac{\partial L}{\partial x} = -2(x - 1) + \mu = 0,$

$$F_2 \equiv \dfrac{\partial L}{\partial y} = -2(y - 1) + \mu = 0,$$

$$F_3 \equiv \dfrac{\partial L}{\partial z} = -2(z - 1) + \mu = 0,$$

$$F_4 \equiv \dfrac{\partial L}{\partial \mu} = x + y + z - 2 - t = 0,$$

where $F_i(x, y, z, \mu, t)$ are functions of the endogenous variables and the parameter t, $i = 1, 2, 3, 4$.
Check the conditions for IFT:
  (i) F_i's are continuously differentiable.
 (ii) $(x, y, z, \mu) = (\frac{2}{3}, \frac{2}{3}, \frac{2}{3}, -\frac{2}{3})$ satisfies all FOC when $t = 0$.
(iii) The Jacobian determinant is nonzero:

$$J = \begin{bmatrix} \dfrac{\partial F_1}{\partial x} & \dfrac{\partial F_1}{\partial y} & \dfrac{\partial F_1}{\partial z} & \dfrac{\partial F_1}{\partial \mu} \\[2mm] \dfrac{\partial F_2}{\partial x} & \dfrac{\partial F_2}{\partial y} & \dfrac{\partial F_2}{\partial z} & \dfrac{\partial F_2}{\partial \mu} \\[2mm] \dfrac{\partial F_3}{\partial x} & \dfrac{\partial F_3}{\partial y} & \dfrac{\partial F_3}{\partial z} & \dfrac{\partial F_3}{\partial \mu} \\[2mm] \dfrac{\partial F_4}{\partial x} & \dfrac{\partial F_4}{\partial y} & \dfrac{\partial F_4}{\partial z} & \dfrac{\partial F_4}{\partial \mu} \end{bmatrix}$$

$$= \begin{bmatrix} -2 & 0 & 0 & 1 \\ 0 & -2 & 0 & 1 \\ 0 & 0 & -2 & 1 \\ 1 & 1 & 1 & 0 \end{bmatrix} = D \text{ of part (a).}$$

So $|J| = D_2 = -12 \neq 0$.
Hence IFT can be applied; i.e., there exist differentiable functions $x(t)$, $y(t)$, $z(t)$, and $\mu(t)$ such that $F_i(x(t), y(t), z(t), \mu(t); t) \equiv 0$

for $i = 1, 2, 3, 4$, for t near 0. Totally differentiating these identities:

$$-2\,dx + d\mu = 0,$$
$$-2\,dy + d\mu = 0,$$
$$-2\,dz + d\mu = 0,$$
$$dx + dy + dz = dt,$$

or

$$\begin{bmatrix} -2 & 0 & 0 & 1 \\ 0 & -2 & 0 & 1 \\ 0 & 0 & -2 & 1 \\ 1 & 1 & 1 & 0 \end{bmatrix} \begin{bmatrix} dx \\ dy \\ dz \\ d\mu \end{bmatrix} = \begin{bmatrix} 0 \\ 0 \\ 0 \\ dt \end{bmatrix},$$

$$\begin{bmatrix} dx \\ dy \\ dz \\ d\mu \end{bmatrix} = \begin{bmatrix} -2 & 0 & 0 & 1 \\ 0 & -2 & 0 & 1 \\ 0 & 0 & -2 & 1 \\ 1 & 1 & 1 & 0 \end{bmatrix}^{-1} \begin{bmatrix} 0 \\ 0 \\ 0 \\ dt \end{bmatrix},$$

yielding $dx(0)/dt = 1/3 = dy(0)/dt = dz(0)/dt$.

8.2 Endogenous variables x, y; exogenous variable z. System of equations defined by

$$F^1(x, y, z) \equiv x^2 + 2y^2 + (z - 1)^2 - 1 = 0, \tag{1}$$
$$F^2(x, y, z) \equiv x - y + z^2 - 2 = 0. \tag{2}$$

Check IFT conditions:
(a) $(x, y, z) = (1, 0, 1)$ satisfies (1) and (2).
(b) F^1 and F^2 are continuously differentiable.
(c) Jacobian of first partials with respect to endogenous variables is nonzero at $(1, 0, 1)$:

$$J = \begin{bmatrix} 2x & 4y \\ 1 & -1 \end{bmatrix}.$$

So $|J| = -2 \neq 0$.

Hence IFT holds, and the intersection of the surfaces can be written as $x = g(z)$, $y = h(z)$ near $(1, 0, 1)$. Totally differentiating (1) and (2):

$$\begin{bmatrix} 2g(z) & 4h(z) \\ 1 & -1 \end{bmatrix} \begin{bmatrix} dg(z) \\ dh(z) \end{bmatrix} = \begin{bmatrix} -2(z - 1)\,dz \\ -2\,dz \end{bmatrix},$$

where $x = g(z)$ and $y = h(z)$. Evaluating above at $(1, 0, 1)$, we get

$$dg(1) = \frac{1}{|J|} \begin{vmatrix} 0 & 0 \\ -2\,dz & -1 \end{vmatrix} \Rightarrow \frac{dg(1)}{dz} = 0.$$

Similarly,

$$dh(1) = \frac{1}{|J|} \begin{vmatrix} 2 & 0 \\ 1 & -2dz \end{vmatrix} \Rightarrow \frac{dh(1)}{dz} = 2.$$

8.3 $F(x, y) = x^2 y + x \ln y = 0.$
(i) $(x, y) = (e, 1/e)$ satisfy equation.
(ii) Continuously differentiable function.
(iii) Also $\partial F / \partial y \neq 0$.
Therefore IFT holds, and implicit differentiation is valid for "$y(x)$."
Totally differentiating F, we get

$$2xy\,dx + x^2\,dy + \ln y\,dx + \frac{x}{y}\,dy = 0 \quad \text{or} \quad \frac{dy}{dx} = \frac{-(2xy + \ln y)}{x^2 + x/y}$$

or, at $(e, 1/e)$, slope $= dy/dx = -1/2e^2$.

8.4 (a) Profit function: $\Pi(q) = R(q) - c(q) - T = q(4 - q^5/6) - q - q^2/2 - 1(q).$
FOC: $d\Pi/dq = 2 - q - q^5 = 0$ or $(q - 1)(q^4 + q^3 + q^2 + q + 2) = 0.$
Since $q \geq 0$, $q^* = 1$ is only potential solution. Furthermore, $d^2\Pi/dq^2 = -1 - 5q^4 < 0$ for all $q \geq 0$, and $d^2\Pi/dq^2 = -6$ when $q = 1$. Thus the profit function is strictly concave $\Rightarrow q^* = 1$ is unique global profit maximizer.

(b) Introducing tax rate t: $\Pi(q, t) = q(4 - q^5/6) - q - q^2/2 - tq.$
FOC: $d\Pi/dq = 3 - t - q^5 - q = 0.$
Let $F(q, t) \equiv 3 - t - q^5 - q.$ Check IFT conditions:
(i) $F(1, 1) = 0$ holds.
(ii) F is continuously differentiable.
(iii) $\partial F(1, 1)/\partial q = -6 \neq 0.$
So IFT holds, and there exists a continuously differentiable optimal output function $q(t)$ for t in the neighborhood of $t = 1$. Totally differentiating FOC:

$$-5q^4\,dq - dq = dt, \quad \text{or}$$

$$\frac{dq}{dt} = -\frac{1}{5q^4 + 1},$$

which implies $dq(1)/dt = -1/6$.

8.5 Let

$$F^1(x, y; z) = x^2 + y + z^2 - 4 = 0, \tag{1}$$

$$F^2(x, y; z) = y - xz - 1 = 0. \tag{2}$$

(i) F^1 and F^2 are continuously differentiable.

(ii) $F^1(1, 2; 1) = 0$ and $F^2(1, 2; 1) = 0$.

(iii)

$$|J| = \begin{vmatrix} \dfrac{\partial F^1}{\partial x} & \dfrac{\partial F^1}{\partial y} \\[2mm] \dfrac{\partial F^2}{\partial x} & \dfrac{\partial F^2}{\partial y} \end{vmatrix} = \begin{vmatrix} 2 & 1 \\ -1 & 1 \end{vmatrix} = 3 \neq 0 \quad \text{at } (1, 2, 1).$$

Hence, IFT holds, and endogenous variables can be written in terms of exogenous variable z in the form $x = g(z)$ and $y = h(z)$. Totally differentiating (1) and (2),

$$2x\,dx + dy + 2z\,dz = 0,$$
$$-z\,dx + dy - x\,dz = 0$$

or

$$\begin{pmatrix} 2x & 1 \\ -z & 1 \end{pmatrix}\begin{pmatrix} dx \\ dy \end{pmatrix} = \begin{pmatrix} -2z\,dz \\ x\,dz \end{pmatrix}.$$

Evaluated at $(1, 2; 1)$,

$$\begin{pmatrix} dx \\ dy \end{pmatrix} = -\begin{pmatrix} 2 & 1 \\ -1 & 1 \end{pmatrix}^{-1}\begin{pmatrix} 2dz \\ -dz \end{pmatrix} = -\frac{1}{3}\begin{pmatrix} 1 & -1 \\ 1 & 2 \end{pmatrix}\begin{pmatrix} 2dz \\ -dz \end{pmatrix}.$$

Hence $dg(1)/dz = -1$ and $dh(1)/dz = 0$.

8.6 (a) Min $x^2 + y^2 + z^2$ s.t. $x \geq 0$, $y \geq 0$, $x + y + 2z = 6$.

$$L = -x^2 - y^2 - z^2 + \lambda_1 x + \lambda_2 y - \mu(6 - x - y - 2z).$$

FOC:

$$\frac{\partial L}{\partial x} = -2x + \lambda_1 + \mu = 0,$$

$$\frac{\partial L}{\partial y} = -2y + \lambda_2 + \mu = 0,$$

$$\frac{\partial L}{\partial z} = -2z + 2\mu = 0,$$

$$\frac{\partial L}{\partial \lambda_1} = x \geq 0, \qquad \lambda_1 \geq 0, \lambda_1 x = 0,$$

$$\frac{\partial L}{\partial \lambda_2} = y \geq 0, \qquad \lambda_2 \geq 0, \lambda_2 y = 0,$$

$$\frac{\partial L}{\partial \mu} = x + y + 2z - 6 = 0.$$

The only potential solution is $(x^*, y^*, z^*, \lambda_1^*, \lambda_2^*, \mu^*) = (1, 1, 2, 0, 0, 2)$.

SOC: $n = 3$, $s = 1 \Rightarrow n - s = 2$, and two determinants to check:

$$D = \begin{bmatrix} -2 & 0 & 0 & 1 \\ 0 & -2 & 0 & 1 \\ 0 & 0 & -2 & 2 \\ 1 & 1 & 2 & 0 \end{bmatrix}.$$

$D_1 = 10 \Rightarrow (-1)^{1+1}D_1 = 10 > 0$, and $D_2 = -24 \Rightarrow (-1)^{1+2}D_2 = 24 > 0$. So SOC holds, and $(x, y, z) = (1, 1, 2)$ is a local minimizer.

Global: Hessian of original function:

$$H = \begin{bmatrix} 2 & 0 & 0 \\ 0 & 2 & 0 \\ 0 & 0 & 2 \end{bmatrix} = \begin{bmatrix} f_{11} & f_{12} & f_{13} \\ f_{21} & f_{22} & f_{23} \\ f_{31} & f_{32} & f_{33} \end{bmatrix},$$

$$f_{11} = 2 > 0, \qquad \begin{vmatrix} f_{11} & f_{12} \\ f_{21} & f_{22} \end{vmatrix} = 4 > 0, \qquad |H| = 8 > 0.$$

Thus, H is positive definite $\Rightarrow$ strictly convex objective function. The feasible set is convex; hence, $(x, y, z) = (1, 1, 2)$ is unique, global minimizer.

(b) Only the third constraint is binding for t near 0, so rewrite the Lagrangian as $L = -x^2 - y^2 - z^2 - \mu(6 + t - x - y - 2z)$. Using the envelope theorem,

$$\frac{\partial f^*}{\partial t} = \frac{\partial L}{\partial t}(1, 1, 2) = -\mu^* = -2 \Rightarrow \frac{\partial f}{\partial t} = 2.$$

Note that the transformed objective function decreases by 2 in optimum $\Rightarrow$ minimized value of original function increases by 2.

8.7 (a) Binding constraints are $x - y \geq -2$ and $0 \geq x$.

$$L^*(x, y, \lambda_2, \lambda_3; t) = (x + 3)(y + t) - \lambda_2(-2 - x + y) - \lambda_3(x).$$

System of equations:

$$L_x^* = y + t + \lambda_2 - \lambda_3 = 0,$$

$$L_y^* = x + 3 - \lambda_2 = 0,$$

$$L_{\lambda_2}^* = 2 + x - y = 0,$$

$$L_{\lambda_3}^* = x = 0.$$

(b) When $t = 0$ these are the original constraints. Again the constraint $y \geq 0$ is not binding. Write the Lagrangian as

$$L^*(x, y, \lambda_2, \lambda_3; t) = (x + 3)(y + 1) - \lambda_2(-2 - 2t - x + y)$$
$$- \lambda_3(x - t)$$

Note: $\partial L^*/\partial t = 2\lambda_2 + \lambda_3$ and $\partial L^*(0, 2, 3, 6; 0)/\partial t = 12$. By the envelope theorem,

$$\frac{df^*(0)}{dt} = \frac{\partial L^*}{\partial t}(0, 2, 3, 6; 0) = 12.$$

8.8 (a) x and y are endogenous; z is exogenous, and $(3, 1, 1)$ is on both surfaces. Let $F^1(x, y; z) = xyz - 3$ and $F^2(x, y; z) = x^2 + y^2 + (z - 1)^2 - 10$. The F^i are differentiable, and

$$\begin{bmatrix} \dfrac{\partial F^1(3, 1; 1)}{\partial x} & \dfrac{\partial F^1(3, 1; 1)}{\partial y} \\ \dfrac{\partial F^2(3, 1, 1)}{\partial x} & \dfrac{\partial F^2(3, 1; 1)}{\partial y} \end{bmatrix} = \begin{bmatrix} 1 & 3 \\ 6 & 2 \end{bmatrix}.$$

Since

$$\text{Det}\begin{bmatrix} 1 & 3 \\ 6 & 2 \end{bmatrix} \neq 0$$

the intersection can be written in the desired form.

(b) x and z are endogenous; y is exogenous, and $(1, 3, 1)$ is on both surfaces. Let $F^1(x, z; y) = xyz - 3$ and $F^2(x, z; y) = x^2 + y^2 + (z - 1)^2 - 10$. The F^i are differentiable, and

$$\begin{bmatrix} \dfrac{\partial F^1(1, 1; 3)}{\partial x} & \dfrac{\partial F^1(1, 1; 3)}{\partial z} \\ \dfrac{\partial F^2(1, 1; 3)}{\partial x} & \dfrac{\partial F^2(1, 1; 3)}{\partial z} \end{bmatrix} = \begin{bmatrix} 3 & 3 \\ 2 & 0 \end{bmatrix}$$

with nonzero determinant.

$$\begin{pmatrix} \dfrac{dx^*(3)}{dy} \\ \dfrac{dz^*(3)}{dy} \end{pmatrix} = -\begin{bmatrix} 3 & 3 \\ 2 & 0 \end{bmatrix}^{-1}\begin{pmatrix} 1 \\ 6 \end{pmatrix} = \begin{pmatrix} -3 \\ 8/3 \end{pmatrix}.$$

8.9 (a) At $t = 1$, this is the original problem. The $y \geq 0$ constraint is not binding, so $L^*(x, y, \lambda_1, \lambda_3; t) = (2x + y)^t - \lambda_1(x) - \lambda_3((x - 1)^2 + (y + 1)^2 - 10)$. The system of equations is the FOC with equality for binding inequality constraints:

$$L_x = 2t(2x + y)^{t-1} - \lambda_1 - 2\lambda_3(x - 1) = 0,$$

$$L_y = t(2x + y)^{t-1} - 2\lambda_3(y + 1) \qquad = 0,$$

$$L_{\lambda_1} = -x \qquad = 0,$$

$$L_{\lambda_3} = -(x - 1)^2 - (y + 1)^2 + 10 \qquad = 0.$$

(b) At $t = 0$, this is the original problem. The $y \geq 0$ constraint is not binding so $L^*(x, y, \lambda_1, \lambda_3; t) = 2x + yt + y - \lambda_1(x - t) - \lambda_3((x - 1)^2 + (y + 1)^2 - 10 - t)$.

$$\frac{\partial L^*}{\partial t} = y + \lambda_1 + \lambda_3,$$

$$\frac{df^*(0)}{dt} = \frac{\partial L^*}{\partial t}(x^*(0), y^*(0), \lambda_1^*(0), \lambda_3^*(0); 0),$$

$$= y^*(0) + \lambda_1^*(0) + \lambda_3^*(0),$$

$$= 2 + 7/3 + 1/6 = 9/2 \quad \text{by the envelope theorem.}$$

8.10 Let

$$F^1(x, y, z) = xy + xz + yz - 11,$$

$$F^2(x, y, z) = z^2 + y \ln x - 4.$$

Conditions of IFT:
1. $F^1(1, 3, 2) = F^2(1, 3, 2) = 0$.
2. F^1 and F^2 are differentiable.
3.

$$\det \begin{bmatrix} \dfrac{\partial F^1(1,3,2)}{\partial x} & \dfrac{\partial F^1(1,3,2)}{\partial z} \\[2mm] \dfrac{\partial F^2(1,3,2)}{\partial x} & \dfrac{\partial F^2(1,3,2)}{\partial z} \end{bmatrix} = \det \begin{bmatrix} 5 & 4 \\ 3 & 4 \end{bmatrix} \neq 0$$

Thus differentiable $x^*(y)$ and $z^*(y)$ exist near $(1, 3, 2)$.

$$\begin{pmatrix} \dfrac{dx^*(3)}{dy} \\[2ex] \dfrac{dz^*(3)}{Ady} \end{pmatrix} = -\begin{bmatrix} 5 & 4 \\ 3 & 4 \end{bmatrix}^{-1} \begin{pmatrix} \dfrac{\partial F^1(1,3,2)}{\partial y} \\[2ex] \dfrac{\partial F^2(1,3,2)}{\partial y} \end{pmatrix}$$

$$= -\frac{1}{8}\begin{bmatrix} 4 & -4 \\ -3 & 5 \end{bmatrix}\begin{pmatrix} 3 \\ 0 \end{pmatrix} = \begin{pmatrix} -3/2 \\ 9/8 \end{pmatrix}.$$

8.11 At $p = 1$ this is the original problem, and only the first constraint is binding.

$$L^* = (x - 2)(y + p) - \lambda_1(-p - x - py),$$

$$L_x^* = y + p + \lambda_1 = 0,$$

$$L_y^* = x - 2 + p\lambda_1 = 0,$$

$$L_{\lambda_1}^* = p + x + py = 0 \quad \text{since the first constraint is binding.}$$

(a) At $p = 1$,

$$[L_{ij}^*] = M = \begin{bmatrix} 0 & 1 & 1 \\ 1 & 0 & 1 \\ 1 & 1 & 0 \end{bmatrix},$$

which has nonzero determinant, and all conditions of the IFT are satisfied.

$$M \begin{pmatrix} \dfrac{dx^*(1)}{dp} \\[2ex] \dfrac{dy^*(1)}{dp} \\[2ex] \dfrac{d\lambda_1^*(1)}{dp} \end{pmatrix} = -\begin{pmatrix} 1 \\ \lambda_1^*(1) \\ 1 + y^*(1) \end{pmatrix}$$

$$= \begin{pmatrix} -1 \\ -1 \\ 1 \end{pmatrix} \quad \text{or} \quad \begin{pmatrix} \dfrac{dx^*(1)}{dp} \\[2ex] \dfrac{dy^*(1)}{dp} \\[2ex] \dfrac{d\lambda_1^*(1)}{dp} \end{pmatrix} = \begin{pmatrix} 1/2 \\ 1/2 \\ -3/2 \end{pmatrix}.$$

(b) $L^*(x, y, \lambda_1; p) = (x - 2)(y + p) - \lambda_1(-p - x - py)$.
By the envelope theorem,

$$\frac{df^*(1)}{dp} = \frac{\partial L^*(x^*(1), y^*(1), \lambda_1^*(1); 1)}{\partial p},$$

$$\frac{\partial L^*}{\partial p} = x - 2 - \lambda_1(-1 - y),$$

and $(x^*(1), y^*(1), \lambda_1^*(1)) = (1, -2, 1)$, so $df^*(1)/dp = 1 - 2 - 1(-1 - (-2)) = -2$.

8.12 (a) At $t = 1$ this is the original problem. Only $x \geq 0$ and $y \geq 0$ are binding.

$$L^* = (3 - tx)(5 - y) - \lambda_1(-x) - \lambda_2(-y).$$

System of equations is

$$L_x = -t(5 - y) + \lambda_1 = 0,$$

$$L_y = -(3 - tx) + \lambda_2 = 0,$$

$$L_{\lambda_1} = x = 0,$$

$$L_{\lambda_2} = y = 0.$$

(b) $L^* = (3 - tx)(5 - y) - \lambda_1(-x) - \lambda_2(-y)$.

$$\frac{\partial L^*}{\partial t} = -x(5 - y).$$

By the envelope theorem,

$$\frac{df^*(1)}{dt} = \frac{\partial L^*(x^*(1), y^*(1), \lambda_1^*(1), \lambda_2^*(1), 1)}{\partial t}$$

$$= -0(5 - 0) = 0.$$

8.13 First, check IFT conditions: Let $F^1 = x^2 + zy - 7$, $F^2 = xy - z - 5$.
1. $F^1(2, 3, 1) = 4 + 3 - 7 = 0$ and $F^2(2, 3, 1) = 6 - 1 - 5 = 0$.
2. F^1 and F^2 are continuously differentiable.
3.

$$\det \begin{bmatrix} \dfrac{\partial F^1(2,3,1)}{\partial y} & \dfrac{\partial F^1(2,3,1)}{\partial z} \\[4mm] \dfrac{\partial F^2(2,3,1)}{\partial y} & \dfrac{\partial F^2(2,3,1)}{\partial z} \end{bmatrix} = \det \begin{bmatrix} 1 & 3 \\ 2 & -1 \end{bmatrix} \neq 0.$$

All conditions of IFT hold, so the intersection can be written in the desired form.

$$
\begin{pmatrix} \dfrac{dy^*(2)}{dx} \\ \dfrac{dz^*(2)}{dx} \end{pmatrix} = -\begin{bmatrix} 1 & 3 \\ 2 & -1 \end{bmatrix}^{-1} \begin{pmatrix} \dfrac{\partial F^1(2,3,1)}{\partial x} \\ \dfrac{\partial F^2(2,3,1)}{\partial x} \end{pmatrix}
$$

$$
= \frac{1}{7}\begin{bmatrix} -1 & -3 \\ -2 & 1 \end{bmatrix}\begin{pmatrix} 4 \\ 3 \end{pmatrix} = \begin{pmatrix} -13/7 \\ -5/7 \end{pmatrix}.
$$

8.14 (a) When $p = 1$, the problem is the original problem. Only the third constraint is binding, so the appropriate Lagrangian is $L^* = px^4y - \lambda_3(px^2 + y^2 - 5p)$. The system of equations for comparative statics is

$$
4px^3 - 2\lambda_3 px = 0,
$$

$$
px^4 - 2\lambda_3 y = 0,
$$

$$
-px^2 - y^2 + 5p = 0.
$$

The conditions of the IFT hold, so

$$
\begin{pmatrix} \dfrac{dx^*(1)}{dp} \\ \dfrac{dy^*(1)}{dp} \\ \dfrac{d\lambda^*(1)}{dp} \end{pmatrix} = -\begin{bmatrix} 32 & 32 & -4 \\ 32 & -16 & -2 \\ -4 & -2 & 0 \end{bmatrix}^{-1} \begin{pmatrix} 4x^{*3}y^* - 2\lambda_3^* x^* \\ x^{*4} \\ -x^{*2} + 5 \end{pmatrix}
$$

$$
= \frac{-1}{640}\begin{bmatrix} -4 & 8 & -128 \\ 8 & -16 & -64 \\ -128 & -64 & -1536 \end{bmatrix}\begin{pmatrix} 0 \\ 16 \\ 1 \end{pmatrix} = \begin{pmatrix} 0 \\ 1/2 \\ 4 \end{pmatrix}.
$$

(b) By the envelope theorem,

$$
\frac{df^*(1)}{dp} = \frac{\partial L^*(x^*(1), y^*(1), \lambda_3^*(1), 1)}{\partial p}
$$

$$
= x^{*4}y^* - \lambda_3^*(x^{*2} - 5) = 24.
$$

A.10 SOLUTIONS FOR CHAPTER 10

10.1 (a) Given system is $\dot{x} = f(x) = -x^3$. Linear approximation system is then

$$\dot{x} = \frac{df}{dx}(x^*)(x - x^*) = -3x^{*2}(x - x^*).$$

At $x^* = 0$, get $\dot{x} = 0 \Rightarrow$ eigenvalues of this system equal $0 \Rightarrow$ no conclusion can be made about local stability using linear approximation. Note that strictly negative real part of eigenvalue is sufficient but not necessary for local asymptotic stability.

(b) Given $V(x) = x^2$,
   (i) $V(x)$ is continuously differentiable, $V(x) > 0 \; \forall x \neq x^* = 0$ and $V(x^*) = 0$.
   (ii) Given $\nabla V(x) = 2x$ and $f(x) = -x^3$, $\dot{V} = \nabla V(x)f(x) = -2x^4 < 0 \; \forall x \neq x^* = 0$.

Hence $V(x) = -x^2$ satisfies both conditions and can be used as a Liapunov function to show local asymptotic stability of the system.

10.2 (a) $\dot{x} = -2x + y$ and $\dot{y} = 2x - 3y$.

$$\begin{vmatrix} -2 - \lambda & 1 \\ 2 & -3 - \lambda \end{vmatrix} = 0 \Rightarrow \lambda = -1, -4.$$

Both eigenvalues strictly negative $\Rightarrow$ system is globally asymptotically stable.

(b) $\dot{x} = x - 5y$ and $\dot{y} = x - 3y$.

$$\begin{vmatrix} 1 - \lambda & -5 \\ 1 & -3 - \lambda \end{vmatrix} = 0 \Rightarrow \lambda = -1 \pm i.$$

Since eigenvalues have strictly negative real part (-1), system is globally asymptotically stable.

(c) $\dot{x} = x - 4y$ and $\dot{y} = 4x - 7y$.

$$\begin{vmatrix} 1 - \lambda & -4 \\ 4 & -7 - \lambda \end{vmatrix} = 0$$

$\Rightarrow \lambda = -3$ with multiplicity $2 \Rightarrow$ negative real parts. Hence globally asymptotically stable.

10.3 (a) $d(p \cdot p)/dt = 2p \, dp/dt = 2p \cdot z(p)$. By Walras' law, $p \cdot z(p) = 0 \; \forall p \in P$, so $d(p \cdot p)/dt = 0$.

(b) Let $V(p) = (p - p^*) \cdot (p - p^*)$. Then $V(p) > 0$ for $p \neq p^*$; V is continuously differentiable everywhere, and $V(p^*) = 0$.

$$\dot{V}(p) = \nabla V(p) f(p)$$
$$= 2(p - p^*) z(p)$$
$$= 2pz(p) - 2p^* z(p)$$
$$= -2p^* z(p) \quad \text{(since } pz(p) = 0 \text{ by (a))}$$
$$< 0 \qquad \text{(by the weak axiom of revealed preference).}$$

Hence $V(p)$ can be used as a Liapunov function, which implies that the equilibrium is locally stable.

10.4 Writing the system as

$$\begin{bmatrix} -3 & 2 & 0 \\ 2 & -4 & 0 \\ 0 & 0 & -3 \end{bmatrix} \begin{bmatrix} x \\ y \\ z-1 \end{bmatrix} = \begin{bmatrix} \dot{x} \\ \dot{y} \\ \dot{z} \end{bmatrix},$$

$$-3 < 0, \quad \begin{vmatrix} -3 & 2 \\ 2 & -4 \end{vmatrix} = 8 > 0, \quad \begin{vmatrix} -3 & 2 & 0 \\ 2 & -4 & 0 \\ 0 & 0 & -3 \end{vmatrix} = -24 < 0.$$

Matrix is symmetric and negative definite. $\Rightarrow$ all eigenvalues are strictly negative $\Rightarrow$ local asymptotic stability of the equilibrium $(0, 0, 1)$.

10.5 Given $H(x, y) = (x^2 - 1)^2 + (y - 2)^2$ let,

$$\begin{pmatrix} \dot{x} \\ \dot{y} \end{pmatrix} = -\nabla H(x, y) \quad \text{or} \quad \nabla H(x, y) = \begin{bmatrix} 4x(x^2 - 1) \\ 2(y - 2) \end{bmatrix}.$$

For equilibrium, need $\nabla H(x, y) = 0 \Rightarrow$ solve for x and y to get three equilibria.
(a) $x = 0$, $y = 2$
(b) $x = 1$, $y = 2$
(c) $x = -1$, $y = 2$
    SOC matrix for minimizing $H(x, y)$ is

$$B(x, y) = \begin{bmatrix} 12x^2 - 4 & 0 \\ 0 & 2 \end{bmatrix},$$

$$B(0, 2) = \begin{bmatrix} -4 & 0 \\ 0 & 2 \end{bmatrix} \Rightarrow \text{not PSD} \Rightarrow \text{unstable,}$$

$$B(1, 2) = B(-1, 2) = \begin{bmatrix} 8 & 0 \\ 0 & 2 \end{bmatrix}$$

$\Rightarrow B$ is PD $\Rightarrow$ both $(1, 2)$ and $(-1, 2)$ are strict local minimizers of $H(x, y) \Rightarrow$ both are locally asymptotically stable equilibria. Since we have multiple equilibria the dynamic system is not globally stable.

10.6 Write as

$$\begin{pmatrix} \dot{x} \\ \dot{y} \\ \dot{z} \end{pmatrix} = \begin{pmatrix} -3 & 4 & 0 \\ 0 & -2 & -6 \\ 0 & 0 & -4 \end{pmatrix} \begin{pmatrix} x + 4 \\ y + 3 \\ z - 1 \end{pmatrix},$$

$$|A - \lambda I| = \begin{vmatrix} -3 - \lambda & 4 & 0 \\ 0 & -2 - \lambda & -6 \\ 0 & 0 & -4 - \lambda \end{vmatrix}$$

$$= [-(3 + \lambda)][-(2 + \lambda)][-(4 + \lambda)] = 0$$

$\Rightarrow \lambda = -2, -3, -4$. Since $\lambda_i < 0 \; \forall i = 1, 2, 3$, the equilibrium $(-4, -3, 1)$ is asymptotically stable.

10.7 False. Given $g(x, y) = x^4 - 2x^2 + y^2$, note that

$$\begin{pmatrix} \dot{x} \\ \dot{y} \end{pmatrix} = f(x, y) = -\nabla g(x, y) \quad \text{where } \nabla g(x, y) = \begin{bmatrix} 4x^3 - 4x \\ 2y \end{bmatrix}.$$

Clearly, $\dot{g} = -\|\nabla g(x, y)\|^2 < 0 \; \forall (x, y)$ such that $\nabla g(x, y) \neq (0, 0)$. Now checking for condition (i) i.e., $g(x, y) > 0 \; \forall (x, y) \neq (0, 0)$, get SOC matrix as

$$B(x, y) = \begin{bmatrix} 12x^2 - 4 & 0 \\ 0 & 2 \end{bmatrix}$$

$\Rightarrow$

$$B(0, 0) = \begin{bmatrix} -4 & 0 \\ 0 & 2 \end{bmatrix}$$

$\Rightarrow$ not PSD $\Rightarrow (0, 0)$ is not local minimizer of $g(x, y) \Rightarrow$ not locally stable.

10.8 False. The linear approximation system may fail to be stable while the true system is stable. As a counterexample consider

$$\dot{x} = f(x) = -x^3, \qquad Ax = -3x^{*2}(x - x^*).$$

Here, though the eigenvalue of the linear approximation system is not negative, the function x^2 can be used as a Liapunov function to show local asymptotic stability of the true system.

10.9 True. Define the function $h(x) = 10 - g(x)$. Then $h(0) = 10 - 10 = 0$, while $h(x) > 0 \; \forall x \neq 0$. Furthermore,

$$\dot{h} = \nabla h(x) f(x) = -\nabla g(x) f(x) < 0 \; \forall x \neq 0.$$

Hence $x^* = 0$ is locally asymptotically stable.

10.10 To find equilibrium, solve $\dot{x} = \dot{y} = \dot{z} = 0$ to obtain $(x^*, y^*, z^*) = (10, 4, -2)$. The system

$$\begin{pmatrix} \dot{x} \\ \dot{y} \\ \dot{z} \end{pmatrix} = \begin{pmatrix} -2 & 1 & -8 \\ 2 & -3 & 4 \\ 0 & 0 & -5 \end{pmatrix} \begin{pmatrix} x - 10 \\ y - 4 \\ z + 2 \end{pmatrix}$$

is stable iff the real parts of the eigenvalues of the matrix are negative. To find the eigenvalues,

$$\begin{aligned} \det &\begin{bmatrix} -2 - \lambda & 1 & -8 \\ 2 & -3 - \lambda & 4 \\ 0 & 0 & -5 - \lambda \end{bmatrix} \\ &= (-5 - \lambda)((-2 - \lambda)(-3 - \lambda) - 2) \\ &= (-5 - \lambda)(\lambda + 4)(\lambda + 1) = 0. \end{aligned}$$

Eigenvalues are $\lambda = -1, -4, -5$ so the equilibrium is stable.

10.11 h is differentiable, $h(1, 0) = 0$, and

$$\dot{h} = \nabla h \cdot (\dot{x}, \dot{y}) = (4x^3 - 12x^2 + 16x - 8, 2y) \cdot (\dot{x}, \dot{y})$$
$$= -\nabla h \cdot \nabla h < 0 \text{ if } \nabla h \neq \mathbf{0}.$$

Since this is a gradient system, h can be used as a Liapunov function if $(1, 0)$ is an isolated minimizer of h. $\nabla h(1, 0) = \mathbf{0}$ so $(1, 0)$ is an equilibrium.

$$[h_{ij}] = \begin{bmatrix} 12x^2 - 24x + 16 & 0 \\ 0 & 2 \end{bmatrix}$$

so

$$[h_{ij}(1, 0)] = \begin{bmatrix} 4 & 0 \\ 0 & 2 \end{bmatrix},$$

which is positive definite, so $(1, 0)$ is a strict local minimizer of h, and h can be used as a Liapunov function.

10.12 At any equilibrium, $\dot{x} = \dot{y} = \dot{z} = 0$. $-3x + 6 = 0$ or $x^* = 2$. Then $2x^* - 4z^* = 0$ or $z^* = x^*/2 = 1$. Also $x^* - y^{*2} + 7z^* = 0$ so $y^{*2} = x^* + 7z^* = 9$ and $y^* = 3$ or $y^* = -3$. Since there are two equilibria. $(2, 3, 1)$ and $(2, -3, 1)$, neither can be globally stable. The linear approximation system has matrix

$$\begin{bmatrix} -3 & 0 & 0 \\ 1 & -2y^* & 7 \\ 2 & 0 & -4 \end{bmatrix}$$

At $(2, 3, 1)$ this is

$$\begin{bmatrix} -3 & 0 & 0 \\ 1 & -6 & 7 \\ 2 & 0 & -4 \end{bmatrix},$$

which has eigenvalues $-3, -6, -4$, all strictly negative. Thus $(2, 3, 1)$ is locally stable. At $(2, -3, 1)$ the matrix is

$$\begin{bmatrix} -3 & 0 & 0 \\ 1 & 6 & 7 \\ 2 & 0 & -4 \end{bmatrix},$$

which has eigenvalues $-3, 6, -4$. Since one eigenvalue is strictly positive, $(2, -3, 1)$ is not locally stable.

A.11 SOLUTIONS FOR CHAPTER 11

11.1 Bellman's equation is

$$V(k, x) = \max_{u \geq 0} \{ g(k, x, u) + V(k + 1, f(k, x, u)) \}.$$

Here

$$g(k, x, u) = \delta^k \sqrt{u} \ \forall \ 0 \leq k < N$$

$$= \delta^N \sqrt{b} \quad \text{for} \quad k = N, b = x(N)$$

and $f(k, x, u) = (1 + r)(x(k) - u(k))$. Hence $V(k, x) =$ Max$_{u \geq 0}\{\delta^k \sqrt{u} + V(k + 1, (1 + r)(x(k) - u(k))\}$.
For $k = N$: $V(N, x) = \delta^N \sqrt{x}$.
For $k = N - 1$:

$$V(N - 1, x) = \max_{u} \left\{ \delta^{N-1} \sqrt{u} + V(N, (x - u)(1 + r)) \right\}$$

$$= \max_{u} \left\{ \delta^{N-1} \sqrt{u} + \delta^N \sqrt{(x - u)(1 + r)} \right\}.$$

FOC:

$$\frac{\delta^{N-1}}{2\sqrt{u}} - \frac{\delta^N \sqrt{1 + r}}{2\sqrt{x - u}} = 0.$$

Note SOC holds everywhere. Thus $(x - u) = \delta^2(1 + r)u$ or $u[1 + (1 + r)\delta^2] = x$. So

$$u = \frac{x}{1 + \delta^2(1 + r)} = \frac{x}{1 + \delta^2 + \delta^2 r},$$

$V(N - 1, x)$

$$= \delta^{N-1}\sqrt{\frac{x}{1 + \delta^2(1 + r)}} + \delta^N\sqrt{(1 + r)\left(x - \frac{x}{1 + \delta^2(1 + r)}\right)}$$

$$= \delta^{N-1}\left\{\sqrt{\frac{x}{1 + \delta^2(1 + r)}} + \delta\sqrt{\frac{(1 + r)\delta^2(1 + r)}{1 + \delta^2(1 + r)}x}\right\}$$

$$= \delta^{N-1}\left\{\sqrt{\frac{x}{1 + \delta^2(1 + r)}} + \delta^2(1 + r)\sqrt{\frac{x}{1 + \delta^2(1 + r)}}\right\}$$

$$= \delta^{N-1}\left[(1 + \delta^2(1 + r))\sqrt{\frac{x}{1 + \delta^2(1 + r)}}\right],$$

$$V(N - 1, x) = \delta^{N-1}\sqrt{\{1 + \delta^2(1 + r)\}x}.$$

For $k = N - 2$

$V(N - 2, x)$

$$= \underset{u}{\text{Max}}\left\{\delta^{N-2}\sqrt{u} + V(N - 1, (1 + r)(x - u))\right\}$$

$$= \underset{u}{\text{Max}}\left\{\delta^{N-2}\sqrt{u} + \delta^{N-1}\sqrt{[1 + \delta^2(1 + r)](x - u)(1 + r)}\right\}.$$

FOC:

$$\frac{\delta^{N-2}}{2\sqrt{u}} - \frac{\delta^{N-1}\sqrt{(1 + r)[1 + \delta^2(1 + r)]}}{2\sqrt{x - u}} = 0.$$

Note SOC holds everywhere. Thus

$$(x - u) = \delta^2(1 + r)[1 + \delta^2(1 + r)]u,$$

or

$$u\left[1 + \delta^2(1 + r)\left[1 + \delta^2(1 + r)\right]\right]$$

$$= x \Rightarrow u = \frac{x}{1 + \delta^2(1 + r) + \delta^4(1 + r)^2} = \varphi(N - 2, x),$$

$V(N - 2, x)$

$$= \delta^{N-2}\sqrt{\frac{x}{1 + \delta^2(1 + r) + \delta^4(1 + r)^2}}$$

$$+ \delta^{N-1}\sqrt{\left[1 + \delta^2(1 + r)\right](1 + r)\left(x - \frac{x}{1 + \delta^2(1 + r) + \delta^4(1 + r)^2}\right)}$$

$$= \delta^{N-2}\left\{\sqrt{\frac{x}{1 + \delta^2(1 + r) + \delta^4(1 + r)^2}}\right.$$

$$\left. + \delta\sqrt{\frac{\left[1 + \delta^2(1 + r)\right](1 + r)\left[\delta^2(1 + r) + \delta^4(1 + r)^2\right]x}{1 + \delta^2(1 + r) + \delta^4(1 + r)^2}}\right\}$$

$$= \frac{\delta^{N-2}\sqrt{x}}{\sqrt{1 + \delta^2(1 + r) + \delta^4(1 + r)^2}}$$

$$\times\left\{1 + \delta\sqrt{\left[1 + \delta^2(1 + r)\right]\delta^2(1 + r)^2\left[1 + \delta^2(1 + r)\right]}\right\}$$

$$= \delta^{N-2}\sqrt{\frac{x}{1 + \delta^2(1 + r) + \delta^4(1 + r)^2}}$$

$$\times\left\{1 + \delta\left[1 + \delta^2(1 + r)\right]\delta(1 + r)\right\}$$

$$= \delta^{N-2}\sqrt{\frac{x}{1 + \delta^2(1 + r) + \delta^4(1 + r)^2}}$$

$$\times\left[1 + \delta^2(1 + r) + \delta^4(1 + r)^2\right]$$

$$\Rightarrow V(N - 2, x) = \delta^{N-2}\sqrt{\left[1 + \delta^2(1 + r) + \delta^4(1 + r)^2\right]x}.$$

We then have

$$\varphi(N - 1, x) = \frac{x}{1 + \delta^2(1 + r)},$$

$$V(N - 1, x) = \delta^{N-1} \sqrt{\{1 + \delta^2(1 + r)\}x},$$

$$\varphi(N - 2, x) = \frac{x}{1 + \delta^2(1 + r) + \delta^4(1 + r)^2},$$

$$V(N - 2, x) = \delta^{N-2} \sqrt{\left[1 + \delta^2(1 + r) + \delta^4(1 + r)^2\right]x}.$$

So guess

$$\varphi(N - j, x) = \frac{x}{\sum_{i=0}^{j}\delta^{2i}(1 + r)^i},$$

$$V(N - j, x) = \delta^{N-j} \sqrt{x \sum_{i=0}^{j} \delta^{2i}(1 + r)^i}.$$

Assume formula holds for $N - (j - 1)$. Then

$$V(N - j, x)$$
$$= \max_{u} \left\{ \delta^{N-j} \sqrt{u} + \delta^{N-j+1} \sqrt{(1 + r)(x - u)\sum_{i=0}^{j-1}\delta^{2i}(1 + r)^i} \right\}.$$

From FOC:

$$\frac{\delta^{N-j}}{\sqrt{u}} = \frac{\delta^{N-j+1} \sqrt{(1 + r)\sum_{i=0}^{j-1}\delta^{2i}(1 + r)^i}}{\sqrt{x - u}}.$$

Note SOC holds everywhere. Thus $(x - u) = \delta^2(1 + r)\sum_{0}^{j-1}\delta^{2i}(1 + r)^i \cdot u$ or

$$x = u\left[1 + \delta^2(1 + r)\left[1 + \delta^2(1 + r) + \cdots + \delta^{2j-2}(1 + r)^{j-1}\right]\right].$$

So, we get

$$u\left\{1 + \delta^2(1 + r) + \delta^4(1 + r)^2 + \cdots + \delta^{2j}(1 + r)^j\right\} = x$$

or

$$u = \frac{x}{\sum_{i=0}^{j}\delta^{2i}(1 + r)^i} = \varphi(N - j, x),$$

and $\varphi(N - j, x)$ agrees with our guess.

Now see if formula for $V(N - j, x)$ works:

$$V(N - j, x) = \delta^{N-j} \sqrt{\frac{x}{\sum_{i=0}^{j} \delta^{2i}(1 + r)^i}}$$

$$+ \delta^{N-j+1} \sqrt{(1 + r) \sum_{i=0}^{j-1} \delta^{2i}(1 + r)^i \left[x - \frac{x}{\sum_{0}^{j} \delta^{2i}(1 + r)^i}\right]}$$

$$= \delta^{N-j} \sqrt{\frac{x}{\sum_{i=0}^{j} \delta^{2i}(1 + r)^i}}$$

$$\times \left\{1 + \delta \sqrt{(1 + r)\left\{\sum_{i=0}^{j-1} \delta^{2i}(1 + r)^i\right\}\left\{\sum_{i=1}^{j} \delta^{2i}(1 + r)^i\right\}}\right\}$$

$$= \delta^{N-j} \sqrt{\frac{x}{\sum_{i=0}^{j} \delta^{2i}(1 + r)^i}}$$

$$\times \left\{1 + \sqrt{\left[\delta^2(1 + r) + \cdots + \delta^{2j}(1 + r)^j\right] \sum_{i=1}^{j} \delta^{2i}(1 + r)^i}\right\}$$

$$= \delta^{N-j} \sqrt{\frac{x}{\sum_{i=0}^{j} \delta^{2i}(1 + r)^i}} \left\{1 + \sum_{i=1}^{j} \delta^{2i}(1 + r)^i\right\}$$

or

$$V(N - j, x) = \delta^{N-j} \sqrt{\frac{x}{\sum_{i=0}^{j} \delta^{2i}(1 + r)^i}} \left\{\sum_{i=0}^{j} \delta^{2i}(1 + r)^i\right\}$$

$$= \delta^{N-j} \sqrt{x \sum_{i=0}^{j} \delta^{2i}(1 + r)^i},$$

which agrees with our guess. So,

$$\varphi(k, x) = \frac{x}{\sum_{i=0}^{N-k} \delta^{2i}(1 + r)^i}$$

and

$$V(k, x) = \delta^k \sqrt{x \sum_{i=0}^{N-k} \delta^{2i}(1 + r)^i}.$$

Optimal consumption for $k = 0$ is

$$\varphi(0, w_0) = \frac{w_0}{\sum_{i=0}^{N} \delta^{2i}(1+r)^i} = c_0.$$

Using this, we can get $x_1(w_1)$ as

$$x_1 = (w_0 - c_0)(1+r) = w_0 \left[1 - \frac{1}{\sum_{i=0}^{N} \delta^{2i}(1+r)^i} \right](1+r)$$

$$= \frac{w_0(1+r)}{\sum_{i=0}^{N} \delta^{2i}(1+r)^i} \sum_{i=1}^{N} \delta^{2i}(1+r)^i.$$

So

$$c_1(= u_1) = \frac{x_1}{\sum_{i=0}^{N-1} \delta^{2i}(1+r)^i} = \frac{w_0(1+r)\delta^2(1+r)}{\sum_{i=0}^{N} \delta^{2i}(1+r)^i}.$$

In this way we can get the optimal consumption path:

$$c_j = \frac{w_0 \delta^{2j}(1+r)^{2j}}{\sum_{i=0}^{N} \delta^{2i}(1+r)^i}.$$

Maximized utility with $x_0 = w_0$ is

$$V(0, w_0) = \delta^0 \sqrt{\sum_{i=0}^{N} \delta^{2i}(1+r)^i w_0} = \sqrt{w_0 \sum_{i=0}^{N} \delta^{2i}(1+r)^i},$$

while bequest is

$$b = \frac{w_0 \delta^{2N}(1+r)^{2N}}{\sum_{i=0}^{N} \delta^{2i}(1+r)^i}.$$

11.2 Bellman's (optimality) equation is

$$V(k, n) = \underset{u \geq 0}{\text{Max}} \{ g(k, x, u) + V(k+1, f(k, x, u)) \}$$

Here $g(k, x, u) = \sqrt{u}$ for $0 \leq k \leq N - 1$ and $g(k, x, u) = \sqrt{x}$ for $k = N$ while $f(k, x, u) = x - u$. The dynamic programming problem then is to

$$\underset{u_i \geq 0}{\text{Max}} \sum_{i=1}^{N-1} \sqrt{u_i} + \sqrt{x(N)} \quad \text{s.t.} \quad x(k+1) = x(k) - u(k), \quad \text{and}$$

$$x(0) = x_0.$$

Bellman's equation is

$$V(k, x) = \underset{u \geq 0}{\text{Max}} \left\{ \sqrt{u} + V(k + 1, x(k) - u(k)) \right\}.$$

For last period, $k = N$, $V(N, x) = h(x) = \sqrt{x}$.
For $k = N - 1$,

$$V(N - 1, x) = \max_u \left\{ \sqrt{u} + V(N, x - u) \right\} = \max_u \left\{ \sqrt{u} + \sqrt{x - u} \right\}.$$

FOC for maximization:

$$\tfrac{1}{2} u^{-1/2} + \tfrac{1}{2} (x - u)^{-1/2} (-1) = 0.$$

SOC:

$$\left(-\frac{1}{2} \right) \left(\frac{1}{2} \right) u^{-3/2} + \left(-\frac{1}{2} \right) \left(\frac{1}{2} \right) (x - u)^{-3/2} (-1)(-1) < 0 \quad \forall u \geq 0.$$

From FOC we get

$$\frac{1}{2\sqrt{u}} = \frac{1}{2\sqrt{x - u}} \Rightarrow u = x - u \Rightarrow u = \frac{x}{2}.$$

Thus

$$\varphi(N - 1, x) = \frac{x}{2} \quad \text{and} \quad V(N - 1, x) = \sqrt{\frac{x}{2}} + \sqrt{x - \frac{x}{2}} = \sqrt{2x}.$$

For $k = N - 2$,

$$V(N - 2, x) = \max_u \left\{ \sqrt{u} + V(N - 1, x - u) \right\}$$

$$= \max_u \left\{ \sqrt{u} + \sqrt{2(x - u)} \right\}.$$

FOC:

$$\frac{1}{2} u^{-1/2} + \sqrt{2} \cdot \frac{1}{2} (x - u)^{-1/2} \cdot (-1) = 0 \quad \text{or} \quad \frac{1}{2\sqrt{u}} = \frac{1}{\sqrt{2}\sqrt{x - u}}.$$

Note SOC holds everywhere. Thus, $2u = x - u \Rightarrow u = x/3$,

$$\varphi(N - 2, x) = \frac{x}{3},$$

$$V(N - 2, x) = \sqrt{\frac{x}{3}} + \sqrt{2\left(x - \frac{x}{3} \right)} = \sqrt{3x}.$$

We then have

$$\varphi(N - 1, x) = \frac{x}{2}, V(N - 1, x) = \sqrt{2x},$$

$$\varphi(N - 2, x) = \frac{x}{3}, V(N - 2, x) = \sqrt{3x}.$$

We may guess

$$V(N - j, x) = \sqrt{(j + 1)x},$$

$$\varphi(N - j, x) = \frac{x}{j + 1}.$$

Assume formula is correct for $N - (j - 1)$, i.e.,

$$V(N - (j - 1), x) = \sqrt{(j - 1 + 1)x} = \sqrt{jx},$$

then

$$V(N - j, x) = \underset{u}{\text{Max}} \left\{ \sqrt{u} + V(N - j + 1, x - u) \right\}$$

$$= \underset{u}{\text{Max}} \left\{ \sqrt{u} + \sqrt{j(x - u)} \right\}.$$

FOC:

$$\frac{1}{2\sqrt{u}} - \frac{1}{2}\sqrt{j}\,\frac{1}{\sqrt{x - u}} = 0.$$

Note SOC holds everywhere. Thus $1/u = j/(x - u) \Rightarrow x - u = ju$ or $u = x/(j + 1) = \varphi(N - j, x)$. So

$$V(N - j, x) = \sqrt{\frac{x}{j + 1}} + \sqrt{j\left(x - \frac{x}{j + 1}\right)}$$

$$= \sqrt{\frac{x}{j + 1}} + \sqrt{j\frac{(jx + x - x)}{j + 1}}$$

$$= \sqrt{\frac{x}{j + 1}} + j\sqrt{\frac{x}{j + 1}}$$

$$= (j + 1)\sqrt{\frac{x}{j + 1}} = \sqrt{(j + 1)x}.$$

This agrees with our guess for $V(N - j, x)$ and $\varphi(N - j, x)$, and by induction we have found the value function and optimal control as

$$V(k, x) = \sqrt{(N - k + 1)x},$$

$$\varphi(k, x) = \frac{x}{N - k + 1} \quad \forall \; 0 \le k \le N - 1.$$

11.3 (a) $\text{Max}_{(y_0, y_1, \ldots, y_N)} \sum_{t=0}^{N} \alpha^t \ln y_t$ subject to $\sum_{t=0}^{N} y_t = 100$. Bellman's equation here is

$$V(j, x) = \underset{y}{\text{Max}} \{\alpha^j \ln y + V(J + 1, x - y)\},$$

$$j = 0, 1, \ldots, N - 1,$$

$$V(N, x) = \alpha^N \ln x.$$

(b) Putting $\alpha = 1$ and $N = 99$, we get $V(99, x) = 1^N \ln x = \ln x$. But

$$\ln x = (100 - 99)\ln\left(\frac{x}{100 - 99}\right),$$

which is consistent with given $V(j, x)$ for $j = N$. Now suppose formula holds for $(j + 1)$. Then

$$V(J + 1, x) = (100 - j - 1)\ln\left(\frac{x}{100 - j - 1}\right).$$

So

$$V(j, x) = \underset{y}{\text{max}} \{(\ln y + V(j + 1, x - y))\}$$

$$= \underset{y}{\text{max}} \left\{\ln y + (100 - j - 1)\ln\left(\frac{x - y}{100 - j - 1}\right)\right\}.$$

FOC:

$$\frac{1}{y} + (100 - j - 1)\frac{1}{(x - y)/(100 - j - 1)}\left(\frac{-1}{100 - j - 1}\right) = 0,$$

or $1/y = (100 - j - 1)/(x - y)$, or $y = x/(100 - j)$. Note SOC holds everywhere so $\varphi(j, x) = x/(100 - j)$. Thus,

$$V(j, x) = \ln\left(\frac{x}{100 - j}\right) + (100 - j - 1)\ln\left(\frac{x - \dfrac{x}{100 - j}}{100 - j - 1}\right)$$

$$= \ln\left(\frac{x}{100 - j}\right) + (100 - j - 1)\ln\left[\frac{(100 - j - 1)x}{(100 - j - 1)(100 - j)}\right]$$

$$= \ln\left(\frac{x}{100 - j}\right) + (100 - j - 1)\ln\left(\frac{x}{100 - j}\right)$$

$$= (100 - j)\ln\left(\frac{x}{100 - j}\right).$$

Hence the proposition is true.

11.4 Bellman's equation:

$$V(k, x) = \max_{y}\{y - e^{-y} + V(k + 1, x - y)\}.$$

For $k = N$, $V(N, x) = x - e^{-x}$. For $k = N - 1$,

$$V(N - 1, x) = \max_{y}\{y - e^{-y} + V(N, x - y)\}$$

$$= \max_{y}\{y - e^{-y} + (x - y) - e^{-(x-y)}\}.$$

FOC: $e^{-y} - e^{-(x-y)} = 0 \Rightarrow -y = y - x$ or $y = x/2 = \varphi(N - 1, x)$. Note SOC holds everywhere.
Then $V(N - 1, x) = -e^{-x/2} + x - e^{-(x-x/2)} = x - 2e^{-x/2}$. We may guess $V(N - j, x) = x - (j + 1)e^{-x/(j+1)}$. This holds for $j = 0$ and $j = 1$. Assume this formula is true for $N - (j - 1)$:

$$V(N - j + 1, x) = x - (j - 1 + 1)e^{-x/(j-1+1)} = x - je^{-x/j}$$

Then

$$V(N - j, x) = \max_{y}\{y - e^{-y} + V(N - j + 1, x - y)\}$$

$$= \max_{y}\{y - e^{-y} + (x - y) - je^{-(x-y)/j}\}$$

or

$$V(N - j, x) = \max_{y}\{-e^{-y} + x - je^{-(x-y)/j}\}.$$

FOC: $e^{-y} - je^{-(x-y)/j}(1/j) = 0$ or $-y = -((x-y)/j)$ or $(j+1)y = x \Rightarrow y = x/(j+1) = \varphi(N-j, x)$. Note SOC holds everywhere. Value function:

$$V(N-j, x) = -e^{-x/(j+1)} + x - je^{-(1/j)(x-x/(j+1))}$$

$$= -e^{-x/(j+1)} + x - je^{-(1/j)((xj+x-x)/(j+1))}$$

$$= -e^{-x/(j+1)} + x - je^{-x/(j+1)}$$

or $V(N-j, x) = x - (j+1)e^{-x/(j+1)}$, which agrees with our guess.

11.5 (a) Writing all values discounted to $t = 0$, $V(T, K) = \beta^T \sqrt{K}$.

$$V(T-1, K) = \max_{i \geq -K} \left\{ \beta^{T-1}(\sqrt{K} - K - i) + \beta^T \sqrt{K+i} \right\}.$$

FOC:

$$\beta^{T-1}\left(-1 + \frac{\beta}{2\sqrt{K+i}} \right) = 0.$$

SOC:

$$\beta^{T-1}\left(-\frac{\beta}{4(K+i)^{3/2}} \right) < 0.$$

Solution: $i^* = \beta^2/4 - K$.

$$V(T-1, K) = \beta^{T-1}(\sqrt{K} - K - i^*) + \beta^T \sqrt{K+i^*}$$

$$= \beta^{T-1}\left(\sqrt{K} + \frac{\beta^2}{4} \right),$$

$$V(T-2, K) = \max_{i \geq -K} \left\{ \beta^{T-2}(\sqrt{K} - K - i) \right.$$

$$\left. + \beta^{T-1}\left(\sqrt{K+i} + \frac{\beta^2}{4} \right) \right\}.$$

Again $i^* = \beta^2/4 - K$ and

$$V(T-2, K) = \beta^{T-2}\left(\sqrt{K} + \frac{\beta^2}{4}(1 + \beta) \right).$$

Hypothesis:

$$V(T - j, K) = \beta^{T-j}\left(\sqrt{K} + \frac{\beta^2}{4}\sum_{t=0}^{j-1}\beta^t\right) \quad \text{and}$$

$$\varphi(T - j, K) = \frac{\beta^2}{4} - K.$$

$$V(T - j - 1, K) = \max_{i \geq -K}\left\{\beta^{T-j-1}(\sqrt{K} - K - i)\right.$$

$$\left. + \beta^{T-j}\left(\sqrt{K + i} + \frac{\beta^2}{4}\sum_{t=0}^{j-1}\beta^t\right)\right\}.$$

Solution $i^* = \beta^2/4 - K$ and the guess works:

$$V(T - j, K) = \beta^{T-j}\left(\sqrt{K} + \frac{\beta^2}{4}\sum_{i=0}^{j-1}\beta^i\right) \quad \text{and}$$

$$\varphi(T - j, K) = \frac{\beta^2}{4} - K.$$

(b) Given $K_0, i_0 = \varphi(0, K_0) = \beta^2/4 - K_0$ and $K_1 = K_0 + i_0 = \beta^2/4$. Then

$$i_1 = \varphi\left(1, \frac{\beta^2}{4}\right) = \frac{\beta^2}{4} - \frac{\beta^2}{4} = 0.$$

and $K_2 = K_1 + i_1 = \beta^2/4$. Then

$$i_2 = \varphi\left(2, \frac{\beta^2}{4}\right) = \frac{\beta^2}{4} - \frac{\beta^2}{4} = 0$$

and $K_3 = K_2 + i_2 = \beta^2/4$. Then

$$i_{T-1} = \varphi\left(T - 1, \frac{\beta^2}{4}\right) = 0.$$

$$K_T = K_{T-1} + i_{T-1} = \frac{\beta^2}{4},$$

$$(K_0, K_1, K_2, \ldots, K_T) = \left(K_0, \frac{\beta^2}{4}, \frac{\beta^2}{4}, \ldots, \frac{\beta^2}{4}\right),$$

and

$$(i_0, i_1, \ldots, i_{T-1}) = \left(\frac{\beta^2}{4} - K_0, 0, 0, \ldots, 0\right).$$

In the initial period the firm adjusts its capital stock to $\beta^2/4$ and holds that level, with no further net investment, for all remaining periods.

11.6 Discounting to period 0, $V(N, x) = \delta^N x^2$.

$$V(N - 1, x) = \max_{0 \le c \le x} \left\{\delta^{N-1} c^2 + V(N, (1 + r)(x - c))\right\}.$$

Solving the optimization problem, note $\delta^{N-1} c^2 + \delta^N[(1 + r)(x - c)]^2$ is convex in c so the solution will be a corner solution, i.e., either $c^* = 0$ or $c^* = x$. Comparing the values at 0 and x, $c^* = 0$ is optimal if $\delta(1 + r)^2 \ge 1$ and $c^* = x$ is optimal if $\delta(1 + r)^2 \le 1$.

Case 1. $\delta(1 + r)^2 > 1$. Then $c^* = 0$ and $V(N - 1, x) = \delta^N(1 + r)^2 x^2$.

$$V(N - 2, x) = \max_{0 \le c \le x} \left\{\delta^{N-2} c^2 + V(N - 1, (1 + r)(x - c))\right\}.$$

Again the solution is at the corner, $c^* = 0$, and $V(N - 2, x) = \delta^N(1 + r)^4 x^2$. For all j, the solution is $\varphi(N - j, x) = 0$ and $V(N - j, x) = \delta^N(1 + r)^{2j} x^2$. When $\delta(1 + r)^2 > 1$ the consumer saves all her wealth until the final period.

Case 2. $\delta(1 + r)^2 < 1$. Then $c^* = x$ and $V(N - 1, x) = \delta^{N-1} x^2$.

$$V(N - 2, x) = \max_{0 \le c \le x} \left\{\delta^{N-2} c^2 + V(N - 1, (1 + r)(x - c))\right\}.$$

Again the solution is at the corner, $c^* = x$, and $V(N - 2, x) = \delta^{N-2} x^2$. For all j, the solution is $\varphi(N - j, x) = x$ and $V(N - j, x) = \delta^{N-j} x^2$. When $\delta(1 + r)^2 < 1$ the consumer uses all her wealth for current consumption.

Case 3. $\delta(1 + r)^2 = 1$. The consumer is indifferent between $c^* = 0$ and $c^* = x$. Wealth is all consumed in a single period, but the consumer is indifferent about the actual date of consumption.

11.7 From Problem 11.1 we know that the value function for finite horizon case is

$$V(k, x) = \delta^k \sqrt{x \sum_{i=0}^{N-k} \delta^{2i}(1 + r)^i}.$$

Setting $k = 0$, we get

$$V(0, x) = \sqrt{x \sum_{i=0}^{N} \delta^{2i}(1 + r)^i}.$$

Then

$$\lim_{N \to \infty} V(0, x) = \sqrt{x\left[1 - \delta^2(1 + r)\right]^{-1}}.$$

Note: $(1 - a)^{-1} = 1 + a + a^2 + a^3 + \cdots$ for $a < 1$. Here we are using $a = \delta^2(1 + r) < 1$. We can guess

$$V(x) = \sqrt{\frac{x}{1 - \delta^2(1 + r)}} \cdot$$

Similarly, we can guess $\varphi(x) = \text{Lim}_{N \to \infty} \varphi(0, x) = [1 - \delta^2(1 + r)]x$. Checking these formulas:

$$V(x) = \text{Max}_u \left\{ \sqrt{u} + \delta V((x - u)(1 + r)) \right\}$$

$$= \text{Max}_u \left\{ \sqrt{u} + \delta \sqrt{\frac{(x - u)(1 + r)}{(1 - \delta^2(1 + r))}} \right\} \cdot$$

FOC:

$$\frac{1}{2\sqrt{u}} - \delta \sqrt{\frac{1 + r}{1 - \delta^2(1 + r)}} \frac{1}{2\sqrt{x - u}} = 0.$$

Note SOC holds everywhere. Thus

$$\frac{1}{u} = \delta^2 \frac{1 + r}{1 - \delta^2(1 + r)} \cdot \frac{1}{x - u},$$

or $\delta^2(1 + r)u = [1 - \delta^2(1 + r)]x - [1 - \delta^2(1 + r)]u$, or $u = [1 - \delta^2(1 + r)]x = \varphi(x)$, which agrees with our formula.
Checking for $V(x)$:

$$V(x) = \sqrt{[1 - \delta^2(1 + r)]x}$$

$$+ \delta \sqrt{\frac{(1 + r)}{1 - \delta^2(1 + r)} (x - (1 - \delta^2(1 + r))x)}$$

$$= \sqrt{[1 - \delta^2(1 + r)]x} + \delta^2(1 + r) \sqrt{\frac{x}{1 - \delta^2(1 + r)}}$$

$$= \sqrt{[1 - \delta^2(1 + r)]x} \left\{ 1 + \delta^2(1 + r) \frac{1}{1 - \delta^2(1 + r)} \right\}$$

$$= \sqrt{[1 - \delta^2(1 + r)]x} \left\{ \frac{1 - \delta^2(1 + r) + \delta^2(1 + r)}{1 - \delta^2(1 + r)} \right\}$$

$$= \sqrt{\frac{x}{1 - \delta^2(1 + r)}} = V(x), \quad \text{which agrees with our guess.}$$

So, maximized utility is

$$V(w_0) = \sqrt{\frac{w_0}{1 - \delta^2(1 + r)}}$$

with optimal wealth and consumption streams $w_i = w_0[\delta(1 + r)]^{2i}$ and $c_i = w_0[\delta(1 + r)]^{2i}[1 - \delta^2(1 + r)]$.

11.8 The firm's problem is to

$$\text{Max} \sum_{t=0}^{\infty} \delta^t(p_t q_t - 100 q_t) \quad \text{subject to } q_t \geq 0 \text{ and } \sum_{t=0}^{\infty} q_t = A$$

Marginal profit in period t is $d\pi_t/dq_t = p_t - 100$ where 100 is marginal cost. For any $s > t$, marginal profit in period s discounted back to period t is $\delta^{s-t}(p_s - 100)$. In particular when $s = t + 1$, the firm will extract in periods t and $t + 1$ only if $\delta(p_{t+1} - 100) = p_t - 100$. For positive extraction in every period we must have

$$p_0 - 100 = \delta(p_1 - 100)$$

$$= \delta^2(p_2 - 100) = \cdots = \delta^s(p_s - 100) = \cdots.$$

Defining m_t = markup over marginal cost in period $t = p_t - mc = p_t - 100$ we get

$$\frac{m_{t+1}}{m_t} = \frac{p_{t+1} - 100}{p_t - 100} = \frac{1}{\delta}.$$

Let $\delta = 1/(1 + r)$ (the discount rate) $\Rightarrow m_{t+1} = (1 + r)m_t$ for all $t \Rightarrow$ mark up grows at the "interest rate" r.

11.9 Bellman's optimality equation is

$$V(k, x) = \max_{y}\{-e^{-y} + V(k + 1, x - y + w)\} \quad \text{for } 0 \leq k < N$$

and $V(N, x) = -e^{-x}$
Since $w = \lambda$ (given) for $k = N - 1$, get

$$V(N - 1, x) = \max_{y}\{-e^{-y} + V(N, x - y + \lambda)\}$$

$$= \max_{y}\{-e^{-y} - e^{-(x-y+\lambda)}\}.$$

FOC: $-e^{-y}(-1) - e^{-(x-y+\lambda)} = 0$. Note SOC holds everywhere. Thus $-y = -x - \lambda + y$ or $y = (x + \lambda)/2 = \varphi(N - 1, x)$. Then,

$$V(N - 1, x) = -e^{-(x+\lambda)/2} - e^{-(x-(x+\lambda)/2+\lambda)} = -2e^{-(x+\lambda)/2}.$$

For $k = N - 2$,

$$V(N - 2, x) = \underset{y}{\text{Max}}\{-e^{-y} + V(N - 1, x - y + \lambda)\}$$

$$= \underset{y}{\text{Max}}\{-e^{-y} - 2e^{-1/2[x-y+\lambda+\lambda]}\}.$$

FOC: $e^{-y} - 2e^{-1/2[x-y+2\lambda]}(\frac{1}{2}) = 0$. Note SOC holds everywhere. Thus

$$-y = -\frac{x}{2} + \frac{y}{2} - \lambda \quad \text{or} \quad \frac{3}{2}y = \frac{x + 2\lambda}{2} \quad \text{or}$$

$$y = \frac{x + 2\lambda}{3} = \varphi(N - 2, x).$$

So,

$$V(N - 2, x) = -e^{-(x+2\lambda)/3} - 2e^{-[x-(x+2\lambda)/3+2\lambda]/2} = -3e^{-(x+2\lambda)/3}.$$

Guess $V(N - j, x) = -(j + 1)e^{-(x+j\lambda)/(j+1)}$ and $\varphi(N - j, x) = (x + j\lambda)/(j + 1)$. Assume formula holds for $N - (j - 1)$. To show that $V(N - j, x)$ agrees with guess: By formula,

$$V(N - j + 1, x) = -(j - 1 + 1)e^{-(x+(j-1)\lambda)/(j-1+1)}$$

$$= -je^{-(x+(j-1)\lambda)/j}.$$

By Bellman's equation,

$$V(N - j, x) = \underset{y}{\max}\{-e^{-y} + V(N - j + 1, x - y + \lambda)\}$$

$$= \underset{y}{\max}\{-e^{-y} - je^{-[x-y+\lambda+(j-1)\lambda]/j}\}$$

$$= \underset{y}{\max}\{-e^{-y} - je^{-(x-y+j\lambda)/j}\}).$$

FOC: $-e^{-y}(-1) - je^{-(x-y+j\lambda)/j}(1/j) = 0$. Note SOC holds everywhere. Thus

$$-y = -\frac{(x + j\lambda)}{j} + \frac{y}{j} \quad \text{or} \quad \left(\frac{j + 1}{j}\right)y = \frac{x + j\lambda}{j} \quad \text{or}$$

$$y = \frac{x + j\lambda}{j + 1} = \varphi(N - j, x),$$

which agrees with our guess. Now checking for the value function:

$$
\begin{aligned}
V(N-j, x) &= -e^{-(x+j\lambda)/(j+1)} - je^{-(x-(x+j\lambda)/(j+1)+j\lambda)/j} \\
&= -e^{-(x+j\lambda)/(j+1)} - je^{-(jx-j\lambda+j(j+1)\lambda)/(j+1)j} \\
&= -e^{-(x+j\lambda)/(j+1)} - je^{-(x-\lambda+(j+1)\lambda)/(j+1)} \\
&= -(j+1)e^{-(x+j\lambda)/(j+1)},
\end{aligned}
$$

which corresponds with our guess. Hence,

$$
V(N-j, x) = -(j+1)e^{-(x+j\lambda)/(j+1)}
$$

is the desired value function.

REFERENCES AND
FURTHER SOURCES

Some of the topics in this book are standard and don't really need a further source. They are covered in most calculus, or differential equations, or analysis, or linear algebra texts. Other topics, such as correspondences, do not have good sources available at the appropriate level. Most treatments are either detailed and very advanced or quite brief and sketchy. There are, however, a few books which overlap with some of our main topics and provide more in depth treatment. In particular, K. G. Binmore's *Calculus* (1983) covers linear algebra topics including hyperplanes, differential calculus of several variables, integration, and differential equations. The book has many economic examples and applications. Two other books by Binmore, *Mathematical Analysis* (1982) and *Topological Ideas* (1981), provide an increasingly advanced approach to the material or cover more advanced topics. At an advanced level, Murata's *Mathematics for Stability and Optimization of Economic Systems* (1977) provides a comprehensive and detailed treatment of many related topics.

Binmore, K. G. (1981). *Topological Ideas*. Cambridge: Cambridge University Press.
Binmore, K. G. (1982). *Mathematical Analysis*, Second Edition. Cambridge: Cambridge University Press.
Cornes, R. (1992). *Duality and Modern Economics*. Cambridge: Cambridge University Press.
Murata, Y. (1977). *Mathematics for Stability and Optimization of Economic Systems*. New York: Academic Press.

INDEX

Economic Theory, Econometrics, and Mathematical Economics

Edited by Karl Shell, *Cornell University*

Printed in the United States
98673LV00002B/246/A